FINANCIAL MODELING USING LOTUS™ 1-2-3™

FINANCIAL MODELING USING LOTUS™ 1-2-3™

Charles W. Kyd

Osborne **McGraw-Hill**
Berkeley, California

Osborne **McGraw-Hill**
2600 Tenth Street
Berkeley, California 94710
U.S.A.

For information on translations and book distributors outside of the U.S.A., please write to Osborne **McGraw-Hill** at the above address.

Lotus, 1-2-3, and Symphony are trademarks of Lotus Development Corporation.

FINANCIAL MODELING USING
LOTUS™ 1-2-3™

234567890 DODO 89876

ISBN 0-07-881213-5

Cynthia Hudson, Acquisitions Editor
Lyn Cordell, Project Editor
Pamela Webster, Text Design
Yashi Okita, Cover Design

To Marilyn

ACKNOWLEDGMENTS

My most sincere thanks to Chris Morgan and the rest of the staff of *Lotus* magazine. Without their support, this book would not have been possible.

CONTENTS

INTRODUCTION

Lotus 1-2-3 has brought a significant change to the working lives of business professionals. Until the computer spreadsheet, most of us used green paper, a yellow pencil, a big eraser, and a clunky calculator to plan, analyze, and summarize the finances of our companies. Even if a multimillion dollar computer installation generated our data, we analyzed it by hand.

This process worked, of course, but it was slow and boring. Worse, it was incomplete. We seldom had the time to test other assumptions, add further data, try another approach, graph partial results, or update old forecasts to reflect new information.

Lotus 1-2-3 has made all these things not just possible, but easy, once the models are built. Creating the initial model, however, is frequently time-consuming. This book was written to simplify that task.

CONTENTS OF THE BOOK

The 16 chapters in this book show how to create 1-2-3 spreadsheets that will help you in the following areas.

- *Sales forecasting.* Two chapters show three different methods of forecasting your sales: time series analysis, polling the sales force, and forecasting the performance of sales representatives and a dealer network.
- *Cash forecasting, reporting, and control.* Five chapters discuss many of the different aspects of cash: forecasting future cash flows, reporting past cash flows, controlling periodic cash requirements, generating useful loan amortization schedules, and saving cash when buying inventories.

- *Performance analysis.* Four chapters show how to answer questions like: How likely are we or our customers to go bankrupt? How fast can we afford to grow? What is our break-even point and why does it matter? Why did our profits decrease when our sales increased?
- *Management reporting.* Six chapters discuss the Data Bank, a new system that will allow you to create—and your clerks to produce—new and informative management reports. Are you paying your vendors too quickly? Are your customers paying you too slowly? What was your cash flow for the last month, the last quarter, the last three years? What are the trends in major areas of performance that affect your firm? These questions and many more can be answered each month by the reports in these chapters.

WHAT YOU SHOULD KNOW

When you begin to use this book, you should be familiar with Lotus 1-2-3 and its most frequently used commands and formulas. For example, when you read "copy," you should think of /Copy; when you read "move," you should think of /Move; and when you read "@SUM," you should know how the function works. But you don't have to be an expert in the program. Figures and explanations will show you how to create each spreadsheet.

If you would rather not create the spreadsheets yourself, you can obtain them on disk. Ordering information follows this introduction.

SYSTEM REQUIREMENTS

To create all of the spreadsheets described in this book, you will need 1-2-3 Version 2. If you use Version 1A, the reports in Chapter 5 will be difficult to create and those in Chapter 13 will be impossible. With minor exceptions, the remaining reports can be generated using either version.

You will need an IBM PC, or compatible, with graphics capabilities and at least 512K of memory. (The report in Chapter 13 requires a full 640K.) A hard disk is not required, but it is recommended.

WHAT TO DO IF PROBLEMS OCCUR

If you have problems with a spreadsheet, start by printing it and comparing it to the figures and formulas in the book. Remember that in a formula, one misplaced $ or) can cause errors, and in a macro, a forgotten ~

can cause the macro to fail. Usually, simple errors like these will be the cause of your spreadsheet problems.

If you have checked for all such possibilities and you still have problems with a spreadsheet, please write to me at the address on the disk order form. Be sure to include a copy of your spreadsheet, a printout of your cell formulas, and a complete description of your problem. With this information, I will do everything I can to find a solution.

Also, if you find any errors in this book or have suggestions for improvements to future editions, please write to me at the same address.

HOW TO ORDER DISKS

Instead of keying in the spreadsheets discussed in this book, you can purchase them on disks for use with Version 1A or Version 2.

Here's what each disk contains:

	Chapter	*Description*
Disk #1	1 & 2	The Data Bank
Disk #2	3	A/R Collections Analysis
	4	Economic Order Quantity
	5*	A/P Management Analysis
	6	Changes in Financial Position
	7	Scheduled Payments Calendar
	8	Amortization System
	9	Analyzing Sales Variances
	10	Break-Even Analysis
	12	Sustainable Growth Analysis
Disk #3	11	Forecasting Bankruptcy With Z Scores
	13*	The Mini Graph Management Report
	14	Sales Forecasting—Time Series Analysis
	15	Sales Forecasting—Other Methods
	16	Projecting Cash Flows, Income, and the Balance Sheet Accounts

* Not included on disks for 1-2-3 Version 1A

ORDER FORM

Item	*Description*	*Quantity*
1.1	Disk #1—Version 1A	________
2.1	Disk #2—Version 1A	________
3.1	Disk #3—Version 1A	________
1.2	Disk #1—Version 2	________
2.2	Disk #2—Version 2	________
3.2	Disk #3—Version 2	________
	Total quantity ordered	________
	Price per disk	**$19.95**
	Subtotal	$________
	Plus shipping and handling	**$ 3.00**
	Washington residents add 7.9% sales tax	$________
	Grand total	$________

Method of Payment

____ Check ______ VISA ____ MasterCard ______ Money order

Card number ______________________________ Exp. date __________

Cardholder's name ____

Ship to name ____

Company ____

Ship to address ____

City ________________________ State ________ ZIP __________

Check if: Company address ____________ Home address __________

Mail orders to: CashMaster Business Systems
12345 Lake City Way, NE
Suite 220
Seattle, WA 98125

If you can't wait, you can order by phone 24 hours every day by calling (800) 634-2255 or, in California, (800) 847-4663. Ask for extension 123.

All prices subject to change without notice.

Chapter
One

MANAGING FINANCIAL DATA: THE DATA BANK

In the early 1970s I was the young controller of a firm that was purchased by a Fortune 500 company. Since it was my job to report our performance each month to the new owners, the corporate controller invited me to corporate headquarters to see what the firm did with my data.

When I arrived, he took me directly to the War Room. This was a large room with easy chairs in its center and chalkboards covering the walls. These boards displayed hand-written graphs and charts showing the financial results from all divisions. During the night of the eighth working day of each month, I was told, little elves updated all the chalkboards. On the ninth working day, management sat in the chairs and reviewed the results for the entire company.

I was envious. Our little division couldn't afford a pack of elves, and our time-share computer system could hardly produce an income statement without complaint. There was no way that I could produce similar reports and analyses for my own division managers.

AN OVERVIEW OF THE DATA BANK

This chapter describes a Lotus-based system that I call the Data Bank. It *can* produce the reports that most managers would like to see, and it can do so with surprisingly little professional involvement. Here are some of the reports that this Data Bank system can produce.

Figure 1-1 shows an Accounts Receivable Collections analysis. Far superior to monitoring the days of sales in accounts receivable, it summarizes and illustrates true collection performance over the past year. It also provides accurate information that is critically needed in forecasting cash flows. Chapter 3 describes this report.

Figure 1-2 shows an Accounts Payable Management analysis. This report helps you to learn whether you are paying your bills too early, too

Accounts Receivable Collections Analysis
Dec-85

Section 1

Month Of Sale	Percent of Sales Collected in Each 30-Day Period: 0-30 DAYS	30-60 DAYS	60-90 DAYS	% Uncollected After 90 Days	A/R Over 90 Days As a Percent Of 12-Mos Sales
Dec-84	5% +	43% ++++++++++	42% ++++++++++	10% ++	0.76% +++
Jan-85	8% ++	42% ++++++++++	38% +++++++++	12% +++	1.56% ++++++
Feb-85	6% +	48% +++++++++++	30% +++++++	16% ++++	1.17% +++++
Mar-85	11% +++	53% ++++++++++++	21% +++++	15% +++	0.24% +
Apr-85	7% ++	44% ++++++++++	46% +++++++++++	3% +	0.24% +
May-85	1% .	46% +++++++++++	38% +++++++++	15% +++	1.00% ++++
Jun-85	11% +++	57% +++++++++++++	21% +++++	11% +++	0.41% ++
Jul-85	6% +	27% ++++++	35% ++++++++	32% +++++++	0.63% +++
Aug-85	2% .	15% +++	48% +++++++++++	35% ++++++++	1.27% +++++
Sep-85	1% .	28% ++++++	63% ++++++++++++++	8% ++	1.72% +++++++
Oct-85	3% +	34% ++++++++	36% ++++++++	27% ++++++	0.99% ++++
Nov-85	1% .	45% ++++++++++		54% (Incomplete)	2.63% +++++++++++
Dec-85	2% .			98% (Incomplete)	1.82% +++++++

This Month's Amount Over 90 Days = $38

Section 2

Average of Original Sale Collected Each Period	0-30 DAYS	30-60 DAYS	60-90 DAYS	% Uncollected After 90 Days	A/R Over 90 Days As a Percent Of 12-Mos Sales
Previous 6-Mos	7% ++	48% +++++++++++	32% +++++++	13% +++	0.77% +++
Most recent 6-Mos	3% +	30% +++++++	46% +++++++++++	21% +++++	1.51% ++++++
Improvement	-4%	-18%	14%	-8%	-0.74%

Section 3

Average Total Interest Cost, at 12%, For Receivables Less Than 90 Days Old	
Previous 6-Mos	1.47%
Most recent 6-Mos	2.02%
Improvement	-0.55%

Average Collection Period For Sales Less Than 90 Days Old	
Previous 6-Mos	44 Days
Most recent 6-Mos	61 Days
Improvement	-17 Days

Figure 1-1. An Accounts Receivable Collections analysis

```
                              Accounts Payable Management Analysis
                                            Dec-85
How We Pay
================

                 Percent of Our Purchases We Paid in Each 30-Day Period
  Month    ------------------------------------------------------------------------------
 Of Purch  0-30  30-60  60-90   Pd>90            30       60       90     Pd>90            Avg Days Outstanding
 --------- ------------ ------  ------          ++++++  ------  ******  ======           ----------------------
   Dec-84    7%    29%    50%    14%   +++-------------***********************=======     66   DaysDaysDaysD
   Jan-85   13%    48%    28%    11%   ++++++----------------------*************=====     56   DaysDaysDay
   Feb-85   17%    34%    39%    10%   ++++++++---------------******************====     58   DaysDaysDays
   Mar-85   10%    40%    37%    13%   +++++------------------*****************======     61   DaysDaysDays
   Apr-85   33%    38%    17%    12%   +++++++++++++++-----------------********======     47   DaysDaysD
   May-85   23%    35%    16%    26%   +++++++++++----------------*******============     59   DaysDaysDays
   Jun-85   12%    44%    28%    16%   ++++++--------------------*************=======     59   DaysDaysDays
   Jul-85   28%    35%    23%    14%   +++++++++++++----------------***********======     52   DaysDaysDa
   Aug-85    7%    26%    29%    38%   +++------------*************=================     74   DaysDaysDaysDay
   Sep-85   11%    25%    33%    31%   +++++-----------***************==============     70   DaysDaysDaysDa
   Oct-85   26%    24%    43%     7%   ++++++++++++-----------*******************===     54   DaysDaysDay
   Nov-85   10%    23%            67%  +++++----------==============================
   Dec-85   20%                   80%  +++++++++====================================

Average % of Purchases We Paid in the Three-Month Period Ending on Date Shown
------------------------------------------------------------------------------------------------
   Mar-85   13%    41%    35%    11%   ++++++------------------****************=====     58   DaysDaysDays
   Jun-85   23%    39%    20%    18%   +++++++++++-----------------*********========     55   DaysDaysDay
   Sep-85   15%    29%    28%    28%   +++++++-------------*************============     66   DaysDaysDaysD
   Dec-85   19%    24%    43%    14%   +++++++++-----------*******************======     61   DaysDaysDays

How Our A/P Balance is Changing
===================================
                                                                                               Balance in A/P
                                                                              ----------------------------------------------
 Month   Purch   Pmts         Purchases      Payments        Change in A/P       Total   120+     30    60    90  120+
 ------- --------------------------------------------------  ---------------    ------- ------  ++++ ---- **** ====
 Dec-84   $92    $92              +++++++|-------                $0      |       $196    $29    +++++++------*===
 Jan-85   $76   $117               ++++++|---------            ($41)     |---    $155    $15    +++++------*=
 Feb-85   $89   $112              +++++++|--------             ($23)     |--     $132    $15    +++++++--*==
 Mar-85  $101    $80             ++++++++|------                $21    ++|       $153    $10    +++++++-----=
 Apr-85  $126   $131           ++++++++++|----------            ($5)     |       $148     $5    +++++++-----=
 May-85  $106   $108             ++++++++|--------              ($2)     |       $146    $15    ++++++++--*==
 Jun-85  $131    $82           ++++++++++|------                $49  ++++|       $195    $20    +++++++++-----*==
 Jul-85  $139   $133          +++++++++++|----------             $6      |       $201    $15    ++++++++------**=
 Aug-85  $160   $123         ++++++++++++|---------             $37   +++|       $238    $18    ++++++++++++-----**=
 Sep-85  $161   $104         ++++++++++++|--------              $57 +++++|       $295    $24    ++++++++++++----------**==
 Oct-85  $135   $137           ++++++++++|----------            ($2)     |       $293    $30    ++++++++----------******==
 Nov-85  $181   $175       ++++++++++++++|--------------         $6      |       $299    $18    +++++++++++++-----*****==
 Dec-85  $144   $175          +++++++++++|--------------       ($31)     |--     $268    $22    +++++++++------------*=
```

Figure 1-2. An Accounts Payable Management analysis

late, or both. It also provides information that you will use in forecasting cash flows. This report is described in Chapter 5.

Figure 1-3 shows a report of Changes in Financial Position. It analyzes cash flows for the past month and for the period to date and compares this performance with that of previous periods. Chapter 6 describes this report in detail.

Figure 1-4 shows a Mini Graph Management report. Similar to the

Acme Computers, Inc.
Changes in Financial Position

	Current		Comparison	
	Month	YTD Jan-85	Month	YTD Jan-84
	Dec-85	Dec-85	Dec-84	Dec-84
Net Income After Taxes	19	202	15	96
Add: Depreciation & Amortization	11	102	8	75
Cash Generated From Operations	30	304	23	171
Source (Applications) of Cash From (To) Working Capital				
(Inc) Dec Accounts Receivable	-10	-165	-25	3
(Inc) Dec Inventory	-9	-59	-15	-12
(Inc) Dec Ppd Exp & Other Cur Exp	0	0	-3	-3
Inc (Dec) Accounts Payable	-31	72	0	10
Inc (Dec) P/R Taxes & Benefits	-1	13	1	-1
Inc (Dec) Accrued Income Tax	13	114	12	-24
Inc (Dec) Other Accrued Expenses	5	37	4	11
Total Sources (Applications) of Cash From (To) Working Capital	-33	12	-26	-16
Other Sources (Applications) of Cash				
Net (Purch) Sale of Fixed Assets	0	-262	0	-75
Other Sources (Applications)	1	-2	0	0
Total Other Sources (Applications)	1	-264	0	-75
Net Inc (Dec) in Cash From Operations	-2	52	-3	80
Inc (Dec) in Bank Loan				
Inc (Dec) In Notes Payable	18	32	9	-40
Inc (Dec) in Long Term Loans	-3	-32	-2	-28
Net Increase (Decrease) In Bank Loans	15	0	7	-68
Payment of Dividends	-15	-38	-3	-9
Net Inc (Dec) in Cash	-2	14	1	3
Beginning Cash Balance	45	29	28	26
Ending Cash Balance	43	43	29	29

Figure 1-3. Changes in Financial Position report

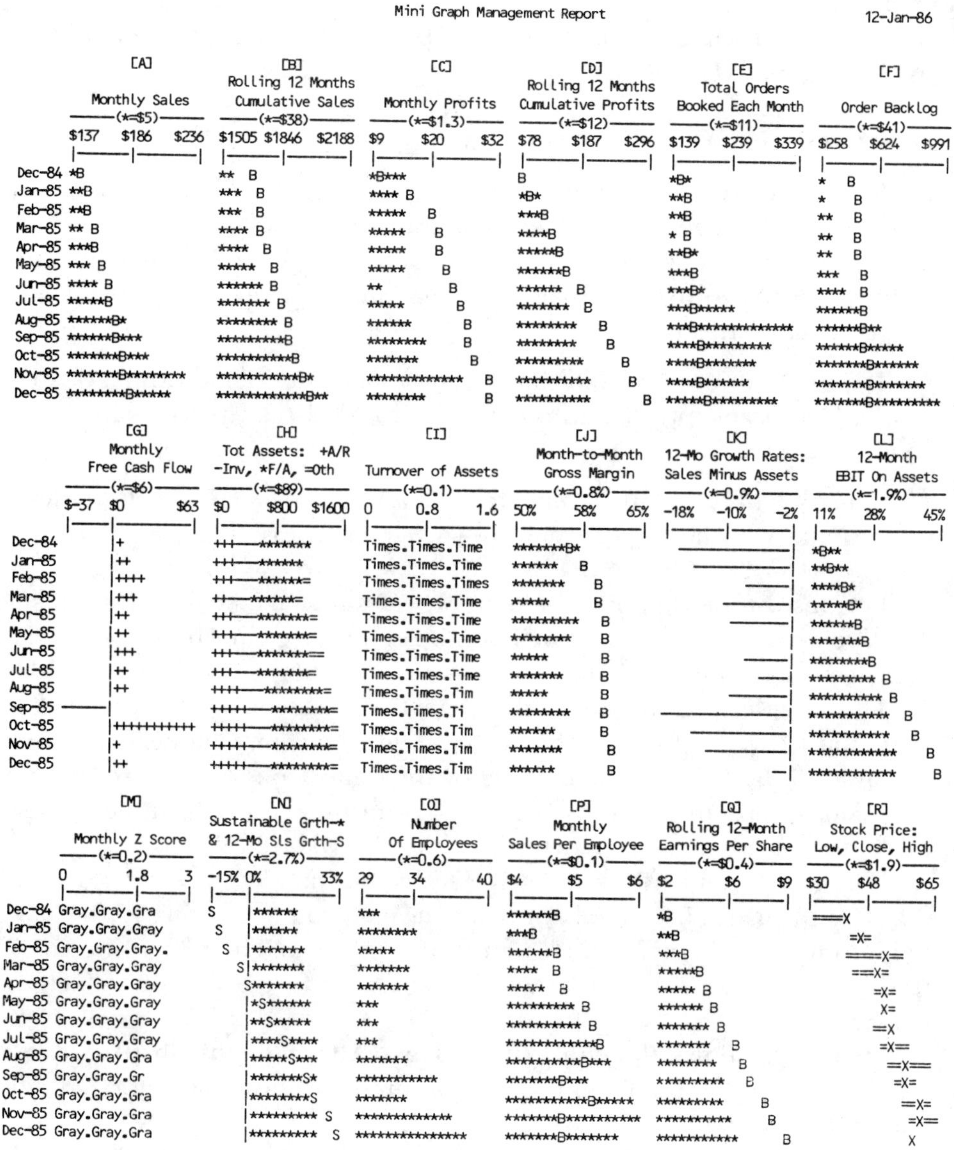

Figure 1-4. A Mini Graph Management report

War Room graphs that were used so effectively, these graphs show at a glance how your company is performing. This report is described in Chapter 13.

As you can see, the Data Bank is a powerful system, especially when you consider the following:

1. All these reports use the same file of historical data.

2. Since this file can contain both accounting data (such as sales, expenses, and accounts payable) and nonaccounting data (for example, number of employees, the price of our stock, and the number of units shipped), virtually any data that is available monthly can be reported using this Data Bank file.

3. Reports that use the Data Bank can be printed one at a time, or they can be loaded and printed automatically from a list of report names that you create.

4. This system is designed to be updated and run by a clerk or lower level professional who has a minimal knowledge of Lotus 1-2-3.

In short, use of the Data Bank system provides management with sophisticated, reliable, timely reports with a minimum of continuing professional involvement in the details of producing those reports.

This chapter explains how the Data Bank system works and how to build the section of the Data Bank that holds the data. Chapter 2 lists and explains all the macros that are used by the Data Bank to assist in entering new data, preparing new reports, and printing reports. Chapter 2 also explains how to enter your own data into the Data Bank.

Chapters 3, 5, 6, and 13 will discuss specific Data Bank reports. Appendix A, at the back of the book, presents the data you must enter in the Data Bank to test the reports you create in these chapters.The remaining chapters describe other ways to analyze, report, and forecast business performance.

Figure 1-5 shows the entire Data Bank. Although this display is less than one-tenth the size of a normal printout, it will give you a good idea of what the Data Bank looks like.

The data section, at the top of the Data Bank, holds several years' worth of monthly data about your firm. As shown in the detail of this figure, the two leftmost columns are Data Bank numbers and descriptions. To their right are columns for summary data (columns C through J in the detail) and columns for monthly data.

	A	B	C	D	E	F	G	H	I	J	K	L	M
1		The DATA BANK	—Current Mo—		—Current PTD—		—Last Per Mo—		—Last PTD—		START_COL		
2	Management Reporting System				From:	Jan-85			From:	Jan-84	11		
3			Month:	Dec-85	To:	Dec-85	Month:	Dec-84	To:	Dec-84	START_MO		
4	DB#	Description	Balance	Change	Total	Change	Balance	Change	Total	Change	Dec-82	Jan-83	Feb-83
5	100.010	Sales	216	-9	2084	72	144	6	1584	12	153	158	164
6	100.020	Cost of Goods Sold	98	-2	931	37	61	2	747	-3	73	80	81
7	100.030	Research & Development	23	0	216	7	16	0	192	0	16	16	16
8	100.040	Marketing	32	5	294	11	21	1	243	-5	24	23	23
9	100.050	General & Admin	28	2	265	11	17	-1	206	-2	20	19	22
10	100.055	Gain (Loss) on Sale of F/A	0	0	1	0	0	0	2	0	0	0	0

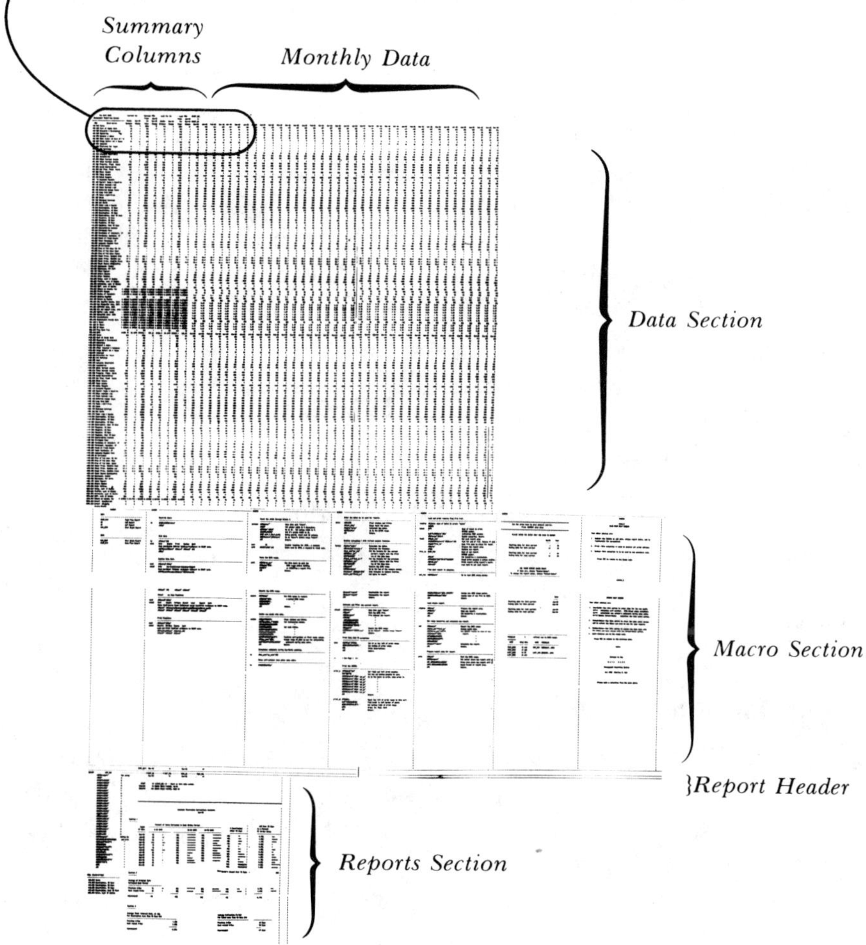

Figure 1-5. The Data Bank

The macro section, in the middle, consists of macros and a few standard calculations. The report header, at the bottom of the macro section, holds several of these calculations and separates the macros from the reports section. The data and macro sections make up the Data Bank spreadsheet.

The reports section, at the bottom of Figure 1-5, shows the Accounts Payable report described in Chapter 3. This section temporarily holds each report when the report is combined into the Data Bank, calculated, and printed, until it is erased from memory to make room for another report.

The Data Bank on Disk

Unfortunately, you cannot create the Data Bank system in ten minutes. It may take several days to get the Data Bank set up and the first few applications working. If you prefer not to invest the time necessary to create the complete Data Bank system, you may be interested in the disk set available for this book. It includes both the complete Data Bank system and the other reports that this book discusses.

REPORTING MONTHLY PERFORMANCE WITH THE DATA BANK

Each month, after the financial statements and other monthly reports have been produced, a clerk updates the Data Bank and prints the Data Bank reports. Figure 1-6 shows an outline of the steps in this monthly reporting cycle that are now described in detail.

Retrieving the Data Bank

To begin a new month, use /**F**ile **R**etrieve to retrieve the most current Data Bank (Figure 1-6a). Then, as explained in Chapter 2, use ALT-M Update New-Month to set the titles and position the cell pointer in the Data Bank to accept data for the new month.

If you have a floppy disk system, replace the Data Bank disk with a formatted blank disk as soon as you retrieve this file. The blank disk will hold the Data Bank for the new month. Since the Data Bank used in this book requires approximately 230 kilobytes of disk memory, this file will consume nearly the entire disk.

Store the month-old disk in a safe place with the Data Bank disks of previous months. Keep these backup disks for at least one year. They will

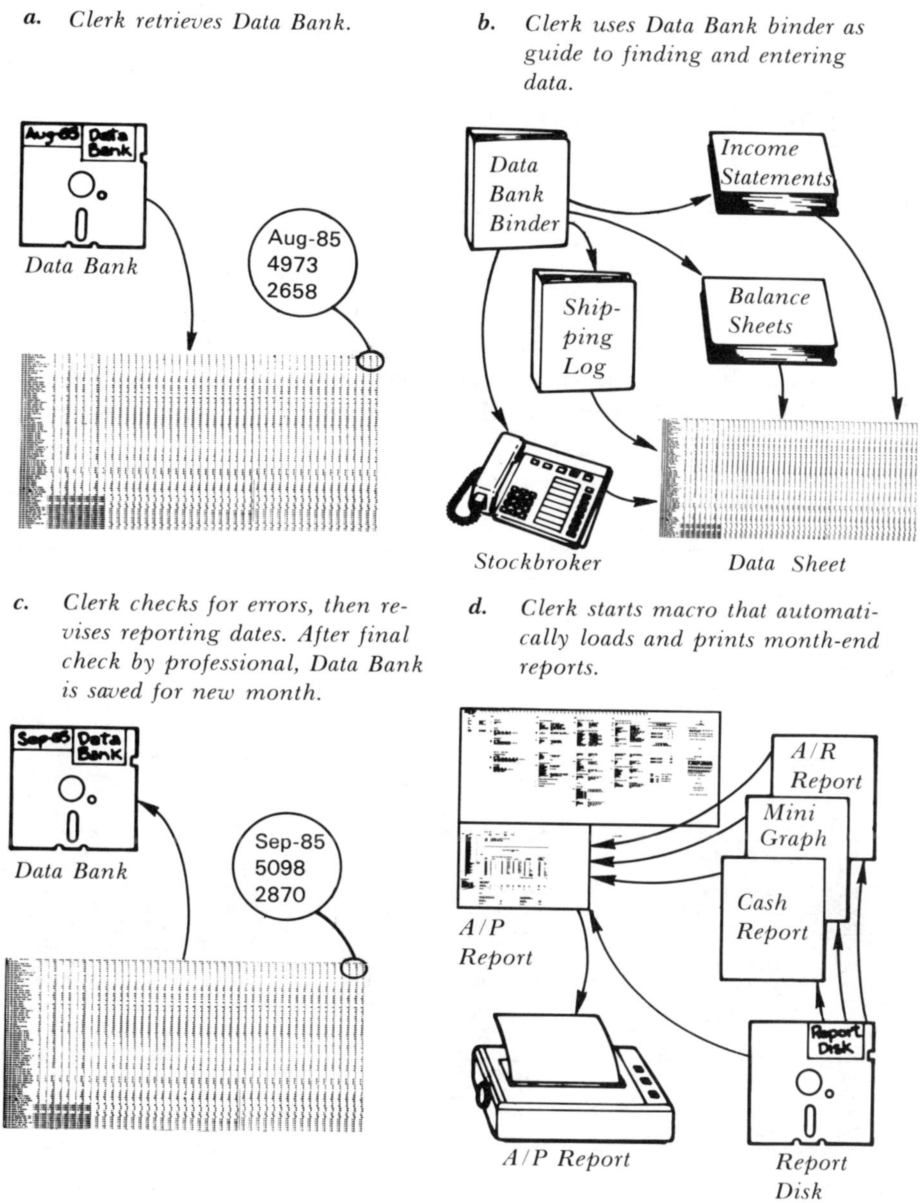

Figure 1-6. The steps in reporting monthly performance

allow you to recover most of your data if the current disk is damaged, even if the damage had existed for months before you discovered the problem.

If you have a hard disk, keep the current version of the Data Bank on the hard disk and maintain floppies as backups.

Using the Binder as a Data Entry Guide

The Data Bank binder is a three-ring binder containing all the documentation necessary to update and maintain the Data Bank. The Data Bank will be very difficult to maintain if you do not assemble this binder.

Figure 1-7 illustrates one page from the binder belonging to Acme Widgets, Inc. This copy of an income statement has three purposes: (1) it explains where to find the current report; (2) it illustrates the report; and (3) it shows which data in the current report must be entered into the Data Bank. This copy will remain in the Data Bank binder until the format of

Available in the monthly "Management Reports" binder in Ms. Davidson's office.

05/31/84
Period 5

ACME WIDGETS, INC.
INCOME STATEMENT
CURRENT–HISTORICAL COMPARISON
MAY 31, 1984

ACCT NO	DESCRIPTION	CURRENT PERIOD THIS YEAR	%	LAST YEAR	%	YEAR TO DATE THIS YEAR	%	LAST YEAR	%
	REVENUE								
301	SALES, WIDGETS	7283.05	41.9	7219.90	43.3	45610.61	48.0	41117.17	46.9
302	SALES, GIDGETS	3955.87	22.8	3767.62	22.6	21165.70	22.3	19235.22	21.9
303	SALES, FIDGETS	1192.88	6.9	1155.12	6.9	7747.48	8.1	7195.35	8.2
304	SALES, MIDGETS	1343.65	7.7	1274.57	7.6	7327.73	7.7	7230.08	8.2
305	SALES, DIDGETS	3478.69	20.0	3161.95	18.9	12607.70	13.3	12356.93	14.1
320	FREIGHT SALES	30.30	0.2	29.80	0.2	155.97	0.2	141.51	0.2
321	MISC SALES	0.00	0.0	0.00	0.0	0.00	0.0	0.00	0.0
349	LESS SALES DISCOUNTS	80.01	0.5	76.90	0.5	452.93	0.5	423.62	0.5
	TOTAL REVENUE 100.010	~~17364.45~~	100.0	16685.84	100.0	95068.11	100.0	87699.88	100.0
	COST OF SALES								
351	COST OF GOODS SOLD	7764.36	44.7	7627.71	45.7	42506.65	44.7	40114.60	45.7
370	FREIGHT	232.93	1.3	211.34	1.3	1275.20	1.3	1202.48	1.4
371	MISC PAID	57.00	0.3	55.08	0.3	57.00	0.1	52.10	0.1
393	SALES TAX PAID	171.56	1.0	163.95	1.0	171.56	0.2	157.26	0.2
396	PURCHASE DISCOUNTS	0.00	0.0	0.00	0.0	0.00	0.0	0.00	0.0
	TOTAL COST OF SALES 100.020	~~8225.85~~	47.4	8058.07	48.3	44010.41	46.3	41526.44	47.3
	GROSS PROFIT ON SALES	9138.60	52.6	8627.77	51.7	51057.71	53.7	46173.44	52.6

Figure 1-7. An Income Statement from the Data Bank binder

	OPERATING EXP									
401	R&D SALARIES		529.00	3.0	482.33	2.9	3318.99	3.5	3151.81	3.6
402	R&D PAYROLL TAXES		79.35	0.5	78.33	0.5	290.00	0.3	267.91	0.3
410	R&D RENT		296.00	1.7	271.81	1.6	1529.25	1.6	1484.91	1.7
420	R&D SUPPLIES		36.00	0.2	33.61	0.2	152.23	0.2	141.26	0.2
430	R&D DEPRECIATION		57.00	0.3	56.90	0.3	191.83	0.2	179.47	0.2
	TOTAL R&D EXPENSE	100.030	997.35	5.7	922.97	5.5	5482.30	5.8	5225.38	6.0
501	SALES SALARIES		2975.36	17.1	2807.73	16.8	13842.09	14.6	12736.52	14.5
502	SALES PAYROLL TAXES		446.30	2.6	422.90	2.5	2070.89	2.2	1923.65	2.2
510	SALES RENT		358.00	2.1	334.75	2.0	1507.79	1.6	1486.71	1.7
520	SALES SUPPLIES		129.00	0.7	123.01	0.7	693.76	0.7	630.72	0.7
530	SALES DEPRECIATION		22.33	0.1	22.31	0.1	117.01	0.1	111.93	0.1
540	ADVERTISING		79.00	0.5	73.29	0.4	471.22	0.5	462.16	0.5
	TOTAL SALES EXPENSE	100.040	4009.99	23.1	3783.99	22.7	18702.77	19.7	17351.69	19.8
601	OFFICE SALARIES		1194.56	6.9	1115.65	6.7	7637.76	8.0	6980.70	8.0
602	OFFICE PAYROLL TAXES		179.18	1.0	174.99	1.0	644.57	0.7	596.69	0.7
610	OFFICE RENT		157.00	0.9	155.78	0.9	473.65	0.5	443.93	0.5
620	OFFICE SUPPLIES		62.50	0.4	58.02	0.3	224.45	0.2	218.75	0.2
630	OFFICE DEPRECIATION		10.00	0.1	9.41	0.1	51.60	0.1	49.40	0.1
650	ACCOUNTING COSTS		783.00	4.5	715.43	4.3	4110.77	4.3	4011.25	4.6
	TOTAL OFFICE EXPENSE	100.050	2386.24	13.7	2229.28	13.4	13142.81	13.8	12300.73	14.0
	TOTAL OPERATING EXPENSE		7393.59	42.6	6936.24	41.6	37327.88	39.3	34877.80	39.8
	TOTAL OPERATING PROFIT		1745.01	10.0	1691.53	10.1	13729.83	14.4	11295.64	12.9
	OTHER INC & EXP	100.060 = (A + B)								
801	INTEREST INCOME		57.20	0.3	51.77	0.3	306.15	0.3	304.77	0.3
802	FINANCE CHARGES RECEIVED		0.20	0.0	0.19	0.0	1.37	0.0	1.24	0.0
851	INTEREST EXPENSE	100.070 (B)	282.20	1.6	263.64	1.6	1479.90	1.6	1431.73	1.6
859	LOSS (GAIN) ON F/A SALES	100.055	0.00	0.0	0.00	0.0	0.00	0.0	0.00	0.0
	TOTAL OTHER INC & (EXP)		-224.80	-1.3	-211.68	-1.3	-1531.50	-1.6	-1481.66	-1.7
	NET PROFIT									
	EARNINGS BEFORE TAXES	(A)	1520.21	8.8	1479.85	8.9	12198.33	12.8	9813.98	11.2
902	LESS: PROVISION FOR TAXES	100.080	456.06	2.6	443.95	2.7	3659.50	3.8	2944.19	3.4
	NET PROFITS AFTER TAXES	100.090	1064.14	6.1	1035.89	6.2	8538.83	9.0	6869.79	7.8

Figure 1-7. An Income Statement from the Data Bank binder (*continued*)

the monthly Income Statement changes or until the copy is so marked up and torn that it must be replaced.

Each month, a clerk at Acme turns to this page and enters data from the current report that corresponds with the numbers marked in the figure. The circle in this figure shows which number to use from the current report. The data within the circle is crossed out. This reduces the tendency to enter the data from the binder rather than from the current report.

Each circled data item has a Data Bank number (DB#) assigned to it, which represents the framework on which the Data Bank is built. This number is similar to a general ledger account number but with one important difference: general ledger account numbers specify where the data will be reported; Data Bank numbers specify where the data is documented.

You can use any numbering system that you wish to generate your Data Bank numbers. But once you have assigned a number, be prepared to use it for a long time—many different reports will use each Data Bank number.

Figure 1-8 shows a list of all Data Bank numbers and descriptions in the sample Data Bank. The system used to generate the Data Bank numbers in this list seems to work well; each number it produces refers to a section and item number in the Data Bank binder.

```
         A                B
 1            The DATA BANK
 2     Management Reporting System
 3  ===================================
 4      DB#           Description
 5   100.010 Sales
 6   100.020 Cost of Goods Sold
 7   100.030 Research & Development
 8   100.040 Marketing
 9   100.050 General & Admin
10   100.055 Gain (Loss) on Sale of F/A
11   100.060 Erngs Before Int & Taxes
12   100.070 Interest
13   100.080 Provision for Taxes
14   100.090 Net Earnings
15   105.005 Cash
16   105.010 Accounts Receivable
17   105.020 Inventories
18   105.030 Other Current Assets
19   105.040 Total Current Assets
20   105.050 Property, Plant, Equip
21   105.060 Accum Depreciation
22   105.070 Net Prop, Plant, Equip
23   105.080 Other Assets
24   105.090 Total Assets
25   105.100 Notes Payable
26   105.110 Accounts Payable
27   105.120 Payroll Taxes & Benefits
28   105.130 Other Accrued Liab
29   105.140 Total Current Liab
30   105.150 Deferred Income Taxes
31   105.160 Long Term Debt
32   105.170 Total Liabilities
33   105.180 Stock
```

Figure 1-8. The Data Bank numbers and their descriptions

	A	B
34	105.190	Retained Earnings
35	105.200	Net Worth
36	105.210	Total Liab & Equity
37	110.010	Receivables, 30 Days
38	110.020	Receivables, 60 Days
39	110.030	Receivables, 90 Days
40	110.040	Receivables, Over 90 Days
41	115.010	Payables, 30 Days
42	115.020	Payables, 60 Days
43	115.030	Payables, 90 Days
44	115.040	Payables, Over 90 Days
45	120.010	Depreciation Expense
46	199.010	Dividends Paid
47	199.020	Purchases of Inventory, AP
48	199.022	Purchases, Expenses, AP
49	199.023	Purch of Fixed Assets
50	199.029	Total Purchases, AP
51	199.030	Accounts Payable Paid
52	199.040	AR Collected
53	199.060	Disp of Fxd Asts--Bk Val
54	199.070	Disp of Fxd Asts--Depr
55	199.080	Disp of Fxd Asts--Sales
56	200.010	Stock Price, Monthly High
57	200.020	Stock Price, Monthly Low
58	200.030	Stock Price, Monthly Close
59	200.040	Stock Shares Outstanding
60	300.010	Employees, Number
61	300.020	Employees, Vol Quit
62	300.100	Total Payroll
63	400.010	Orders Booked
64	400.020	Order Backlog
65	800.010	Sales, Last 12 Months
66	800.020	Profits, Last 12 Months
67	800.030	Dividends, Last 12 Months
68	800.040	EBIT, Last 12 Months
69	810.010	Return on Assets, Cur
70	810.020	Profit Margin
71	810.030	Months of Inventory
72	810.040	Working Capital
73	810.120	Return on Equity
74	815.010	Wrk Cap/Tot Assets, [X1]
75	815.020	Ret Erngs/Tot Asts, [X2]
76	815.030	EBIT/Tot Asts, [X3]
77	815.040	Mkt Val Eqty/T Liab, [X4]
78	815.050	NW/Tot Liab, [X4A]
79	815.060	Sales/Tot Asts, [X5]
80	815.062	Assets/Sales
81	850.010	Sustainable Growth Rate
82	851.010	Z Score
83	851.020	Z1 Score
84	851.030	Z2 Score

Figure 1-8. The Data Bank numbers and their descriptions (*continued*)

	A	B
85	852.010	Free Cash Flow
86	900.010	DATE
87	1100.010	Sales
88	1100.020	Cost of Goods Sold
89	1100.030	Research & Development
90	1100.040	Marketing
91	1100.050	General & Admin
92	1100.055	Other (Income) & Expenses
93	1100.060	Erngs Before Int & Taxes
94	1100.070	Interest
95	1100.080	Provision for Taxes
96	1100.090	Net Earnings
97	1105.005	Cash
98	1105.010	Accounts Receivable
99	1105.020	Inventories
100	1105.030	Other Current Assets
101	1105.040	Total Current Assets
102	1105.050	Property, Plant, Equip
103	1105.060	Accum Depreciation
104	1105.070	Net Prop, Plant, Equip
105	1105.080	Other Assets
106	1105.090	Total Assets
107	1105.100	Notes Payable
108	1105.110	Accounts Payable
109	1105.120	Payroll Taxes & Benefits
110	1105.130	Other Accrued Liab
111	1105.140	Total Current Liab
112	1105.150	Deferred Income Taxes
113	1105.160	Long Term Debt
114	1105.170	Total Liabilities
115	1105.180	Stock
116	1105.190	Retained Earnings
117	1105.200	Net Worth
118	1105.210	Total Liab & Equity
119	1110.010	Receivables, 30 Days
120	1110.020	Receivables, 60 Days
121	1110.030	Receivables, 90 Days
122	1110.040	Receivables, Over 90 Days
123	1115.010	Payables, 30 Days
124	1115.020	Payables, 60 Days
125	1115.030	Payables, 90 Days
126	1115.040	Payables, Over 90 Days
127	1120.010	Depreciation Expense
128	1199.010	Dividends Paid
129	1199.020	Purchases of Inventory, AP
130	1199.022	Purchases, Expenses, AP
131	1199.023	Purch of Fixed Assets
132	1199.029	Total Purchases, AP
133	1199.030	Accounts Payable Paid
134	1199.040	AR Collected
135	1199.060	Disp of Fxd Asts--Bk Val

Figure 1-8. The Data Bank numbers and their descriptions (*continued*)

	A	B
136	1199.070	Disp of Fxd Asts--Depr
137	1199.080	Disp of Fxd Asts--Sales
138	1200.010	Stock Price, Monthly High
139	1200.020	Stock Price, Monthly Low
140	1200.030	Stock Price, Monthly Close
141	1200.040	Stock Shares Outstanding
142	1300.010	Employees, Number
143	1300.020	Employees, Vol Quity
144	1300.100	Total Payroll
145	1400.010	Orders Booked
146	1400.020	Order Backlog
147	1800.010	Sales, Last 12 Months
148	1800.020	Profits, Last 12 Months
149	1800.030	Dividends, Last 12 Months
150	1800.040	EBIT, Last 12 Months
151	1810.010	Return on Assets, Cur
152	9999.010	Error? Assets=Liab
153	9999.020	Error? AR=Aging
154		(Leave Blank)

Figure 1-8. The Data Bank numbers and their descriptions (*continued*)

Section Numbers The numbers before the decimal point refer to sections or pages in the Data Bank binder. Each section is dedicated to a single category of data. For example, section 100, the first section shown in the sample Data Bank in Figure 1-8, is the firm's income statement. The next one is the firm's balance sheet; section 110 is the firm's accounts receivable aging schedule; section 199 contains miscellaneous information from the accounting system; the section numbers in the 400s have marketing and sales data; and so on. Space has been left between these section numbers so that additional categories of data sources may be added later.

In Figure 1-8, the section numbers in the 800s and 900s all refer to formulas explained in Appendix A. These formulas generate totals and ratios that will be used by the reports in Chapters 3, 5, 6, and 13. Also, as discussed later in this chapter, you will use these totals and ratios to find errors in your data.

The Data Bank section numbers in the thousands all refer to budgets. In general, the Data Bank number for a budget category is equal to the DB# for reporting actual performance, plus 1000. For example, the DB# for Sales in Figure 1-8 is 100.010; its budget number is 1100.010. The number for a second set of budgets or forecasts would be equal to the DB# for the actual data plus 2000; for a third set it would be plus 3000, and so on. This approach to numbering budget data makes it easy to compare actual performance to one of several different budgets or to compare one budget to another.

If your firm generates new budget numbers monthly, document budgets in the Data Bank binder just as you did for actual performance data. But if, like most firms, yours generates no more than four budgets each year, you should be able to store them in the Data Bank binder itself. Budgets, therefore, will be the only category of data that you will enter into the Data Bank directly from the Data Bank binder.

Finally, the Data Bank section number 9999 in Figure 1-8 holds several error-checking formulas. Error checking is discussed in greater detail shortly.

Item Numbers Following the decimal point in the Data Bank numbers are item numbers within each section. They usually are assigned sequentially, in increments of ten, as shown in Figures 1-7 and 1-8. This allows for additional numbers in each report to be assigned later. In these figures, for example, the category Gain (Loss) on Sale of Fixed Assets, DB# 100.055, was inserted after the original Data Bank was created.

At times, the item number may take a page or two of documentation to explain fully. For example, DB# 199.020 in Figure 1-8 contains the amount of all purchases of inventory that were charged to accounts payable each month. Since this amount is normally not reported by the accounting system, a full page of detail may be necessary to explain how to extract the amount from reports that *are* produced by your system.

Error Checking, Revising Dates, and Saving the Data Bank

Check for Errors Errors will find their way into the Data Bank; dates must be revised, and the Data Bank must be saved (see Figure 1-6c). You will want to correct errors before your clerk prints and distributes the reports. One way to do so is to compare several numbers from each current report with the corresponding numbers in the Data Bank. This step ensures that your clerk has entered data from the proper report for the current month.

Another way to check for errors is to check the rows of subtotals contained in the data section of the Data Bank. These subtotals fall into three categories:

1. Financial statement subtotals

2. Error-checking formulas

3. Running totals and financial ratios.

In Figure 1-8, Net Earnings (100.090), Total Current Assets (105.040), and Total Liabilities and Equity (105.210) are examples of lines in the financial statements that result from data found in other lines. Allowing a formula to calculate these financial statement subtotals does two things: (1) it saves data entry time, and (2) it allows you and your clerk to check data entry accuracy. If the clerk has entered sales and expenses properly, the Net Earnings amount calculated in the Data Bank should match the amount shown in the monthly report.

Unfortunately, formulas in a cell require more memory and calculation time than do simple values. You can minimize this problem by changing the formulas into values each month after data has been entered. If you have 1-2-3 Version 2, use the /**R**ange **V**alues command to do this. If you have Version 1A, use the /**F**ile **X**tract **V**alues command to save a section of the Data Bank to a temporary file; then use the /**F**ile **C**ombine **C**opy **E**ntire command to load this section of values back into the spreadsheet.

The last two rows in Figure 1-8 illustrate another approach, using the second category of subtotals. These error-checking formulas return an ERR if the numbers don't balance. For example, DB# 9999.010 returns an ERR if the Total Assets for any month (DB# 105.090) don't equal Total Liabilities and Equity (DB# 105.210). If the data balances, the formula returns a zero. As before, these formulas can be changed to a value once the month is entered.

A more thorough way to check for errors is to use the methods described in Chapters 3, 5, 6, and 13 to write an error-checking report for the Data Bank. This report would reconcile every numeric relationship you can think of in your Data Bank. This approach also reduces the memory required for the Data Bank by eliminating the need for error-checking formulas in the data section.

In Figure 1-8 the Data Bank numbers in the 800s and 900s are all in the third category of subtotals, that of running totals and financial ratios. DB#

800.010, for example, shows total Sales each month for the most recent 12 months, and DB# 810.020 shows the monthly profit margin percentage.

These totals and percentages provide an excellent reasonability test of the data your clerk has entered. After recalculating the Data Bank, compare each total and ratio with those of several previous months. If any ratio shows an unusual rise or fall in the current month, an error is often the cause.

The formulas for each row of the 800s and 900s are included in Appendix A. The formulas all are given for column AU, the last column in the sample data base. Why the last column rather than the first? Because many of these formulas won't work in the first year of data. After all, a formula can't sum the most recent 12 months of data if the data doesn't exist.

The Data Bank numbers for these formulas refer to the section numbers in the Data Bank binder where the formulas are explained. Generally, it is easiest to establish a section in the binder for logical groupings of ratios. In Figure 1-8, for example, the 800 section contains the 12-month running totals, the 851 section has the Z Score calculations discussed in Chapter 10 and graphed in Chapter 13, and so on.

Revise the Dates When your clerk has finished finding and entering all the data for the month, he or she selects ALT-M Update Select-Dates. This macro allows your clerk to choose two time periods to report.

Usually the first period is the current fiscal year to date, but it could be the most recent quarter, the most recent 12 months, or even the most recent 36 months. The second period, the comparison period, could be any earlier period that you wish. Generally, it consists of the same months as the current period but from the preceding year.

After selecting the dates to report, your clerk selects ALT-M Update Update-Dates. This option uses the new dates to change the summary formulas in the Data Bank. These formulas calculate the totals and the balance sheet changes that the Data Bank reports will need.

Save the Data Bank Before saving the Data Bank for the first time each month, make sure that the file of the Data Bank for the previous month has been stored in a safe place. Then, to save the Data Bank, simply issue the /**F**ile **S**ave command.

Printing Reports

The Data Bank contains lists of report names. Each list defines a batch of reports that can be loaded and printed automatically. To print the reports, your clerk issues the ALT-M Print Reports command and then tells the macro which list of reports to print. Beginning with the first name in this list, the macro loads each report, calculates it, prints it, and then continues with the next name on the list. When the list is completed, the processing ends.

Chapter 2 discusses how to create the list of report names and how to create the macros to which the ALT-M command gives you access.

ENTERING NEW DATA CATEGORIES INTO THE DATA BANK

From time to time you will want to add additional data categories to the Data Bank. For example, you may want to add a row that shows the price of your major competitor's stock, the total sales price of goods returned each month for warranty repair, the number of active customers at the end of each month, and so on. Figure 1-9 illustrates the steps in this process that are now described in greater detail.

Finding a Reliable Source of New Data

The accuracy of the Data Bank depends upon the accuracy and consistency of the data it contains. A Data Bank analysis can be wrong, in fact, if definitions of data are suddenly changed.

Suppose, for example, that you want to maintain a row in the Data Bank that tracks the number of employees in your firm. Several reports in the personnel and accounting departments contain this data. But they probably won't agree. One report may show the number of people receiving paychecks. Another may show the number of full-time equivalent employees. (This calculation would count two half-time employees as one full-time employee.) A third report may include the number of temporary and contract employees.

a. *Professional finds reliable source of new data.*

b. *Professional adds copy of new report to Data Bank binder, and explains how to obtain a new report each month and what information to use from it.*

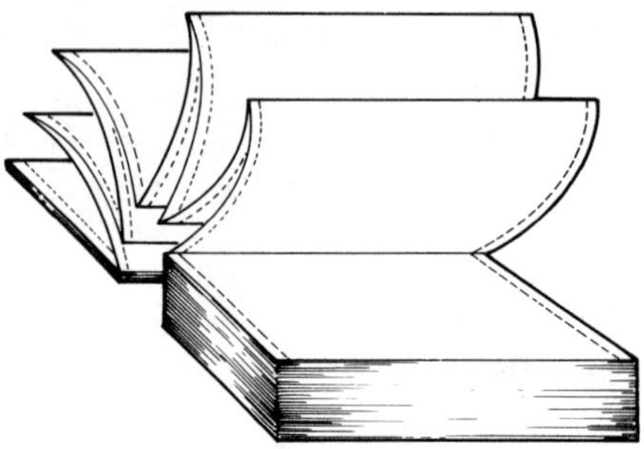

Payroll Report

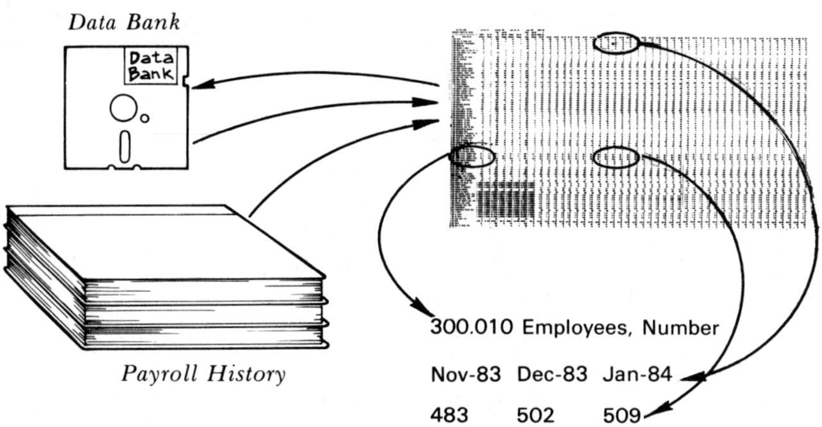

c. *Professional retrieves Data Bank, enters historical data from old report, and then saves Data Bank.*

Figure 1-9. Entering new data categories into the Data Bank

You probably could use any of these reports as a source for your data. But if the report that you use suddenly changes the way it defines an employee, the change would distort any Data Bank reports that reflect this change. So be very careful to find sources of data that you can depend upon.

Documenting the Report in the Data Bank Binder

The method shown in Figure 1-9b is a quick, easy, and effective way to document a new source of data: copy the report; explain where it can be found monthly; with a line and circle, show the places from which corresponding data in new reports should be entered; assign Data Bank numbers; and then three-hole punch the copy and insert it in DB# sequence in the Data Bank binder.

Entering and Saving New Historical Data

The Data Bank allows you to compare trends over periods of at least two years. When you add a new category of data, therefore, you must enter this historical data (Figure 1-9c).

To enter new categories of data, use /**W**orksheet **I**nsert **R**ows to insert the necessary rows. (Be sure to insert the rows in such a way that the Data Bank numbers remain in numerical sequence in the Data Bank.) Enter the DB#s and their descriptions. Then, beginning in column K, as shown in the detail of Figure 1-5, enter data for the first month in the Data Bank through the current month. Finally, copy the formulas for columns C through K into the new rows as necessary. When you have finished, there should be no empty cells in the data section of the Data Bank from column A through the current column of monthly data.

CREATING A NEW DATA BANK REPORT

Chapters 3, 5, 6, and 13 explain in detail how to create new Data Bank reports. Figure 1-10 illustrates the general approach, as follows:

1. Retrieve the Data Bank (Figure 1-10a). As always, when you retrieve the Data Bank, it will be empty of reports.

2. Write your new Data Bank report (Figure 1-10b). If your new report is similar to an existing Data Bank report, you may find it easier to load the existing report and then modify it. Chapter 5 uses this approach to create an Accounts Receivable report from an Accounts Payable report.

3. Save the new report (Figure 1-10c). Each of the four chapters about Data Bank reports explains how to extract and save them. As illustrated in Figure 1-10, this process saves the report separately from the Data Bank itself.

4. Add the new report name to the Data Bank (Figure 1-10d). After you have created the new report, you will probably want to add the report name to the list of reports that are printed monthly. Chapter 2 explains where to add the name of your new report within the macro section of the Data Bank.

When you update the list of names, do not save the copy of the Data Bank in memory that you have been using to create your report. Instead, as shown in Figure 1-10, retrieve a fresh copy of the Data Bank, update the print list, and then save the Data Bank. This extra step ensures that you don't save any accidental changes you may have made to the Data Bank while you created your new report.

USING THE DATA BANK

To get a better idea of how the Data Bank works, let's follow Susan, an assistant controller for Acme Widgets, Inc., and Bill, an accounting clerk, as they use the Data Bank.

Entering New Data Categories

Since Acme's payroll costs have been rising rapidly in recent months, Susan decides to include a sales-per-employee calculation in her monthly management reports. And since her accounting data base can't easily provide this information, she decides to use the Data Bank.

Acme's Data Bank for the accounting department already has monthly sales figures but lacks the number of employees. So Susan must find the best source for this information and then enter it into the Data Bank. She talks with both the payroll and the personnel departments. They show her what information they have that could help her. Finally, Susan decides that

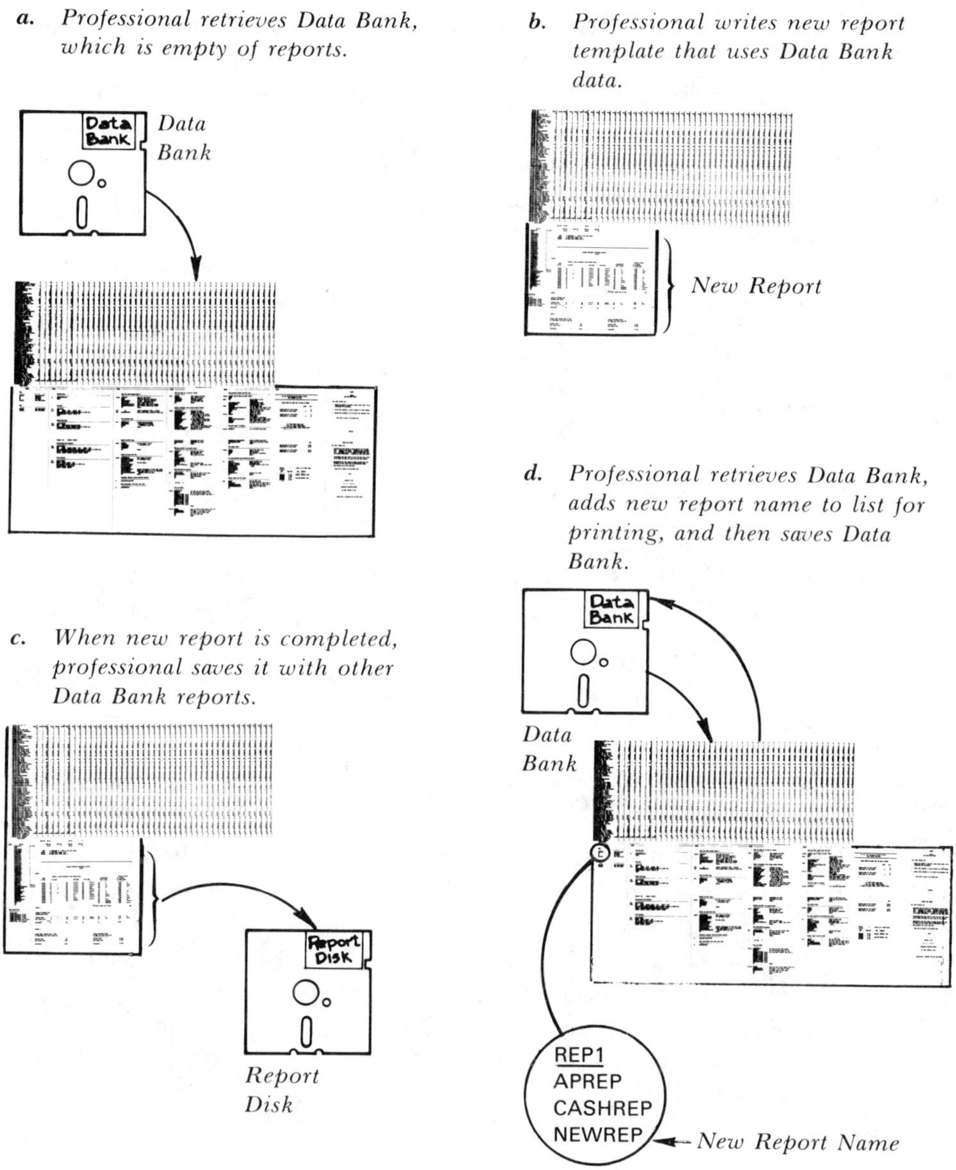

Figure 1-10. Creating new Data Bank reports

a summary report by the payroll department has just the information she needs.

Susan takes a photocopy of a past report on which she writes the name, phone number, and department of the person who keeps the payroll summary on file. This information will tell Bill where to find new payroll reports each month. Also, from old copies of this report, Susan records the number of employees Acme had at the end of each month during the previous two years. Entering this information into the Data Bank will allow her to analyze historical trends.

When Susan returns to the accounting department, she assigns a DB# to the new information and writes this number on her copy of the payroll report. Then she files this copy in the Data Bank binder. Finally, she loads the Data Bank spreadsheet, adds the historical data, and then saves the updated Data Bank.

Creating New Data Bank Reports

Beginning with a Data Bank that is empty of reports, Susan creates the report she needs. When the report is completed, she uses the Data Bank macros to extract and save this report with her file of other Data Bank reports. Finally, Susan adds the name of her new report to the list of other reports that is kept in the Data Bank. From now on, this new report will be produced automatically each month.

The Monthly Reporting Cycle

Bill has been assigned to update and maintain the Data Bank. Though he doesn't know very much about Lotus 1-2-3, he's interested in learning more about computers and isn't afraid to ask questions.

When the monthly reports required by the Data Bank have been completed, Bill knows it's time to run the Data Bank reports. He loads last month's Data Bank and then selects ALT-M Update New-Month. This command prepares the Data Bank to accept data for the new month. To enter the data, Bill begins by turning to the first section of the Data Bank binder.

Figure 1-7 shows the page that Bill sees. Near the bottom of this page, the documentation shows that DB# 100.060 is equal to A+B. Figure 1-8 shows that DB# 100.060 is Earnings Before Interest and Taxes. The income statement shown in Figure 1-7, however, doesn't calculate this amount. DB# 100.060, therefore, is equal to Earnings Before Taxes (marked as A) plus

Interest Expense (marked as B). Notice that letters rather than numbers are used to label these values. This makes sure that Bill doesn't accidentally enter number labels into the Data Bank instead of the values that the labels represent.

As instructed by the note at the top of Figure 1-7, Bill borrows Ms. Davidson's copy of the current income statement and updates the Data Bank with the data corresponding with the numbers marked in the documentation. After returning the income statement, he turns to the next section in the Data Bank binder, gets the current version of that report, enters the current data, returns the current version, turns to the next section of the binder, and so on, until he has entered all the data required by the Data Bank.

Some instructions in other sections of the Data Bank binder are more complex. Some require the use of several reports, numerous calculations, and detailed ways to reconcile the result. (Each company that uses the Data Bank will have different areas of complexity in this regard.) Other instructions are as simple as "Call Mr. Dimple, our stockbroker, at 555-1976, and ask him for the price of Acme's stock." But in all cases, each section describes the exact procedure that Bill must follow to find and enter the required data.

After entering each report in the Data Bank, Bill double checks that he has correctly entered the correct numbers from the correct copy of the correct report.

When Bill has finished finding and entering all the data for the Data Bank, he selects ALT-M Update Select-Dates, which allows him to choose the two time periods that he has been instructed to report. Next, he selects ALT-M Update Update-Dates. This option uses the new dates to change the summary formulas in the Data Bank. These formulas calculate the totals and the balance sheet changes that the Data Bank reports will need.

When the dates have been updated, Bill saves the Data Bank. Since Acme personnel faithfully follow a policy of making backup copies of all computer files, Susan knows that she can always recover the previous month's Data Bank if Bill accidentally destroys the current Data Bank. The worst damage that Bill could do, therefore, would be to lose the current month's data, forcing him to enter it again.

After Bill has entered all the data and updated the periods to report, Susan makes a final check for errors. When she is satisfied that the data is correct, she changes many of the formulas in the Data Bank to values. This step speeds recalculation time and reduces the memory requirements of the spreadsheet.

Finally, after the adjusted Data Bank has been saved, either Susan or Bill will select ALT-M Print Reports. This option, which could run for an hour or more, will print all Data Bank reports contained in the list that Bill or Susan chooses.

HOW TO ASSEMBLE THE DATA BANK BINDER

The Data Bank binder is easy to assemble and maintain. It makes extensive use of the office copier, handwritten notes, and common sense. Include as much documentation as you need. At the minimum, however, your binder should contain the following three major divisions.

Instructions for Updating the Data Bank

The first page of the binder should be a summary of the commands necessary to start the computer, load 1-2-3, retrieve the Data Bank, enter the data, and print the reports. This page isn't intended to teach your clerk how to perform these steps. You must do the teaching. But after you have done so, the page will serve as a quick reference.

To complete the remaining pages, make a copy of every report that will provide data for your Data Bank: the income statement, balance sheet, accounts payable aging schedule, accounts receivable aging schedule, and so on. If these reports are printed on standard 11-inch by 15-inch computer paper, you will need to use a copy machine with reduction capability. As shown in Figure 1-7, explain where to find each report. If necessary, include the title of the binder that contains the report.

Circle every number in these copies that must be entered into the Data Bank and then draw a line through the number. As discussed previously, the line reminds your clerk that you've marked the numbers to help him or her find similar numbers that are to be entered from the current report.

Budgets require a slightly different approach because, unlike actual performance data, budget data often *will* be entered from the Data Bank binder. To enter budgets in the binder, obtain a copy of the budgets, circle the budget numbers you wish to enter in the Data Bank, assign DB#s to these, and then insert the copies in the binder.

As discussed previously, the steps necessary to find and enter other data may be simple or quite complex. In either case, try to keep the instructions for these steps as short and as easy to understand as possible.

Documentation for the Data Section Formulas

The documentation for these formulas can be very simple, as the following two examples show:

- 800.010 Sales, Last 12 Months—@SUM of DB# 100.010 for the current month and for the previous 11 months.
- 815.060 Sales/Tot Asts, [X5]—Equal to this month's Sales, Last 12 Months (800.010) divided by this month's Total Assets (105.090). This is the X5 ratio used by the Z Score calculation.

The documentation in Appendix A for the DB#s in the 800s and 900s provides additional illustrations.

Copies of the Data Bank Reports

This division of the Data Bank binder should contain a sample of each Data Bank report. Reference information about each report can be written on the copy or included on accompanying pages. This reference information would include the file name of the report, which print list or lists it has been included in, the names of the individuals who receive a copy of each report, and so on.

BUILDING THE DATA SECTION

The data section of the Data Bank is the easiest section to build, but it's the most tedious. It's easy because this section isn't very sophisticated; it's tedious because there's a lot of data to enter.

Enter the Headings

Beginning with an empty spreadsheet, issue the /**W**orksheet **G**lobal **R**ecalculation **M**anual command. Set the width of column A to 9 and the width of column B to 26. (The length of the longest description in the sample Data Bank is 26 characters; adjust this width as necessary.) The default global column width of 9 characters will work for the sample data, but you will probably need to widen the global column width for your own data.

Enter **The DATA BANK** in cell A1, preceded by nine spaces, and then enter the remaining headings, other than the dates and numbers, that you see in Figure 1-11.

```
      A                B                 C          D          E          F          G           H          I          J          K          L
1           The DATA BANK             ---Current Mo----  ---Current PTD---  ---Last Per Mo---  -----Last PTD----  START_COL
2     Management Reporting System                           From:    Jan-85                          From:    Jan-84        11
3   ===================================  Month:    Dec-85      To:   Dec-85    Month:    Dec-84      To:   Dec-84  START MO
4        DB#         Description       Balance    Change    Total    Change   Balance    Change     Total    Change    Dec-82    Jan-83
```

Figure 1-11. The headings in the data section of the Data Bank

The following four formulas return the beginning and ending dates for the current period and the comparison period. Suppose, for example, that we wish to report performance for the first five months of 1986, comparing this information with the performance one year earlier. The four cells would contain the dates Jan-86, May-86, Jan-85, and May-85, respectively. The formulas in these cells all refer to values that will be generated in Chapter 2. For now, therefore, they will return Jan-00 after you have formatted the cells as Date 3 as shown. When you complete Chapter 2, these formulas will return the proper date values.

```
F2: (D3) +$BB$184
F3: (D3) +$BB$185
J2: (D3) +$BB$187
J3: (D3) +$BB$188
```

The labels START_COL and START_MO in K1 and K3 are range names for cells K2 and K4, respectively. To assign these names to the appropriate cells, use the /**R**ange **N**ame **L**abel **D**own command, highlighting the range K1..K3.

The formula for the date in cell K4 is simply @DATE(82,12,15). Later, when you enter your own data, you will put the date for the first month of data that you wish to enter in this cell.

Succeeding dates in row 4 are calculated by adding the average number of days per month, or 30.4375 (365.25/12), to the preceding cell. The formula for the date in L4, for example, is +K4+30.4375. It uses the date format /Range Format Date (3). Copy this formula from L4 to M4..AU4.

If you use 1-2-3 Version 2, enter the following formula:

```
K2: @CELL("COL",$K$4..$K$4)
```

This formula returns the column number of the first data column in the Data Bank. This value is used frequently by the macros described in Chapter 2.

If you use 1-2-3 Version 1A, simply enter the number 11 in K2. Remember, however, that if you ever insert or delete columns to the left of column K, you must change this number accordingly.

Enter the Data

Appendix A provides all the data contained in the sample Data Bank. This data needs to be in place for the reports in Chapters 3, 5, 6, and 13 to work properly.

To begin, enter the Data Bank numbers and descriptions shown in Figure 1-8. Make sure that you enter the (Leave Blank) description shown for row 154. This is the only entry you make in this row.

Next, move your cell pointer to column C. Issue the /**W**orksheet **T**itles **V**ertical command. Then turn to Appendix A and enter the numbers shown there. The following macro should help you to enter this data.

```
\E  {?}{DOWN}
    /XG \E~
```

To use this macro, place your cell pointer where you wish to enter the first number and then press ALT-E. After you enter the number and press ENTER, the cell pointer will move down to the next cell. If you make a data entry mistake, use the arrow keys to reposition the cell pointer. Use CTRL-BREAK to stop the execution of the macro.

If you wish to postpone the data entry step, enter the values for Sales in row 5. This will allow you to continue with the following narrative. Later, you can go back and enter the data as required. Of course, if you wish to skip the data entry step entirely, you may wish to purchase the disk set available for this book.

Enter the Formulas for the Summary Columns

Data Bank reports often need to summarize different sections of the data. For example, the funds flow report in Chapter 6 compares information about the current month and year to date to comparable information for a previous month and year to date. It would be a simple matter to write a similar report that could produce comparative income statements.

The Data Bank summary columns, which are updated when you select ALT-M Update Update-Month, make this information available to the reports. This macro calculates four numbers that are used in the summary columns. The range names of these numbers are as follows:

THIS_ENDC This range contains the column number where the data for the ending month of the current period can be found. For example, if we were reporting the period of January through May 1986 and comparing it to January through May 1985, the number of the spreadsheet column containing May 1986 would appear in this cell. And if the data for May 1986 were contained in column AA, the value 27 would appear.

LAST_ENDC This range contains the column number where the data for the ending month of the last period (the comparison period) can be found. Continuing the previous example, this cell would contain the value 16, showing that data for May 1985 can be found in column P.

THIS_BEGC This range contains the column number where the data for the beginning month of the current period can be found. For example, it might contain the value 23, showing that data for January 1986 can be found in column W.

LAST_ENDC This range contains the column number where the data for the beginning month of the last period (the comparison period) can be found. For example, it might contain the value 12, showing that data for January 1985 can be found in column L.

The formulas shown for columns C through J use these range names to generate the summaries. These formulas will be copied from row 5 as shown to the remaining rows of the summary section of the Data Bank. However, since these ranges will be named in Chapter 2, you will not be able to enter the summary formulas. For now, therefore, read the following description of the formulas. After you complete the macros discussed in Chapter 2, you can easily enter these formulas.

The formulas in columns C through J also use the range name DATA. In Chapter 2 this range will be defined as the entire data section of the Data Bank, from cell A5 through the end of the data.

The following formula shown for C5 finds the balance for the ending month of the current period. The formula in G5 finds the balance for the ending month of the previous period. When copied to rows containing Income Statement data, these formulas will return the income or expenses for the month. When copied to rows containing Balance Sheet data, they will return the balance data for the end of the month.

Here's how the formula shown for C5 works: it looks up in the DATA range the DB# found in A5; then it returns the value found a certain number of columns to the right of the leftmost column in the DATA range (column A). This number is equal to THIS_ENDC minus 1. We subtract 1 from THIS_ENDC because lookup formulas number columns beginning with the value zero. As a consequence, for example, the eleventh column in the Data Bank is equivalent to the tenth column in a @LOOKUP formula.

C5: @VLOOKUP(A5,$DATA,$THIS_ENDC−1)
G5: @VLOOKUP(A5,$DATA,$LAST_ENDC−1)

In the two formulas that follow, D5 and H5 show the changes that have occurred during the current and comparison months. When copied to the row for Accounts Receivable, for example, they would show how much Accounts Receivable has increased (or decreased) during the current month (column D) or during the comparison month (column H). When copied to the row for Interest Expense, they would show how much greater (or less) Interest Expense was compared to that of the previous month.

D5: @VLOOKUP(A5,$DATA,$THIS_ENDC−1)−@VLOOKUP(A5,$DATA,$THIS_ENDC−2)
H5: @VLOOKUP(A5,$DATA,$LAST_ENDC−1)−@VLOOKUP(A5,$DATA,
$LAST_ENDC−2)

The following formulas for cells E5 and I5 contain the sum of the data in the columns encompassed by the current period and by the previous period, respectively. For example, if the current period were January through May 1985, cell E5 would show the sum of the sales for those five months. When copied to E6, the formula in E6 would show the sum of the Cost of Sales for the five-month period. When copied to rows containing Balance Sheet accounts, the sums in columns E and I are of little direct use. However, dividing these sums by the number of months in the period does allow us to calculate the average monthly balance during the period.

The lookup formula in C5, described previously, lets us find the sales for any month by entering the column number of the month we wish to view into a cell with the range name THIS_ENDC. The other lookup formulas work similarly. Unfortunately, we can't follow the same approach with @SUM formulas. That is, we cannot change an @SUM range by changing the column numbers in certain cells. Instead, the @SUM function requires that we use a specific range when we write an @SUM formula. To change that range, we must physically change the formula.

The macros in Chapter 2, therefore, create @SUM formulas with the specific ranges that we need and copy them to columns E and I. For now, however, enter the following two formulas. The formula in E5 sums the last year in the sample Data Bank, and I5 sums the previous year. These time periods were chosen at random, so don't be concerned about the reasons that these formulas reference the columns that they do. When you have completed Chapter 2, the Data Bank macros will change the formulas in columns E and I to give us the sums of any two periods (any two ranges) that we require.

```
E5: @SUM(AJ5..AU5)
I5: @SUM(X5..AI5)
```

Columns F and J show the changes that have occurred during the current and previous periods, respectively. For example, when copied to a row containing Inventory data, the formulas might show how much inventory has grown (or decreased) during the calendar year. This change would be calculated by subtracting the inventory balance at the end of last December from the inventory balance at the end of this December.

```
F5: @VLOOKUP(A5,$DATA,$THIS_ENDC-1)-@VLOOKUP(A5,$DATA,$THIS_BEGC-2)
J5: @VLOOKUP(A5,$DATA,$LAST_ENDC-1)-@VLOOKUP(A5,
    $DATA,$LAST_BEGC-2)
```

A PREVIEW OF CHAPTER 2

The next chapter will discuss the two major steps that remain in completing the Data Bank. First, it will show you how to write the macros that we will need. Second, it will discuss how to enter your own data into the Data Bank, allowing you to create your own reports.

Chapter
Two

CREATING THE DATA BANK MACROS AND ENTERING YOUR DATA

Two steps remain before the Data Bank is complete. First, you must enter the macros that control the operation of the Data Bank. Second, you must enter your own data. We treat both topics in this chapter, starting with the macros.

THE PHYSICAL ARRANGEMENT OF THE MACRO SECTION

As Figure 2-1 shows, the macro section of the Data Bank extends from rows 155 through 254. Rows 250 through 254 contain the report header area of the macro section. This area is much like a tall fence containing several mailboxes. The fence protects the permanent macro section to the north from the transient Data Bank reports to the south. The mailboxes—specific cells, actually—provide a way for the macros and the reports to communicate.

The macro section looks somewhat like seven pages from a book laid side by side. The pages, each of which contains several macros, are numbered from MACRO0 (macro zero) at the left to MACRO6 at the right. Each one is discussed in this chapter.

When you are using the Data Bank, your macro section can begin and end with any row. But to make the discussion easier to follow, we'll assume that the report header always starts at row 250, as shown in Figure 2-1.

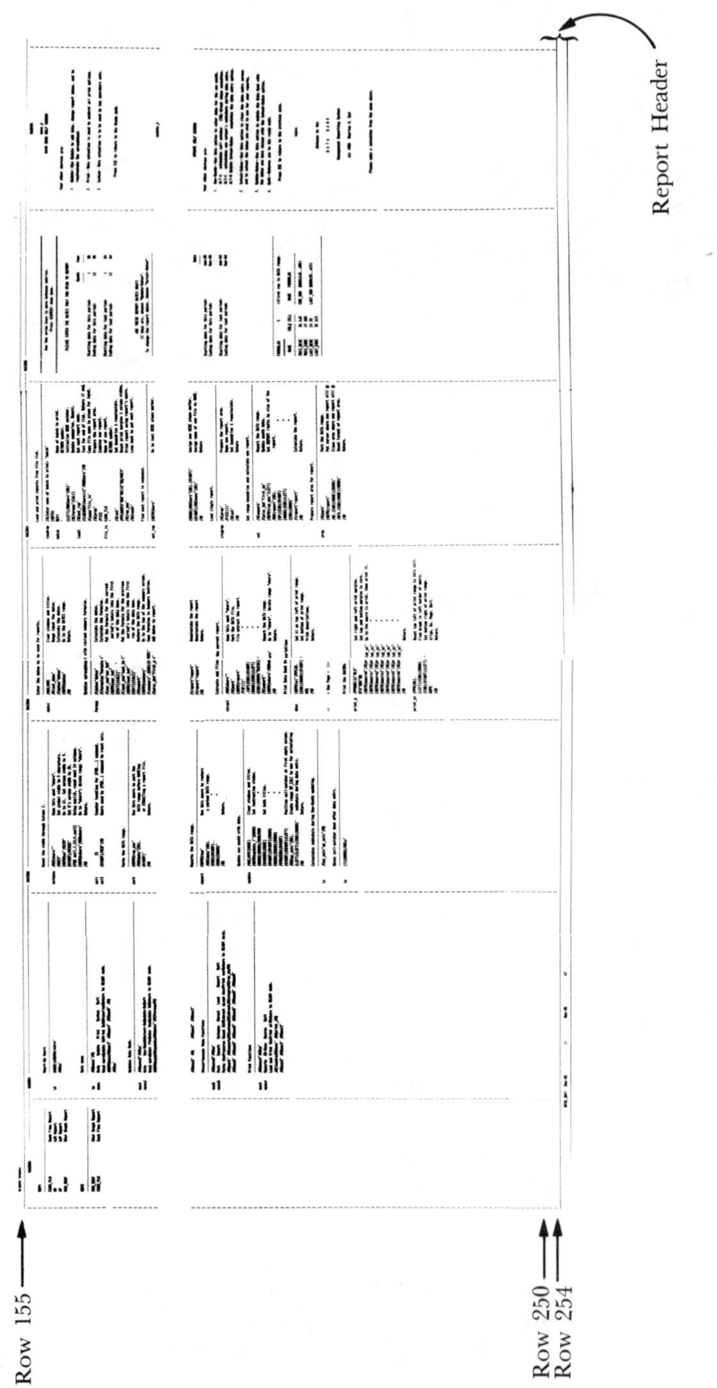

Figure 2-1. The macro section of the Data Bank

AN INTRODUCTION TO THE DATA BANK MACROS

As you can see in Figure 2-2, when you first load the Data Bank, your screen displays a message of introduction and asks you to choose from one of five menu selections.

- Help
- Update
- Print
- System
- Quit.

Before we discuss how these selections work, let's see what they do.

```
BF202: [W76]                                                                MENU
Help  Update  Print  System  Quit
Need more information about your options?
                                   BF
202
203
204
205                             Welcome to the
206
207                           D A T A   B A N K
208
209                        Management Reporting System
210
211                        (c) 1985  Charles W. Kyd
212
213
214
215                   Please make a selection from the menu above.
216
217
218
219
220
221
30-Nov-85  09:18 AM                            CMD        CALC
```

Figure 2-2. The Data Bank Welcome screen

Help

Selecting Help, as shown in Figure 2-3, displays a screen that briefly explains your other menu selections. In your own Data Bank, it would be a simple task to expand this Help screen to provide as much information as you wish.

Update

Your clerk will use the Update selection to update the Data Bank monthly. This selection provides a menu of the following five options:

Help This Help screen explains the other options within the Update menu.

```
BF159: [W76]                         MAIN MENU HELP SCREEN                  MENU
Help  Update  Print  System  Quit
Need more information about your options?
                                                  BF
159                                     MAIN MENU HELP SCREEN
160
161
162        Your other choices are:
163
164        1.  Update--Use Update to add data, change report dates, and to
165            recalculate the spreadsheet.
166
167        2.  Print--This selection is used to control all print options.
168
169        3.  System--This selection is to be used by key operators only.
170
171
172              Press ESC to return to the Ready mode.
173
174
175
176
177
178
30-Nov-85  09:19 AM                          CMD        CALC
```

Figure 2-3. The Main menu Help screen

New-Month This selection is used to enter new data for the month. The macro begins by using /Worksheet Titles Both to set the left and top titles. As you can see in Figure 2-4, setting the left title allows you to read the Data Bank numbers and descriptions in columns A and B, no matter how far to the right you move your cell pointer. Similarly, the top title allows you to read the dates in row 4, no matter how far down you move your pointer. After the titles are set, the macro positions the cell pointer at the top of the first empty column and returns the program to the Ready mode.

As shown in rows 186 through 188 of the figure, this option also displays a mini Help screen at the top of the display. The Help screen reminds your clerk how to use a macro to help position the cell pointer, how to recalculate the current column, and what to do when all the data has been entered.

```
AV5:                                                                      READY

                                    BF
186          ALT-A   automates cell pointer.  CTRL-Break stops execution.
187          ALT-C   calculates new column's subtotals during data entry.
188          ALT-M Update Select-Dates    completes the data entry option.
         A               B                   AT        AU        AV       AW
1            The DATA BANK
2        Management Reporting System
3      ===================================
4         DB#          Description         Nov-85    Dec-85    Jan-86   Feb-86
5       100.010 Sales                         225       216
6       100.020 Cost of Goods Sold            100        98
7       100.030 Research & Development         23        23
8       100.040 Marketing                      27        32
9       100.050 General & Admin                26        28
10      100.055 Gain (Loss) on Sale of F/A      0         0
11      100.060 Erngs Before Int & Taxes       49        35
12      100.070 Interest                        1         1
13      100.080 Provision for Taxes            22        15
14      100.090 Net Earnings                   26        19
15      105.005 Cash                           45        43
16      105.010 Accounts Receivable           413       423
30-Nov-85  09:21 AM                                  CALC      NUM
```

Figure 2-4. The Update New-Month screen

```
BA168: U 1                                                                  READY

          AV        AW        AX        AY        AZ        BA        BB        BC
157
158
159 ===============================================================================
160              Use the arrow keys to move between entries.
161                         Press <ENTER> when done.
162 ===============================================================================
163
164              PLEASE ENTER THE DATES THAT YOU WISH TO REPORT
165
166                                                          Month      Year
167                                                          -----      ----
168           Starting date for this period:                     1        85
169           Ending date for this period:                      12        85
170
171           Starting date for last period:                     1        84
172           Ending date for last period:                      12        84
173
174
175
176
30-Nov-85  09:23 AM                            CMD        CALC      NUM
```

a

```
AV175:                                                                       MENU
Help  New-Month  Select-Dates  Update-Dates  Quit
Need more information about your options?
          AV        AW        AX        AY        AZ        BA        BB        BC
175
176
177                       ARE THESE REPORT DATES OKAY?
178                    If they are, choose "Update-Dates".
179              To change the report dates, choose "Select-Dates".
180           ------------------------------------------------------
181
182                                                                   Date
183                                                                  -----
184           Starting date for this period:                        Jan-85
185           Ending date for this period:                          Dec-85
186
187           Starting date for last period:                        Jan-84
188           Ending date for last period:                          Dec-84
189
190
191
192
193
194
30-Nov-85  09:24 AM                            CMD        CALC      NUM
```

b

Figure 2-5. The two Select-Dates screens

Select-Dates As shown at the top of Figure 2-5, this selection displays the date settings for the current period and comparison period, and it provides the opportunity to change these dates. After you enter new dates and press ENTER, the macro displays these dates in a month-year format. The bottom of Figure 2-5 shows this screen.

Update-Dates This selection changes the @SUM formulas in columns E and I to summarize the two periods that you have selected with the Select-Dates option. Then it recalculates the entire summary section, columns C through J. When this macro has completed, the summary section contains the data your reports will need when they report the periods you have chosen.

Quit This selection ends the macro execution, returning the program to the Ready mode.

```
BF202: [W76]                                                          MENU
Reports  DB-Desc  Macros  Quit
Load and print a batch of reports
                                        BF
202
203
204
205                                 Welcome to the
206
207                               D A T A   B A N K
208
209                           Management Reporting System
210
211                            (c) 1985  Charles W. Kyd
212
213
214
215                  Please make a selection from the menu above.
216
217
218
219
220
221
30-Nov-85  09:37 AM                       CMD      CALC     NUM
```

Figure 2-6. The Print menus selected from the Welcome screen

Print

As Figure 2-6 illustrates, the Print selection offers the following four choices:

Reports The Reports option asks for the name of the batch of reports to be printed; then it loads, calculates, and prints the reports in the batch one at a time.

DB-Desc This selection provides a convenient way to print the complete list of Data Bank numbers and descriptions.

Macros This selection prints the Data Bank macros in an easy-to-read format. This is a convenient option for documenting your Data Bank, but it is one that your clerk will seldom use.

Quit This selection returns you to the Ready mode. Use ESC if you wish, instead, to return to the Data Bank Main menu.

```
BF202: [W76]                                                          MENU
Park  Unpark  Columns  Xtract  Load  Report  Quit
Parks the data ranges needed by the reports.
                                    BF
202
203
204
205                              Welcome to the
206
207                            D A T A    B A N K
208
209                         Management Reporting System
210
211                         (c) 1985  Charles W. Kyd
212
213
214
215                  Please make a selection from the menu above.
216
217
218
219
220
221
30-Nov-85  09:36 AM                         CMD       CALC      NUM
```

Figure 2-7. The System menus selected from the Welcome screen

System

As shown in Figure 2-7, the System option offers the following five choices that you will use when you create new Data Bank reports:

Park and Unpark There could not be a Data Bank if the macros used by these two selections did not exist. Figures 2-8a and 2-8b illustrate the problem that these macros solve.

Rows 3 through 7 in Figure 2-8a represent a simplified data section of the Data Bank. (Both the summary section and the macro section are ignored.) The report, shown for rows 8 and 9, returns the value 20. As shown at the bottom of this figure, the formula in A9 looks up the Data Bank number with a value of 1 in the highlighted DATA range and returns the value found in column 2. (Remember that the LOOKUP functions begin counting from zero. What is column 3 to us is therefore column 2 to the LOOKUP function.) The Range Name Table shows the limits of the DATA range.

Suppose that after we extract and save the report in rows 8 and 9 of Figure 2-8a, we add an additional row to the Data Bank. Figure 2-8b shows that a problem arises when we combine the report back into the Data Bank. The problem is that the lookup formula, now in A10, does not know that it has been shifted downward or that the DATA range has been expanded. This formula still expects to find the top of the DATA range five rows above the formula and the bottom of the range one row below the top row. In other words, the formula has no idea where the DATA range actually is.

Figures 2-8c through 2-8e show the three steps we take to let the formula keep track of the DATA range. Figure 2-8c shows the results of the first step. Before we extract and save the report, we use /Range Name Create to redefine, or "park," the DATA range in cells B8..C8. Since the new range is smaller than the formula expects and contains no data, the formula in A9 returns an ERR. We ignore this temporary condition when we extract and save the report.

Figure 2-8d illustrates the Data Bank after we have added a new row and combined the report back into the Data Bank. Unlike the problem shown in Figure 2-8b, however, the parked DATA range is just where the formula expects it to be. The DATA range still begins one row up and one column to the right of the formula.

The final step is to use /Range Name Create to properly define, or "unpark," the DATA range. Figure 2-8e shows that after we do this, the formula in A10 will reference the proper range and return the proper value.

Before a new Data Bank report can be saved, therefore, the dimensions

```
       A         B         C         D

 1
 2
 3    DB#       Jul       Aug
 4      1        19        20
 5      2        36        37
 6  (Blank)
 7  ------------------
 8  Report
 9  '   20
10

    A9: @VLOOKUP(1,$DATA,2)

    Range Name Table
    ------------------
    DATA   A4..C5
```

a.

```
       A         B         C         D

 1
 2
 3    DB#       Jul       Aug
 4      1        19        20
 5      2        36        37
 6      3        77        19
 7  (Blank)
 8  ------------------
 9  Report
10    ERR

    A10: @VLOOKUP(1,$A$5..$C$6,2)

    Range Name Table
    ------------------
    DATA   A4..C6
```

b.

```
       A         B         C         D

 1
 2
 3    DB#       Jul       Aug
 4      1        19        20
 5      2        36        37
 6  (Blank)
 7  ------------------
 8  Report
 9    ERR
10

    A9: @VLOOKUP(1,$DATA,2)

    Range Name Table
    ------------------
    DATA   B8..C8
```

c.

```
       A         B         C         D

 1
 2
 3    DB#       Jul       Aug
 4      1        19        20
 5      2        36        37
 6      3        77        19
 7  (Blank)
 8  ------------------
 9  Report
10    ERR

    A10: @VLOOKUP(1,$DATA,2)

    Range Name Table
    ------------------
    DATA   B9..C9
```

d.

```
       A         B         C         D

 1
 2
 3    DB#       Jul       Aug
 4      1        19        20
 5      2        36        37
 6      3        77        19
 7  (Blank)
 8  ------------------
 9  Report
10    20

    A10: @VLOOKUP(1,$DATA,2)

    Range Name Table
    ------------------
    DATA   A4..C6
```

e.

Figure 2-8. An illustration of the need for the PARK and UNPARK macros

of the DATA range must be "parked" in a consistent location. After a report is combined into the Data Bank, the DATA range is "unparked," or redefined, to include the cell locations where the actual data can be found.

The parking and unparking of the DATA range is all done automatically by the other macro selections. Occasionally, however, you will want to use /File Xtract or /File Combine to save or load a Data Bank report. These Park and Unpark selections allow you to redefine the DATA range dimensions as necessary when you use these 1-2-3 commands.

Columns Each Data Bank report sets column widths to its own requirements. Often when you are writing a new report, you need to reset these widths to the global width. This selection resets those columns.

Xtract and Load These selections use the /File Extract and /File Combine commands, respectively, to save and load Data Bank reports. Both selections activate the PARK and UNPARK macros so that you don't have to do it yourself.

Report This selection executes the macro in the current Data Bank report. Generally, this macro does two things: (1) it sets the column widths that the report needs, and (2) it sets the print range and then prints the report. When you wish to load and print just one Data Bank report, you will use the Load option to load the report and the Report option to print it. As Chapters 3, 5, 6, and 13 explain, you also will use this option frequently when you create a report.

Quit As always, use the Quit selection to return to the Ready mode and use the ESC key to return to the Data Bank Main menu.

Quit

When you are in the Data Bank Main menu, use either the Quit option or the ESC key to return to the Ready mode.

THE DATA BANK MENU STRUCTURE

Figure 2-9 shows MACRO1, the page of the macro section containing the Data Bank menus. As with most menu macros, the labels overlap each other, making the macros unreadable. Figure 2-10, therefore, shows the

```
             E         F         G         H         I         J         K         L         M         N         O         P         Q

155 --------------------------------------------------------------------------------------------------------------------------------
156 --------- MACRO1  --------------------------------------------------------------------------------------------------------------
157        |                                                                                                                        |
158        |                                                                                                                        |
159        |                 Start-Up Macro                                                                                         |
160        |                 -------------------------------------------------------------------------------------                  |
161        |        \0       {HOME}{GOTO}intro~                                                                                     |
162        |                 /XG\m~                                                                                                 |
163        |                                                                                                                        |
164        |                                                                                                                        |
165        |                                                                                                                        |
166        |                 Main menu                                                                                              |
167        |                 -------------------------------------------------------------------------------------                  |
168        |        \m       /XMmenu~/XQ                                                                                            |
169        |        menu     Help      Update    Print     System    Quit                                                           |
170        |                 Need moreUpdate thPrint DatMiscellanReturn to READY mode.                                              |
171        |                 {GOTO}men/XGmac3~ /XGmac4~ /XGmac8~ /XQ                                                                |
172        |                 /XG\m~                                                                                                 |
173        |                                                                                                                        |
174        |                                                                                                                        |
175        |                 Updates Data Bank.                                                                                     |
176        |                 -------------------------------------------------------------------------------------                  |
177        |        mac3     /XMmenu3~/XG\m~                                                                                        |
178        |        menu3    Help      New-MonthSelect-DaUpdate-DaQuit                                                              |
179        |                 Need moreEnter finEnter theUpdate thReturn to READY mode.                                              |
180        |                 {GOTO}upd/XCupdate/XCdate1~/XCformup/XQ                                                                |
181        |                 /XGmac3~ /XQ      /XGmac3~ /XGmac3~                                                                    |
182        |                                                                                                                        |
183        |                 Miscellaneous Menu Functions                                                                           |
184        |                 -------------------------------------------------------------------------------------                  |
185        |        mac8     /XMmenu8~/XG\m~                                                                                        |
186        |        menu8    Park      Unpark    Columns   Xtract    Load      Report    Quit                                       |
187        |                 Parks thePrepares Reset DATExtract aLoad desiPrint curReturn to READY mode.                            |
188        |                 /XCpark~ /XCunpark/XCcolumn/XCxtract/XCsingre/XCrep_ma/XQ                                              |
189        |                 /XCmac8~ /XCmac8~ /XCmac8~ /XCmac8~ /XCmac8~ /XCmac8~                                                  |
190        |                                                                                                                        |
191        |                                                                                                                        |
192        |                 Print Functions                                                                                        |
193        |                 -------------------------------------------------------------------------------------                  |
194        |        mac4     /XMmenu4~/XG\m~                                                                                        |
195        |        menu4    Reports   DB-Desc   Macros    Quit                                                                     |
196        |                 Load and Print thePrint allReturn to READY mode.                                                       |
197        |                 /XCloadre/XCdesc~ /XCprint_/XQ                                                                         |
198        |                 /XGmac3~ /XGmac3~ /XGmac3~                                                                             |
199        |                                                                                                                        |
200                                                                                                                                 |
201        |                                                                                                                        |
202        |                                                                                                                        |
203        |                                                                                                                        |
```

Figure 2-9. The MACRO1 page

```
=============================
Detail of the menus in MACRO1
=============================


G159: 'Start-Up Macro
------------------------------------------------------------------------------------
F161: '\0
G161: '{HOME}{GOTO}intro~
G162: '/XG\m~


G166: 'Main menu
------------------------------------------------------------------------------------
F168: '\m
F169: 'menu
G168: '/XMmenu~/XQ

G169: 'Help
G170: 'Need more information about your options?
G171: '{GOTO}menu_h~
G172: '/XG\m~

H169: 'Update
H170: 'Update the Data Bank with new information.
H171: '/XGmac3~

I169: 'Print
I170: 'Print Data Bank reports
I171: '/XGmac4~

J169: 'System
J170: 'Miscellaneous functions for key operators.
J171: '/XGmac8~

K169: 'Quit
K170: 'Return to READY mode.
K171: '/XQ


G175: 'Updates Data Bank.
------------------------------------------------------------------------------------
F177: 'mac3
F178: 'menu3
G177: '/XMmenu3~/XG\m~

G178: 'Help
G179: 'Need more information about your options?
G180: '{GOTO}update_h~

G181: '/XGmac3~

H178: 'New-Month
H179: 'Enter financial information about the new month.
H180: '/XCupdate~
H181: '/XQ

I178: 'Select-Dates
I179: 'Enter the dates to be used for printing reports.
I180: '/XCdate1~
I181: '/XGmac3~

J178: 'Update-Dates
J179: 'Update the Data Bank with the dates you have chosen.
J180: '/XCformup~
J181: '/XGmac3~
```

Figure 2-10. Detail of the menus in the MACRO1 page

```
K178: 'Quit
K179: 'Return to READY mode.
K180: '/XQ

G183: 'Miscellaneous Menu Functions
------------------------------------------------------------------------------------------------
F185: 'mac8
F186: 'menu8
G185: '/XMmenu8~/XG\m~

G186: 'Park
G187: 'Parks the data ranges need by the reports.
G188: '/XCpark~
G189: '/XCmac8~

H186: 'Unpark
H187: 'Prepares data ranges so they can be used by the reports.
H188: '/XCunpark~
H189: '/XCmac8~

I186: 'Columns
I187: 'Reset DATA BANK column widths.
I188: '/XCcolumns~
I189: '/XCmac8~

J186: 'Xtract
J187: 'Extract and save new report.  Warning!  Make sure report boundries are set!

J188: '/XCxtract~
J189: '/XCmac8~

K186: 'Load
K187: 'Load designated report file.
K188: '/XCsingrep~
K189: '/XCmac8~

L186: 'Report
L187: 'Print current report format using macro with the report.
L188: '/XCrep_mac~
L189: '/XCmac8~

M186: 'Quit
M187: 'Return to READY mode.
M188: '/XQ


G192: 'Print Functions
------------------------------------------------------------------------------------------------
F194: 'mac4
F195: 'menu4
G194: '/XMmenu4~/XG\m~

G195: 'Reports
G196: 'Load and print a batch of reports
G197: '/XCloadrep~
G198: '/XGmac3~

H195: 'DB-Desc
H196: 'Print the DATA BANK numbers and descriptions.
H197: '/XCdesc~
H198: '/XGmac3~
```

Figure 2-10. Detail of the menus in the MACRO1 page (*continued*)

```
I195: 'Macros
I196: 'Print all macros.  (Be sure the right borders are marked.)
I197: '/XCprint_m~
I198: '/XGmac3~

J195: 'Quit
J196: 'Return to READY mode.
J197: '/XQ
```

Figure 2-10. Detail of the menus in the MACRO1 page *(continued)*

same macro section in a cell-formula format. When you create the macros for your own Data Bank, use Figure 2-9 to see how each macro is positioned and Figure 2-10 to see how to enter each line of the macro.

Macro Section Titles

In Figure 2-9, MACRO1 is the title for this macro page. With your cell pointer on F156, use /**R**ange **N**ame **C**reate to assign this range name. Having this name does two things: (1) it allows you to GO TO this page from any point in the spreadsheet, and (2) it tells the macro-print routine where to find this page when you print the macros.

The Auto-Execute Macro

When the Data Bank is loaded, the START-UP macro in Figure 2-9 uses the Auto-Execute command to display the Introduction and call the Main menu. As your 1-2-3 user's manual explains, the special \0 (backslash zero) macro name cannot be executed from the keyboard. It is executed only when the Data Bank spreadsheet is loaded.

Using the ESC Key With Macro Menus

As you know, 1-2-3's command menus use the ESC key to return to prior menus. Figures 2-9 and 2-10 demonstrate how we add this convenience to our Data Bank menus.

When 1-2-3 encounters the /XM command in any menu, it pauses to display your custom menu. When you press the ESC key during this pause, 1-2-3 executes the macro commands following the /XM command. Therefore, if we want the macro to stop execution when we press the ESC key, we follow the /XM command with the /XQ command. And if we want a prior menu to be called, we follow the /XM command with the /XG command, referencing the prior menu. In other words, when we use this approach, we imitate the way 1-2-3 uses the ESC key with its command menus.

To get a better idea of how this method works, look again at Figure 2-9. When we issue the ALT-M command, 1-2-3 begins execution of the macro at G168. Since /XMmenu~ is the first command in this cell, the program pauses and displays the custom menu that follows the range name MENU. If we press ESC at this point, the program executes the next command that it sees, the /XQ command. This of course stops the macro execution.

Suppose, however, that we select the Update menu option. The program continues execution at MAC3, where it sees the /XMmac3~ command. Here, if we press ESC, the program finds the macro command /XG \m~ , which sends us back to the Main menu.

Macro Names

As you look through Figure 2-9 and the other figures of macros in this chapter, you will probably wonder what system was used to name these macros. If a macro is to be executed from the keyboard, its name must be two characters long. The first character of the name must be a \ (backslash), and the second character may be any letter. Therefore, no more than 26 names can be executed from the keyboard.

However, if a macro is to be executed by another macro, its name can be any legal range name. This wide range of choices raises the question, What strategy should we use to name our macros?

Figure 2-9 shows one approach. I named the Main menu macro \M and the custom menu range MENU. The other macros were named in sequence, MAC1, MAC2, and so on, and their menu ranges were named MENU1, MENU2, and so on. As a close reading will show, eight menus were created, of which only four have survived.

Occasionally, when I use numbered macro names, I'll use numbers for the lower-level names as well. For instance, MAC1 may call MAC10, MAC11, and MAC12. MAC12 may call MAC120 and MAC121. You get the idea. The problem with this approach is that nothing ever stays organized. As macros are created, erased, and changed, their names soon get out of sequence (as Figure 2-9 again shows). And their numbers become meaningless.

An alternative approach is to name a macro for what it does. This approach works well when you have one PRINT macro or one UPDATE macro, but not so well when you have three or four printing macros and a dozen macros that do things difficult to describe with one word. The macro names quickly begin to look rather creative.

Since the macro names often contribute so little information, make a special effort to document your macros as you write them. With good documentation, it won't matter if you use a strange name like, say, GLUB for one of your macros. A quick look at the documentation surrounding the macro would remind you that GLUB stands for General Ledger, Update Balances.

THE MACRO PAGES

Now that we have had an overview of the Data Bank macros, it is time to create them. The following figures show each page of macros and describe what each line of the macro does.

Notice that these macro pages are described out of numerical sequence. The numerical order begins with the print list (MACRO0), follows with the Main menu (MACRO1) and the lower-level macros, and ends with the Help screens (MACRO6). These macros will be easier to understand, however, if we discuss them in a different sequence.

Macros in Versions 1A and 2

If you have read the documentation for 1-2-3 Version 2, you know that Version 2 has two different macro formats.The /X macro commands are the same commands used by Version 1A. The macro keywords, similar to the Symphony command language, duplicate the /X features while adding new power.

Wherever possible, the /X version has been used in this chapter, and throughout the book, for two reasons. First, like most users of Version 2, you are probably more familiar with the /X macros than with the keyword versions. Using /X, then, should help you to concentrate on what the macros are doing, without having to struggle with an unfamiliar syntax. Second, the /X version is the only one available to 1A users.

Entering the Macros

Two steps are necessary to make the following macros work properly: (1) enter the macros and the borders as shown, and (2) make sure that all range names are properly defined. Most range names will be easy to define, however, because they are associated with macros. Simply use the /**R**ange **N**ame **L**abels **R**ight command, highlighting the columns of range names in each macro page.

Although the following pages discuss many of the other Data Bank range names in detail, some range names are not discussed. Figure 2-11 lists all Data Bank range names, shows their addresses, and describes their uses. As you create the Data Bank, use this figure as a checklist to ensure that you've properly defined all ranges.

The MACRO2 Page

Figure 2-12 shows the MACRO2 page. The macros on this page generally are used for organizing the Data Bank and for entering data.

COLUMNS This command sets the column widths for columns A and B; then it resets the next 24 columns to the global column width setting. This is one of two macros in the Data Bank that uses a command not available to Version 1A users. This command, the {FOR...} command, is similar to a FOR-NEXT command in the BASIC programming language. It allows us to easily change the number of columns to be reset. That is, if you find that additional columns need to be reset, replace the number 24 in cell S165 with the appropriately higher number.

The {FOR...} macro command is new to Version 2. It uses the following format: "{FOR *counter-location,start-number,stop-number,step-number, starting-location*}".

In Figure 2-12, cell S169 is the counter location. Whenever the command is executed, this cell takes the value of the start number; then the macro continues execution at the starting location, cell S170. When the macro in S170 has completed, the /XR command returns processing to the {FOR...} command. The step number is added to the counter location; then execution returns to the starting location. This process continues until the counter location equals the stop number, when macro execution stops with the macro command following the {FOR...} command, cell S166.

Appendix B provides a macro that Version 1A users can substitute for this macro.

```
==========================
DATA BANK RANGE NAMES
==========================

Range names found in the data section of the Data Bank.
==========================================================================================
TOP          A5            Marks the top left corner of the DATA range.
SUMMARY      C5..J5        The first row of the Data Bank summary formulas.
CUR_TOT      E5            Destination for current period's summary formula.
LAST_TOT     I5            Destination for previous period's summary formula.
START_COL    K2            The column number of first column of monthly data.
START_MO     K4            The date serial number of the first column of monthly data.

Range names found in the macro section of the Data Bank.
==========================================================================================

MACRO0       B156          Macro page title.
------------------------------------------------------------------------------------------
REP1         B159          Name of first batch of reports to print.
REP2         B167          Name of second batch of reports to print.


MACRO1       F156          Macro page title.
------------------------------------------------------------------------------------------
\0           G161          Macro names, and range names used within the macros.
\M           G168                              "
MENU         G169                              "
MAC3         G177                              "
MENU3        G178                              "
MAC8         G185                              "
MENU8        G186                              "
MAC4         G194                              "
MENU4        G195                              "
```

Figure 2-11. The Data Bank range names

```
MACRO2      R156          Macro page title.
--------------------------------------------------------------------------------
COLUMNS     S161          Macro names, and range names used within the macros.
COL1        S169                             "
COL2        S170                             "
PARK        S176                             "
UNPARK      S183                             "
UPDATE      S192                             "
\C          S206                             "
\A          S210                             "

MACRO3      AB156         Macro page title.
--------------------------------------------------------------------------------
DATE1       AC160         Macro names, and range names used within the macros.
FORMUP      AC169                            "
XTRACT      AC188                            "
DESC        AC201                            "
PRINT_M     AC212                            "
PRINT_M1    AC223                            "

MACRO4      AL156         Macro page title.
--------------------------------------------------------------------------------
LOADREP     AM160         Macro names, and range names used within the macros.
BATCH       AM162                            "
LOAD1       AM165                            "
FILE_IN     AM170                            "
NXT_REP     AM179                            "
SINGREP     AM186                            "
SET         AM193                            "
PREP        AM205                            "

MACRO5      AV156         Macro page title.
--------------------------------------------------------------------------------
ENT_DATE    AV157..BC175  Range for entering report dates.
DATES       AV175..BC194  Range of new report dates in date format.
FORMULAS    AW197..BC206  Range of column formulas derived from dates.
```

```
THIS_BEGC     AX202          Holds col# for beginning month of current period.
THIS_ENDC     AX203          Holds col# for ending month of current period.
LAST_BEGC     AX204          Holds col# for beginning month of previous period.
LAST_ENDC     AX205          Holds col# for ending month of previous period.
FST_ROW       AY198          Holds number of first row which contains data.
CUR_SUM       BA202          Holds first @SUM formula for current period.
LAST_SUM      BA204          Holds first @SUM formula for previous period.
REP_MO        BB185          Date serial number for the Report Month.

MACRO6        BF156          Macro page title.
-----------------------------------------------------------------------------
MENU_H        BF159          First cell for main menu help screen.
UPDATE_H      BF181          First cell for update help screen.
UPDATE_I      BF186          First cell for mini help screen during data input.
INTRO         BF202          First cell for Data Bank introduction.

Range names used in the report header.
=============================================================================
REP_MAC       B254           First cell in the report macro.
MISC_DAT      F251..M251     Holds miscellaneous data needed by the reports.
FIRST_MO      F254           Date serial number for the first month in Data Bank.
THIS_MO       J254           Date serial number for the current month.
THIS_COL      L254           Column number of current month.

Range names created by the macros.
=============================================================================
DATA          A5..Misc       Source of data for all reports.  Dimensions set by UNPARK macro.
  "           B254..C254     Parked position of DATA.  Dimensions set by PARK macro.
REPORT        A254..Misc     Range holding current report.  Created by SET macro.
UP_CALC       Misc           Recalc range during data entry.  Created by UPDATE macro.
NAME          Misc           Holds name of current report during batch printing.
                               Created by NXT_REP macro.
WHERE         Misc           Created and deleted by various macros to mark temporary
HERE          Misc             positions in the spreadsheet.
```

Figure 2-11. The Data Bank range names (*continued*)

```
            Q          R          S          T          U          V          W          X          Y          Z          AA

155  ------------------------------------------------------------------------------------------------------------------------
156  ---------  MACRO2  ----------------------------------------------------------------------------------------------------
157         |                                                                                                            |
158         |                                                                                                            |
159         |                    Reset the width through Column Z.                                                       |
160         |                    ------------------------------------------------------------------------------          |
161         |       columns      /RNCwhere~~                    Name this spot "where".                                  |
162         |                    /WGC9~                         Set global width to 9 characters.                        |
163         |                    {GOTO}a1~/WCS9~                Go to A1.  Set column width to 9.                        |
164         |                    {RIGHT}/WCS26~                 Set B's column width to 26.                              |
165         |                    {FOR col1,1,24,1,col2}         Using mac110, reset next 24 columns.                     |
166         |                    {GOTO}where~/RNDwhere~         Go to "where"; delete range "where".                     |
167         |                    /XR                            Return.                                                  |
168         |                                                                                                            |
169         |       col1                 25                     Counter location for {FOR...} command.                   |
170         |       col2         {RIGHT}/WCR~/XR                Macro used by {FOR..} command to reset cols.             |
171         |                                                                                                            |
172         |                                                                                                            |
173         |                                                                                                            |
174         |                    Parks the DATA range.                                                                   |
175         |                    ------------------------------------------------------------------------------          |
176         |       park         {GOTO}rep_mac~                 Use this macro to park the                               |
177         |                    /RNCdata~{BS}.                   DATA range before SAVEing                              |
178         |                    {RIGHT}~                         or XTRACTing a report file.                            |
179         |                    /XR                            Return.                                                  |
180         |                                                                                                            |
181         |                    Unparks the DATA range.                                                                 |
182         |                    ------------------------------------------------------------------------------          |
183         |       unpark       {GOTO}top~                     Use this macro to restore                                |
184         |                    /RNCdata~{BS}.                   a parked DATA range.                                   |
185         |                    {END}{RIGHT}..                             "                                            |
186         |                    {END}{DOWN}~                               "                                            |
187         |                    /XR                            Return.                                                  |
```

```
188
189
190             Update new month with data.
191             -----------------------------------------------------------------------
192   update    /WWC/WTC{HOME}               Clear windows and titles.
193             {GOTO}update_i~{DOWN}        Set instruction window.
194             {DOWN}{DOWN}/WWH/WWU                   "
195             {WINDOW}{HOME}               Set both titles.
196             {RIGHT}{RIGHT}{DOWN}                   "
197             {DOWN}{DOWN}{DOWN}                     "
198             /WTB{END}{RIGHT}                       "
199             {RIGHT}{RIGHT}{LEFT}         Position cell-pointer at first empty column.
200             /RNCup_calc~{BS}.            Create range UP_CALC to use for calculating
201             {LEFT}{LEFT}{END}{DOWN}~       subtotals during data entry.
202             /XR                          Return.
203
204             Calculates subtotals during New-Month updating.
205             -----------------------------------------------------------------------
206   \c        /Cup_calc~up_calc~/XQ
207
208             Moves cell-pointer down after data entry.
209             -----------------------------------------------------------------------
210   \e        {?}{DOWN}/XG\e~
211
212
213
214
215
216
```

Figure 2-12. The MACRO2 page

PARK and UNPARK These two macros use a little-known trick in cells S177 and S184. When a formula references a range name, that range name has "captured" the formula. That is, if you use the proper method to redefine the range, the dimensions of all formulas that reference that range will be redefined also.

To redefine the range, we use the /Range Name Create command. When we enter the name of the range we wish to redefine, and then press ENTER, 1-2-3 highlights the old range. Pressing BACKSPACE (shown as {BS} in S177 and S184) will cancel this highlight, allowing us to redefine the range name as we wish.

The /Range Name Label command works differently. If we used that command to redefine range names, formulas would continue to reference the dimensions represented by the old range. However, there is one limitation to this use of the /Range Name Create command that you should remember. If you define a one-cell range, this command cannot capture the range and expand it into a multicell range. This is why the PARK macro uses the {RIGHT} command in S178 to keep the parked DATA range a two-cell range.

UPDATE This macro begins by clearing windows and titles. Unfortunately, 1-2-3 emits a single beep if there are no windows to be cleared. Don't let this noise bother you. There's nothing wrong.

After the windows and titles are cleared, the macro sets new windows and titles. As shown in Figure 2-4, the additional window is used to display three lines of the Update Help screen. The titles display the dates at the top of the work area and the Data Bank numbers and descriptions at the left.

\C Your data will often include totals and subtotals for categories like Total Current Assets, Total Operating Expenses, and Net Income. Chapter 1 explains why it is useful to include rows of formulas within the Data Bank to calculate these totals.

This short macro uses a simple trick to recalculate these totals: copying a range onto itself will recalculate that range. The recalculation is executed in column order, beginning with the top cell of the left-hand column.

\E This data entry macro pauses to accept data and then moves the cell pointer to the next lower cell. If you make a mistake or wish to reposition the pointer, use your cursor control keys to move the cell pointer where you wish. To cancel this macro, press CTRL-BREAK. The ERROR indicator will blink, and you then press ESC.

The MACRO3 and MACRO5 Pages

Figure 2-13 shows the MACRO3 page. These macros generally are used for updating and printing the Data Bank. The MACRO5 page, shown in Figure 2-14, contains the screens and formulas used by the first few macros in Figure 2-13.

DATE1 Your clerk should select this macro when he or she is finished entering data in the Data Bank. As you can see in Figure 2-13, the first line of DATE1 clears the windows and titles that were created by UPDATE.

The /Range Input command in AC161 restricts cursor movement to only those cells within the specified range that have been unprotected. This restriction makes it easy to move to those cells and update them.

The range specified in AC161 is ENT_DATE. Figure 2-11 tells us that this range is in MACRO5 (Figure 2-14) and has the dimensions AV157..BC175. After you define this range, use /**R**ange **P**rotect to protect it; then use /**R**ange **U**nprotect to unprotect the ranges BA168..BB169 and BA171..BB172. As Figure 2-14 shows, these two ranges contain the numbers for the months and years you wish to report.

The next row of the macro in Figure 2-13 calculates the range DATES. As you might suspect, this is the range for the second screen shown in Figure 2-14, the range AV175..BC194.The only formulas in this range are in column BB.

```
BB184:  (D3) @DATE($BB$168,$BA$168,15)
BB185:  (D3) @DATE($BB$169,$BA$169,15)
BB187:  (D3) @DATE($BB$171,$BA$171,15)
BB188:  (D3) @DATE($BB$172,$BA$172,15)
```

The DATE1 macro goes to the DATES range, displaying the new dates on the screen. This allows you to review these dates and correct them if need be, before you use them to update the formulas in the Data Bank.

FORMUP This macro updates the summary formulas in the Data Bank to reflect the dates that you have chosen. As Chapter 1 explains this macro is necessary because 1-2-3 does not have a function that lets us alter the range we have specified in the @SUM formula. Neither @SUM nor @DSUM will do the job. The macro that substitutes for this missing command depends upon a string function that is unavailable to users of 1-2-3 Version 1A. Appendix C suggests an alternative approach for Version 1A users.

The first line of FORMUP recalculates the DATES range. The next line

```
          AA       AB        AC        AD        AE        AF        AG        AH        AI        AJ        AK

155 ------------------------------------------------------------------------------------------------------------
156 --------- MACRO3   -----------------------------------------------------------------------------------------
157      |                                                                                                  |
158      |                   Enter the dates to be used for reports.                                       |
159      |                   -----------------------------------------------------------------------        |
160      |       date1       /WWC/WTC                      Clear windows and titles.                        |
161      |                   /RIent_date~                  Range Input the dates.                           |
162      |                   /Cdates~dates~                Calculate the dates.                             |
163      |                   {GOTO}dates~                  Go to the DATES range.                           |
164      |                   /XR                           Return.                                          |
165      |                                                                                                  |
166      |                                                                                                  |
167      |                   Updates spreadsheet with revised summary formulas.                             |
168      |                   -----------------------------------------------------------------------        |
169      |       formup      /Cdates~dates~                Calculate the dates.                             |
170      |                   /Cformulas~formulas~          Calculate the formulas.                          |
171      |                   /Ccur_sum~cur_tot~            Put the formula for the current                  |
172      |                   {GOTO}cur_tot~                  period's totals into the first                 |
173      |                   {EDIT}{CALC}~                   row of the data base.                          |
174      |                   /Clast_sum~last_tot~          Put the formula for the previous                 |
175      |                   {GOTO}last_tot~                 period's totals into the first                 |
176      |                   {EDIT}{CALC}~                   row of the data base.                          |
177      |                   /XCunpark~                    Restore the DATA range.                          |
178      |                   {GOTO}summary~                Go to the top of the summary column.             |
179      |                   /Csummary~.{END}{DOWN}~       Copy formulas to Summary Section.                |
180      |                   /Cmisc_dat~first_mo~          Add dates to report.                             |
181      |                   /Creport~report~              Recalculate the report                           |
182      |                   /Creport~report~              Recalculate the report                           |
183      |                   /XR                           Return.                                          |
184      |                                                                                                  |
185      |                                                                                                  |
186      |                   Extracts and files the current report.                                         |
187      |                   -----------------------------------------------------------------------        |
188      |       xtract      /RNCwhere~~                   Name this spot "where".                          |
189      |                   /XCpark~                      Park the DATA file.                              |
190      |                   {GOTO}report~                 File extract the report.                         |
191      |                   /FXF{?}~                            "                                          |
192      |                   .{UP}{END}{RIGHT}                   "                                          |
```

```
193 |            {DOWN}{END}{LEFT}                 "
194 |            {END}{DOWN}~R{ESC}~               "
195 |            /XCunpark~                  Unpark the DATA range.
196 |            {GOTO}where~/RNDwhere~      Go to "where".  Delete range "where".
197 |            /XR                         Return.
198 |
199 |            Print Data Bank Descriptions
200 |            ------------------------------------------------------------
201 |  desc      {GOTO}a1~/PPCAR.            Set A1 as top left of print range.
202 |            {END}{DOWN}{RIGHT}~         Set bottom of print range.
203 |            AGQ                         Print descriptions.
204 |            /XR                         Return.
205 |
206 |
207 |  ::        = New Page =  |::
208 |
209 |
210 |            Print the MACROs
211 |            ------------------------------------------------------------
212 |  print_m   /PPOMR132~ML8~              Set right and left print margins.
213 |            MTO~MBO~QQ                  Set top and bottom margins to zero.
214 |            {GOTO}macro0~/XCprint_m1~   Go to the macro to print, then print it.
215 |            {GOTO}macro1~/XCprint_m1~         "
216 |            {GOTO}macro2~/XCprint_m1~         "
217 |            {GOTO}macro3~/XCprint_m1~         "
218 |            {GOTO}macro4~/XCprint_m1~         "
219 |            {GOTO}macro5~/XCprint_m1~         "
220 |            {GOTO}macro6~/XCprint_m1~         "
221 |            /XR                         Return.
222 |
223 |  print_m1  /PPR{BS}.                   Reset top left of print range to this cell.
224 |            {LEFT}{END}{DOWN}           Find break in left border of macro.
225 |            {END}{RIGHT}{LEFT}~         Set bottom right of print range.
226 |            AGPQ                        Align, Go, Page, Quit.
227 |            /XR                         Return.
228 |
229
230 |
231 |
```

Figure 2-13. The MACRO3 page

```
           AU        AV        AW        AX        AY        AZ        BA        BB        BC        BD        BE

155 ----------------------------------------------------------------------------------------------------------------
156 ---------- MACROS  ----------------------------------------------------------------------------------------------
157       |                                                                                                       |
158       |                                                                                                       |
159       |    ==============================================================================                     |
160       |               Use the arrow keys to move between entries.                                            |
161       |                          Press <ENTER> when done.                                                     |
162       |    ==============================================================================                     |
163       |                                                                                                       |
164       |               PLEASE ENTER THE DATES THAT YOU WISH TO REPORT                                          |
165       |                                                                                                       |
166       |                                                          Month      Year                              |
167       |                                                          -----      ----                              |
168       |            Starting date for this period:                    1        85                              |
169       |            Ending date for this period:                     12        85                              |
170       |                                                                                                       |
171       |            Starting date for last period:                    1        84                              |
172       |            Ending date for last period:                     12        84                              |
173       |                                                                                                       |
174       |                                                                                                       |
175       |                                                                                                       |
176       |                                                                                                       |
177       |                        ARE THESE REPORT DATES OKAY?                                                   |
178       |                     If they are, choose "Update-Dates".                                               |
179       |               To change the report dates, choose "Select-Dates".                                      |
180       |            ------------------------------------------------------                                     |
181       |                                                                                                       |
```

```
182   |                                                     Date          |
183   |                                                     -----         |
184   |     Starting date for this period:                  Jan-85        |
185   |     Ending date for this period:                    Dec-85        |
186   |                                                                   |
187   |     Starting date for last period:                  Jan-84        |
188   |     Ending date for last period:                    Dec-84        |
189   |                                                                   |
190   |                                                                   |
191   |                                                                   |
192   |                                                                   |
193   |                                                                   |
194   |                                                                   |
195   |                                                                   |
196   |                                                                   |
197   |     ------------------------------------------------------------  |
198   |     FORMULAS          5        <<First row in DATA range.        |
199   |     =========                                                     |
200   |       NAME        COL# CELL      NAME    FORMULAS                 |
201   |     ----------------- ----     ---------------------------        |
202   |     THIS_BEGC       36 AJ5     CUR_SUM  @SUM(AJ5..AU5)            |
203   |     THIS_ENDC       47 AU5                                        |
204   |     LAST_BEGC       24 X5      LAST_SUM @SUM(X5..AI5)             |
205   |     LAST_ENDC       35 AI5                                        |
206   |     ------------------------------------------------------------  |
207   |                                                                   |
208                                                                       |
209   |                                                                   |
210   |                                                                   |
211   |                                                                   |
```

Figure 2-14. The MACRO5 page

recalculates the FORMULAS range shown at the bottom of Figure 2-14. Let's look at this section in more detail.

The first row of data in the Data Bank is row 5. It is possible, however, that for some reason you could insert or delete rows in the heading, changing this row number. The following formula simply "looks" at the range name assigned to the top of the data and returns the string representation of its row number.

```
AY198:  @STRING(@CELL("ROW",$TOP),0)
```

The following formulas calculate the column numbers where we can find the data for the beginning and ending months of the current period and of the comparison period. Each formula begins by checking the dates. The formulas return an ERR if the beginning dates are earlier than the earliest date in the Data Bank or if the ending date in a period is earlier than the beginning date. If the dates are acceptable, the formulas calculate how many months have elapsed between the starting month in the Data Bank and each of the dates entered at the top of MACRO5. Adding this number of months to the column number containing the starting month produces the column number for each of the dates.

Although the following formulas occupy more than one line on the page, be sure to enter the entire formula in the cell shown and to leave no spaces between any characters in the formula.

```
AX202:  @IF($BB$184<$START_MO,@ERR,
          12*$BB168+$BA168-12*@YEAR($START_MO)-@MONTH
          ($START_MO)+$START_COL)
AX203:  @IF($REP_MO<$BB$184,@ERR,
          12*$BB169+$BA169-12*@YEAR($START_MO)-@MONTH
          ($START_MO)+$START_COL)
AX204:  @IF($BB$187<$START_MO,@ERR,
          12*$BB171+$BA171-12*@YEAR($START_MO)-@MONTH
          ($START_MO)+START_COL)
AX205:  @IF($BB$188<$BB$187,@ERR,
          12*$BB172+$BA172-12*@YEAR($START_MO)-@MONTH
          ($START_MO)+START_COL)
```

The next four string formulas calculate the cell locations of the first row of data for each of the four dates entered at the top of MACRO5. The formulas change the column number to a column letter: given the number 26, for example, they would return Z; given 27, they would return AA. Finally, the formulas add the string representing the first row in the Data Bank to the end of the column letter(s).

```
AY202:  @IF(THIS_BEGC<27,"",@CHAR(@INT((THIS_BEGC-1)/26)+64))
          &@CHAR(64+@MOD(THIS_BEGC-1,26)+1)&$FST_ROW
AY203:  @IF(THIS_ENDC<27,"",@CHAR(@INT((THIS_ENDC-1)/26)+64))
          &@CHAR(64+@MOD(THIS_ENDC-1,26)+1)&$FST_ROW
AY204:  @IF(LAST_BEGC<27,"",@CHAR(@INT((LAST_BEGC-1)/26)+64))
          &@CHAR(64+@MOD(LAST_BEGC-1,26)+1)&$FST_ROW
AY205:  @IF(LAST_ENDC<27,"",@CHAR(@INT((LAST_ENDC-1)/26)+64))
          &@CHAR(64+@MOD(LAST_ENDC-1,26)+1)&$FST_ROW
```

The preceding nine formulas were created to make the following formulas possible. These two formulas return strings that look like the @SUM formulas that we need. In other words the @SUM formulas shown in cells BA202 and BA204 of Figure 2-14, are not actual formulas at all. They are the results of these two string formulas:

```
BA202:  +"@SUM("&$AY$202&".."&$AY$203&")"
BA204:  +"@SUM("&$AY$204&".."&$AY$205&")"
```

Now we can see what the FORMUP macro does in Figure 2-6. The macro command in cell AC171 copies CUR_SUM, the formula in BA202, to CUR_TOT. This destination is the top cell in the column of the Data Bank that holds the current period totals. The next two lines of this macro use the {EDIT}{CALC} commands to turn the string formula into an actual @SUM formula.

FORMUP follows the same approach to create the @SUM formula for the comparison period's total. Next, this macro copies all the summary formulas in the top row of the Data Bank to the rest of the rows in the summary columns. This step updates the summary columns with the two @SUM formulas and recalculates the remaining summary columns.

Finally, the macro recalculates the range containing the Data Bank reports. This step lets you see how a change in the reporting dates affects the data in any report you may have in the Data Bank.

XTRACT This macro uses /File Xtract to extract and save the report contained in the report section of the Data Bank. When you read Chapters 3, 5, 6, and 13, you will see that we carefully position a border down the right side of each report. This border is very important because the XTRACT macro uses the border as a guide for setting the range for the /File Extract command. If this border is improperly positioned or missing, the XTRACT macro will not save what you expect.

Cell AC194 uses another handy trick. When you save a file that already exists, 1-2-3 asks if you want to replace this file. The "R" in AC194 tells the

```
        AK       AL        AM         AN         AO         AP         AQ         AR         AS         AT         AU

155 ------------------------------------------------------------------------------------------------------------------
156 --------- MACRO4 -------------------------------------------------------------------------------------------------
157     |                                                                                                        |
158     |                Load and print reports from file list.                                                  |
159     |                ------------------------------------------------------------------------------          |
160     |       loadrep  /XLEnter name of batch to print: ~batch~                                                |
161     |                {GOTO}                                                                                  |
162     |       batch    REP1                                      Name of batch to print.                       |
163     |                ~                                         RETURN symbol.                                |
164     |                {LEFT}/RNChere~{BS}~                      Initialize HERE pointer.                      |
165     |                /XCformup~{CALC}                          Update summaries. Recalc.                     |
166     |       load1    /XCnxt_rep~                               Get next report name.                         |
167     |                /XI@COUNT(here)<2~/RNDhere~/XR            Test for end of list. Return if end.          |
168     |                /Cname~file_in~                           Copy file name to place for input.            |
169     |                /XCprep~                                  Prepare the report area.                      |
170     |                /FCCE                                     Combine new report.                           |
171     |       file_in  CASH_FLO                                  Name of new report.                           |
172     |                ~                                         RETURN symbol.                                |
173     |                /XCset~                                   Set boundaries & recalculate.                 |
174     |                /PPCAOMTO~MBO~MR132~QQ/WGC9~              Reset print margins & column widths.          |
175     |                /XCrep_mac~                               Print report using report's macro.            |
176     |                /XGload1~                                 Loop back to get next report.                 |
177     |                                                                                                        |
178     |                Find next report in sequence.                                                           |
179     |                ------------------------------------------------------------------------------          |
180     |       nxt_rep  {GOTO}here~                               Go to last HERE place marker.                 |
181     |                {DOWN}/RNChere~{BS}.{RIGHT}~              Assign new HERE place marker.                 |
182     |                {RIGHT}/RNCname~{BS}~                     Assign name of new file to NAME.              |
183     |                /XR                                       Return                                        |
```

```
184
185              Load single report.
186              --------------------------------------------------------------------
187   singrep    /XCprep~                             Prepare the report area.
188              /FCCE{?}~                            Name new report.
189              /XCset~                              Set boundaries & recalculate.
190              /XR                                  Return
191
192              Set range boundries and calculate new report.
193              --------------------------------------------------------------------
194   set        /XCunpark~                           Unpark the DATA range.
195              /Cmisc_dat~first_mo~                 Update month data.
196              {GOTO}rep_mac~{LEFT}                 Set REPORT limits to size of the
197              /RNCreport~{BS}.                       report.
198              {UP}{END}{RIGHT}                                  "
199              {DOWN}{END}{LEFT}                                 "
200              {END}{DOWN}~                                      "
201              /Creport~report~                     Calculate the report.
202              /XR                                  Return.
203
204              Prepare report area for report.
205              --------------------------------------------------------------------
206   prep       /XCpark~                             Park the DATA range.
207              {GOTO}report~                        Put cursor where new report will go.
208              /RE.{END}{HOME}{DOWN}~               Erase area where new report will go.
209              /RFR.{END}{HOME}{DOWN}~              Reset Format of report area.
210              /XR                                  Return.
211
212
213
214
215
```

Figure 2-15. The MACRO4 page

program to Replace. In this instance, the {ESC} command has no effect. On the other hand, if you are saving the file for the first time, 1-2-3 asks no questions and the "R" isn't needed. In this instance, {ESC} erases the unneeded "R." So, whether the file name you have assigned exists or not, including "R{ESC}" in the macro command will save that file with no further questions asked.

DESC This simple macro prints the Data Bank numbers and descriptions.

New Page See |:: contained in cell AB207. This set of symbols is new to 1-2-3 Version 2. When found in the left-hand border of a print range, it sends a form-feed command to the printer. This embedded print command is used by the following macro, which prints all the macros.

When you assign range names for the macros on this page, you will use the /Range Name Labels Right command, highlighting the column of range names. Since the embedded print command is also in this column, the range name :: also will be assigned. Use /**R**ange **N**ame **D**elete to delete this range.

PRINT_M Notice that the vertical border in cell AA229 is blank and that this blank is below the last line of the macros in MACRO3. When you issue the command to print the macros (ALT-M Print Macros), PRINT_M uses this blank to set the print range for MACRO3.

Also notice that this macro sets the right print column width to 132 characters but does not initiate the Condensed Print mode. Since each printer requires different commands to set condensed print, you must add the command to this macro that sets condensed print for your own printer.

The MACRO4 and MACRO0 Pages And the Report Header

All the macros in MACRO4 (Figure 2-15) are used to load and print Data Bank reports. When these reports are printed as a batch, the macros use the list of reports in MACRO0 (Figure 2-16) to find each report.

In Figure 2-15 LOADREP is the macro that updates the report header; loads each report, recalculates it, and prints it; and then loads the next report. To do this, it uses other macros included in Figure 2-15. LOADREP will be easier to understand, therefore, if we look first at the report header and then at those other macros.

```
           A                B                    C         D         E

155 -------------------------------------------------------------------------
156 |                    MACRO0              ----------------------------------
157 |                                                                      |
158 |          REP1                                                        |
159 |          ------------------------------------------                  |
160 |          CASH_FLO                       Cash Flow Report             |
161 |          AR                             A/R Report                   |
162 |          AP                             A/P Report                   |
163 |          MIN_GRAF                       Mini Graph Report            |
164 |                                                                      |
165 |                                                                      |
166 |          REP2                                                        |
167 |          ------------------------------------------                  |
168 |          MIN_GRAF                       Mini Graph Report            |
169 |          CASH_FLO                       Cash Flow Report             |
170 |                                                                      |
171                                                                        |
172 |                                                                      |
173 |                                                                      |
174 |                                                                      |
```

Figure 2-16. The MACRO0 page

The Report Header Figure 2-17 shows the left side of the report header and the rows just above and below it.

Rows 242 through 249 show the bottom of the borders for MACRO0. The top of this macro page is shown in Figure 2-16. The vertical borders for the other MACRO pages all end, like MACRO0, in row 249. Rows 250 through 254 constitute the report header. Each label shown in row 253 is the range name for the cell below it in row 254. Rows 254 through 260 show the top of the Accounts Receivable Collections analysis. This report is discussed in Chapter 3.

Notice that the report and the header overlap at row 254. Any range defined for the last row in the Data Bank—here row 254—"belongs" to both the Data Bank and its reports. To understand why it is important that this be the case, remember why the Park and Unpark menu options are necessary. Recall that when a Data Bank report is extracted and saved, the report can lose track of any cell references outside its boundaries. To be assured that the reports keep track of the cell references, we must "park" the DATA range within the boundaries of the report. We therefore park the

```
          A              B          C    D    E    F    G    H    I    J    K    L    M    N

242 |                                         |
243 |                                         |
244 |                                         |
245 |                                         |
246 |                                         |
247 |                                         |
248 |                                         |
249 |                                         |
250 ---------------------------------------------------------------------------------------------
251                                       MISC_DAT Dec-82        11        Dec-85        47
252 ---------------------------------------------------------------------------------------------
253 REPORT          REP_MAC     ------------------FIRST_MO------FIRST_CO------THIS_MO ------THIS_COL-----------
254             {GOTO}report~   Set colu             Dec-82          11        Dec-85          47
255             /WCS9~          A
256             {RIGHT}/WCS26~  B
257             {RIGHT}/WCS20~  C                 START     34 +$THIS_COL-13 -- Start w/ this data column.
258             {RIGHT}/WCS8~   D               SCALE30     23 GRAPH SCALE FACTOR, 30-90
259             {RIGHT}/WCR~    E               SCALE90    400 GRAPH SCALE FACTOR, OVER 90
260             {RIGHT}/WCS7~   F
```

Figure 2-17. The left side of the report header

range in the first row of the report—row 254. To the Data Bank, row 254 is a row of range names in the last row of the spreadsheet. No data can be stored here permanently because data is erased whenever a new report is added. But the range names survive. Row 254 therefore acts as a way to communicate, or translate, information between the Data Bank and its reports.

To enter the report header, begin by entering the labels and underlines shown in rows 250 through 253. Next, copy the underlines in the range N250..N253 to O250..BG250. Then put your cell pointer on A253 and issue the /**R**ange **N**ame **L**abels **D**own command, highlighting the range A253..L253. This command assigns range names to row 254 that are defined by the labels in row 253. Then use /**R**ange **N**ame **D**elete to delete the range name —. This range was created by the underlines (just as the range :: was created in MACRO3 by the embedded print command).

Enter the label **MISC_DAT** in E251.Then use /**R**ange **N**ame **C**reate to create the range name MISC_DAT, highlighting the range F251..M251. Finally, enter the following formulas:

F251: (D3) +$START_MO

This is the month and year of the oldest data in the Data Bank.

H251: +$START_COL

This is the column where the data for the starting month can be found.

J251: (D3) +$REP_MO

This is the month and year of the current reporting month.

L251: 12*@YEAR(J251-F251)+@MONTH(J251-F251)+$START_COL

This is the column where the data for the current reporting month can be found.

PREP Shown at the bottom of Figure 2-15, this macro prepares the report area for a new report. After parking the DATA range in the last row of the Data Bank, it erases and resets the format of the spreadsheet from the last row of the Data Bank (row 254 again) through the bottom of the spreadsheet.

SET After a new report has been loaded into the Data Bank, this macro unparks the DATA range. Next, as shown in cell AM195 of Figure 2-15, it copies the miscellaneous data from row 251 to row 254. Remember, PREP erased everything from row 254 downward. But the new report will need the month and column data that had been stored in row 254. The command in AM195 restores this information.

Finally, the SET macro sets the limits of the REPORT range to the size of the newly added report. The most frequent use of the REPORT range is to copy it onto itself, thus recalculating the report. This use is shown in cell AM201 of Figure 2-15.

SINGREP When you issue the command ALT-M System Load, the menu sends you to this macro for loading single reports. The macro uses PREP to prepare the report area; then it uses the command /File Combine Copy Entire-File to load the file that you specify. Finally, it uses SET to set the REPORT range and then returns control to the macro menus.

LOADREP This macro, at the top of Figure 2-15, loads and prints reports in a batch from a file list. The first few commands in this macro set up the spreadsheet for the real work that follows. The setup begins by asking for the name of the batch to print. This macro command, in AM160, enters your response into the range name BATCH, found in AM162. In the figure, REP1 is the name of one such batch.

The macro then goes to the range you have specified. The range name REP1 is found in cell B159 of MACRO0 (Figure 2-16). All batches of report names are maintained in this MACRO page.

If you look back at Figure 2-11, you will see that the address for the range name REP1 is B159. This cell contains the underline immediately below REP1 and above CASH_FLO, the name of the first report to print. Assign this range name by putting your cell pointer on REP1 and using the /**R**ange **N**ame **L**abels **D**own command.

The next setup command in LOADREP moves the cell pointer one cell to the left of B159 and assigns the range name HERE to cell A159. Finally, the last setup commands rerun the FORMUP macro and then calculate the spreadsheet. The FORMUP command, remember, updated the summary columns of the spreadsheet to reflect the new report dates. If your clerk has remembered to issue this command, issuing it again won't hurt anything. It merely recalculates the summary columns one additional time.

The real work begins at LOAD1. The first command at this point is to use the NXT_REP macro. This macro shifts the HERE range down one row, assigning two cells to this range. The macro also assigns the range NAME to the first name in the print list.

The next row of the macro counts the number of entries in HERE. At the moment, the count equals two. (The name CASH_FLO in column B counts as one, and the vertical line in column A counts as the other.) But when the HERE range has shifted to below the last name on the list, the count will be less than two since the range now includes only the vertical line. If the count is less than two, the macro deletes the HERE range and then returns control to the menu.

If the count equals two, the macro copies the NAME of the report in the list to the FILE_IN range, shown in AM171 of Figure 2-15. Next, the macro runs PREP to prepare the report area for the report. Then it uses the name in FILE_IN to /File Combine the new report.

Once the report has loaded, the macro runs SET to assign the REPORT boundaries and recalculate. Then the macro assigns the print settings. Again, remember that the macro does *not* include a setup string to use the compressed print feature of your printer. You must add the command that works with your specific printer.

Next the macro runs the REP_MAC macro. This macro, which is loaded with each report, sets the column widths unique to the report, assigns the print range, calculates the report again, if necessary, and then prints the report.

Finally, the command in AM176 of Figure 2-15 returns control to LOAD1, where the next report name is found, and the processing continues until the last name has been printed.

The MACRO6 Page

The final MACRO page, MACRO6, shown in Figure 2-18, holds the Help screens. As you can see, the page is only three columns wide. Columns BE and BG hold the page borders. Column BF, which has a width of 76 characters, holds the Help screen information.

To create this section, simply enter the information that you see and then use /**R**ange **N**ame **C**reate to assign the range names and addresses specified for MACRO6 in Figure 2-11.

```
          BE                         BF                                   BG
155 -------------------------------------------------------------------------------
156 ---------                     MACRO6                                      |
157     |                                                                     |
158     |                         menu_h                                      |
159     |               MAIN MENU HELP SCREEN                                 |
160     |                                                                     |
161     |                                                                     |
162     |      Your other choices are:                                        |
163     |                                                                     |
164     |      1.  Update--Use Update to add data, change report dates, and to|
165     |          recalculate the spreadsheet.                               |
166     |                                                                     |
167     |      2.  Print--This selection is used to control all print options.|
168     |                                                                     |
169     |      3.  System--This selection is to be used by key operators only.|
170     |                                                                     |
171     |                                                                     |
172     |            Press ESC to return to the Ready mode.                   |
173     |                                                                     |
174     |                                                                     |
175     |                                                                     |
176     |                                                                     |
177     |                                                                     |
178     |                                                                     |
179     |                                                                     |
180     |                          update_h                                   |
181     |               UPDATE HELP SCREEN                                    |
182     |                                                                     |
183     |      Your other choices are:                                        |
184     |                                                                     |
185     |      1.  New-Month--Use this option to enter data for the new month. |
186     |          ALT-A   automates cell pointer.  CTRL-Break stops execution.|
```

```
187          ALT-C   calculates new column's subtotals during data entry.
188          ALT-M Update Select-Dates    completes the data entry option.
189
190      2.  Select-Dates--Use this option to clear the data entry screen
191          and to select the dates you wish to use for your reports.
192
193      3.  Update-Dates--Use this option to update the Data Bank with
194          the dates you have chosen with the Select-Dates option.
195
196      4.  Quit--Returns you to the ready mode.
197
198            Press ESC to return to the previous menu.
199
200
201                                 intro
202
203
204
205                           Welcome to the
206
207                         D A T A    B A N K
208
209                     Management Reporting System
210
211                      (c) 1985  Charles W. Kyd
212
213
214
215               Please make a selection from the menu above.
216
217
218
219
220
```

Figure 2-18. The MACRO6 page

ENTERING YOUR OWN DATA INTO THE DATA BANK

The whole purpose of the Data Bank is to create your own reports. Here are the steps to follow.

1. Start with a working version of the sample Data Bank. If you have purchased the disk set available for this book, this task is easy. Otherwise, follow the steps outlined in Chapter 1 and this chapter to create the Data Bank. Then follow the steps in Chapters 3, 5, 6, and 13 to create the sample Data Bank reports.

2. Make copies of the Data Bank. Once you have a working system, make copies of the Data Bank and all reports. Store the original disks in a safe place and use only the copies for your future work. With this approach, if you ever damage the copies, the originals will help you to recover.

3. Start your Data Bank binder. Set up a Data Bank binder as described in Chapter 1. Begin with the following data: Income Statement, Balance Sheet, Accounts Receivable Aging, Accounts Payable Aging, Dividends Paid, Accounts Payable Paid (total Debits to Accounts Payable), and Accounts Payable Purchases (total Credits to Accounts Payable). These reports and categories of information are common in a business and should be readily available. As shown in Figure 1-7, assign a Data Bank number to each data item that you expect to use from these reports.

4. Prepare the sample Data Bank for your data. Beginning with cell K5 of a *copy* of the sample Data Bank, erase every cell in the data section that does not contain a formula. This step will ensure that your Data Bank doesn't accidentally contain sample data.

5. Adjust the Data Bank numbers and descriptions. When you prepare to enter each report, begin by adjusting the Data Bank numbers to match the numbers you have assigned in your binder and by modifying the descriptions as necessary. You will often need to add or delete rows to make the Data Bank match your own data categories.

You will want to reduce the number of formulas for ratios and running totals that you have to reenter. Therefore, if the sample Data Bank assigns a category to a particular row, try to use that row for your own data; for example, try to use the row with the sample Current Assets for your own Current Assets data.

6. Enter the subtotal formulas as necessary. If you decide to use formulas within the Data Bank to calculate subtotals such as Total Current Assets, Net Profit, and Net Worth, enter them now. The easiest approach is to go to column C, issue the /**W**orksheet **T**itles **V**ertical command, and then enter your formulas in column K. The titles will make it easy for you to point to the cells in column K that you will want to add, subtract, or @SUM to calculate the subtotals. After you've entered the subtotal formulas for any report, copy them across the Data Bank.

7. Gather old data and enter it into the Data Bank. Enter the month and year of your oldest data into the @DATE formula in cell K4. Continue to use 15 as the day of the month in this cell. When you calculate the Data Bank, the date headings in row 4 should be correct. (At this point many of the ratio calculations, attempting to divide by zero, will return ERR. This problem should end when you enter data.)

To enter your data, use the macro command ALT-M Update New-Month. This command will set titles and then position your cell pointer at the first empty column. Use the macros \C and \E, as necessary, to calculate your subtotals or to move your cell pointer as you enter data.

8. Adjust the formulas for the ratios and running totals. Once you enter the first four reports and recalculate, many of the formulas for the ratios and running totals should return correct information. However, there are two problems to be careful of. First, the formulas for the 12-month running totals will not work within the first 12 months of data. If you can calculate what the numbers should be, enter those values; if not, enter estimates. Second, although you were careful to enter your data into appropriate categories, the formulas for the ratios may no longer be correct. Using the descriptions and the formulas in Appendix A, Table A-1, check each ratio that *should* be correct at this point. Make sure that the formulas are indeed correct.

9. Select reporting dates for a sample report. Use the Data Bank commands ALT-M Update Select-Dates and then Update-Dates to select and update dates for which you have entered data.

10. Adjust the reports to reflect your new data categories. Use ALT-M System Load to load the statement of Changes in Financial Position, described in Chapter 6. Modify the Data Bank numbers in column I to correspond with the numbers that you have assigned. If necessary, add or delete any categories of data in the report. When you recalculate, your funds statement should balance. After you save this report, load and adjust the AR report, described in Chapter 3, and then load the AP report, described in Chapter 5.

The mini graph, described in Chapter 13, will require more data. However, graphs for which you have data will work once you have modified their Data Bank numbers to reflect your own number scheme. To complete the other graphs, either add the data that these graphs seek or modify the graphs to analyze the data that you have already entered.

11. Complete data entry. Once you have the reports working, enter other data that you wish to maintain in the Data Bank. Also, delete from the sample Data Bank those categories of data that you do not wish to use. Note that these steps may require that you delete or modify some of the ratios or running totals.

When you have completed data entry, your Data Bank should contain a solid block of data. You should have no blank rows of data within the Data Bank.

12. Double-check your reports. Before you begin to use the reports you have created, check again that they are correct. Are they picking up the correct data from the correct Data Bank rows? Are the dates correct? Are the ratios correct?

An additional way to check your funds statement is to use a reporting period that encompasses the entire period for which you have data. Not only should this two- or three-year analysis be interesting in its own right, it should provide an additional test of whether your balance sheet balances within the Data Bank.

13. Put your Data Bank into production. By now you will have learned enough about the Data Bank to put it into production. Doing so involves three steps. First, enter the names of the reports that work with your data into the MACRO0 page of the Data Bank. The ALT-M Print Reports command will now be able to print them as a batch. Second, train a clerk to update the Data Bank monthly. And finally, as you need additional reports and analyses, add the necessary data to the Data Bank and write the reports as needed.

Chapter
Three

HOW TO MONITOR ACCOUNTS RECEIVABLE

Several years ago the fire alarm in my house developed a mind of its own. At times, usually in the middle of the night, it would suddenly begin to shake the house with its buzz and clatter. And then, five, ten, fifteen minutes later, it would stop. And all the while, there was no smoke and no fire.

The alarm upset my sleep, of course. And my disposition. Worse, there was always the concern: Will it raise an alarm when it should? This concern finally overcame my Scottish frugality. I replaced the alarm.

MONITORING DAY'S SALES OUTSTANDING (DSO)

Most businesses monitor their Accounts Receivable balances with a device that is much like my old fire alarm, but less reliable. This monitoring device is a number that is found by dividing the Accounts Receivable balance by the firm's average daily sales. It is called the Accounts Receivable Collection Period, or the Day's Sales Outstanding (DSO) in receivables. Whatever it is called, this measure frequently gives a warning when none is needed. Worse, when receivables are growing out of control, the DSO can fail to raise much of an alarm at all.

The DSO fails because its calculation is influenced by two factors that have nothing to do with how quickly customers pay. First, the DSO is strongly influenced by recent trends in the growth or decline in sales. Second, it can swing wildly, depending on the number of months that are used to calculate the average daily sales.

To illustrate, assume that the Acme Corporation has had a constant collection history over the past year. At the end of each month, 90% of that month's sales remain uncollected. By the end of the second month, 40% of these sales have been collected, leaving 60% uncollected. By the end of the third month, 90% of the sales have been collected. The remaining 10% are collected by the end of the fourth month after the sale is made.

Figure 3-1 illustrates the quarterly statistics for Acme's collection history. Since the sales for each month in the first quarter were equal in this figure, the Average Daily Sales and Collection Periods for each calculation method were equal also. Average sales were $2 and the Collection Period was 48 days.

But look at the other quarters. In the second quarter sales start high at $90 and then decrease to $30. Here, depending on the number of days used to calculate the average daily sales, the collection period has deteriorated to 72 days, stayed the same at 48 days, or improved to 36 days. In the third quarter sales start low and then increase. Here the collection period has improved, stayed the same, or deteriorated. And so it goes. These jumbled results have occurred even though customer payments have remained constant through the year.

These confusing signals not only cause unjustified elation or concern about Accounts Receivable collections, they can also disguise real problems. Look, for example, at the Alternative Fourth Quarter in Figure 3-1. In this instance *no* invoices have been paid for November and December, and 40% of October's invoices are still outstanding. This significant drop in customer payments has produced a relatively minor increase in the collection period. Nothing in these figures shows that the deterioration is as significant as it is.

In short the Accounts Receivable collection period does not effectively monitor a firm's collection history. Now let's see what does.

A BETTER WAY

As a financial manager, I have three separate but related goals for Accounts Receivable (A/R) collections.

Acme Corp. Receivables Analysis

		Outstanding Receivables At End of Qtr		Average Daily Sales If Averaging Period Is The Most Recent			End of Quarter Collection Period If Averaging Period Is		
Month	Sales	% of Sales	Dollar Amount	30 Days	60 Days	90 Days	30 Days	60 Days	90 Days
First Quarter									
Jan	$60	10%	$6						
Feb	$60	60%	$36						
Mar	$60	90%	$54						
	$180		$96	$2.00	$2.00	$2.00	48 Days	48 Days	48 Days
Second Quarter									
Apr	$90	10%	$9						
May	$60	60%	$36						
Jun	$30	90%	$27						
	$180		$72	$1.00	$1.50	$2.00	72 Days	48 Days	36 Days
Third Quarter									
Jul	$30	10%	$3						
Aug	$60	60%	$36						
Sep	$90	90%	$81						
	$180		$120	$3.00	$2.50	$2.00	40 Days	48 Days	60 Days
Fourth Quarter									
Oct	$60	10%	$6						
Nov	$30	60%	$18						
Dec	$90	90%	$81						
	$180		$105	$3.00	$2.00	$2.00	35 Days	53 Days	53 Days
Alternative Fourth Quarter									
Oct	$60	40%	$24						
Nov	$30	100%	$30						
Dec	$90	100%	$90						
	$180		$144	$3.00	$2.00	$2.00	48 Days	72 Days	72 Days

Figure 3-1. Day's Sales Outstanding with various sales patterns

1. Collect as much as you can as soon as you can. If you can collect in 10 days, great! If you can collect within 30 days, do it! If it takes 45 days to collect a 30-day invoice, that's borderline. But if it takes 60 or 90 days to collect the invoice, deposit the cash and try to do better in the future.

2. Keep invoices out of the Over-90-Days column. When an invoice hits this column, most lenders who use accounts receivable as collateral will "unqualify" that invoice, which means that we must return to the lender the cash we have borrowed against the invoice. Worse, many lenders will unqualify all invoices for one customer if more than 10% of the customer's A/R balance is more than 90 days old. Even if you don't borrow against your receivables, it is wise to keep invoices out of this column. The chance of collecting an invoice decreases significantly after it is 90 days old.

3. Take immediate action to collect everything that is more than 90 days old. That balance represents cash that should be in your bank, not on your books. Twist arms. Get the cash!

Figure 3-2 illustrates an Accounts Receivable Collections analysis. This report, generated by the Data Bank, shows how well we have performed in these three areas. Even if your collection goals differ from mine, this kind of report will show how you are doing. Let's see what it tells us.

In Section 1 the first line of data tells us that just one year ago, in December 1984, 5% of our sales were collected during the month of the sale. During the following month, we collected 43% of December's sales. During the third month, we collected 42%. And 10% of our December sales were not collected within 90 days. Finally, the report shows that our over-90-days balance was equal to 0.76% of our sales for the most recent 12 months.

The figure displays similar information for each of the 12 months since December 1984. The data for November and December 1985 are shown as incomplete, however, because we haven't had time for November and December sales to fall into the 30-, 60-, and 90-Day columns.

As you can see in the first two sections of the figure the collection percentages are graphed. The first four columns of graphs all use the same scale, which makes it easy to compare collection performance month by month as well as period by period. The graph in the rightmost column uses a different scale. The vertical line separating the data for this column from the remaining columns gives us a sense of this change.

The only dollar amount given in Figure 3-2 is at the bottom of Section

Accounts Receivable Collections Analysis
Dec-85

Section 1

Month Of Sale	Percent of Sales Collected in Each 30-Day Period: 0-30 DAYS		30-60 DAYS		60-90 DAYS		% Uncollected After 90 Days		A/R Over 90 Days As a Percent Of 12-Mos Sales	
Dec-84	5%	+	43%	++++++++++	42%	++++++++++	10%	++	0.76%	+++
Jan-85	8%	++	42%	++++++++++	38%	+++++++++	12%	+++	1.56%	++++++
Feb-85	6%	+	48%	+++++++++++	30%	+++++++	16%	++++	1.17%	+++++
Mar-85	11%	+++	53%	++++++++++++	21%	+++++	15%	+++	0.24%	+
Apr-85	7%	++	44%	++++++++++	46%	+++++++++++	3%	+	0.24%	+
May-85	1%	.	46%	+++++++++++	38%	+++++++++	15%	+++	1.00%	++++
Jun-85	11%	+++	57%	+++++++++++++	21%	+++++	11%	+++	0.41%	++
Jul-85	6%	+	27%	++++++	35%	++++++++	32%	+++++++	0.63%	+++
Aug-85	2%	.	15%	+++	48%	+++++++++++	35%	++++++++	1.27%	+++++
Sep-85	1%	.	28%	++++++	63%	++++++++++++++	8%	++	1.72%	+++++++
Oct-85	3%	+	34%	++++++++	36%	++++++++	27%	++++++	0.99%	++++
Nov-85	1%	.	45%	++++++++++			54%	(Incomplete)	2.63%	+++++++++++
Dec-85	2%	.					98%	(Incomplete)	1.82%	+++++++

This Month's Amount Over 90 Days = $38

Section 2

Average of Original Sale Collected Each Period	0-30 Days		30-60 Days		60-90 Days		Over 90 Days		A/R Over 90 Days	
Previous 6-Mos	7%	++	48%	+++++++++++	32%	+++++++	13%	+++	0.77%	+++
Most recent 6-Mos	3%	+	30%	+++++++	46%	+++++++++++	21%	+++++	1.51%	++++++
Improvement	-4%		-18%		14%		-8%		-0.74%	

Section 3

Average Total Interest Cost, at 12%, For Receivables Less Than 90 Days Old		Average Collection Period For Sales Less Than 90 Days Old	
Previous 6-Mos	1.47%	Previous 6-Mos	44 Days
Most recent 6-Mos	2.02%	Most recent 6-Mos	61 Days
Improvement	-0.55%	Improvement	-17 Days

Figure 3-2. A sample Accounts Receivable Collections Analysis report

1. This is the amount in this month's aging in the Over-90-Days column. It shows us the extent of both the opportunities and risks that the past-due balance represents.

Section 2 of the figure compares the average collection performance for the sales from two six-month periods. As you can see in row 298, collections of sales made from January through June were significantly better than collections from sales in the second half of the year. As the figure shows, the "Improvement" over the past six months was mostly negative.

Section 3 of Figure 3-2 reports collection performance in two other ways. Both sets of figures report the success we have had with the first goal, that of collecting our receivables as quickly as possible.

If someone asked us to interpret the first set of figures in Section 3, we might say "We pay interest on every invoice in Accounts Receivable. We pay it from the day we book the sale until the day we collect the invoice (or until the day the invoice goes over 90 days). Assuming that our interest cost was 1% per month, or 12% per year, we paid an average of 2.02% interest on every credit sale we made during the past six months. This performance was much worse than that of our previous six months.

"Of course, our receivables loan costs us about twice that 12% interest rate. But using 12% lets us monitor our collection performance easily. Besides, it's easy to double that 2.02% to find out what we are really paying."

And if we interpret the second set of figures, we might say, "During the past six months, it took an average of 61 days to collect each invoice or toss it into the 90-day bucket. During the previous six months, we collected each invoice in 44 days—a significantly shorter time."

Notice how this method of calculating a sales collection period differs from the DSO calculation described earlier. Here we average actual collection history for each month. The calculated figure is not affected by any variation in the volume of sales, and there is no need to calculate a daily sales rate.

Now that we have a sound method of measuring our collection performance, let's build the Accounts Receivable Collection analysis.

BUILDING THE REPORT

When you have completed this application, the report section will look like Figure 3-3. The data and macro sections of the Data Bank are above this display, as shown in Figure 1-5. If you haven't built the Data Bank as Chapters 1 and 2 describe, this would be a good time to do so.

The Data

The Data Bank Number Control section begins in A293 of Figure 3-3. This section (described later in detail) shows the categories of data that you will need. If you have entered the sample Data Bank from Appendix A, or have purchased the disk set available for this book, you're set. Otherwise, find the data for these categories in Appendix A and enter it into the Data Bank.

As you can see, there is nothing sophisticated about these categories of data. The data is simply the monthly Sales figure, the Accounts Receivable balance, and the column totals from your monthly Accounts Receivable aging schedule. The Sales, Last 12 Months line represents the sum of the sales for that month and for the previous 11 months. Appendix A describes these categories in detail.

Starting the Report

Let's look at other sections of Figure 3-3. Rows 250 through 253 show the macro header section. These rows hold range names and formulas (described in Chapter 2) that we will use to create the report. Columns B and C from row 254 downward hold the macro (and its description) that we will use to set column widths and print our report. The macro isn't easy to read in Figure 3-3 because the printing is quite small. (Figure 3-4 shows this macro in greater detail.)

Finally, notice again that the macro header section begins in row 250. You will find it easier to understand the following explanation if your macro header section also begins in row 250. In your spreadsheet, put your cursor on this line; then insert the number of rows necessary to put it on row 250. When you have completed the report that follows, delete the rows that you had inserted, if you need to conserve disk space, and save your spreadsheet.

Miscellaneous Data and Parameters

Cells E257 through E259 in Figure 3-3 contain three labels that name ranges in the cells to their right. Since those ranges contain miscellaneous values that we will use frequently when we build this report, assigning names to these values simplifies our task. But remember, 1-2-3 will not save these ranges when we extract and save the report. After this report is

```
      A          B                      C                      D        E        F  G    H     I  J       K          L   M      N          O  P      Q      R  S  T   U          V     W
250 ------------------------------------------------------------------------------------------------------------------------------------------------------------------------------------
251                                                                MISC_DAT:Dec-82       11       **                  47
252 ------------------------------------------------------------------------------------------------------------------------------------------------------------------------------------
253 REPORT         REP_MAC              ----------------------------------------FIRST_M--FIRST_CO-------TH--------------THIS_CO---------------------------------------------------------
254          {GOTO}report~           Set column widths:                           Dec-82       11        **                  47                                                  |        |
255          /WCS9~                  A                                                                                                                                            |        |
256          {RIGHT}/WCS26~          B                                                                                                                                            |        |
257          {RIGHT}/WCS20~          C                                    START      34 +$THIS_COL-13 -- Start w/ this data column.                                               |        |
258          {RIGHT}/WCS8~           D                                  SCALE30      23 GRAPH SCALE FACTOR, 30-90                                                                  |        |
259          {RIGHT}/WCR~            E                                  SCALE90     400 GRAPH SCALE FACTOR, OVER 90                                                                |        |
260          {RIGHT}/WCS7~           F                                                                                                                                            |        |
261          {RIGHT}/WCS2~           G                                                                                                                                            |        |
262          {RIGHT}/WCS8~           H                                                                                                                                            |        |
263          {RIGHT}/WCS7~           I                                                                                                                                            |        |
264          {RIGHT}/WCS2~           J                            ==================================================================================================================|        |
265          {RIGHT}/WCS15~          K                                                                                                                                                     |
266          {RIGHT}/WCS7~           L                                                                                                                                            |        |
267          {RIGHT}/WCS2~           M                                                           Accounts Receivable Collections Analysis                                         |        |
268          {RIGHT}/WCS15~          N                                                                          Dec-85                                                            |        |
269          {RIGHT}/WCS7~           O                                                                                                                                            |        |
270          {RIGHT}/WCS2~           P                                                                                                                                            |        |
271          {RIGHT}/WCS13~          Q                         Section 1                                                                                                          |        |
272          {RIGHT}/WCS1~           R                         ---------                                                                                                          |        |
273          {RIGHT}/WCS7~           S                                                Percent of Sales Collected in Each 30-Day Period                          |   A/R Over 90 Days|        |
274          {RIGHT}/WCS2~           T                                     Month     ----------------------------------------------------------   % Uncollected  |  As a Percent     |        |
275          {RIGHT}/WCS11~          U                                   Of Sale       0-30 DAYS          30-60 DAYS           60-90 DAYS         After 90 Days  |  Of 12-Mos Sales  |        |
276          {RIGHT}/WCR             V                                  ---------    -------------      ----------------     -----------------    -------------- |  ---------------- |        |
277          {RIGHT}/WCR             W                                    Dec-84      5%  +            43%  ++++++++++       42%  ++++++++++      10%  ++        |  0.76%  +++       |        |
278          {GOTO}report~/xq        Define Report Range                  Jan-85      8%  ++           42%  ++++++++++       38%  +++++++++       12%  +++       |  1.56%  ++++++    |        |
279          {UP}{END}{RIGHT}{DOWN}   and print report:                   Feb-85      6%  +            48%  +++++++++++      30%  +++++++         16%  ++++      |  1.17%  +++++     |        |
280          {END}{LEFT}{LEFT}               "                            Mar-85     11%  +++          53%  ++++++++++++     21%  +++++           15%  +++       |  0.24%  +         |        |
281          {END}{DOWN}                     "                            Apr-85      7%  ++           44%  ++++++++++       46%  +++++++++++      3%  +         |  0.24%  +         |        |
282          {END}{LEFT}{LEFT}               "                            May-85      1%  .            46%  +++++++++++      38%  +++++++++       15%  +++       |  1.00%  ++++      |        |
283          {DOWN}/PPR{BS}.                 "                            Jun-85     11%  +++          57%  +++++++++++++    21%  +++++           11%  +++       |  0.41%  ++        |        |
284          {UP}{RIGHT}                     "                            Jul-85      6%  +            27%  ++++++           35%  ++++++++        32%  +++++++   |  0.63%  +++       |        |
285          {END}{RIGHT}{LEFT}              "                            Aug-85      2%  .            15%  +++              48%  +++++++++++     35%  ++++++++  |  1.27%  +++++     |        |
286          {DOWN}{DOWN}                    "                            Sep-85      1%  .            28%  ++++++           63%  ++++++++++++++   8%  ++        |  1.72%  +++++++   |        |
287          {END}{DOWN}{LEFT}~              "                            Oct-85      3%  +            34%  ++++++++         36%  ++++++++        27%  ++++++    |  0.99%  ++++      |        |
288          OMR135~ML5~Q                    "                            Nov-85      1%  .            45%  ++++++++++                            54%  (Incomplete) |  2.63%  +++++++++++|       |
289          AGPQ                            "                            Dec-85      2%  .                                                       98%  (Incomplete) |  1.82%  +++++++   |        |
290          /XR                             "                                                                                                                        |        |
```

```
      A              B                  C              D      E      F  G  H      I  J      K            L  M         N             O  P       Q    R  S   T        U      V      W
291
292                                                  Section 2                                                 This Month's Amount Over 90 Days  =                  $38 |      |
293 Data Bank Number Control                         ---------
294 ==============================================================
295   DB#   DB Description            Data Needed    Average of Original Sale
296 -------------------------------------------------Collected Each Period
297 100.010 Sales                     Monthly Sales  ----------------------------
298 110.010 Receivables, 30 Days      A/R, 30 Days   Previous 6-Mos      7% ++        48% +++++++++++   32% +++++++      13% +++      | 0.77% +++
299 110.020 Receivables, 60 Days      A/R, 60 Days   Most recent 6-Mos   3% +         30% +++++++       46% +++++++++++  21% +++++    | 1.51% ++++++
300 110.030 Receivables, 90 Days      A/R, 90 Days                    -------       -------         -------          -------       |-------
301 110.040 Receivables, Over 90 Days A/R, Over 90   Improvement        -4%          -18%              14%              -8%            -0.74%
302 800.010 Sales, Last 12 Months     Sales, Last 12 Mos
303
304
305                                                  Section 3
306                                                  ---------
307
308                                                  Average Total Interest Cost, at 12%,      Average Collection Period
309                                                  For Receivables Less Than 90 Days Old     For Sales Less Than 90 Days Old
310                                                  -------------------------------------     -------------------------------------
311                                                  Previous 6-Mos               1.47%        Previous 6-Mos               44 Days
312                                                  Most recent 6-Mos            2.02%        Most recent 6-Mos            61 Days
313                                                                              -------                                     -----
314                                                  Improvement                 -0.55%        Improvement                 -17 Days
315
316
317
318
319
```

Figure 3-3. The complete spreadsheet that is attached to the Data Bank to produce the Accounts Receivable Collections Analysis report

```
              A                    B                        C
253  REPORT                    REP_MAC            --------------------
254                   {GOTO}report~               Set column widths:
255                   /WCS9~                      A
256                   {RIGHT}/WCS26~              B
257                   {RIGHT}/WCS20~              C
258                   {RIGHT}/WCS8~               D
259                   {RIGHT}/WCR~                E
260                   {RIGHT}/WCS7~               F
261                   {RIGHT}/WCS2~               G
262                   {RIGHT}/WCS8~               H
263                   {RIGHT}/WCS7~               I
264                   {RIGHT}/WCS2~               J
265                   {RIGHT}/WCS15~              K
266                   {RIGHT}/WCS7~               L
267                   {RIGHT}/WCS2~               M
268                   {RIGHT}/WCS15~              N
269                   {RIGHT}/WCS7~               O
270                   {RIGHT}/WCS2~               P
271                   {RIGHT}/WCS13~              Q
272                   {RIGHT}/WCS1~               R
273                   {RIGHT}/WCS7~               S
274                   {RIGHT}/WCS2~               T
275                   {RIGHT}/WCS11~              U
276                   {RIGHT}/WCR                 V
277                   {RIGHT}/WCR                 W
278                   {GOTO}report~               Define Report Range
279                   {UP}{END}{RIGHT}{DOWN}       and print report:
280                   {END}{LEFT}{LEFT}                     "
281                   {END}{DOWN}                           "
282                   {END}{LEFT}{LEFT}                     "
283                   {DOWN}/PPR{BS}.                       "
284                   {UP}{RIGHT}                           "
285                   {END}{RIGHT}{LEFT}                    "
286                   {DOWN}{DOWN}                          "
287                   {END}{DOWN}{LEFT}~                    "
288                   OMR135~ML5~Q                          "
289                   AGPQ                                  "
290                   /XR                                   "
291
```

Figure 3-4. A listing of the macro in the Accounts Receivable Collections Analysis report that sets the column widths and prints the report

completed and saved, therefore, formulas that had referenced these ranges will reference the cell addresses instead.

The first of the three miscellaneous numbers that we need is the number with the range name START. Most of the information in the A/R report is generated by the @VLOOKUP function, which uses the Data Bank number (DB#) and a column number to find values in the DATA range. START holds the column number that the @VLOOKUP function uses to find the data for the month one year before the report date. In Figure 3-3, for example, the START value of 34 tells us that Dec-84 is the thirty-fourth column in the DATA range.

So, in F257, enter the formula **+$THIS_COL−13**. As you learned in Chapter 2, THIS_COL is the number of the spreadsheet column (where Column A=1, B=2, and so on) that contains the data for the current report month. Subtract 12 from THIS_COL to find the spreadsheet column number for the month one year ago, and then subtract one more to create the number that the @VLOOKUP formula uses to find this column. (Remember that the @VLOOKUP function numbers each column in a range starting with zero. So A=0, B=1, and so on when the @VLOOKUP formulas look up these columns in the DATA range.)

We will also need some graph scale factors. You will see how these are used in a minute. For now, simply enter the numbers 23 and 400 as shown.

Finally, enter the range names to the left of the three numbers, in column E, and their descriptions to the right, in column G; then use the /Range Name Label Right command, highlighting the three range names.

Preparing the Column Widths

Figure 3-4 shows the complete macro for setting the column widths and printing the A/R Collections Analysis. The easiest way to enter rows 257 through 277 is to type **{RIGHT}WCS** into B256, copy this cell to B257..B277, and then edit each cell with the appropriate changes.

The remainder of the macro defines the print range, sets the margins, and prints the report. The way the print range is set will be described at the end of this chapter.

Notice that because the right margin has been set to 135 characters, the report requires use of the compressed print feature of your dot-matrix printer. However, no setup string has been included in this macro to set up your printer for compressed printing. Since different brands of printers require different control codes, you must insert the commands in this macro that your own printer requires.

When I create these reports, I often wish to set the column widths without printing the report. I therefore edit cell B278 to appear as {GOTO}report~/XQ. This added command stops the macro's execution after the column widths are set. When the report is completed, I remove the /XQ and save the report.

Be sure to enter the cell letters as shown in column C. You will want to change column widths occasionally. The letters will tell you which row of the macro to change.

After you have entered the macro, press ALT-M System Report to run it.

HOW TO CREATE THE REPORT

We have three steps left. First, we must create the Data Bank Number Control. Second, we must create the three sections of the report. Finally, we must put a border around the report that will allow us to save and print it easily.

Creating the Data Bank Number Control

The Data Bank Number Control section does two things. First, it provides an easy way to change Data Bank numbers in the report. To illustrate, suppose you decide to replace the DB# 100.010 for Sales with the number 222.2. You would have to change this number not only in your Data Bank data, but in all reports as well. To change the number in the A/R report, you would simply change the DB# shown in A297 of Figure 3-3 to 222.2. Doing this would adjust the entire A/R report to the new number.

Second, if you use 1-2-3 Version 2, the Data Bank Number Control will confirm that the DB# you have used is the one you intend to use. It does this in column B with an @VLOOKUP formula. This formula simply returns the description of the DB# you entered in column A. Comparing this description to the label you have entered in column C gives you quick confirmation that the DB# is correct. The first string formula in this section is

B297: @VLOOKUP(A297,$DATA,1)

Copy this formula down column B as needed.

Creating Section 1

As shown in Figure 3-3, enter \= in E264; then copy this cell from column F through column U. The report will start below this line.

Enter the report heading in I267. The formula for the report date in

L268 is simply +THIS_MO. Next, enter the headings for Section 1 as shown in rows 271 through 276 of Figure 3-3.

The Month of Sale Column The formula for Dec-84 in E277 is +THIS_MO−365. The formula for Jan-85 is equal to 30 days plus this date, or 30+E277. Copy this cell from E278 to E279..E289.

The 0-30-Days Columns The formula for the 5% amount in F277 is

```
F277: @ROUND(1−(@VLOOKUP($A$298,$DATA,$START+@COUNT($E$277..$E277)−1)/
      @VLOOKUP($A$297,$DATA,$START+@COUNT($E$277..$E277)−1)),2)
```

Be particularly careful of the dollar signs as shown. For example, look at the function @COUNT($E$277..$E277), which appears twice in this formula. This function provides a count of the number of months since the first month in the table, December 1984. Dollar signs precede both of the Es. Wherever the formula is copied, therefore, the new formulas will continue to reference column E. This is called an *absolute* cell address.

The first row number also has an absolute cell address. But the second row number has no dollar sign. It has a *relative* cell address. When you copy F277 to F278..F289, the second row number in the @COUNT function will change accordingly. In F278, for example, the function will be @COUNT($E$277..$E278).

Let's take a closer look at the formula in F277: This formula says "Look up the 30-Day Receivables for December 1984, and look up the sales for that month; divide the former by the latter. This tells us the percent of December sales that were uncollected by the end of the month. Subtract this amount from 1. This tells us the percent that *was* collected. Finally, round off the result to two decimal places."

The portion of the formula that looks up the December 1984 sales is

```
@VLOOKUP($A$298,$DATA,$START+@COUNT($E$257..$E27)−1)
```

Let's take a closer look at what this means. The formula tells 1-2-3 to find the row of data in the DATA range with a DB# equal to the number in cell A298. Figure 3-3 shows that this cell contains the DB# for 30-day-old accounts receivable.

Finally, the @VLOOKUP formula says to find the value located a designated number of columns to the right of the first column in the row that we have chosen. In the preceding formula, this number is equal to the

START value plus an @COUNT value minus 1. As you remember, START is the number of columns to the right of the DB# where we will find the December 1984 information. This is the number that we want. The @COUNT function merely adds one to the total, and then −1 takes it away again. The @COUNT function, combined with −1, looks like excess baggage. Why use it?

Think about what will happen when we copy this formula to the cell below it, the row for January 1985. On this row, the @COUNT function will look like this: @COUNT($E$277..$E278). In other words, it will have a value of two. So, we have told the @VLOOKUP function to find January by taking the START value (December's value), adding two, and then subtracting one. Bingo! When we copy the formula down the column, from February 1985 to December 1985, the @COUNT function will make sure that the @VLOOKUP function pulls data from the proper month.

The formula for the plus sign in H277 is @ROUND(F277*$SCALE30,0). Format this cell as /Range Format +/−, and copy the cell from H277 to H278..H289. This format command will create a bar graph by printing the number of plus or minus symbols that is equal to the integer value in the cell. If the value in the cell is 4, for instance, ++++ will be printed; if the value is −3, −−− will be printed, and so on. If the number of symbols is too large to fit into the cell, the overflow symbol, *, will fill the cell. Finally, a single dot in the cell indicates that the number is zero.

You now see why the $SCALE30 factor is necessary. It does two things. First, it changes numbers like the 0.05 for December 1984 into a value large enough for the +/− format to display. Second, it allows us to easily change all values using the same bar graph scale to produce the largest number of symbols that will fit in the space available.

The 30-60-Days Columns The following formula is for the 43% in cell I277:

```
I277:  @ROUND(1-(@VLOOKUP($A$299,$DATA,$START+1+@COUNT($E$277..$E277)-1)/
         @VLOOKUP($A$297,$DATA,$START+@COUNT($E$277..$E277)-1))-F277,2)
```

Copy this formula from I277 to I278..I289. This formula is similar to the 0-30-Days formula. It says, "Look up 60-Day Receivables one month from now and divide the amount by this month's sales. This operation tells us the percentage of this month's sales that was uncollected after 60 days. Subtract this amount from 1 to find the percentage that *was* collected during the first 60 days; then subtract the amount that was collected during the first 30 days (F277). This leaves the percentage that was collected during the 30-60-day period. Finally, round the result to two decimal places."

The formula @ROUND(I277*$SCALE 30,0) is for the bar graph in K277. To enter this, just copy the formula from H277..H289 to K277.

The 60-90-Days Columns The following formula is for the 42% in cell L277:

```
L277: @ROUND(1-(@VLOOKUP($A$300,$DATA,$START+2+@COUNT ($E$277..$E277)
        -1)/@VLOOKUP($A$297,$DATA,$START+@COUNT($E$277..$E277)-1))-I277
        -F277,2)
```

Copy this formula from L277 to L278..L289. This formula is similar to those in F277 and I277. It says, "Look up 90-Day Receivables two months from now and divide that amount by this month's sales. This tells us the percentage of this month's sales that was uncollected after 90 days. Subtract this amount from 1 to find the percentage that *was* collected during the first 90 days; then subtract the amount that was collected during the first 30 days (F227) and the first 60 days (I277). This leaves the percentage that was collected during the 60-90 day period. Finally, round the result to two decimal places."

The formula for the bar graph in N277 is @ROUND(L277* $SCALE30,0). To enter this, just copy the formula from K277..K289 to N277.

The %-Uncollected-After-90-Days Columns The formula for O277 is simply 1−(L277+I277+F277). And the formula for the bar graph in Q277 follows the same pattern as before. It is @ROUND(O277*$SCALE30,0).

The A/R Over 90 Days as % of 12-Mos Sales Columns Since these columns report receivables information in a different format than the previous four sets of columns, we want to set them apart from the other columns. Therefore, in R277, enter '| (apostrophe and vertical line). Here is the formula for the 0.76% in S277:

```
S277: @VLOOKUP($A$301,$DATA,$START+@COUNT($E$277..$E277)-1)/@VLOOKUP
        ($A$302,$DATA,$START+@COUNT($E$277..$E277)-1))
```

Compared to the other similar formulas, this one's easy. It simply says, "Look up this month's receivables that are more than 90 days old and divide them by the sales for the last 12 months."

The formula for the bar graph in U277 is @ROUND(S277*$SCALE90,0). Notice that we use a different scaling factor than we used before because the numbers in this column will be smaller than the previous numbers. We need to use a larger scaling factor to make the graphs of these numbers appear at all. After you have entered this formula, copy it from U277 to U278..U289.

Completing Section 1 To complete Section 1, we must adjust the display for Nov-85 and Dec-85. December 1985 is the current month of the report. We don't yet know what percentage of our sales will be paid in 60 days, or in 90 days. We must therefore erase cells in the Dec-85 row for those two sets of columns. For a similar reason, we must erase the cell in the Nov-85 row in the 60-90-Days columns. To let people know what we've done, we type **(Incomplete)** as shown in Q288 and Q289 of the figure.

Finally, go to U291 and enter **@VLOOKUP($A$301,$DATA,$START+12)**. This returns the amount from the December 1985 aging that is more than 90 days old. Format the cell as currency and label it as shown.

Creating Section 2

Enter the headings and row labels as shown. The formulas for the values in column F in this section are

F298: @ROUND(@AVG(F283..F278),2)
F299: @ROUND(@AVG(F289..F284),2)
F300: \-
F301: +F299−F298

Format these values as Percent (0). The formulas for the bar graphs are

H298: @ROUND(F298*$SCALE30,0)
H299: @ROUND(F299*$SCALE30,0)

Format these as +/−.

The easiest way to complete the rest of Section 2 is to copy F298..H301 to I298, to L298, to O298, and to S298. However, after you have done this, you must change several of the formulas.

In column O, the most recent six months' average includes the two values for incomplete months. Also, the signs for the Improvement line must be reversed. Therefore, change the formulas in column O to read

O298: 1−(L298+I298+F298)
O299: 1−(L299+I299+F299)
O301: +O298−O299

Finally, the signs for the Improvement line, row 301, must be reversed in column S as well:

S301: +S298−S299

The reason for changing O301 and S301 is obvious when you look at the trend and ask yourself if it has gotten better or worse. If the trend is worse, the signs need to be negative.

Creating Section 3

Enter the headings as shown. The formulas for column I are

I311: .005*(1−$F298)+0.015*(1−$I298−$F298)+0.025*O298
I312: .005*(1−$F299)+0.015*(1−$I299−$F299)+0.025*O299
I313: \−
I314: +I311−I312

The formulas in I311 and I312 assume that sales were constant during the month. On average, therefore, we paid a 1/2 month's interest on sales in the 30-Day column, 1 1/2 month's interest on sales in the 60-Day column, and 2 1/2 month's interest on sales in the 90-Day column. With interest at 1% per month, the decimal fractions are as you see them.

The formulas for column S are

S311: 3000*I311
S312: 3000*I312
S313: \−
S314: +S311−S312

In I311 and I312 we assumed that we paid interest for 1/2 month, 1 1/2 months, and 2 1/2 months. In S311 and S312, we multiply I311 and I312 by 100. This eliminates the interest calculation, telling us the average number of months that our customers took to pay. Then we multiplied by 30, to convert months to days. And therefore 100*30 = 3000 in S311 and S312.

COMPLETING THE REPORT

We need to recalculate the report. But if you press CALC (F9) the process would take several minutes if you have a large Data Bank. There is a quicker way. When we load a report, the macro SET (found in Figure 2-15) sets the boundaries of the REPORT range to the size of our report. To recalculate only this REPORT range, simply copy it onto itself. In other words, we /**C**opy from REPORT to REPORT. However, we haven't used this macro yet to load a report, so we must define the REPORT range manually. Use /**R**ange **N**ame **C**reate to define the range REPORT from A253 to U320. Then use this range to recalculate the report.

After you've calculated the report, print it. If you find errors, this will be the easiest time to correct them.

Setting the Borders

As Chapter 2 explains, we must set two borders. The outer border lets the Data Bank Xtract macro know the limits of the report. Without this knowledge, the macro won't extract and save your report properly. The inner border defines the print range for the printing macro.

To understand why these borders are necessary, think of the borders as pathways. The Xtract and print macros shown in Figure 3-4 both start with the cell pointer below the word RECORD in cell A254 of Figure 3-3. To begin to print or extract, the macros move the pointer up one cell and then use {END}{RIGHT} to send the pointer to the extreme right-hand side of the macro header section. (For this step to work properly, make sure that every cell from A253 through BG253 contains either a label or an underline.)

By sending the cell pointer to the right-hand side of the Data Bank, we know it has passed the right-hand border of our report. Next, both macros move the cell pointer down to row 254 and then use {END}{LEFT} to send the pointer back to the report, ending at W254.

To extract the file, the Xtract macro uses {END}{DOWN} to travel down the path in column W to cell W319 in Figure 3-3. (This cell should be several rows beneath the last line of your report.) Since the Xtract macro has previously anchored cell A254 as one point of the extract range, cell W319 completes the extract range definition.

To define the print range, the macro in Figure 3-4 moves left from W254 to V254. Then {END}{DOWN} sends the pointer to V264. (This is the last cell before the blank cell in V265.) Then {END}{LEFT} sends the cell pointer to the left-hand side of the double lines in row 264. Next, the print macro sets the top left point of the print range with respect to the end point of the double lines.

Once the top left of the print range is set, the cell pointer returns to the double lines, travels back to the vertical lines, moves past the empty cell in

V265 and then moves down the vertical line to V319. The bottom right point of the print range is one cell to the left of V319, or U319.

At first, using these pathways may appear to be needlessly involved. It's not. Remember, when we extract this report, range names will not survive, and when the size of the Data Bank changes, cell references will change. So there is no practical way to specify the ranges for printing or extracting the report. We must find the ranges as we have done here.

Saving the Report

Finally, it's time to save the completed report. To do this, simply select ALT-M System Xtract. The first time you do this with a new report, it is best to run the macro one step at a time. Therefore, after selecting ALT-M System, press STEP. Then select **X**tract. Each time you press any key, one additional step of the macro will be executed. (Turn back to Figure 2-13 to see a listing of this macro.) Finally, after many steps, the program will ask you for a file name. After you enter the name, you will see how the cell pointer goes to A254 and defines the Xtract range.

If you want to stop the macro at any point, press CTRL-BREAK. After the screen responds with an ERROR message, press ESC.

Chapter
Four

ECONOMIC ORDER QUANTITIES WITH PRICE BREAKS FOR QUANTITY PURCHASES

How much inventory should we buy? Buying too little takes too much effort and increases the risk of shortages. Buying too much takes too much cash and increases the risk of damage and obsolescence. How do we find a balance between these extremes?

The Economic Order Quantity (EOQ) calculation is one of the few mathematical tools available to answer this question. The purpose of this calculation is to find a middle ground between buying too much of an item and buying too little.

In practice, however, the EOQ calculation isn't widely used, principally because the traditional calculation can't accurately evaluate the effect of price breaks for quantity purchases. And it is these fiendishly seductive price breaks that lure many companies into buying more inventory than they should.

This chapter will discuss the concept of the EOQ and then review the traditional EOQ calculation. Finally, we'll see how to use a 1-2-3 spreadsheet to evaluate the effects of quantity price breaks in the inventory purchase decision.

THE ECONOMIC ORDER QUANTITY (EOQ)

To find the Economic Order Quantity, consider all of the costs relating to the purchase and ownership of the part in question. Then order the quantity that produces the lowest total cost. Generally, these costs of purchase and ownership are classified as ordering costs and carrying costs.

Ordering Costs

Ordering costs are all of the costs incurred in ordering, shipping, and receiving parts into inventory. Generally, these are assumed to vary more with the quantity of orders placed by a company than with the quantity or price of the goods purchased. Specifically, these costs include the following:

1. The cost of ordering, including telephone expenses, purchase order forms, computer charges, and relevant wages and salaries.

2. Shipping costs, including freight, insurance, expediting charges, and freight damage.

3. Receiving costs, including relevant material-handling labor, stockroom labor, and computer charges.

Carrying Costs

Carrying costs are the costs of owning inventories. They generally are assumed to be a function of the dollar value of the goods in inventory and are expressed (much as interest is) as a yearly percentage. These costs include the following:

1. The labor and overhead costs of storing and handling inventories, including rent and depreciation of warehouse facilities, shelving, computer charges, forklift expenses, and so on.

2. Insurance and taxes on inventory. Usually, these costs are a function of the total inventory value on particular dates, not a cumulative cost over time. However, we assume that every part in inventory shares in this cost over time.

3. Scrap, waste, material handling damage, and obsolescence. The longer a part is kept in inventory, the more likely it is to suffer these costs.

4. The costs of capital tied up in inventory. Generally, this is the largest carrying cost. Expressed as a percentage, the cost of capital is a function of a firm's interest costs, the return that the firm's stockholders expect on their investment, and the return expected from other investment opportunities available to the firm.

A Simplified EOQ Analysis

We must make trade-offs to control ordering and carrying costs. If we maintain a small inventory, we keep our carrying costs low but experience high purchasing costs. If we maintain a large inventory, we keep our purchasing costs low but have high carrying costs. The purpose of the EOQ is to find the combination of ownership options that leads to the lowest total cost.

Figure 4-1 shows a typical EOQ example in a simple spreadsheet. Here the Price per Unit, Carrying Cost, Ordering Cost, Yearly Usage, and Safety Stock are the values shown in rows 5 through 7. The values were given the range names shown by the capitalized labels.

In the figure, the Price is assumed to be constant no matter what quantity is purchased, and rate of use is assumed to be constant over time. Safety Stock is the minimum quantity of parts that we plan to keep in inventory. This quantity helps to ensure that inventory will still be available if we use more parts than we had planned.

Most of the formulas in the bottom half of the figure should be easy to understand. The calculation of Average Inventory assumes that parts are used uniformly throughout the year. Total Carrying Costs are equal to the Average Inventory multiplied by the annual cost per dollar of inventory. Ordering Costs are equal to the cost per order times the number of orders. And Total Inventory Costs are equal to the sum of Total Carrying Costs and Total Ordering Costs.

Column G is a handy column. The asterisks identify the row with the lowest Total Inventory Cost value. As you can see from the formulas in the figure, the formula in G returns a 99 if the value in that row of the F column is the lowest value in the whole F column. If not, the formula returns a zero. The column uses a +/− format (symbolized by (+) in the figure). This format option displays a zero as a period and tries to display a bar graph of 99 plus signs when the value in the cell is 99. But since column G is only seven characters wide, the cell is filled with asterisks, the common overflow symbol.

If you have 1-2-3 Version 2, you can improve the appearance of column

```
        A         B         C         D         E         F         G
 1
 2            Determination of the Lowest-Cost Order Quantity
 3                   Using Traditional EOQ Assumptions
 4 -------------------------------------------------------------------
 5               PRICE      $50                 USAGE     3,600
 6             CAR_CST        30%               SAFETY       60
 7             ORD_CST     $150
 8 -------------------------------------------------------------------
 9 Graph:
10      X                             A         B         C
11 ===================================================================
12      Qty                         Total     Total      Total
13       to    Safety   Average   Carrying  Ordering  Inventory  Least
14    Purch     Stock  Inventory   Costs     Costs      Costs    Cost
15 -------------------------------------------------------------------
16      100        60       110     1,650     5,400     7,050 .
17      200        60       160     2,400     2,700     5,100 .
18      300        60       210     3,150     1,800     4,950 *******
19      400        60       260     3,900     1,350     5,250 .
20      500        60       310     4,650     1,080     5,730 .
21      600        60       360     5,400       900     6,300 .
22 ===================================================================


    Cell    (Format) [Column Width] and Formula
   ----------------------------------------------------------
        A16: [W7] 100
        B16: +$SAFETY
        C16: @ROUND(+A16/2+B16,0)
        D16: +C16*$PRICE*$CAR_CST
        E16: +$ORD_CST*($USAGE/A16)
        F16: +E16+D16
        G16: (+) [W7] @IF(F16=@MIN($F$16..$F$21),99,0)

        Global column width = 9.
        Global format = (,0) (comma, zero decimal places).


            Range Names
            ------------
            PRICE     C5
            CAR_CST   C6
            ORD_CST   C7
            USAGE     F5
            SAFETY    F6
```

Figure 4-1. A typical EOQ spreadsheet

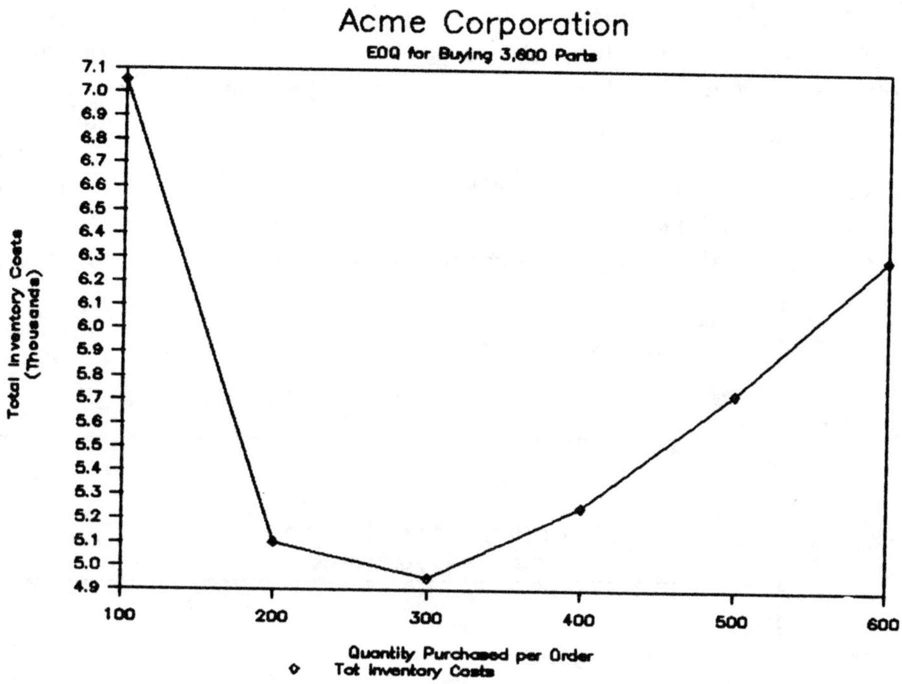

Figure 4-2. A graph of the Total Inventory Costs line from a typical EOQ spreadsheet

G by using the /Worksheet Global Zero Yes command to make the dots disappear.

Graphing the EOQ

A graph of Figure 4-1 will give a clearer picture of why Total Inventory Costs fall and then begin to climb.

It is easy to get a quick view of the total costs. Display the Graph menu by issuing the /Graph command. To enter the values for the horizontal axis, press X and then point to the range A16 to A21. To enter the values for Total Inventory Costs, press C and then point to cells H16 to H21. (The Graph heading lines in row 10 of Figure 4-1 will remind you which columns belong to which graph letters.) When you press VIEW, you can see how costs change as the quantity of your purchase varies. Figure 4-2 shows this graph. (Titles and legends have been added to make the figure easier to read.)

Figure 4-3 shows the final graph. To create it, press ENTER to return to the Graph menu. Then, as you did with X and C, enter graph letters **A** and **B**, pointing to the data for the columns shown in Figure 4-1. To assign

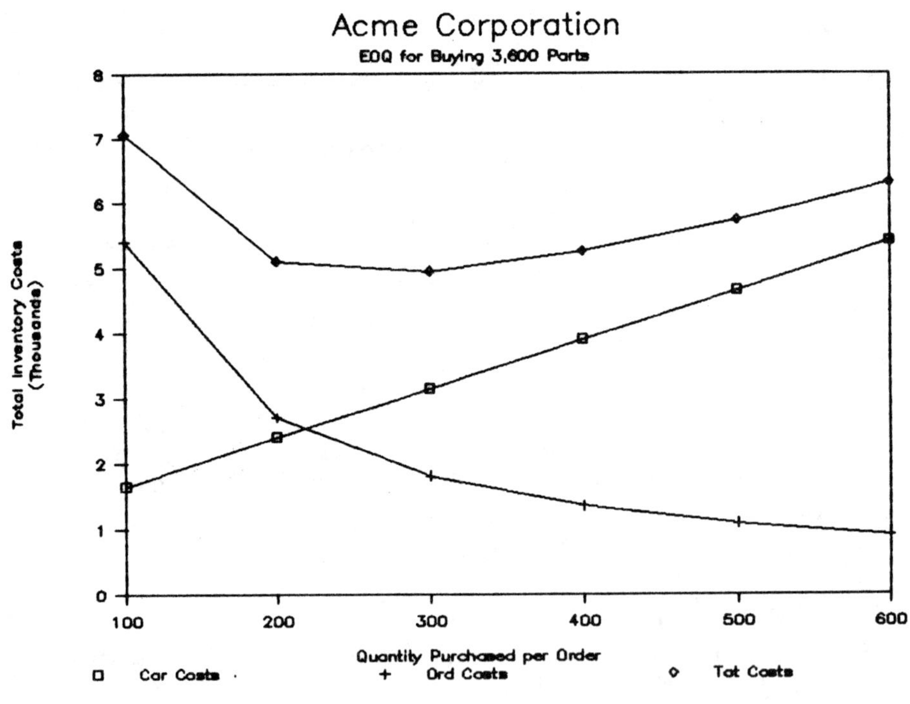

Figure 4-3. A graph of Carrying Costs, Ordering Costs, and Total Inventory Costs from a typical EOQ spreadsheet

labels to the lines A, B, and C as shown in Figure 4-3, use Options Legend. Using Options Titles will let you fill in the titles as shown.

When you compare these two graphs, you will see that Figure 4-2 appears to show significantly more variation in Total Costs than does Figure 4-3. The reason that the scales in these two graphs differ considerably is because Figure 4-3 must display the two additional sets of costs. The Total Cost data is the same in both graphs.

Figure 4-3 makes it easier to see why the Total Cost line is changing. We can see how the Carrying Costs increase with the quantity purchased and how the Ordering Costs decline. The point where the Total Cost line is at its lowest is the EOQ. To see how different values change the EOQ, change the Carrying Costs or the Ordering Costs and then recalculate. When you press F10, you can see the results of your changes.

The Problems With the Traditional EOQ

Although the version of the EOQ just described is convenient for understanding the approach, it isn't of much use in practice. There are several reasons why.

1. There is no obvious way to fold price breaks for quantity purchases into the EOQ analysis.

2. Lumping interest cost in with the other carrying costs means that Total Carrying Costs will reflect simple interest, not compound interest. Therefore, a significant carrying cost, that of interest on interest, has been ignored.

3. The EOQ model assumes uniform parts usage. But in the real world, usage of a part can vary significantly from week to week. Ordering quantities recommended by the EOQ model, therefore, can cause excess inventory in some periods and shortages in others.

4. For many businesses the assumption that future prices will remain unchanged is false. For example, the cost of many electronic components is quite high when the components are first marketed. But the price drops continually until the product is replaced by another one that costs more but does more. Then the cycle repeats itself. Many basic industries, on the other hand, face constantly increasing prices.

5. Some purchasing costs—freight for example—vary significantly with the size of the order. If such costs are large, they should be included as an explicit part of the model.

1-2-3 enables us to create an EOQ spreadsheet that deals with these objections to standard EOQ calculations.

THE PRACTICAL EOQ ANALYSIS

We will now create a spreadsheet that analyzes one year of purchases under each of several different assumptions about order quantity. For each quantity we will consider price breaks, interest calculations, freight rates, and any other special costs. Finally, we will use a Data Table to compare the costs associated with each order quantity and choose the quantity that seems right for us.

Entering the Parameters and Lookup Tables

Start with an empty spreadsheet. Set the recalculation mode to manual and the global format to , (comma) with zero decimal places. The global column width should already be 9 characters.

Enter the information that you see in Figure 4-4 except the four formulas in column G, rows 15 through 18. (These are the only formulas in the figure.) When you have entered everything but the formulas, create the range names. Use the /Range Name Label Left command on the labels in columns F and H of the Order Parameters section. Use /Range Name Create to assign the range name DATA to B32 through D37. Use the same command to assign the range name PCHANGE to G30 through H33. Now enter the formulas.

Cell G15 The PRICE formula should be clear. The formula finds the PRICE by looking up the ORDER size in the Quantity (Qty) column of the DATA Lookup Table. The PRICE is in the middle column of that table.

G15: `@VLOOKUP(ORDER,DATA,1)`

Cell G16 The weekly CAR_CST (carrying cost) is equal to the yearly miscellaneous carrying cost percentage divided by 52. This percentage excludes interest costs. Interest is handled explicitly in cell G17.

G16: `+E11/52`

Cell G17 The INT (weekly interest rate) formula is slightly more involved. It reflects how U.S. bankers calculate interest charges. They divide the annual interest rate by 12 to calculate a monthly rate that is used for compounding. When interest compounds for a year, therefore, the effective annual rate exceeds the stated yearly interest rate.

The next two paragraphs explain the weekly interest calculation in more detail. If you wish, you may skip these paragraphs and simply enter the formula shown for G17.

Suppose that the stated annual interest rate is 15%. This produces a

```
        A         B         C         D         E         F         G         H         I
 1
 2                      Determination of the Lowest-Cost Order Quantity
 3                               Using Detailed EOQ Assumptions
 4 ============================================================================
 5 Order Parameters
 6 ======================                 Enter Data          Calculations
 7                                        ----------------    ------------------
 8        Minimum Order Size                 5,000     ORDER
 9        Safety Stock                          25    SAFETY
10        Order Costs                          $50   ORD_CST
11        Misc Carrying Costs/Year             20%
12        Yearly Interest Rate                 15%
13        Yearly Usage Growth Rate             30%
14
15        Price                                                    $70     PRICE
16        Misc Carrying Costs/Week                               0.38%  CAR_CST
17        Weekly Interest Rate                                   0.29%      INT
18        Weekly Usage Growth Rate                               0.51%   GROWTH
19
20
21 ============================================================================
22 Lookup Tables
23 ================
24
25        DATA                                                PCHANGE
26        ---------                                           ---------
27        Quantity Purch Info                                 Expected Prices
28        ------------------------                            As a % of Today's
29                                 Frt                        ------------------
30           Qty    Price          Cst                          01-Jan        100%
31        ------   -----          ----                          30-Mar         95%
32            50     100            25                          30-Jun         90%
33           100      95            35                          30-Sep         85%
34           250      90            50
35           500      80            75
36         1,000      75           100
37         5,000      70           150
38
39
40
41 ============================================================================
```

Figure 4-4. The Order Parameters and the Lookup Tables sections of the practical EOQ spreadsheet

monthly rate of 0.15/12, or 1.25%. To compound this amount for 12 months, we add 1, take this to the twelfth power, then subtract 1. So (1.0125)^12−1 produces an effective annual rate of about 16.08%.

To find the weekly rate that will yield this effective annual rate, we take 1 plus the effective annual rate to the 1/52nd power, then subtract 1. That is, (1.1608)^(1/52)−1 equals the 0.29% weekly interest rate that you see in Figure 4-4. The formula in G17 combines these two steps.

G17: (1+(+E12/12))^(12/52)−1

Cell G18 If you do not have a specific forecast of requirements for a part, cell E13 allows you to enter an estimated annual growth rate in the number of parts that you will use. Cell G18 translates that annual growth rate to a weekly rate. If you do have a forecast of requirements, you will be able to enter it in the Purchase Forecast Data Base, which will be discussed shortly.

G18: (1+E13)^(1/52)−1

Starting the EOQ Analysis Section

Figure 4-4 contains facts and assumptions about order costs, price breaks, interest rates, and so on. Figure 4-6 provides a 52-week schedule of projected inventory activity. Figure 4-5, which lies between these two schedules, is an EOQ Analysis Section generated by 1-2-3's Data Table command. Using the assumptions in Figure 4-4, it takes each Quantity to Purchase we will enter in column A of Figure 4-5 and inserts it into the schedule shown in Figure 4-6. By looking at this table of results in Figure 4-5, we can see which purchase option is lowest for us.

When you have finished creating Figure 4-4, enter the headings shown in Figure 4-5. Before you can enter formulas in this section of the spreadsheet, however, you must enter the purchase schedule shown in Figure 4-6. This schedule generates the data the formulas require in Figure 4-5.

Building the Purchase Forecast Data Base

Figure 4-6 shows the top and bottom portions of a data base that contains 52 weeks of projected inventory activity. Enter all labels, underlines, and such that are shown in this figure. Then enter the data and formulas described in the following paragraphs.

```
        A         B         C         D         E         F         G         H         I
41 ================================================================================
42 EOQ Analyis
43 ================
44    X         A        B         C     <<Graph
45 ===============================
46 -------    Data Table  ---------                      This Purchase In
47              (In Thousands)                    Savings Mos of Inventory       This
48  Purch    Purch Carry    Total    Least   vs 4-Wk ------------------       Purch
49   Qty      Cost  Cost     Cost     Cost Purchase     Next       Plan  (1000s)
50 -------                         ---------------------------------------------
51
52
53
54
55
56
57
58
59
60
61 ================================================================================
```

Figure 4-5. The EOQ Analysis section of the practical EOQ spreadsheet before the formulas have been added

In some columns, you will see one formula to be entered in row 74 and another to be entered in row 75. This need for two formulas arises from a quirk caused by an improvement in 1-2-3 Version 2. Unlike Version 1A, Version 2 includes string formulas. Thus, in Version 2 adding a cell with "Hi" to a cell with "There" returns a value of "Hi There." But say you tried to add a cell with the value of 5 to a cell with the label "Hi," Version 2 would return an ERR; Version 1A would evaluate "Hi" as zero and return a value of 5.

This is why sometimes we need two formulas in Figure 4-6. We must change formulas in the first row of a data base that try to add values to the labels appearing in the preceding row.

Therefore, when you have finished entering the following formulas, copy row 74 to row 75 through row 126. However, if a formula for row 75 is shown below, copy it, instead, down the rest of the data base to row 126.

The following information should help you to understand and build this data base. The formulas that follow the descriptions show column widths in brackets if the widths differ from the global widths.

```
            A        B        C        D         E         F         G         H         I         J         K        L          M
 61 ===================================================================================================================
 62 Purchase Forecast
 63 =================
 64          MONTH    202 <--Quantity Purchased in First Four Weeks
 65
 66       Column Totals                              Column Totals in Thousands
 67       ---------------         ---------------------------------------------------------------
 68          3,030 3,030                 0       233       233        51        62       113       346
 69
 70                                                               Misc                Total               USAGE      Time
 71          Units Units    Ending     Order       Inv     Total     Carry       Int     Carry     Total   Runing   Elapsed
 72           Prch  Used  Unit Inv     Costs     Purch     Purch     Costs      Cost      Cost     Costs    Total    In Mos
 73 ---------------------------------------------------------------------------------------------------- ----------------
 74 01-Jan   5,000    50     4,950       200   350,000   350,200     1,339     1,009     2,349   352,549       50       0.2
 75 08-Jan       0    50     4,900         0         0         0     1,326     1,016     2,342     2,342      100       0.5
 76 15-Jan       0    51     4,849         0         0         0     1,312     1,023     2,335     2,335      151       0.7

    X X X X X X X X X X X X X X X X X X X X X X X X X X X X X X X X X X X X X X X X X X X X X X X X X X X X X X X X X X

125 23-Dec       0    65     2,035         0         0         0       556     1,320     1,877     1,877    2,965      12.0
126 30-Dec       0    65     1,970         0         0         0       539     1,326     1,865     1,865    3,030  1 Year +
127 30-Dec (1,970)               0         0 (117,187)(117,187)          0         0         0 (117,187)
```

Figure 4-6. The top and bottom of the Purchase Forecast from the practical EOQ spreadsheet

Column A Use the Data Fill command here. Specify the range as A74 through A126. The Start Value is 1, the Step Value is 7, and the Ending Value is 365. Format the numbers as Dates, option 2.

Column B The formula in B75 shows a requirement for parts if that week's ending inventory ends with a quantity less than the safety stock. If the week's requirement exceeds the Minimum Order Size, the amount of the requirement is shown. Otherwise, the Minimum Order Size is shown. The formula in B74 assumes that we start with no inventory on hand. It therefore shows the calculated requirement. (Both SAFETY and ORDER appear in Figure 4-4.)

```
B74:  @MAX(+$C74+$SAFETY,$ORDER)
B75:  @IF($D74-$C75<$SAFETY,@MAX(+$C75+$SAFETY-$D74,
          $ORDER),0)
```

Column C In Figure 4-6, the Units Used data start at the arbitrary quantity of 50 units and then grow at the rate specified in the Order Parameters section in Figure 4-4. Actually, you could show the specific quantities required on specific weeks, or you could insert your own beginning Units Used figure and enter an appropriate growth rate in the Order Parameters. If you have a negative growth rate, the @MAX function keeps your usage from falling below zero.

```
C74:  [W6] 50
C75:  [W6] @MAX(+C74*(1+$GROWTH),0)
```

Column D Ending Inventory is equal to Beginning Inventory, plus Units Purchased, less Units Used.

```
D74:  -C74+B74
D75:  +D74-C75+B75
```

Column E If a quantity of parts is purchased for the week, this formula calculates the cost of the order. This cost is the sum of Order Costs from the Order Parameters section and Freight Cost from the DATA lookup table.

```
E74:  @IF(B74>0,$ORD_CST+@VLOOKUP(B74,$DATA,2),0)
```

Column F The Inventory Purchased cost is equal to the product of the quantity purchased, its price, and the adjustment for any expected price changes. This value is normally excluded from EOQ calculations. We have added it so that we can evaluate price discounts as well as expected price changes.

F74: +B74*$PRICE*@VLOOKUP(A74,$PCHANGE,1)

Column G Total Purchasing Costs are equal to the sum of Order Costs and the cost of Inventory Purchases.

G74: +F74+E74

Column H Miscellaneous Carrying Costs are equal to the product of the average quantity of parts on hand during the week, the weekly carrying cost percentage, and the price. Expected price changes are ignored here because the formula would have to find the price actually paid for the inventory now on hand. This small refinement isn't worth the effort.

H74: (C74/2+D74)*CAR_CST*PRICE

Column I The Interest Costs balance in I75 is equal to the sum of (1) the interest on the current week's Purchasing and Carrying Costs and (2) last week's interest charges plus interest. Think of these interest charges as either interest on the loan or rent on the capital you have invested in inventory. (We are not double counting when we add in last week's interest: last week we paid one week's interest on the inventory costs paid to date; this week we must pay this week's interest on those old costs.)

I74: +$INT*(H74+G74)
I75: +$INT*(H75+G75)+(1+$INT)*I74

Column J Total Carrying Costs are simply the sum of Miscellaneous Carrying Costs and Interest Costs.

J74: +I74+H74

Column K Total Costs are equal to Total Carrying Costs plus Total Purchasing Costs. Notice that unlike the traditional EOQ formula, Total Costs *do* include the invoice cost of the product.

K74: +J74+G74

Column L The EOQ Analysis section uses this and the next column to look up how many months it will take to use the quantity of inventory you are planning to buy. When you have completed these two columns, use the /**R**ange **N**ame **C**reate command to define the range USAGE from L74 through M126. In this column, the Running Total of units used is equal to the previous total plus current units used, rounded to zero decimal places.

L74: [W8] @ROUND(+C74,0)
L75: [W8] @ROUND(+C75+L74,0)

Column M Use the **D**ata **F**ill command to create the column of Time Elapsed in Months. The range is M74 through M125. The Start and Step Values both equal 12/52; the End Value is 12. When the @VLOOKUP function searches for usage in excess of the number in L126, it returns the value in M126. We therefore want to put an indicator in M126 that we have exceeded one year's usage. With 1-2-3 Version 2, the label "1 Year +" should do. With Version 1A, use the value 999.

Row 127 The EOQ analysis assumes that every purchase quantity that we compare ends with no inventory on hand. Row 127 therefore adjusts the Ending Inventory balance to zero. Since this is an arbitrary adjustment, we need to make sure that it doesn't cause us to calculate some negative Purchasing or Carrying Costs. The formulas for row 127 are:

A127: [W7] +A126
B127: −D126
D127: +D126−C127+B127
F127: +B127*$PRICE*@VLOOKUP(A127,$PCHANGE,1)
G127: +F127+E127
K127: +J127+G127

Row 68 After completing the data base, we need to accumulate some subtotals for the EOQ analysis. These appear in row 68. In B68 type the formula **@SUM(B74..B127)**. Copy this to C68. In E68 type the formula **@SUM(E74..E127)*.001**. Copy this from F68 to K68.

Row 64 If you haven't yet done so, enter **MONTH** in B64. Then use /**R**ange **N**ame **L**abel **R**ight to assign this as the range name for C64. In C64 enter the formula **@SUM(C74..C77)**. This puts our total expected usage for the next four weeks into the range named MONTH.

If you calculate your spreadsheet now, your balances in rows 68 and 64 should equal the balances shown in Figure 4-6. If you insert a value other than 5,000 in E8—1,000, for example—you should get the same values in

G68, J68, and K68 as are shown in Figure 4-7 for B57, C57, and D57, respectively. If you get an ERR or other values, check all formulas and range name assignments.

Completing the EOQ Analysis Data Table

Once your spreadsheet produces the values in Figure 4-6, it is time to have 1-2-3 complete the Data Table shown in Figure 4-7. Enter the Purchase Quantities shown in column A, and then enter the formulas shown in B50, C50, and D50. These three cells have been formatted as Text, but once you have your spreadsheet working, you may want to format the cells as +/−. This format will display a row of stars rather than the cell formulas—a neater appearance for future work.

Next, issue the /**D**ata **T**able **1** command. The table range is A50 to D59. The input cell is E8, shown in Figure 4-4. When you issue this command, 1-2-3 will substitute each purchase quantity in column A of the table into E8 (the ORDER quantity). Then it will calculate the totals for row 68, put these into the appropriate line of the Data Table, and go to the next purchase quantity. When the Data Table command has completed, you should have the same values as shown in Figure 4-7.

```
         A        B       C        D         E         F         G         H         I
41 ==========================================================================================
42 EOQ Analyis
43 ==================
44    X         A       B        C     <<Graph
45 ===================================
46 -------    Data Table  ---------                        This Purchase In
47             (In Thousands)                    Savings Mos of Inventory            This
48  Purch     Purch Carry     Total     Least   vs 4-Wk -------------------------   Purch
49    Qty      Cost  Cost      Cost      Cost Purchase         Next       Plan   (1000s)
50 -------+F68      +J68  +K68      ----------------------------------------------------
51      50      279    24       307 .                -4%        0.2        0.2        $5
52     100      266    25       293 .                 1%        0.5        0.5       $10
53     200      267    27       295 .                 0%        1.0        0.7       $19
54     250      252    26       279 .                 6%        1.2        0.9       $23
55     500      226    27       254 .                16%        2.5        2.1       $40
56     700      228    30       259 .                14%        3.5        3.0       $56
57   1,000      216    33       249 *********        18%        5.0        4.4       $75
58   2,500      221    60       281 .                 5%       12.4       10.2      $188
59   5,000      233   113       346 .               -15%       24.8   1 Year +      $350
60
61 ==========================================================================================
```

Figure 4-7. The completed EOQ Analysis section

Completing the EOQ Analysis

All that remains is to enter a few formulas to help us analyze our results.

Column E E51 contains the same pointing formula that we used in Figure 4-1. It points to the purchase quantity that has the lowest total cost. Format this cell as +/− and then copy it down the column.

E51: @IF(@MIN(D$51..D$59)=D51,99,0)

Column F Suppose you ignored the EOQ analysis and decided to purchase a four-week supply of inventory whenever you ran low. Column F shows what you would have saved during the year if you had chosen each of the purchase quantities shown. Format this column as Percentage with zero decimal places. Before entering this formula, create the range name TABLE, pointing from A51 to D59. Table 4-1 lists all range names and their cell addresses.

F51: @ROUND((@VLOOKUP($MONTH,$TABLE,3)/D51)−1,2)

Column G Although the EOQ analysis is evaluating a purchasing policy throughout the year, you are evaluating the immediate purchase

Range Name	***Address***	***Figure***
ORDER	E8	4-4
SAFETY	E9	4-4
ORD_CST	E10	4-4
PRICE	G15	4-4
CAR_CST	G16	4-4
INT	G17	4-4
GROWTH	G18	4-4
PCHANGE	G30..H33	4-4
DATA	B32..D37	4-4
TABLE	A51..D59	4-7
MONTH	C64	4-6
USAGE	L74..M126	4-6

Table 4-1. The Range Names Used in the Practical EOQ Spreadsheet

decision. This column divides each Purchase Quantity that you entered in column A by the quantity of parts you expect to use over the next four weeks. The result tells you how many months of inventory, at current usage, each choice represents. Format this column as Fixed with one decimal place.

G51: @ROUND(+$A51/$MONTH,1)

Column H This column is similar to column G. However, it tells you how many months of inventory the choices represent under the plan that you have entered in the Purchase Forecast Data Base (Figure 4-6). Format this column as Fixed with one decimal place.

H51: @VLOOKUP(A51,$USAGE,1)

Column I This column answers an obvious question: How much would each quantity cost? It is simply the product of each quantity and the price for that quantity, in thousands of dollars. It is formatted as Currency with zero decimal places.

I51: @VLOOKUP(A51,$DATA,1)*A51*0.001

Graphing the EOQ

Row 44 of Figure 4-7 shows the axes that I use to graph the EOQ analysis. The setup and interpretation of the graph are similar to the setup for the graphs of the previous EOQ model, Figures 4-2 and 4-3. However, I often graph only columns X and C, just as in Figure 4-2. This gives a better-defined picture of how my total costs vary. Try both approaches.

USING THE EOQ ANALYSIS

It's a simple process to enter your own data into the EOQ analysis. Enter assumptions about your firm into rows 8 through 13 of the Order Parameters table, as shown in Figure 4-4. Adjust the Lookup Tables in that figure to reflect the price breaks and price changes that you expect for the part you wish to analyze. (Make sure to expand the DATA and PCHANGE ranges if your tables are larger than those in the figure.)

If a schedule of requirements exists for the part you wish to analyze, enter this in column C of Figure 4-6. (Since entering data in column C will destroy the formula in that column, make sure to save your spreadsheet before you enter the data.) If you don't have a schedule of requirements, enter your current usage in C74; then make sure that expected usage growth rate of the part has a correct value in E13.

Next, as shown in Figure 4-7, enter possible quantities to purchase. If the formulas in column F are to work properly, these quantities must be in ascending order. Finally, issue the /**D**ata **T**able **1** command.

Once you have graphed your data, you can view the graph by pressing F10. And once you have issued the /**D**ata **T**able **1** command, you can enter new facts and assumptions and then recalculate the Data Table by pressing F8.

NOTES ON USING THE EOQ ANALYSIS

This chapter is meant to be a practical approach to the EOQ. You can change any part of it except the basic idea that you must make trade-offs between the cost of owning inventory and the cost of buying it.

If a one-year horizon is too long or too short for your business, change it. If you incur other large costs to buy or own inventory, add a table of these and change the formulas accordingly.

Remember, EOQ analysis offers guidance, but it should not be followed blindly. In fact the Economic Order Quantity is frequently not the quantity that you should buy, for reasons given in the following section.

Capital Rationing

Whatever the EOQ formula may say, most firms have a limited amount of cash available for investing in inventories and cannot afford to buy the quantities that the EOQ suggests. The EOQ Analysis section was designed with this fact in mind. It offers information that will be helpful in making compromise decisions.

For example, I would not buy the Economic Order Quantity of 1000 units in Figure 4-7. I hesitate to spend $75,000 to buy four to five months of inventory, whatever the excuse. I probably would buy 500 units instead. I would effect a 16% savings over a one-month buy, instead of an 18% savings for the EOQ, but would be committed to no more than two and one-half months of inventory.

Inventory Obsolescence

Inventory can become obsolete at the stroke of an engineer's pen or at the whim of a capricious customer (never mind what you tell the auditors). The more of a part you have on hand, the greater the risk of obsolescence. In other words, when there is a good chance that a part will soon be obsolete, the EOQ becomes irrelevant. You don't save money buying last year's calendars at discounted prices.

Chapter
Five

MONITORING ACCOUNTS PAYABLE

Not much is written about managing Accounts Payable (A/P). This is a shame. If you manage A/P properly, your Payables can represent a significant amount of interest-free debt. As a controller, I've tried to reconcile three conflicting goals while managing A/P.

First, I've tried to pay as late as is practical. This means that I try never to pay early, to qualify for all the trade credit I can, and to eliminate all CODs. If I take a trade discount, I pay as late as possible within its terms. And, at times, I *do* pay late.

Second, I've attempted to keep my vendors satisfied—not ecstatic, but satisfied. This has often meant nothing more than consistently paying each vendor on the day I promise.

Third, I've worked to keep my overdue invoices from getting out of control. By stretching payables too far, you can dig a hole that may be difficult to climb out of. It can also slow deliveries and increase CODs.

Unfortunately, it hasn't always been easy to know whether I've done a good job or a bad job in meeting these goals. If no vendors complain, I may be paying too early. If many vendors complain, I may be paying some vendors too late while paying others too early. And the trend in my purchases and payments isn't easy to spot.

AN A/P PERFORMANCE ANALYSIS

Figure 5-1 shows a way to monitor your A/P performance. Let's see what this report tells us.

```
          D       E    F   G    H   I   J   K   L          M            N      O     P       Q      R   S     T      U       V
265
266
267                                                  Accounts Payable Management Analysis
268                                                                Dec-85
269
270 How We Pay
271 ==============
272
273                                Percent of Our Purchases We Paid in Each 30-Day Period
274    Month    ---------------------------------------------------------------------
275 of Purch  0-30  30-60  60-90   Pd>90             30     60     90    Pd>90                  Avg Days Outstanding
276 -------- -----  ------ ------  ------          ++++++ ------ ****** =====                 ----------------------
277   Dec-84    7%    29%    50%    14%  +++---------------*************************=======     66   DaysDaysDaysD
278   Jan-85   13%    48%    28%    11%  ++++++------------------------**************======     56   DaysDaysDay
279   Feb-85   17%    34%    39%    10%  ++++++++-----------------********************=====     58   DaysDaysDays
280   Mar-85   10%    40%    37%    13%  +++++--------------------*******************======     61   DaysDaysDays
281   Apr-85   33%    38%    17%    12%  ++++++++++++++++-------------------*********======     47   DaysDaysD
282   May-85   23%    35%    16%    26%  ++++++++++++-----------------********=============     59   DaysDaysDays
283   Jun-85   12%    44%    28%    16%  ++++++----------------------**************========     59   DaysDaysDays
284   Jul-85   28%    35%    23%    14%  ++++++++++++++-----------------************=======     52   DaysDaysDa
285   Aug-85    8%    25%    30%    37%  ++++-------------***************==================     74   DaysDaysDaysDay
286   Sep-85   11%    25%    33%    31%  +++++-------------****************================     70   DaysDaysDaysDa
287   Oct-85   26%    24%    43%     7%  +++++++++++++------------**********************===     54   DaysDaysDay
288   Nov-85   10%    23%           67%  +++++------------=================================
289   Dec-85   20%                  80%  ++++++++++========================================
290
291
```

```
292 Average % of Purchases We Paid in the Three-Month Period Ending on Date Shown
293 ------------------------------------------------------------------------------------------
294   Mar-85    13%    41%    35%    11%  ++++++--------------------****************=====      58   DaysDaysDays
295   Jun-85    23%    39%    20%    18%  +++++++++++-------------------*********=======        55   DaysDaysDay
296   Sep-85    16%    28%    29%    27%  +++++++--------------*************============       65   DaysDaysDaysD
297   Dec-85    19%    24%    43%    14%  +++++++++------------*******************======       61   DaysDaysDays
298
299
300
301 How Our A/P Balance is Changing
302 ==================================
303                                                                                                     Balance in A/P
304                                                                                          ------------------------------------------
305   Month  Purch   Pmts          Purchases     Payments       Change in A/P    Total    >90     30   60   90   >90
306 -------- ------------------------------------------------  ---------------  -------  ------  ++++ ---- **** ====
307   Dec-84   $92    $92            +++++++|-------              $0         |     $196    $29    +++++++------*===
308   Jan-85   $76   $117             ++++++|---------          ($41)        |---  $155    $15    +++++------*=
309   Feb-85   $89   $112            +++++++|--------           ($23)        |--   $132    $15    ++++++---*==
310   Mar-85  $101    $80           ++++++++|------              $21       ++|     $153    $10    +++++++----=
311   Apr-85  $126   $131         ++++++++++|----------          ($5)        |     $148     $5    +++++++----=
312   May-85  $106   $108           ++++++++|--------            ($2)        |     $146    $15    +++++++--*==
313   Jun-85  $131    $82         ++++++++++|------              $49     ++++|     $195    $20    +++++++++----*==
314   Jul-85  $139   $133        +++++++++++|----------           $6         |     $201    $15    ++++++++-----**=
315   Aug-85  $160   $123       ++++++++++++|---------           $37      +++|     $238    $18    ++++++++++++----**=
316   Sep-85  $161   $104       ++++++++++++|--------            $57    +++++|     $295    $24    ++++++++++++----------**==
317   Oct-85  $135   $137         ++++++++++|----------          ($2)        |     $293    $30    ++++++++----------*****==
318   Nov-85  $181   $175     ++++++++++++++|--------------       $6         |     $299    $18    +++++++++++++------****==
319   Dec-85  $144   $175        +++++++++++|--------------     ($31)        |-    $268    $22    +++++++++-------------*=
```

Figure 5-1. A sample Accounts Payable Management Analysis report

The graph titled Balance in A/P, in the bottom right corner of the report, presents traditional data in an untraditional way. The Total column shows the total A/P balance for each of the past 13 months. The >90 column shows the amount in A/P each month that was more than 90 days old.

The remaining column in this section is a stacked bar graph of each month's A/P balance. (The source of this data is the Accounts Payable Aging report that is produced by nearly every accounting system.) As the headings in row 305 show, the + sign graphs the amount in A/P each month that was within 30 days, the − sign graphs the amount owed that was 30-60 days old, the * sign graphs the amount 60-90 days old, and the = sign graphs the amount more than 90 days old. The length of the complete bar graph each month represents the total balance in A/P.

At the top of Figure 5-1, in columns E, G, I, and K, we see the percentage of each month's purchases that was paid during each aging period. For example, we paid 7% of our December 1984 purchases within 30 days, 29% in more than 30 but less than 60 days, and so on. The graph beginning in column M illustrates these percentages.

As you can see from this section, our payments have been quite erratic. In some months, like August 1985, we paid very little within the first 30 days. In other months, like April 1985, we paid 33% of our purchases within 30 days. In view of our slow payments in the previous months, much of April's 30-day payments were probably CODs.

The graph titled Average Days Outstanding, at the top right of Figure 5-1, shows the reason we are on COD. It shows that we've been paying vendors in about 60 days during the past year. From a creditor's standpoint, this poor payment record is made even worse by our erratic performance. As you can see, our A/P aging has varied from a low of 47 days to a high of 74 days.

Rows 292 through 297 show that the trend isn't improving much. The graph in this section again demonstrates our inconsistent payment policies.

The bottom section of the report is titled How Our A/P Balance Is Changing. It illustrates the trend in our purchases, payments, and A/P balances during the past year. As you can see, purchases have nearly doubled. This may be one reason for our problems. Also, the Payments graph illustrates a strange pattern to our payments. Notice that during the first nine months of 1985, we made large A/P payments on the first month of each quarter, made lower payments the next month, and made even lower payments the following month. We need to research the reason for this performance.

The columns titled Change in A/P, beginning in row 305, show the net change in A/P for each of the past 13 months. (The positive numbers show an increase in A/P; the negative numbers show a decrease.) These columns demonstrate a tendency to increase our Payables in spurts. As the graph highlights, A/P increased only 4 months during the past 13. The increase in two of those months (June and September), however, totaled more than $100 ($49 + $57).

In short, the report has given us a better idea of what's happening with our Payables. The next step is to find out *why* we are getting these results and what we can do to improve them. If this were a report for a real company, we would have some work ahead of us.

CREATING THE A/P REPORT

The A/P Management Analysis in Figure 5-1 is very similar to the Accounts Receivable Collections Analysis presented in Chapter 3 as Figure 3-2. Many of the formulas, in fact, are similar. For 1-2-3 users, however, there *is* one major difference between the two reports: the graphs in Figure 5-1 can be generated only by users of 1-2-3 Version 2. If you have Version 1A, you must adapt the graphics techniques described in Chapter 3.

We will take a shortcut in creating this report. Since Figure 5-1 is so similar to Figure 3-2, we will start with Figure 3-2 and change it into Figure 5-1. Creating the report involves five steps.

1. Enter data in the Data Bank for the A/P report to analyze.

2. Erase what we don't want from the A/R report in Figure 3-2.

3. Put the remaining columns where we want them, and change their headings.

4. Change the old formulas and add some new ones.

5. Add graphs to the report.

ENTER A/P DATA INTO THE DATA BANK

Figure 5-2 shows the complete Accounts Payable Management Analysis report. As you create this report, you may want to return to this figure occasionally to guide you in your work.

```
         A           B                      C                D      E  F  G  H  I  J  K  L          M              N   O   P    Q     R  S   T    U    V     W   X   Y   Z   AA  AB
250 ------------------------------------------------------------------------------------------------------------------------------------------------------------------
251                                                              MISC_D*        *     *     **
252 ------------------------------------------------------------------------------------------------------------------------------------------------------------------
253 REPORT           REP_MAC          -------------------------------F------F-----T-----TH---------------------------------------------
254            {GOTO}report~          Set column widths:                *      *     *     **
255            /WCS9~                 A                                                                          Symbols:
256            {RIGHT}/WCS26~         B                                                                          SYMB1  +
257            {RIGHT}/WCS20~         C              START     34  +$THIS_COL-13 — Start w/ this data column.    SYMB2  -
258            {RIGHT}/WCR            D              SCALE1    46  GRAPH SCALE FACTOR, How We Pay, +++---***===  SYMB3  *
259            {RIGHT}/WCS6~          E              SCALE2  0.08  GRAPH SCALE FACTOR, AP Activity, ++++|--- & +++---***===   SYMB4  =
260            {RIGHT}/WCS1~          F              SCALE3   0.2  GRAPH SCALE FACTOR DaysDays               SYMB5  Days
261            {RIGHT}/WCS6~          G              SHIFT1    21  LEFT-RIGHT SHIFT  ++++|---
262            {RIGHT}/WCS1~          H              SHIFT2     6  LEFT-RIGHT SHIFT  ++++|
263            {RIGHT}/WCS6~          I
264            {RIGHT}/WCS1~          J                    ==================================================================
265            {RIGHT}/WCS6~          K
266            {RIGHT}/WCS2~          L
267            {RIGHT}/WCS23~         M                                       Accounts Payable Management Analysis
268            {RIGHT}/WCS7~          N                                                      Dec-85
269            {RIGHT}/WCS5~          O
270            {RIGHT}/WCS6~          P              How We Pay
271            {RIGHT}/WCS7~          Q              ==========
272            {RIGHT}/WCS7~          R
273            {RIGHT}/WCS2~          S                        Percent of Our Purchases We Paid in Each 30-Day Period
274            {RIGHT}/WCS9~          T               Month    -------------------------------------------------------------
275            {RIGHT}/WCS5~          U              Of Purch  0-30 30-60 60-90 Pd>90            30    60    90   Pd>90          Avg Days Outstanding
276            {RIGHT}/WCS14~         V              --------  ---- ----- ----- -----          ++++++ ---- ****** ====          --------------------
277            {RIGHT}/WCR~           W                Dec-84    7%   29%   50%   14%  +++---------------***********************=====   66  DaysDaysDaysD
278            {GOTO}report~/XQ       Define Report Range  Jan-85  13%  48%   28%   11%  ++++++-------------------------*************=====   56  DaysDaysDay
279            {UP}{END}{RIGHT}{DOWN}  and print report:  Feb-85  17%  34%   39%   10%  ++++++++---------------------******************====   58  DaysDaysDays
280            {END}{LEFT}{END}{LEFT}    "                Mar-85   10%   40%   37%   13%  +++++----------------------******************=====   61  DaysDaysDays
281            {END}{DOWN}               "                Apr-85   33%   38%   17%   12%  ++++++++++++++----------------------*********=====   47  DaysDaysD
282            {END}{LEFT}{LEFT}         "                May-85   23%   35%   16%   26%  +++++++++++--------------------*******=============   59  DaysDaysDays
283            {DOWN}/PPR{BS}.           "                Jun-85   12%   44%   28%   16%  ++++++------------------------**************=====   59  DaysDaysDays
284            {UP}{RIGHT}               "                Jul-85   28%   35%   23%   14%  +++++++++++++-----------------************=====   52  DaysDaysDa
285            {END}{RIGHT}              "                Aug-85    8%   25%   30%   37%  ++++--------------***************================   74  DaysDaysDaysDay
286            {DOWN}{DOWN}              "                Sep-85   11%   25%   33%   31%  +++++--------------****************==============   70  DaysDaysDaysDa
287            {END}{DOWN}{LEFT}~        "                Oct-85   26%   24%   43%    7%  ++++++++++++------------*********************===   54  DaysDaysDay
288            OMR135~ML5~Q              "                Nov-85   10%   23%          67%  +++++-------------==================================
289            AGPQ                      "                Dec-85   20%                80%  +++++++++=========================================
290            /XR                       "
291
```

	A	B	C
292			
293	Data Bank Number Control		
294			
295	DB#	DB Description	Data Needed
296			
297	105.110	Accounts Payable	A/P Balance
298	115.010	Payables, 30 Days	A/P, 30 Days
299	115.020	Payables, 60 Days	A/P, 60 Days
300	115.030	Payables, 90 Days	A/P, 90 Days
301	115.040	Payables, Over 90 Days	A/P, Over 90
302	199.029	Total Purchases, AP	Tot A/P Purch
303	199.030	Accounts Payable Paid	A/P Paid
304			
305–322			

Average % of Purchases We Paid in the Three-Month Period Ending on Date Shown

D	E–F	G–H	I–J	K–L	M–Q	R	S–U
Mar-85	13%	41%	35%	11%	++++++——————****************====	58	DaysDaysDays
Jun-85	23%	39%	20%	18%	+++++++++++——————*********=====	55	DaysDaysDay
Sep-85	16%	28%	29%	27%	+++++++————*************=======	65	DaysDaysDaysD
Dec-85	19%	24%	43%	14%	+++++++++————*******************====	61	DaysDaysDays

How Our A/P Balance is Changing

Month	Purch	Pmts	Purchases	Payments	Change in A/P		Total	>90	Balance in A/P: 30 (++++) 60 (——) 90 (****) >90 (==)
Dec-84	$92	$92	+++++++|	————	$0	|	$196	$29	++++++——*==
Jan-85	$76	$117	++++++|	—————	($41)	|—	$155	$15	+++++——*=
Feb-85	$89	$112	+++++++|	————	($23)	|—	$132	$15	++++++—*==
Mar-85	$101	$80	++++++++|	———	$21	++|	$153	$10	+++++++——=
Apr-85	$126	$131	++++++++++|	—————	($5)	|	$148	$5	+++++++——=
May-85	$106	$108	++++++++|	————	($2)	|	$146	$15	+++++++—*==
Jun-85	$131	$82	++++++++++|	———	$49	++++|	$195	$20	+++++++++——*==
Jul-85	$139	$133	+++++++++++|	—————	$6	|	$201	$15	++++++++——**=
Aug-85	$160	$123	++++++++++++|	————	$37	+++|	$238	$18	++++++++++++——**=
Sep-85	$161	$104	++++++++++++|	————	$57	+++++|	$295	$24	++++++++++++————**==
Oct-85	$135	$137	++++++++++|	—————	($2)	|	$293	$30	++++++++————*****==
Nov-85	$181	$175	++++++++++++++|	———————	$6	|	$299	$18	+++++++++++++———****==
Dec-85	$144	$175	+++++++++++|	———————	($31)	|—	$268	$22	+++++++++————*=

W	X	Y	Z	AA	AB
	6.88	5.24	1.36	2.68	
	5.28	5	1.2	1.4	
	5.92	2.32	1.36	1.56	
	7.28	3.8	0.44	1.24	
	6.72	3.72	0.44	0.84	
	6.56	2.44	1.48	1.68	
	9.2	3.8	1	1.6	
	8	4.64	1.88	1.08	
	11.84	3.92	1.6	1.04	
	11.52	8.08	1.68	1.6	
	8	8.24	5.04	2.44	
	13.04	5.48	4.48	1.92	
	9.2	9.96	0.68	1.44	

Figure 5-2. The complete spreadsheet that attaches to the Data Bank to produce the Accounts Payable Management Analysis report

The Data Bank Number Control, beginning in cell A293 of Figure 5-2, shows the categories of data that this report expects to find in the Data Bank. If you have entered the sample Data Bank data from Appendix A, or have purchased the disk set available for this book, you're set. Otherwise, you must enter these data categories into your Data Bank before continuing.

Although most of these data categories can be found in most accounting systems, the Total Purchases category will need some explanation. *Purchases* is a vague term, although it sounds specific. Some firms use it to refer only to purchases of inventory. Others use it to refer to all credits to Accounts Payable. Still others use it to refer to all operating costs other than payroll, whether it involves cash payments or credit.

For our purposes, this definition should be as broad as possible. The purpose of this report, after all, is to monitor and help control the trends in our commitments and payments. We therefore need to include all operating commitments in the analysis. We could, however, create subsidiary reports that would more closely analyze various categories of our purchases and payments.

ERASE SECTIONS OF THE ACCOUNTS RECEIVABLE REPORT

To begin the A/P report, retrieve the Data Bank. Use ALT-M System Load to load your Accounts Receivable Collections Analysis. Then change floppy disks or your hard disk directories so that you won't accidentally save your new A/P report under the name of your old A/R report.

Using ALT-M System Columns, reset your Data Bank columns to the global column width. Now use **/R**ange **E**rase to erase everything in the body of the A/R report except what you see in Figure 5-3.

Move the Columns and Change the Headings

Next move the remaining columns of data as follows:

- Move the data in columns E and F, Month of Sale and 0-30 Days, to columns D and E.
- Move the data in column I, 30-60 Days, to column G.
- Move the data in column L, 60-90 Days, to column I.
- Move the data in column O, % Uncollected After 90 Days, to column K.

	D	E	F	G	H	I	J	K	L	M	N	O	P	Q
263														
264														
265														
266														
267						Accounts Receivable Collections Analysis								
268									Dec-85					
269–272														
273				Percent of Sales Collected in Each 30-Day Period										
274		Month										% Uncollected		
275		Of Sale	0-30 DAYS				30-60 DAYS		60-90 DAYS			After 90 Days		
276														
277		Dec-84	5%			43%			42%			10%		
278		Jan-85	8%			42%			38%			12%		
279		Feb-85	6%			48%			30%			16%		
280		Mar-85	1,1%			53%			21%			15%		
281		Apr-85	7%			44%			46%			3%		
282		May-85	1%			46%			38%			15%		
283		Jun-85	11%			57%			21%			11%		
284		Jul-85	6%			27%			35%			32%		
285		Aug-85	2%			15%			48%			35%		
286		Sep-85	1%			28%			63%			8%		
287		Oct-85	3%			34%			36%			27%		
288		Nov-85	1%			45%						54%		
289		Dec-85	2%									98%		
290–297														
298			7%			48%			32%			13%		
299			3%			30%			46%			21%		

Figure 5-3. The Accounts Receivable Collections Analysis report after removal of graphs and many headings

Next change the macros that set the column widths and print the report. As you remember from Chapter 3, you will find these in column B. Figure 5-4 shows the new macro. Notice the /XQ in row 278. This command stops the macro's execution at that point. When you have finished building the report, edit 278 and remove /XQ, leaving {GOTO}report untouched. For now, use ALT-M System Report to run this macro, thus setting the new column widths.

Finally, change the report headings to those you see in Figure 5-5. Don't worry if you don't have the spacing just right for these headings. You can clean up the headings when the rest of the report is finished.

```
            A                  B                        C
253  REPORT              REP_MAC             --------------------
254              {GOTO}report~               Set column widths:
255              /WCS9~                      A
256              {RIGHT}/WCS26~              B
257              {RIGHT}/WCS20~              C
258              {RIGHT}/WCR                 D
259              {RIGHT}/WCS6~               E
260              {RIGHT}/WCS1~               F
261              {RIGHT}/WCS6~               G
262              {RIGHT}/WCS1~               H
263              {RIGHT}/WCS6~               I
264              {RIGHT}/WCS1~               J
265              {RIGHT}/WCS6~               K
266              {RIGHT}/WCS2~               L
267              {RIGHT}/WCS23~              M
268              {RIGHT}/WCS7~               N
269              {RIGHT}/WCS5~               O
270              {RIGHT}/WCS6~               P
271              {RIGHT}/WCS7~               Q
272              {RIGHT}/WCS7~               R
273              {RIGHT}/WCS2~               S
274              {RIGHT}/WCS9~               T
275              {RIGHT}/WCS5~               U
276              {RIGHT}/WCS14~              V
277              {RIGHT}/WCR~                W
278              {GOTO}report~/XQ            Define Report Range
279              {UP}{END}{RIGHT}{DOWN}       and print report:
280              {END}{LEFT}{END}{LEFT}                 "
281              {END}{DOWN}                            "
282              {END}{LEFT}{LEFT}                      "
283              {DOWN}/PPR{BS}.                        "
284              {UP}{RIGHT}                            "
285              {END}{RIGHT}                           "
286              {DOWN}{DOWN}                           "
287              {END}{DOWN}{LEFT}~                     "
288              OMR135~ML5~Q                           "
289              AGPQ                                   "
290              /XR                                    "
```

Figure 5-4. The macro that sets the column widths and prints the A/P Management Analysis report

Change and Add Formulas

Chapter 3 explained that the Data Bank Number Control provides an easy way to change Data Bank numbers and helps you confirm that the DB# you have used is the DB# you intend to use.

Update the Data Bank Number Control

Cell A297 of Figure 5-2 shows the first of the Data Bank numbers that you must enter into your A/P report. When you have entered the numbers as shown in this figure, copy the formula in B302 to B303. Next, recalculate column B by issuing the /**C**opy command, copying the range B297..B303 to B297. Finally, modify the descriptions in column C to match those in Figure 5-2.

Change the Accounts Receivable Formulas

In Chapter 3 we assigned range names to frequently used values. Then, after the report was completed, we deleted these range names. Later in this chapter we will add a number of these range names. For now, however, we need one of the ranges that we used in Chapter 3. Cell E257 still should contain the range name START. Issue the /**R**ange **N**ame **L**abel **R**ight command to assign this range name to cell F257. This cell still should contain the value 34.

Notice that the macro header section in Figure 5-2 begins in row 250. You will find it easier to understand the following explanation if your macro header section begins on row 250 also. In your spreadsheet, put your cursor on this line of the macro header. Then insert the number of rows necessary to put it on row 250. When you have completed the report that follows, delete the rows that you had inserted, if you need to conserve disk space, and then save your report.

Figure 5-5 shows what our report will look like once we have changed the formulas and added new ones. The circled numbers on this report refer to the following paragraphs, which explain the formulas.

1. Since we have changed the Data Bank numbers in the Data Bank Number Control, these formulas should now produce the accounts payable information that we need. Check each of these formulas, however, to make sure they appear as follows:

```
E277:  @ROUND(1-(@VLOOKUP($A$298,$DATA,$START+@COUNT
         ($D$277..$D277)-1)/@VLOOKUP($A$302,$DATA,$START+@COUNT
         ($D$277..$D277)-1)),2)
G277:  @ROUND(1-(@VLOOKUP($A$299,$DATA,$START+1+@COUNT
         ($D$277..$D277)-1)/@VLOOKUP($A$302,$DATA,$START+@COUNT
         ($D$277..$D277)-1))-E277,2)
I277:  @ROUND(1-(@VLOOKUP($A$300,$DATA,$START+2+@COUNT
         ($D$277..$D277)-1)/@VLOOKUP($A$302,$DATA,$START+@COUNT
         ($D$277..$D277)-1))-G277-E277,2)
```

Row	D	E–L					M–Q				R–V	
263												
264		================										
265												
266												
267							Accounts Payable Management Analysis					
268							Dec-85					
269												
270	How We Pay											
271	==========											
272												
273		Percent of Our Purchases We Paid in Each 30-Day Period										
274	Month											
275	Of Purch	0-30	30-60	60-90	Pd>90		30	60	90	Pd>90	Avg Days Outstanding	
276							++++++	———	******	====		
277	Dec-84	7%	29%	50%	14%	(4)					66	(6)
278	Jan-85	13%	(1) 48%	28%	11%						56	
279	Feb-85	17%	34%	39%	10%						58	
280	Mar-85	10%	40%	37%	13%						61	
281	Apr-85	33%	38%	17%	12%						47	
282	May-85	23%	35%	16%	26%						59	
283	Jun-85	12%	44%	28%	16%						59	
284	Jul-85	28%	35%	23%	14%						52	
285	Aug-85	8%	25%	30%	37%						74	
286	Sep-85	11%	25%	33%	31%						70	
287	Oct-85	26%	24%	43%	7%						54	
288	Nov-85	10%	23%		67%							
289	Dec-85	20%			80%							
290												
291	(2)	(3)			(5)							
292	Average % of Purchases We Paid in the Three-Month Period Ending on Date Shown										(7)	
293												
294	Mar-85	13%	41%	35%	11%						58	
295	Jun-85	23%	39%	20%	18%						55	
296	Sep-85	16%	28%	29%	27%						65	
297	Dec-85	19%	24%	43%	14%						61	
298												
299												

Columns: D E F G H I J K L M N O P Q R S T U V W X Y Z AA AB

	D	E	F–L	M	N–P	Q	R	S	T	U	V	W	X	Y	Z	AA	AB
300																	
301	How Our A/P Balance is Changing																
302																	
303						(12)	(13) Balance in A/P										
304	(8)	(9)	(10)		(11)												
305	Month	Purch	Pmts Purchases	Payments	Change in A/P	Total	>90	30	60	90	>90			(14)			
306								++++	——	****	═══						
307	Dec-84	$92	$92		$0	$196	$29						6.88	5.24	1.36	2.68	
308	Jan-85	$76	$117		($41)	$155	$15						5.28	5	1.2	1.4	
309	Feb-85	$89	$112		($23)	$132	$15						5.92	2.32	1.36	1.56	
310	Mar-85	$101	$80		$21	$153	$10						7.28	3.8	0.44	1.24	
311	Apr-85	$126	$131		($5)	$148	$5						6.72	3.72	0.44	0.84	
312	May-85	$106	$108		($2)	$146	$15						6.56	2.44	1.48	1.68	
313	Jun-85	$131	$82		$49	$195	$20						9.2	3.8	1	1.6	
314	Jul-85	$139	$133		$6	$201	$15						8	4.64	1.88	1.08	
315	Aug-85	$160	$123		$37	$238	$18						11.84	3.92	1.6	1.04	
316	Sep-85	$161	$104		$57	$295	$24						11.52	8.08	1.68	1.6	
317	Oct-85	$135	$137		($2)	$293	$30						8	8.24	5.04	2.44	
318	Nov-85	$181	$175		$6	$299	$18						13.04	5.48	4.48	1.92	
319	Dec-85	$144	$175		($31)	$268	$22						9.2	9.96	0.68	1.44	
320																	
321																	
322																	

Figure 5-5. The Accounts Payable Management Analysis report before graphs have been added

If changes to these formulas were necessary, format them as Percent, with zero decimal places, and then copy them down the remaining rows of this section. Remember to erase the formulas in G289, I288, and I289. These attempt to @VLOOKUP values that we won't know until early next year.

2. Format these four cells as /Range Date (3). To enter the Mar-85 value, type **+** and then point to cell D280, containing Mar-85. To enter Jun-85, point to D283, and so on, for the other two dates.

3. The 13% value for Mar-85 is the numerical average of the values for January through March above in the same column, rows 278-280. Type **@AVG(**; point to January's 0-30-Day value, type **.** (period); point to March's 0-30-Day value, type **)**; press ENTER. Follow a similar approach for the rows for June, Aug, and Dec. Finally, copy these four cells into columns G and I. This should give you the values shown.

4. No changes should be necessary in this formula. Each cell in this column is equal to the value of 1 minus the sum of the three cells to the left. If a change is necessary, do not use the @SUM formula. When we include graphs in the report, this formula would include string values in the @SUM range, which would create an ERR. Instead, type **1−(**, point to the cell with the 50% value, type **+**, point to the cell with the 29% value, type **+**, point to the cell with the 7% value, type **)**, and press ENTER. Finally, copy this formula down the column.

5. This formula is the same as for step 4. Copy it from there.

6. The value for the Average Days Outstanding assumes that the 0-30-Day payments took an average of 15 days to pay, that the 30-60-Day payments averaged 45 days, that the 60-90-Day payments averaged 75, and that the Over-90-Day payments averaged 105 days. Create the formula by entering the appropriate values and pointing to the appropriate cells. Finally, copy this formula down the column as shown. The formula is

R277: @ROUND(15*E277+45*G277+75*I277+105*K277,0)

7. This formula is the same as in step 6. Copy it from R277.

8. This column of dates has been copied from the comparable section of dates above it. Before you copy, however, make sure that the cell with Dec-84 uses an absolute reference. That is, it should read +$THIS_MO, not +THIS_MO.

9. This formula is repeated with only minor modifications across the entire row of numbers. After you enter it, copy it down the column. The formula is

E307: @VLOOKUP($A$302,$DATA,$START+@COUNT($D$277..$D277)−1)

10. Copy this formula from column E and then change the cell to be looked up from $A$302 to $A$303. Copy it down the column. The new formula is

G307: @VLOOKUP($A$303,$DATA,$START+@COUNT($D$277..$D277)−1)

11. This column is equal to the Purchases on each row less the Payments. Enter this formula by pointing and then copy it down the column.

12. Copy the formula from column E into this column and the next, column R. Much as you did with column G, change the cell to be looked up from $A$302 to $A$297. Copy the formula down the column. The formula is

Q307: @VLOOKUP($A$297,$DATA,$START+@COUNT($D$277..$D277)−1)

13. The cell to be looked up here is $A$301. The formula to be copied down the column is

R307: @VLOOKUP($A$301,$DATA,$START+@COUNT($D$277..$D277)−1)

14. The purpose of these four columns is to accumulate the data to be graphed in the detailed Balance in A/P graph. The formula in column X is the result of looking up the 0-30-Day balance from the Data Bank and multiplying that balance by the appropriate scale value. (This value fits the graph to the space available.) The remaining three columns follow the same approach. However, they also adjust for the cumulative rounding error. This adjustment makes the total graph more accurate.

The SCALE value is one of several graph parameters that will be discussed in the following section on graphs. When you have entered the values and range names for these parameters, enter the following formulas:

```
X307:  +$SCALE2*@VLOOKUP($A$298,$DATA,$START+@COUNT
          ($D$277..$D277)-1)
Y307:  +$SCALE2*@VLOOKUP($A$299,$DATA,$START+@COUNT
          ($D$277..$D277)-1)+ X307-@ROUND(X307,0)
Z307:  +$SCALE2*@VLOOKUP($A$300,$DATA,$START+@COUNT
          ($D$277..$D277)-1)+Y307-@ROUND(Y307,0)
AA307: +$SCALE2*@VLOOKUP($A$301,$DATA,$START+@COUNT
          ($D$277..$D277)-1)+ Z307-@ROUND(Z307,0)
```

ADD GRAPHS TO THE SPREADSHEET

Until Version 2 was introduced, we had only two ways to generate graphs in 1-2-3. We could use the /Graph command, or we could format cells of a spreadsheet as a bar graph with the /Range Format +/− command. But Version 2 also gives us string graphics, a significant improvement over the +/− format for spreadsheet bar graphs.

Look again at Figure 5-1. In many ways this report looks like a typical spreadsheet, but the graphs aren't typical. These graphs show some of the flexibility and power that string graphics can provide.

Functions for Graphing With Strings

The following functions are used frequently with string graphics.

@REPEAT(string,number) This function makes spreadsheet graphics possible. It returns the string repeated the number of times.

```
@REPEAT("Hi",3) = "HiHiHi"
@REPEAT("Bill",0) = ""
@REPEAT("Walla ",2.99) = "Walla Walla "
```

@LEFT(string,number) This function returns the leftmost number of characters in the string.

```
@LEFT("Hi There",5) = "Hi Th"
@LEFT(@REPEAT("Walla ",3),14) = "Walla Walla Wa"
@LEFT("Nevermore",5.8) = "Never"
```

@RIGHT(string,number) This returns the rightmost number of characters in the string.

```
@RIGHT("Madam, I'm Adam",8) = "I'm Adam"
@RIGHT(@REPEAT("Sam",3),5) = "amSam"
@RIGHT("Mad Hatter",@ROUND(5.9,0)) = "Hatter"
```

Establish Some Parameters

Rows 255 through 262 of Figure 5-2 show the report parameters above our A/P report. The parameters allow easy maintenance of the graphs that we make.

The START parameter is the only parameter in this section that has nothing to do with graphs. Created in Chapter 3 for our A/R report, it is also needed here. Notice, however, that START, its value, and description have been shifted one cell to the left. This makes the parameters easier to read. Use the /**M**ove command to move E257..6257 to D257.

The SCALE values squeeze our graphs down to a size that will fit into our report. This A/P report uses the three different scales for the graphs described.

You use a SHIFT value when you have graphs like the one for Purchases in Figure 5-1, which adds symbols to the left when values increase. The SHIFT value opens up a space to accommodate these symbols. When a SHIFT value is used in a graph, increasing it by a value of 1 moves the graph to the right by one character. You will better understand how to use the SHIFT value after working through the illustrations that follow.

One powerful feature of string graphics is the ability to use any symbol for your graphs that the computer can generate. This report uses five different symbols, SYMB1 through SYMB5. Changing any of these symbols in the parameters section will change the symbol throughout the report when the report is recalculated.

After you have entered the Parameters section as shown in Figure 5-2, use the /**R**ange **N**ame **L**abel **R**ight command on both columns of range names, assigning the names as shown to the cells at the right of each label.

Now it's time to create the graphs.

A Stacked Bar Chart

The top of Figure 5-1 shows the percent of our purchases that we paid in each 30-day period. For example, in Dec-84 we paid 7% of our purchases in less than 30 days.We paid 29% in 30-60 days and 50% in 60-90 days. Finally, 14% of our invoices were unpaid after 90 days. This stacked bar chart illustrates these percentages.

```
      E    F  G     H  I     J  K    L                M              N      O     P      Q
275  0-30   30-60  60-90    Pd>90                    30       60     90     Pd>90
276  -----  ------ ------  ------                  ++++++  ------ ******  ======
277     7%     29%    50%     14%  +++-------------***********************======
278    13%     48%    28%     11%  ++++++----------------------*************====
```

Since each bar represents 100% of the total purchases for each month, each is the same length. The formula for the bar chart in M277 is long, but its pattern is easy to see.

M277:
```
@LEFT(@REPEAT($SYMB1,@ROUND($SCALE1*E277,0))
      &@REPEAT($SYMB2,@ROUND($SCALE1*G277,0))
      &@REPEAT($SYMB3,@ROUND($SCALE1*I277,0))
      &@REPEAT($SYMB4,$SCALE1),$SCALE1)
```

Each line @REPEATS its own symbol a number of times. The number of repetitions is the @ROUNDed value of $SCALE1 times the appropriate percentage. However, the first and last lines are a little different to correct for the slight inaccuracies that rounding contributes. Without this correction, the bar graphs would be different lengths—one might graph 99%, another 102%, and so on.

We take two steps to ensure that each bar graph will be the same length. First we make the last line a filler. It @REPEATs the $SYMB4 symbol by a number representing 100% of $SCALE1, which of course is equal to $SCALE1. Second, we surround everything with an @LEFT formula. This returns the leftmost number of characters in the string equal to $SCALE1.

Of course, when you write the formula in M277, you will write it all on one line, with no spaces. It is divided into four lines on the page so that you can better see how the formula works. Keep this in mind when you see other formulas similarly split up in the following paragraphs.

How to Enter These Formulas More Easily

The previous formulas and many of the formulas that follow are a combination of several shorter formulas. Here is an easy way to save time and typing when you enter these formulas.

Suppose you are ready to enter the formula given for M277. Start by entering **@REPEAT($SYMB1,@ROUND($SCALE1*E277,0)**). When you press ENTER, this formula should give you the first section of your graph.

Turn this formula into a label by pressing EDIT HOME ' (apostrophe) and ENTER. Then copy it into the three cells below M277.

To move these copies into M277, use the **/R**ange **J**ustify command. Highlight all four cells that contain your formula. Also highlight enough columns to the right of these cells for all formulas to fit on the same line within the highlight. (Don't worry if there is data in the other cells that you are highlighting to the right. The /Range Justify command will justify only the cells in the leftmost column of the highlighted area.) When you press ENTER, all four copies of M277 should be in M277. If they aren't, you probably didn't highlight enough space to the right. Try again.

Now, with four copies of the basic formula in M277, it's an easy matter to edit this cell as required. Substitute the & sign for the space between each formula and then change the formulas as needed. Finally, insert **@LEFT(** at the beginning of the formula and attach **,$SCALE1)** to the end.

Another Stacked Bar Chart

The bar chart titled Balance in A/P in Figure 5-1, Q307 through V319, shows another example of the stacked bar graph. The graph uses the formulas listed in section 14 of the discussion of Figure 5-5. If you haven't entered these formulas you can do so now.

```
        Q       R   S     T       U         V          W          X          Y          Z          AA          AB
303                    Balance in A/P              |                                                       |
304 -------------------------------------------|                                                       |
305  Total     >90    30    60    90    >90        |                                                       |
306 ------- ------   ++++  ----  ****  ====        |                                                       |
307   $196     $29   ++++++++-----*===             |                 6.88       5.24       1.36       2.68 |
308   $155     $15   +++++-----*=                  |                 5.28          5        1.2        1.4 |
```

The formula that produces this graph is very similar to that of the previous bar chart. But since the lines in this stacked bar chart are supposed to be different lengths, there is no need for the @LEFT function.

```
T307: @REPEAT($SYMB1,@ROUND($X259,0))
      &@REPEAT($SYMB2,@ROUND($Y307,0))
      &@REPEAT($SYMB3,@ROUND($Z307,0))
      &@REPEAT($SYMB4,@ROUND($AA307,0))
```

As you can see, the formula is merely four of the @REPEAT functions, similar to those we've already seen. But unlike the previous formula, this one uses no $SCALE factor. This is because the SCALE has already been used to create the values in columns X,Y,Z, and AA that we are graphing.

A Back-to-Back Graph

The graph at the bottom of Figure 5-1 in columns L and M illustrates what I call a back-to-back graph. We use it here to juxtapose monthly purchases, which increase A/P, and payments, which decrease A/P. This graph makes it easy to follow the trend of purchases and payments separately while simplifying the comparison of purchases and payments with each other.

```
       E     F   G    H   I   J   K    L                 M
305 Purch        Pmts               Purchases         Payments
306 ----------------------------------------------------------------
307    $92       $92                     +++++++|-------
308    $76      $117                      ++++++|---------
```

The formula in H307 that produces this graph follows.

```
H307:  @RIGHT(@REPEAT(" ",$SHIFT1)
           &@REPEAT($SYMB1,$E307*$SCALE2),$SHIFT1)
           &"|"
           &@REPEAT($SYMB2,$G307*$SCALE2)
```

We are @REPEATing the $SYMB1 symbol by a value equal to $E307*$SCALE2, adding a vertical line as a divider, and then @REPEATing the $SYMB2 symbol by $G307*$SCALE2. But to keep the center line straight, we add to the first section a number of blanks equal to $SHIFT1 and then take the rightmost number of characters that are equal to $SHIFT1.

If $SHIFT1 is greater than $E307*$SCALE2, the @RIGHT function includes some of the blanks we have added. If $SHIFT1 is less than $E307*$SCALE2, not all of the Purchases graph is displayed. It is nevertheless easy to see whether $SHIFT1 is large enough. Just make sure that no graph symbols for Purchases touch the left edge of column H.

Graphing Changes

When we compare our Payments and Purchases, it isn't easy to see which is larger. Therefore, we can't always tell from the graph whether our Accounts Payable balance increased or decreased each month. The following graph from Figure 5-1 highlights this monthly change in A/P.

```
        N      O     P
305  Change  in  A/P
306  ----------------
307      $0         |
308    ($41)        |---
309    ($23)        |--
310     $21       ++|
```

Here, as you can see, we get + to the left if A/P increased and – to the right if it decreased. As always, we could have used any symbols we wished.

The formula for this graph is

```
O307:  @RIGHT(@REPEAT(" ",$SHIFT2)
           &@REPEAT($SYMB1,($N307>0)*@ROUND(@ABS($N307)*$SCALE2,0)),
           $SHIFT2)&"|"
           &@REPEAT($SYMB2,($N307<0)*@ROUND(@ABS($N307)*$SCALE2,0))
```

This formula is similar to the back-to-back graph but with two major differences. First, we have added a way to "turn off" whichever side of the graph we don't want printed. We do this by multiplying our value to be graphed by ($N307>0) for the left side and by ($N307<0) for the right side of the graph.

If the value in $N307 is positive, ($N307>0) returns a value of 1 and ($N307<0) returns a value of 0. This leaves unchanged the value to be graphed on the left side of the graph but zeros out the value to be graphed on the right side. If the value of $N307 is negative, just the opposite happens.

The second difference is that the formula uses the absolute value of $N307. The string functions won't accept negative values.

Graphing With Words

The graph at the top right of Figure 5-1, columns R through V, shows the approximate number of days that invoices have remained outstanding for each month in the past year. For example, it took us about 66 days to pay the invoices we received in December 1984.

```
        R   S     T      U      V
275        Avg Days Outstanding
276      ------------------------
277      66    DaysDaysDaysD
278      56    DaysDaysDay
```

T277: @LEFT(@REPEAT($SYMB5,15),@ROUND($SCALE3*R277,0))

The formula in T277 should be easy to understand by now We @REPEAT the label in $SYMB5 enough times to have an adequate supply of symbols (I chose 15 times). Then we graph the leftmost number of characters that is equal to the rounded value of $SCALE3*R277.

SETTING THE BORDERS

As the conclusion of Chapter 3 explains, we must set two borders. The outer border lets the Data Bank Xtract macro know the limits of the report. Without this knowledge, the macro won't extract and save your report properly. The inner border defines the print range for the printing macro.

Figure 5-2 shows these borders. Enter them as shown. As explained in Chapter 3, make sure that row 253 has no empty cells from column A through column BG. Also, make sure that you erase cell W265 as shown in Figure 5-2, and that the vertical lines in columns W and AB extend below the last lines of the report as shown.

COMPLETING AND SAVING THE REPORT

To save the Accounts Payable Management Analysis report, press ALT-M System Xtract. The first time you use these commands to save a new report, however, it is wise to use the STEP key to step through the macro execution. Chapter 3 explains this approach.

When you extract the report, only cell addresses are saved, not range names. The range names "belong" to the Data Bank spreadsheet. But the Data Bank has no need for the range names of the parameters (START, SCALE, and so on) that you have created. Therefore, if you intend to /File Save the current generation of your Data Bank, use /**R**ange **N**ame **D**elete to delete the range names shown in D257..D262 and Q256..Q260 of Figure 5-2.

Chapter
Six

REPORTING CASH FLOWS

Quoth the Banker, "Watch Cash Flow"

Once upon a midnight dreary as I pondered weak and weary
Over many a quaint and curious volume of accounting lore,
Seeking gimmicks (without scruple) to squeeze through some new
tax loophole,
Suddenly I heard a knock upon my door,
Only this, and nothing more.

Then I felt a queasy tingling and I heard the cash a-jingling
As a fearsome banker entered whom I'd often seen before.
His face was money-green and in his eyes there could be seen
Dollar-signs that seemed to glitter as he reckoned up the score.
"Cash flow," the banker said, and nothing more.

I had always thought it fine to show a jet black bottom line,
But the banker sounded a resounding, "No,
Your receivables are high, mounting upward toward the sky;
Write-offs loom. What matters is cash flow."
He repeated, "Watch cash flow."

Then I tried to tell the story of our lovely inventory
Which, though large, is full of most delightful stuff.
But the banker saw its growth, and with a mighty oath
He waved his arms and shouted, "Stop! Enough!
Pay the interest, and don't give me any guff!"

Next I looked for non-cash items which could add ad infinitum
To replace the ever-outward flow of cash,
But to keep my statement black I'd held depreciation back,
And my banker said that I'd done something rash.
He quivered, and his teeth began to gnash.

When I asked him for a loan, he responded, with a groan
That the interest rate would be just prime plus eight,
And to guarantee my purity he'd insist on some security—
All my assets plus the scalp upon my pate.
Only this, a standard rate.

Though my bottom line is black, I am flat upon my back,
My cash flows out and customers pay slow.
The growth of my receivables is almost unbelievable:
The result is certain—unremitting woe!
And I hear the banker utter an ominous low mutter,
"Watch cash flow."

Herbert S. Bailey, Jr.

Good advice. Owners of businesses, investors, managers, controllers, and bankers should try to follow it. But how? What are we supposed to watch? Where do we look? After all, accounting theorists have never produced a financial statement that clearly reports cash flows.

At first glance, producing a cash flow report does not seem like a major task. If our bank account balance increased one month, some might say that we had a positive cash flow; if it decreased, we had a negative cash flow.

But what if we had to borrow from the bank or sell some equipment to raise enough cash for payroll? Even if our bank account balance had increased somewhat by these efforts to raise cash, we would certainly seem to be suffering from negative cash flow. And what if the bank wouldn't loan us the cash, and no one could buy our equipment? If we persuaded our employees to accept our company's stock one week instead of cash, should this noncash payroll expense be classified as a "cash flow"?

Or what if we wanted to report the reasons for our cash outflows? Reporting that all our cash was used to reduce accounts payable explains very little. We would like to know instead the amount of cash we paid for inventory, for office expenses, and so on. Unfortunately, few accounting systems can give us this information.

The statement that comes closest to reporting, or explaining, what happened to our cash is the statement of changes in financial position. Some call it the statement of sources and uses of funds or, simply, the funds statement.

What does "funds" mean? The term is loosely defined as any means of payment. For example, you are said to have used funds if an asset increases. After all, for those assets you have exchanged cash, or a promise, or other assets, or *something*. Similarly, a decreasing asset is said to be a source of funds; directly or indirectly you receive something in exchange for the assets you've given up.

The funds statement represents a compromise. Though it doesn't tell us everything we would like to know about how we used our cash, it does tell us a great deal. In this chapter we will look at the standard funds statement, see how to automate its production by using the Data Bank, and then look at several ways to improve its ability to explain cash flows.

CREATING THE FUNDS STATEMENT

In its simplest form the funds statements shows the changes in the balance sheet accounts. This statement uses the following logic:

- Decreases in asset accounts and increases in liability accounts are a *source* of funds. We might cut our accounts receivable in half, for example, by receiving a large amount of customer payments. Or our loans payable might double because we have borrowed an additional amount of cash.
- Increases in asset accounts and decreases in liability accounts are a *use* of funds. If we drastically increase our inventory, for example, we will use a large amount of funds. Also, we must use funds to reduce our accounts payable.
- Since the balance sheet must always balance, the sum of the sources will always equal the sum of the uses of funds.

Before we use the Data Bank to produce a funds statement, let's produce a simplified version to illustrate the approach. Figure 6-1 shows the first step. When you begin this spreadsheet, set the global format to ,0 (comma zero) and set the width of column A to 25 characters.

Rows 3 through 10 of this figure show a simplified Income Statement; cells B17 through B30 show a beginning Balance Sheet; and cells C17 through C30 show an ending Balance Sheet. For every account in the Balance Sheet, the Change column (D) shows the ending balance minus the beginning balance.

The columns for the Source and Use of funds (E and F) use column G

```
                A                 B        C        D        E        F        G        H        I
 1 FIN1
 2
 3 Income Statement
 4 ========================
 5 Sales                               3,000
 6 COS                                 1,500
 7 MG&A                                  900
 8 Interest                               20
 9 Taxes                                 315
10 Profit                                265
11
12
13 Balance Sheet                                                        1=Asset
14 ========================                                            -1=Liab      B/S    Funds
15                              Begin.    End   Change   Source    Use  0=Total      Seq      Seq
16                        ------------------------------------------------------------------------
17 Cash                            30      10     (20)      20       0       1        1       10
18 Receivables                    410     500      90        0      90       1        2        3
19 Inventory                      235     300      65        0      65       1        3        4
20 Fixed Assets                   180     250      70        0      70       1        4        7
21 Accum Depr                     (80)   (100)    (20)      20       0       1        5        2
22 Total Assets                   775     960     185        0       0       0        6       99
23 A/P                            335     250     (85)       0      85      (1)       7        5
24 Other Liabilities               45      50       5        5       0      (1)       8        6
25 Long Term Debt                 170     160     (10)       0      10      (1)       9        8
26 Total Liabilities              550     460     (90)       0       0       0       10       99
27 Common Stock                    75      85      10       10       0      (1)      11        9
28 Retained Earnings              150     415     265      265       0      (1)      12        1
29 Net Worth                      225     500     275        0       0       0       13       99
30 Total                          775     960     185        0       0       0       14       99
31                                                    ------------------
32                                                         320     320

                             D17: +C17-B17
                             E17: @IF($G17*$D17<0,@ABS($D17),0)
                             F17: @IF($G17*$D17>0,@ABS($D17),0)
                             E32: @SUM(E31..E16)
                             F32: @SUM(F31..F16)
```

Figure 6-1. A statement of sources and uses of funds in balance sheet sequence

for guidance. There we have entered a value of 1 for asset accounts and a value of −1 for liability accounts. To understand why this guidance is necessary, look at cell D17. Cash has decreased by 20. If Cash were an asset, the decrease would represent a Source of funds and appear in column E. If Cash were a liability, the decrease would represent a Use of funds and appear in column F. With its value of 1, column G tells the formulas in E17 and F17 that Cash is indeed an asset.

Notice that column G also contains zeros. When we add up the sources and uses, we must ensure that we don't add the same account twice—once when it appears by itself and once when it is included as part of a total or subtotal. Therefore, as the title of column G shows, we have inserted a zero in column G for every row that contains a subtotal.

If your own balance sheet showed debits as positive and credits as negative, column G would still show the value of 0 for all totals and subtotals but would show the value of 1 for all other balance sheet accounts. If your balance sheet also excluded totals and subtotals, as in a typical trial balance, column G would contain the value of 1 throughout. In this case column G could be eliminated if the formulas for cells E17 and F17 were changed as follows and then copied down the remainder of their columns.

```
E17:  @IF($D17<0,@ABS($D17),0)
F17:  @IF($D17>0,$D17,0)
```

The final two columns in Figure 6-1 show sequence numbers. Column H shows the original Balance Sheet Sequence; its data was generated using the Data Fill command. Column I shows the sequence for the funds statement; its numbers were entered at the keyboard. What determines the sequence that we insert in column I? Though the sequence will vary from company to company, the funds statement usually begins with funds provided or used by activities having the most to do with the firm's operations and concludes with activities having the least to do with operations. Since the funds statement will use different subtotals than the balance sheet, we also insert 99s in all rows of column I that contain subtotals. This will move the subtotals out of our way when we sort on column I.

Figure 6-2 shows the balance sheet data from Figure 6-1 but sorted in the sequence of column I. The change in Retained Earnings is shown first. Largely, this change is equal to our operating income for the period. The change in Accumulated Depreciation, a noncash expense, is next. As in most funds statements, working capital accounts (current assets and current liabilities) follow.

Some statements then show external financing transactions and costs

	A	B	C	D	E	F	G	H	I	J
13	Balance Sheet						1=Asset			
14	======================						-1=Liab	B/S	Funds	Funds
15		Begin	End	Change	Source	Use	0=Total	Seq	Seq	Stmt
16										
17	Retained Earnings	150	415	265	265		(1)	12	1	265
18	Accum Depr	(80)	(100)	(20)	20		1	5	2	20
19	Receivables	410	500	90		90	1	2	3	(90)
20	Inventory	235	300	65		65	1	3	4	(65)
21	A/P	335	250	(85)		85	(1)	7	5	(85)
22	Other Liabilities	45	50	5	5		(1)	8	6	5
23	Fixed Assets	180	250	70		70	1	4	7	(70)
24	Long Term Debt	170	160	(10)		10	(1)	9	8	(10)
25	Common Stock	75	85	10	10		(1)	11	9	10
26	Cash	30	10	(20)	20		1	1	10	20
27	Total Assets	775	960	185				6	99	
28	Total Liabilities	550	460	(90)				10	99	
29	Net Worth	225	500	275				13	99	
30	Total	775	960	185				14	99	
31					----------	----------				
32					320	320				

Figure 6-2. A statement of sources and uses of funds sorted in the sequence that will be used in the final funds statement

before showing new investments; other statements instead show new investments, producing a subtotal for free cash flow—the cash flow generated by a firm before consideration of external financing costs and transactions. In Figure 6-2, however, we have only three additional transactions (shown in rows 23 through 25). When we produce this funds statement, therefore, we will group these together under the general heading of Other Sources and Uses.

Cash is shown as the last account, because it is essentially the result of the foregoing transactions. Below Cash, in rows 27 through 30, are the subtotals and totals used in the balance sheet. As explained previously, these have been sorted to the bottom so that they can be ignored in the analysis.

```
                          A                                B
 1 FIN2
 2
 3 Funds Statement
 4 =====================================
 5
 6
 7 Net Income After Taxes                                265
 8 Add: Depreciation                                      20
 9                                                 ---------
10 Funds Provided By Operations                          285
11
12
13 (Inc) Dec in Accounts Receivable                     (90)
14 (Inc) Dec in Inventory                               (65)
15 Inc (Dec) in Accounts Payable                        (85)
16 Inc (Dec) in Other Liabilities                         5
17                                                 ---------
18 Total Sources (Applications) of
19    Cash From (To) Working Capital                   (235)
20
21
22 (Purch) Sale of Fixed Assets                         (70)
23 Inc (Dec) of Long Term Debt                          (10)
24 Sell (Buy) Stock                                      10
25                                                 ---------
26 Total Other Sources (Uses) of Cash                   (70)
27
28                                                 ---------
29 Net Increase (Decrease) in Cash                      (20)
30
31 Beginning Cash                                        30
32
33 Ending Cash                                           10
```

Figure 6-3. A funds statement generated without using the Data Bank

Notice that a column J has been added in this figure. It is equal to the Sources minus the Uses. The data in this column is all that will survive when we produce the funds statement. To produce the column enter **+E17−F17** in cell J17. Copy this cell from J18 through J30. Notice that blanks appear where we would expect to see cells with zero balances. This is because, in order to produce Figure 6-2, the command /Worksheet Global Zero Yes was used. This command is found in 1-2-3 Version 2 but not in Version 1A.

Figure 6-3 shows our final funds statement. To create it, use **/F**ile **E**xtract **V**alues to save the range A13..J25 in Figure 6-2 as the file FIN2. Then retrieve FIN2 and delete columns **B** through **I**. Next, insert rows in the data, as shown in the figure, to make room for new subtotals and labels. Finally, increase the width of column A to 45, enter the descriptions as shown, and calculate the subtotals and totals that you see in rows 10, 19, 26, 29, and 33.

The formula for the Net Increase (Decrease) in Cash in row 29 is equal to the sum of the funds provided by operations plus the working capital sources plus the other sources. Ending Cash is equal to the value shown in Figure 6-1 for Beginning Cash (cell B17) plus the value calculated for Net Increase (Decrease) in Cash (cell B29 of Figure 6-3).

According to Figure 6-3, the firm earned $265. Adding Depreciation (a noncash expense) to this amount shows that the firm generated cash of approximately $285. It used this cash to increase its working capital by $235 and to buy fixed assets of $70. In all the firm used $20 more cash than it generated, so its cash balance fell from $30 to $10.

This approach can generate detailed and informative funds statements; however, each report takes too much professional time. Using the Data Bank to generate funds statements will reduce this problem.

USING THE DATA BANK TO PRODUCE THE FUNDS STATEMENT

Figure 6-4 shows a monthly funds statement produced by the Data Bank. The statement explains cash flow activity for the current month and current period to date, and for a preceding month and period to date. (The period can include any number of months for which you have data.) When we have completed this report, the entire spreadsheet will look like Figure 6-5. Let's see how we build it.

Acme Computers, Inc.
Changes in Financial Position

	Current Month Dec-85	Current YTD Jan-85 Dec-85	Comparison Month Dec-84	Comparison YTD Jan-84 Dec-84
Net Income After Taxes	19	202	15	96
Add: Depreciation & Amortization	11	102	8	75
Cash Generated From Operations	30	304	23	171
Source (Applications) of Cash From (To) Working Capital				
(Inc) Dec Accounts Receivable	-10	-165	-25	3
(Inc) Dec Inventory	-9	-59	-15	-12
(Inc) Dec Ppd Exp & Other Cur Exp	0	0	-3	-3
Inc (Dec) Accounts Payable	-31	72	0	10
Inc (Dec) P/R Taxes & Benefits	-1	13	1	-1
Inc (Dec) Accrued Income Tax	13	114	12	-24
Inc (Dec) Other Accrued Expenses	5	37	4	11
Total Sources (Applications) of Cash From (To) Working Capital	-33	12	-26	-16
Other Sources (Applications) of Cash				
Net (Purch) Sale of Fixed Assets	0	-262	0	-75
Other Sources (Applications)	1	-2	0	0
Total Other Sources (Applications)	1	-264	0	-75
Net Inc (Dec) in Cash From Operations	-2	52	-3	80
Inc (Dec) in Bank Loan				
Inc (Dec) In Notes Payable	18	32	9	-40
Inc (Dec) in Long Term Loans	-3	-32	-2	-28
Net Increase (Decrease) In Bank Loans	15	0	7	-68
Payment of Dividends	-15	-38	-3	-9
Net Inc (Dec) in Cash	-2	14	1	3
Beginning Cash Balance	45	29	28	26
Ending Cash Balance	43	43	29	29

Figure 6-4. A funds statement generated by the Data Bank

Enter the Data

Table 6-1 shows the categories of data that we will need for this report. If you have entered the sample Data Bank data from Appendix A, then you are ready to proceed. Otherwise, enter the data for these categories into your Data Bank.

```
          A                B                C  D   E   F   G   H     I                            J                         K         L        M         N         O         P    Q
250 -------------------------------------------------------------------------------------------------------------------------------------------------------------------------------------
251                                                MISC****     11                                            Dec-85                  47
252 -------------------------------------------------------------------------------------------------------------------------------------------------------------------------------------
253 REPORT            REP_MAC              ----------FIRS----FIRS--------              THIS_MO                         ---------- THIS_COL ------------------------------------------
254             {GOTO}a1~/WCR~             A           ****     11                                            Dec-85                  47                                     |        |
255             {RIGHT}/WCS26~             B                                                                                                                                 |        |
256             {RIGHT}/WCS2~              C -Summary Column-             Preliminary Calculations                                                                           |        |
257             {RIGHT}/WCS4~              D  Cur      Comp  Sign         ========================================                                                           |        |
258             {RIGHT}/WCS4~              E Mo  YTD  Mo  YTD Adj    DB#                                                                                                     |        |
259             {RIGHT}/WCS4~              F  2   2    6   6    1 100.100 Ending Cash Balance                            43        43                  29        29        |        |
260             {RIGHT}/WCS4~              G  3   5    7   9    1 100.100 Less: Change During the Period                 -2        14                   1         3        |        |
261             {RIGHT}/WCS4~              H                                                                    --------------------          --------------------           |        |
262             {RIGHT}/WCS8~              I                              Beginning Cash Balance                         45        29                  28        26        |        |
263             {RIGHT}/WCS40~             J                                                                                                                                 |        |
264             {RIGHT}/WCS10~             K                                                                                                                                 |        |
265             {RIGHT}/WCS10~             L                              ========================================================================================           |        |
266             {RIGHT}/WCS10~             M                                                                         Acme Computers, Inc.                                        |        |
267             {RIGHT}/WCS10~             N                                                                    Changes in Financial Position                                    |        |
268             {RIGHT}/WCS10~             O                                                                                                                                 |        |
269             {GOTO}REPORT~                                                                                          Current                      Comparison               |        |
270             /PPOML10~QR{BS}                                                                                 Month           YTD           Month          YTD             |        |
271             {UP}{END}{RIGHT}                                                                                             Jan-85                         Jan-84           |        |
272             {DOWN}{END}{LEFT}                                                                               Dec-85       Dec-85           Dec-84        Dec-84           |        |
273             {LEFT}{END}{DOWN}{END}                                                                                                                                       |        |
274             {LEFT}{DOWN}.{UP}             2   4    6   8    1 100.090 Net Income After Taxes                         19       202                  15        96        |        |
275             {END}{RIGHT}{LEFT}            3   5    7   9    1 105.060 Add:  Depreciation & Amortization              11       102                   8        75        |        |
276             {DOWN}{DOWN}{END}                                                                               --------------------          --------------------           |        |
277             {DOWN}{LEFT}~                                             Cash Generated From Operations                 30       304                  23       171        |        |
278             AGPQ/XR                                                                                                                                                      |        |
279                                                                                                                                                                          |        |
280                                                                       Source (Applications) of Cash                                                                      |        |
281                                                                         From (To) Working Capital                                                                        |        |
282                                                                       ----------------------------------------                                                           |        |
283                                           3   5    7   9   -1 105.010   (Inc) Dec  Accounts Receivable          -10      -165                 -25         3        |        |
284                                           3   5    7   9   -1 105.020   (Inc) Dec  Inventory                     -9       -59                 -15       -12        |        |
285                                           3   5    7   9   -1 105.030   (Inc) Dec  Ppd Exp & Other Cur Exp        0         0                  -3        -3        |        |
286                                           3   5    7   9    1 105.110   Inc (Dec)  Accounts Payable             -31        72                   0        10        |        |
287                                           3   5    7   9    1 105.120   Inc (Dec)  P/R Taxes & Benefits          -1        13                   1        -1        |        |
288                                           3   5    7   9    1 105.150   Inc (Dec)  Accrued Income Tax            13       114                  12       -24        |        |
289                                           3   5    7   9    1 105.130   Inc (Dec)  Other Accrued Expenses         5        37                   4        11        |        |
290                                                                                                             --------------------          --------------------           |        |
291                                                                       Total Sources (Applications) of                                                                    |        |
292                                                                         Cash From (To) Working Capital              -33        12                 -26       -16        |        |
293
```

	A	B	C	D	E	F	G	H	I	J	K	L	M	N	O	P	Q
294																	
295										Other Sources (Applications) of Cash							
296																	
297				3	5	7	9	-1	105.050	Net (Purch) Sale of Fixed Assets	0	-262		0	-75		
298				3	5	7	9	-1	105.080	Other Sources (Applications)	1	-2		0	0		
299																	
300										Total Other Sources (Applications)	1	-264		0	-75		
301																	
302																	
303										Net Inc (Dec) in Cash From Operations	-2	52		-3	80		
304																	
305										Inc (Dec) in Bank Loan							
306																	
307				3	5	7	9	1	105.100	Inc (Dec) In Notes Payable	18	32		9	-40		
308				3	5	7	9	1	105.160	Inc (Dec) in Long Term Loans	-3	-32		-2	-28		
309																	
310										Net Increase (Decrease) In Bank Loans	15	0		7	-68		
311																	
312				2	4	6	8	-1	199.010	Payment of Dividends	-15	-38		-3	-9		
313																	
314										Net Inc (Dec) in Cash	-2	14		1	3		
315																	
316										Beginning Cash Balance	45	29		28	26		
317																	
318										Ending Cash Balance	43	43		29	29		
319																	
320																	

Figure 6-5. The complete Data Bank report section for the funds statement

```
          A                  B                 C
250 ------------------------------------------------
251
252 ------------------------------------------------
253 REPORT                 REP_MAC              --
254              {GOTO}a1~/WCR~                 A
255              {RIGHT}/WCS26~                 B
256              {RIGHT}/WCS2~                  C
257              {RIGHT}/WCS4~                  D
258              {RIGHT}/WCS4~                  E
259              {RIGHT}/WCS4~                  F
260              {RIGHT}/WCS4~                  G
261              {RIGHT}/WCS4~                  H
262              {RIGHT}/WCS8~                  I
263              {RIGHT}/WCS40~                 J
264              {RIGHT}/WCS10~                 K
265              {RIGHT}/WCS10~                 L
266              {RIGHT}/WCS10~                 M
267              {RIGHT}/WCS10~                 N
268              {RIGHT}/WCS10~                 O
269              {GOTO}REPORT~/XQ
270              /PPOML10~QR{BS}
271              {UP}{END}{RIGHT}
272              {DOWN}{END}{LEFT}
273              {LEFT}{END}{DOWN}{END}
274              {LEFT}{DOWN}.{UP}
275              {END}{RIGHT}{LEFT}
276              {DOWN}{DOWN}{END}
277              {DOWN}{LEFT}~
278              AGPQ/XR
```

Figure 6-6. The report macros for the funds statement

As you can see, there is nothing sophisticated about these data categories. They are simply condensed versions of the income statements and balance sheets, plus a record of dividend payments and the serial number for each month's date. The financial information that you use, however, could be as complete as you wish.

Set the Columns

Begin with a Data Bank that is empty of reports. Figure 6-6 shows the top left corner of the report that we will add to the Data Bank. Rows 250 through 253 show the bottom of the Data Bank macro section. You will find the following discussion easier to follow if you insert the rows necessary at the bottom of your macro section to make the lines in your Data Bank match those in the figure.

Column B, from row 254 downward, holds the macro that we will use to set column widths and print the report. Enter this macro as shown. Also enter the letters shown for column C. These tell you which column each line of the macro is adjusting.

Notice the /XQ statement in cell B269. When you load an unfinished report, you will want to set the column widths and calculate the report section before you resume construction, but you won't want to print anything yet. Inserting the /XQ statement as shown allows you to do the former without the latter. Remove this temporary command after you finish your report.

After you enter this macro, press ALT-M System Report to use it to set your column widths.

Enter the Descriptions and Lookup Values

Enter the numbers and headings shown for the range D256..J262 in Figure 6-5. Let's take a closer look at what the numbers in this range mean.

The formulas in cells K259 through O262 find the beginning cash balances for each of the four periods that we are reporting. They do so by subtracting the change for each period from the balance at the end of the period.

Cells I259 and I260 hold the Data Bank number that the @VLOOKUP formulas in K259..O259 and K260..O260, respectively, use to find the proper row of data in the Data Bank. Table 6-1 shows that the number 100.100, used in both the cells in column I, is the DB# for the Cash account.

The numbers found in columns D, E, F, and G tell the @VLOOKUP formulas in columns K, L, N, and O, respectively, which column numbers to extract cash data from. For example, the number 2 in cell D259 tells the @VLOOKUP formula in K259 to extract the data from column number 2 of the DATA range. Table 6-2 tells us that column number 2 contains the ending balance for the current month.

The number 7 in cell F260 tells the @VLOOKUP formula in N260 to extract data from column number 7. Table 6-2 explains that this column contains the change from the previous month's balance.

Column H in Figure 6-5 (like column G in Figures 6-1 and 6-2) is used to adjust the signs of the data. Generally, this adjustment is necessary in the body of the report when an increase in a line item represents a use of funds. When you enter your own data, use this rule: if an increase in the balance of the item represents a source of funds, put a 1 in the cell in column H, but if an increase represents a use of funds, put in a −1.

For illustration, look at cell H274, the value for Net Income After Taxes.

DB#	Description
100.090	Net Earnings
100.100	Cash
105.010	Accounts Receivable
105.020	Inventories
105.030	Other Current Assets
105.050	Property, Plant, Equip
105.060	Accum Depreciation
105.080	Other Assets
105.100	Notes Payable
105.110	Accounts Payable
105.120	Payroll Taxes & Benefits
105.130	Other Accrued Liab
105.150	Deferred Income Taxes
105.160	Long Term Debt
199.010	Dividends Paid
900.010	Date (15th of Month)

Table 6-1. Data Bank Numbers Used by the Funds Statement

Since an increase in Net Income After Taxes represents a source of funds, H274 contains a 1. Now look at H283. Since an increase in Accounts Receivable represents a use of funds, H283 contains a −1. However, because we are simply calculating a Beginning Cash Balance in rows 259 and 260, we leave the values positive in column H.

Let's enter the formulas for rows 259 and 260 before continuing with the rest of the report.

Enter the Formulas

Although the following formulas are displayed in two lines, enter them as one line in the cell.

K259: @IF(@VLOOKUP($I259,$DATA,0)=$I259,
@VLOOKUP($I259,$DATA,D259),@NA)*$H259

L259: @IF(@VLOOKUP($I259,$DATA,0)=$I259,
@VLOOKUP($I259,$DATA,E259),@NA)*$H259

N259: @IF(@VLOOKUP($I259,$DATA,0)=$I259,
@VLOOKUP($I259,$DATA,F259),@NA)*$H259

O259: @IF(@VLOOKUP($I259,$DATA,0)=$I259,
@VLOOKUP($I259,$DATA,G259),@NA)*$H259

Current Period	*Comparison Period*	*For Data That Consists Of Account Balances*	*For Data That Consists of Accounting Transactions*
2	6	Ending balance for month. (June's inventory balance.)*	Activity for the month. (June's sales.)
3	7	Change from previous month's balance. (Amount by which inventory increased during June.)	Change from previous month's activity.** (Amount by which June's sales exceeded May's sales.)
4	8	Sum of all ending balances in the period.** (Sum of the inventory balances for April, May, and June.)	The Period-to-Date activity. (The total sales for April, May, and June.)
5	9	Change in the balance from the beginning of the period through the end of the period. (The amount of increase of June inventory over the inventory on the last day of March.)	The amount by which the current month's activity exceeds the activity one month prior to the beginning of the period.** (The amount by which June's sales exceed March's sales.)

*Examples in parentheses reflect the period April-June of any year.

**Seldom used.

Table 6-2. Interpretation of Summary Data Found in Columns 2-9 (C-J) of the DATA Range of the Data Bank

To get an idea of how these formulas work, take a closer look at the formula in K259. Notice that the formula uses two @VLOOKUP functions contained within an @IF function. The first @VLOOKUP function looks up the Data Bank number 100.100 in the Data Bank. If the function finds this number in the Data Bank, the formula looks up the information we need about the Ending Cash Balance. But if the function doesn't find this number in the Data Bank, the formula returns NA.

This two-step approach is the safest way to handle most @VLOOKUP and @HLOOKUP functions, for the following reason: if 1-2-3 doesn't find an exact match for the Data Bank Number you look up, it settles for the previous Data Bank number. Without the two-step test, therefore, you won't know whether the data returned by your lookup function is for the number you want or for a different number entirely.

One problem with this two-step approach is that by doubling the number of lookups, it slows the calculation time. It also makes the formulas longer than we would like, which consumes extra memory. To conserve memory, therefore, most Data Bank reports in this book do not use the two-step approach. After you add the various reports, you may want to change their formulas to this safer approach.

To complete the Preliminary Calculations section, copy the range K259..O259 to K260 and draw the underlines as shown in row 260. Finally, enter +K259−K260 into K262 and then copy this formula to L262, N262, and O262. The resulting numbers should be equal to the ending balances in your cash account for the months preceding the periods you are reporting.

Complete the Report

Draw the double line as shown in row 265 of Figure 6-5; then enter the report headings. Next enter the formulas we use to look up the report dates from the Data Bank. We can look up the report dates because each month we add the date serial number for the fifteenth of that month to the Data Bank. (We use the fifteenth so we can assume, with confidence, that all months have the same number of days: 365/12, or approximately 30.4 days.)

The first two of the following formulas calculate the date for the beginning of the period. They do this by first looking up the date for the ending period and then by looking up and subtracting the time that has elapsed since the beginning of the period. Since the resulting date will always be the month prior to the beginning of the period, we must add 30.4 days to this value. The remaining four formulas simply look up the proper dates. Here are the formulas.

L271: (D3) @VLOOKUP(900.01,$DATA,2)−@VLOOKUP(900.01,$DATA,5)+30.4
O271: (D3) @VLOOKUP(900.01,$DATA,6)−@VLOOKUP(900.01,$DATA,9)+30.4
K272: (D3) @VLOOKUP(900.01,$DATA,2)
L272: (D3) @VLOOKUP(900.01,$DATA,2)
N272: (D3) @VLOOKUP(900.01,$DATA,6)
O272: (D3) @VLOOKUP(900.01,$DATA,6)

Next, enter the headings, numbers, and descriptions that you see in columns D through J. When all numbers and descriptions have been entered, copy the formulas in the range K259..0259 to K274..K275, to K283..K290, to K297..K298, to K307..K308, and to K312. Then enter the underlines as shown.

The formulas beneath the underlines are what you would expect from the descriptions in column J. With four exceptions the formulas are simple @SUMs of the blocks of data above each underline. The exceptions are

K303: +K277+K292+K300
K314: @SUM(K303,K309..K313)
K316: +K262
K318: @IF(K316+K314=K259,K259,@ERR)

The last formula is the only one that may need some explanation. This formula compares the calculated ending cash balance with the actual ending cash balance. If the two results agree, it returns the actual cash balance. If they disagree, it returns an ERR.

When you build this report, you may prefer to use the formula +K316+K314 in cell K318 and then put +K259 in cell K320. Doing so allows you to compare the actual results yourself, using any differences between the numbers to help you to find the errors in your report. When the report checks out, you can change K318 to the final version shown above and erase K320.

These formulas, of course, should be copied to the appropriate cells of columns L, N, and O.

Find and Correct Your Mistakes

When you construct your own report, you will make mistakes. Generally, these fall into three categories.

1. Errors in the formulas. In the Data Bank there are two sets of formulas to worry about: the formulas in columns C through J, which summarize the data, and the @VLOOKUP formulas in the report, which extract the data. If your data looks wrong, follow it from the Data Bank data section through the summary section to the report. Is each formula doing what it should?

2. Errors in the data. Does your balance sheet data balance? Do your assets equal your liabilities and equity? Is your problem a simple data entry error?

3. Errors in using 1-2-3 procedures. When printing the final displays for this chapter, I suddenly realized that one report didn't balance. Panic! I had spent days finding and debugging every conceivable error, and yet the darned thing didn't balance. After a frenzy of checking, I found that I had made the most elementary of spreadsheet errors: I had changed a minor formula and failed to recalculate the report. In a general sense, I should have asked myself, "Is there anything that I've forgotten to do to make the spreadsheet work properly?" More specifically, I should have realized, "When in doubt, recalculate."

Add the Borders

Our final step is to add the two right-hand borders as shown in Figure 6-5. The System-Xtract macro uses the outside border as a path to find the bottom right corner of the range it uses to save the report as a separate spreadsheet. The printing macro, shown in Figure 6-6, uses the inside border as a path for defining the print range.

To add the borders, enter ^| (centered vertical line) in cell Q253. Copy it from Q254 to Q320; then copy Q253..Q320 to P253. Next, use /**R**ange **E**rase to erase cells P266 and P320. Cell P266 marks the top row of the print range; erasing cell P320 allows P319 to mark the bottom row of the print range.

Now when you use ALT-M System Xtract, the macros will save your Changes in Financial Position report under the name you specify.

LIMITATIONS OF THE FUNDS STATEMENT

The funds statement tells us more about the flow of cash within a firm than we can easily obtain by looking at the income statement and balance sheet. It's a help, but it's also flawed in at least two ways.

First, the statement oversimplifies the reasons for the changes in the account balances. In Figure 6-3, for example, the $70 increase in Fixed Asset balance was explained as a purchase of $70 of assets. But each of the following transactions could produce the same results shown in the figure:

- Sold $100 of old fixed assets and purchased $170 of new fixed assets.
- Traded $70 of inventory for $70 of fixed assets and then purchased an additional $135 of inventory.
- Reduced fixed assets by $50 when a vendor repossessed the equipment and bought $120 of fixed assets, paying $110 in cash and $10 in stock.

In other words, many important facts may be hidden by our funds statement.

The second flaw is that the statement doesn't show *cash* flows—it shows *funds* flows. If the statement showed cash flows, it would show collections from customers and then payments for goods sold, for operating expenses, fixed assets, taxes, and so on. As explained earlier however, we must compromise with a funds statement because most accounting systems cannot produce the data that a true cash flow statement needs.

IMPROVING THE FUNDS STATEMENT

If we look at the funds statement *as a funds statement,* there are several things we can do. One is to rearrange the data in the report, producing a version that more closely fits the way your own firm manages its cash. This is equivalent to inserting different sequence numbers in column I of Figures 6-1 and 6-2. The discussions of these figures mentioned a few of the many different ways the data could be arranged.

Another way to improve the report is to produce it monthly. Too often, the funds statement is a report that the auditors produce at year end and that management generally ignores. But when the statement is produced monthly, its summary approach can provide a good overall picture of what is happening with the firm's funds.

If we look at the funds statement as a *cash flow report,* there is one approach we can take to improve it. We can record in the Data Bank, and then the report, the "in and out" transactions that produce many of the changes in the balance sheet accounts.

To illustrate a funds statement showing these changes, suppose our income statement concludes as follows:

Net Income Before Taxes	$100
Provision for Income Taxes	$ 55
Net Income After Taxes	$ 45

Suppose also that our account for accrued income taxes payable decreased from $60 to $20 during the period. In a normal funds statement, we would show these two facts as on the following page.

Funds Provided by Operations	$ 45
Increase (Decrease) In Tax Liability	$ 40
Net Increase in Cash	$ 5

However, the ending tax liability is equal to the beginning tax liability plus provision for taxes less income tax payments. Income tax payments are therefore equal to the provision for taxes minus the increase in tax liability; in our example, then, actual tax payments are equal to $55 minus $−40, or $95. Our revised funds statement can therefore read

Funds Provided by Operations	$100
Payment of Income Taxes	$−95
Net Increase in Cash	$ 5

Although the final number is the same, this approach provides a much clearer idea of what actually happened to our firm's cash. Notice, by the way, that the final example redefines Funds Provided by Operations. Since there is no formal definition of the term, we can use any definition that makes sense to us.

We can show the changes for several different categories of cash transactions. In some cases, as with fixed assets, we must record in the Data Bank the changes in the accounts that were caused by the purchase, sale, and retirement of assets. Recording these changes will allow us to explain clearly just why the balance in our fixed asset account changed as it did.

Unfortunately, we can't easily track the changes that would allow us to calculate, for example, cash paid for inventory purchases, because purchases generally go into accounts payable. When this happens, few accounting systems bother to track the data that tells us the reason for the invoice. Thus, when we write checks, we know who we pay and how much, but not why we are paying each invoice. In other words, most accounting systems cannot tell us how many dollars in checks we have written for inventory purchases, for operating expenses, for the purchase of fixed assets, and so on.

However, some of the newer accounting systems using relational data bases can (with a little programming) generate the reports that we need. If you have such a system, the Data Bank can help you to turn this monthly data into worthwhile information. To use this data for cash reporting add all relevant categories of sources and uses of cash to your Data Bank.

Sources might include cash sales, collection of receivables, sales of assets; uses could include cash paid for inventory, for operating expenses, and for customer refunds. Then, each month, use your accounting system report generator to summarize the activity in these categories. Finally, when you update your Data Bank with this information, you can use the methods described in this chapter to report true cash flows for any period that you wish.

Chapter
Seven

SCHEDULING YOUR CASH REQUIREMENTS

This short chapter describes a template that I have used for several years. It solves two related problems that I once had when I paid company bills.

One problem was that we kept forgetting to pay monthly bills to people who didn't send us monthly invoices. When your landlord or banker calls to ask why no check has been sent, a response like "Well, um, you see, I forgot" tends to complicate the business relationship.

The second problem was that we were short of cash. Occasionally, this was caused by business problems, but usually it was caused by timing problems. If we were short of cash, it was because we hadn't realized that so many bills in addition to accounts payable and payroll were all due in the same week.

Before the age of computerized spreadsheets, I tried to maintain a schedule of these cash requirements by hand. It never worked. I could never take the time to write out new schedules when the old ones expired.

But the microcomputer enables us to solve the problem. Figure 7-1 shows my solution. This Scheduled Payments Calendar lets 1-2-3 do all the work in scheduling payments. I just have to make sure each payment schedule is correct and then find the cash that it tells me to pay.

Though I first created the calendar to control cash obligations for which there are no invoices, I quickly expanded its use. Many services, like telephone and utilities, send invoices requiring payment almost immediately. And many periodic state and local taxes are billed at the last moment. I needed some method to plan for these obligations as well.

Scheduled Payments Calendar

Scheduled Monthly

Payee	Reason	Date to Pay	Pay Every	GL Acct	Amount	Monday 16-Feb-87	Monday 23-Feb-87	Monday 02-Mar-87	Monday 09-Mar-87	Monday 16-Mar-87	Monday 23-Mar-87
1st National Bank	Loan	30	1	Misc	$1,219.50		$1,219.50				
Walter R. Smith	Loan	15	1	Misc	$2,000.00				$2,000.00		
Universal Reostat	Loan	1	1	Misc	$8,550.00		$8,550.00				
Mt Bell	406-555-1234	23	1	6553	$220.00		$220.00				$220.00
GTE	805-555-4431	17	1	7553	$2,300.00	$2,300.00				$2,300.00	
Pac Tel	213-555-9812	26	1	6553	$1,500.00		$1,500.00				$1,500.00
Tri-State Leasing	Bob's Chrysler	2	1	7621	$325.00			$325.00			
Acme Accep Corp	Sam's Olds	30	1	6621	$305.00		$305.00				
City Electronics	Lease Oscilscp	10	1	5672	$275.00				$275.00		
ABS Real Estate	Lodi Rent	1	1	5621	$1,255.16		$1,255.16				
Alex Jones	Sales Off Rent	15	1	7621	$835.00				$835.00		
SW Fidelity	Car Insurance	6	12	2455	$1,150.00						
Wells Insurance	General Liab	20	3	2455	$3,300.00	$3,300.00					
Bibb Electronics	AP Paydown	10	6	2302	$4,817.50						
Universal Milling	AP Paydown	30	2	2302	$3,000.00		$3,000.00				
Cal Edison	Sales Off Elect	22	1	6435	$110.00	$110.00				$110.00	
Schure's Hauling	Lodi Trash	30	4	6527	$63.00						
B. Attkinson	Quar Royalty	1	3	2498	$4,850.88						
Clark County	Midvale Prop Tax	15	12	7805	$7,398.16						
					$43,474.20	$5,710.00	$16,049.66	$325.00	$3,110.00	$2,410.00	$1,720.00

Scheduled Weekly

Payee	Reason	Day to Pay	Pay Every	GL Acct	Amount	16-Feb-87	23-Feb-87	02-Mar-87	09-Mar-87	16-Mar-87	23-Mar-87
Chem Corp	AP Paydown	Mon	3	2303	$1,219.50	$1,219.50			$1,219.50		
Smith Packaging	AP Paydown	Mon	1	2303	$150.00	$150.00	$150.00	$150.00	$150.00	$150.00	$150.00
B. Attkinson	Royalty Payment	Fri	6	2497	$955.00	$955.00					
					$2,324.50	$2,324.50	$150.00	$150.00	$1,369.50	$150.00	$150.00
	Total Cash Requirements Per Week:					$8,034.50	$16,199.66	$475.00	$4,479.50	$2,560.00	$1,870.00

Figure 7-1. An illustration of the Scheduled Payments Calendar

My cash calendar now controls rent and lease payments, loan payments, telephone and utility charges, property taxes, royalty payments, insurance payments, and so on. Each of these items resides in my calendar. When a due date for an item falls within six weeks of the current date, the amount due appears in the schedule. And when the due date falls within the current week, I pay the item. Paying even large obligations has become less of a problem now because I always have six weeks advance notice that an obligation is falling due.

USING THE SCHEDULED PAYMENTS CALENDAR

To use the calendar, I retrieve it and enter the new beginning date. When I CALC the spreadsheet, 1-2-3 inserts the new dates, the weekly increments, at the head of the columns and then drops in the proper amounts to be paid each week. Then I print the calendar, getting something like what is shown in the figure.

I keep a copy of this printout to use in my weekly cash requirements forecast. This handwritten forecast summarizes data from the calendar, from payroll, from our accounts payable aging, and from my list of special cash requirements. In these forecasts I always make sure that the calendar doesn't duplicate obligations that are also included in the accounts payable aging.

Every week or two, the accounts payable supervisor gets two copies of the Scheduled Payments Calendar. She uses one copy as a checklist for making the scheduled payments. In general, when we book an invoice into A/P that is listed on the calendar, the amount on the calendar is marked off with a yellow highlighter. When we pay an obligation directly from the calendar, it is marked off with a green highlighter. This method makes it easy to tell whether an obligation was paid with cash or was simply "paid" by being transferred to A/P.

Within two weeks, this copy is so marked up that it is of no use to anyone but the supervisor who marked it, which is why she gets two copies. On the second copy she maintains any changes that need to be made to update the calendar. There are always changes. Sometimes our estimates for the telephone bills and utilities need to be revised; sometimes we add vendors; and sometimes, glory be, we pay off a loan and eliminate a payment.

Some Explanations

When you look closely at Figure 7-1, some of the rows and columns will need explanation. In the Scheduled Monthly section, the Date to Pay is the day of the month that a check should be sent. The Pay Every column gives the frequency of payment: a bill paid every month has a 1 in this column; a bill paid every other month has a 2; a bill paid yearly has a 12; and so on.

The Pay Every column in the Scheduled Weekly section uses the same approach but refers to weeks, not months. Your company may not need to use the Scheduled Weekly section at all. It is part of my template because I once worked for a company with very seasonal sales. During the hard times, we would talk vendors into accepting small amounts every week or two until their bills were paid. This section kept track of those commitments.

Figure 7-1 uses the /Worksheet Global Zero Yes command to display blanks in all cells containing a zero value. This command is available only to users of Version 2. Figure 7-2 shows what the calendar looks like when this command is not used.

The Beginning Date, shown in column A of Figure 7-2, is the starting point, or anniversary date, for both Pay Every columns. This date need not be the original beginning date. As payment schedules are changed, this date should be changed to represent a reference point for the new schedule.

The GL Acct column solves a minor problem that I have had with periodic payments. Frequently, it isn't obvious to the A/P clerk which General Ledger Account number should be used when a payment is made. An insurance payment, for example, could debit an asset, liability, or expense account. Adding the General Ledger Account number to the schedule allows me to better control this A/P activity. But when multiple account numbers are used for the same payment, we insert Misc as shown.

BUILDING THE CALENDAR TEMPLATE

To start to build a calendar of your own, look at Figure 7-2. This figure shows the complete calendar spreadsheet. Before you do anything else, use the /**W**orksheet **G**lobal **R**ecalculation **M**anual command to go to manual recalculation. Unless you have plenty of time to kill, this should be your first step in nearly every spreadsheet you create.

	A	B	C	D	E	F	G	H	I	J	K	L	M	N
1	CALENDAR				DAYS Table:		Monday	Tuesday	Wednesday	Thursday	Friday	Saturday	Sunday	
2														
3								16-Feb	23-Feb	02-Mar	09-Mar	16-Mar	23-Mar	30-Mar
4														
5		Beginning Date												
6							Pay from:	16	23	2	9	16	23	30
7		Calendar begins with this	>	Day:	16 |		Pay to:	23	32	9	16	23	30	32
8		date. Change it, then	>	Month:	2 |									
9		recalculate.	>	Year:	87 |		Pay from:	16	1	2	9	16	23	1
10							Pay to:	23	2	9	16	23	30	0
11														
12														
13							Scheduled Payments Calendar							
14														
15		Scheduled Monthly												
16														
17	Beginning			Date	Pay	GL		Monday	Monday	Monday	Monday	Monday	Monday	
18	Date	Payee	Reason	to Pay	Every	Acct	Amount	16-Feb-87	23-Feb-87	02-Mar-87	09-Mar-87	16-Mar-87	23-Mar-87	
19														
20	30-Jul-84	1st National Bank	Loan	30	1	Misc	$1,219.50	$0.00	$1,219.50	$0.00	$0.00	$0.00	$0.00	
21	13-Jan-81	Walter R. Smith	Loan	15	1	Misc	$2,000.00	$0.00	$0.00	$0.00	$2,000.00	$0.00	$0.00	
22	03-Nov-78	Universal Reostat	Loan	1	1	Misc	$8,550.00	$0.00	$8,550.00	$0.00	$0.00	$0.00	$0.00	
23	23-Apr-82	Mt Bell	406-555-1234	23	1	6553	$220.00	$0.00	$220.00	$0.00	$0.00	$0.00	$220.00	
24	10-Oct-84	GTE	805-555-4431	17	1	7553	$2,300.00	$2,300.00	$0.00	$0.00	$0.00	$2,300.00	$0.00	
25	01-Jul-83	Pac Tel	213-555-9812	26	1	6553	$1,500.00	$0.00	$1,500.00	$0.00	$0.00	$0.00	$1,500.00	
26	30-Mar-81	Tri-State Leasing	Bob's Chrysler	2	1	7621	$325.00	$0.00	$0.00	$325.00	$0.00	$0.00	$0.00	
27	30-Jan-84	Acme Accep Corp	Sam's Olds	30	1	6621	$305.00	$0.00	$305.00	$0.00	$0.00	$0.00	$0.00	
28	03-Nov-85	City Electronics	Lease Oscilscp	10	1	5672	$275.00	$0.00	$0.00	$0.00	$275.00	$0.00	$0.00	
29	30-Sep-84	ABS Real Estate	Lodi Rent	1	1	5621	$1,255.16	$0.00	$1,255.16	$0.00	$0.00	$0.00	$0.00	
30	15-Jan-80	Alex Jones	Sales Off Rent	15	1	7621	$835.00	$0.00	$0.00	$0.00	$835.00	$0.00	$0.00	
31	04-Nov-84	SW Fidelity	Car Insurance	6	12	2455	$1,150.00	$0.00	$0.00	$0.00	$0.00	$0.00	$0.00	
32	23-Aug-82	Wells Insurance	General Liab	20	3	2455	$3,300.00	$3,300.00	$0.00	$0.00	$0.00	$0.00	$0.00	
33	10-May-84	Bibb Electronics	AP Paydown	10	6	2302	$4,817.50	$0.00	$0.00	$0.00	$0.00	$0.00	$0.00	
34	01-Jun-82	Universal Milling	AP Paydown	30	2	2302	$3,000.00	$0.00	$3,000.00	$0.00	$0.00	$0.00	$0.00	
35	03-Mar-81	Cal Edison	Sales Off Elect	22	1	6435	$110.00	$110.00	$0.00	$0.00	$0.00	$110.00	$0.00	
36	30-Nov-79	Schure's Hauling	Lodi Trash	30	4	6527	$63.00	$0.00	$0.00	$0.00	$0.00	$0.00	$0.00	
37	03-Jan-82	B. Attkinson	Quar Royalty	1	3	2498	$4,850.88	$0.00	$0.00	$0.00	$0.00	$0.00	$0.00	
38	15-Nov-78	Clark County	Midvale Prop Tax	15	12	7805	$7,398.16	$0.00	$0.00	$0.00	$0.00	$0.00	$0.00	
39														
40							$43,474.20	$5,710.00	$16,049.66	$325.00	$3,110.00	$2,410.00	$1,720.00	
41														

	A	B	C	D	E	F	G	H	I	J	K	L	M	N
42														
43		Scheduled Weekly												
44														
45	Beginning			Day	Pay	GL								
46	Date	Payee	Reason	to Pay	Every	Acct	Amount	16-Feb-87	23-Feb-87	02-Mar-87	09-Mar-87	16-Mar-87	23-Mar-87	
47														
48	16-Jul-84	Chem Corp	AP Paydown	Mon	3	2303	$1,219.50	$1,219.50	$0.00	$0.00	$1,219.50	$0.00	$0.00	
49	20-Jul-84	Smith Packaging	AP Paydown	Mon	1	2303	$150.00	$150.00	$150.00	$150.00	$150.00	$150.00	$150.00	
50	25-Jan-82	B. Attkinson	Royalty Payment	Fri	6	2497	$955.00	$955.00	$0.00	$0.00	$0.00	$0.00	$0.00	
51														
52							$2,324.50	$2,324.50	$150.00	$150.00	$1,369.50	$150.00	$150.00	
53														
54														
55														
56			Total Cash Requirements Per Week:					$8,034.50	$16,199.66	$475.00	$4,479.50	$2,560.00	$1,870.00	
57														

Figure 7-2. The complete spreadsheet that produces the Scheduled Payments Calendar

Set the global column width to 11 spaces. Set other column widths as follows:

Column	*Width*
A	10
B	19
C	16
D	6
E	7
F	6

Once you have your own data in the calendar, you will want to adjust these widths. But remember, if you make the first six columns too wide, your printer will not be able to print as many columns of the calendar.

As in most of my spreadsheets, cell A1 has the name of the spreadsheet. I called this one CALENDAR. Enter any name that you wish. Next, fill in the beginning Day, Month, and Year and their values, as shown in D7 through E9. These are the dates that you change to update the calendar. Enter the headings and explanations for these dates as shown.

If you have 1-2-3 Version 2, you can display the days of the week as shown in row 17. To do this, enter the **DAYS Table:** description in E1. Enter " **Monday**" in G1, " **Tuesday**" in H1, and so on. Notice that a space has been inserted between the opening quotation mark and the day. This improves the appearance when the day names are used in row 17. After the day names have been entered, use **/R**ange **N**ame **C**reate to assign the range name DAYS to G1 through M1.

Go to H3. Format this cell and I3 as /Range Format Date 2. The formula in H3 is @DATE($E$9,$E$8,$E$7). The formula in I3 is 7+H3. Copy I3 from J3 through N3.

Each of the formulas in H20 through M38 (which we discuss shortly) decides whether it is time to pay an obligation. To make this decision, the formula asks, "Is the Date to Pay greater than or equal to today's day of the month and less than next week's day of the month?" If all dates fall within the same month, it isn't difficult to write a formula to express this question.

However, column I of Figure 7-2 presents a challenge. In this column we must pay all bills with a Date to Pay of 1 and of 23 through 31. Since two sets of dates belong in this column, the formulas in H20..M38 must make two sets of comparisons. The formulas make one comparison with the numbers in H6..N7 and another comparison with H9..N10.

To enter the range G6..N10, type the labels as shown in G6 through G10. Enter the formulas for H6 through H10 shown in Figure 7-3. (A brief explanation of each formula is included in the figure.) Then copy the formulas from column I through column N.

Notice in Figure 7-2 that the calendar ends in column M. The preceding formulas were copied in one extra column, to column N, because each formula needs to look one column ahead. When you read the formulas and explanations in Figures 7-3 and 7-4, you'll see why this is necessary.

You are now ready to create the Scheduled Monthly section.

The Scheduled Monthly Section

Put in the headings as shown in Figure 7-2. The dates above the columns use the same formulas as in row 3. They are formatted, however, as /Range Format Date 1.

The day names in H17 through M17 serve two purposes. First, they reassure you that the Beginning Date you have entered was indeed a Monday. Second, they remind users of the calendar that each date shown is a Monday. Figure 7-3 shows the formulas for H17 and I17. If you have 1-2-3 Version 2, enter these formulas and then copy I17 to J17 through M17. If you have 1-2-3 Version 1A, you may simply wish to enter " Monday" into these cells.

Enter the first three rows of data from Beginning Date through Amount, columns A through G, rows 20 through 22. Then look at Figure 7-4, which shows the formula contained in H20. Although it's a long formula, it makes more sense when you see it in small pieces as in the figure. When you enter the formula, you can enter it from the pieces. Just make sure that you don't leave any blank spaces in the formula when you enter it.

Two aspects of the @MOD function in this formula may need additional explanation. The first aspect is the @MOD function itself. As the 1-2-3 user's manual explains, @MOD(X,Y) returns the remainder of X/Y. In other words, @MOD(15,7) returns 1; @MOD(28,7) returns 0; and so on. In cell H20 we calculate the number of months since the beginning date; if this number is evenly divisible by the Pay Every amount, it is time to pay again.

The second aspect appears near the end of the @MOD formula: +($D20<H$6). This logical formula returns a value of 1 if the statement is true and 0 if the statement is false. Without this adjustment, the calculation for the number of months would be incorrect when payments are due early in the month and the week in which they are due begins in a previous

Formulas for sets of dates

Formula	Explanation
H6: @DAY(H3)	This Monday's date.
H7: @IF(H6>I6,32,I6)	If next Monday is in a new month, put "32" here, otherwise, put next Monday's date.
H9: @IF(H6>I6,1,H6)	If next Monday is in a new month, put "1" here, otherwise, put this Monday's date.
H10: @DAY(I3)	Next Monday's date.
H17: @INDEX($DAYS,@MOD(H18-@DATE(0,1,2),7),0)	Find the day for H18 in the DAYS table. Its position in the table is equal to the remainder found by dividing the number of days since the first Monday in 1900, January 2, by 7 days per week.
I17: +H17	The day of the week one week ago.

Figure 7-3. Formulas and explanations for the dates at the top of the calendar

month. The need for this adjustment is similar to the need to compare the Date to Pay to two sets of dates rather than one.

After the formula in H20 appears to be working, copy it from I20 to M20; then copy this row from H21 to H22. If you get the same numbers as in Figure 7-2, you've probably entered the formula properly. Once you get the formulas working, enter the rest of your data and then copy the formula down the spreadsheet as necessary.

Next, use the @SUM function to total the columns. When you do so, make sure that your @SUM range does *not* include the date heading the column. The date, remember, has a numeric value which will distort your @SUM. (No sense making your weekly cash requirements look worse than they actually are.) You are now ready to create the Scheduled Weekly section.

The Scheduled Weekly Section

Copy the column headings from the monthly schedule to the weekly schedule. Then, change the Date to Pay column heading in the weekly schedule to read Day to Pay.

Enter the three rows of data from Beginning Date through the Amount. Then enter the formula for H48 as shown in Figure 7-4. As you see, this formula is shorter than the formula for H20. Copy the formula and calculate your @SUMs as shown. As in the monthly section, make sure your @SUM range does not include the date. Put in your Total Cash Requirements per Week, row 56. This row is simply the sum of the monthly section and the weekly section (for example, the formula in H56 is +H40+H52).

If you have 1-2-3 Version 1A, you are done. If you have Version 2, you may want to use the /**W**orksheet **G**lobal **Z**ero **Y**es command. As explained earlier, this command tells your spreadsheet to display and print all zero-value cells as blanks.

When you print your Scheduled Payments Calendar, define your print range so that your calendar displays the rows and columns shown in Figure 7-1. You will have to use the compressed print feature on your printer. And before you print, be sure to CALC your spreadsheet. If you are like me, you'll probably forget to do this. That's why I use a simple little calc-and-print macro like the one that follows. To use the macro, use the /**R**ange **N**ame **C**reate command to define PRINTHIS as the range you want to

Scheduled Monthly formula in H20

```
@IF((($D20>=H$6#AND#$D20<H$7)#OR#($D20>=H$9#AND#$D20<H$10))#AND#@MOD(@MONTH(H$18)-@MONTH($A20)+12*(@YEAR(H$18)-@YEAR($A20))+
($D20<H$6),$E20)=0,$G20,0)
```

```
              Formula                                    Explanation
--------------------------------------     ------------------------------------------------
    @IF(                                   If:
       (($D20>=H$6 #AND# $D20<H$7)           / "Date" is between the first set of dates,
                #OR#                         |     or
        ($D20>=H$9 #AND# $D20<H$10))         \ "Date" is between the second set of dates,

                #AND#                             And:

       @MOD(                                 /
           @MONTH(H$18)                      |  /
          -@MONTH($A20)                      |  |
          +12*(                              |  |the number of months since the Beginning Date,
                @YEAR(H$18)                  |  |
               -@YEAR($A20))                 |  |
          +($D20<H$6),                       |  \
          $E20)                              | divided by the "Pay Every" figure,
        =0,                                  | leaves a remainder of zero,
                                             \
       $G20,                               Then put the "Amount" here;
       0)                                  Otherwise, put Zero.
```

Scheduled Weekly formula in H48

```
@IF(@MOD(@INT((H$46-$A48)/7),$E48)=0,$G48,0)
```

Formula	Explanation
@IF(	If:
@MOD(	/
@INT((H$46-$A48)/7),	| the number of completed weeks since the Beginning Date,
$E48)	| divided by the "Pay Every" figure,
=0,	| leaves a remainder of Zero,
	\
$G48,	Then put the "Amount" here;
0)	Otherwise, put Zero.

Figure 7-4. Formulas and explanations for the calculations within the body of the calendar

print. Then use this macro:

```
\a            {CALC}
              /PPRprinthis~AGPPQ
              /XQ
```

This macro will CALC your spreadsheet, print the range named PRINTHIS, and issue two form-feed commands to your printer.

Once you have everything working, the next steps are easy. Just substitute your own data, print your own schedule, and pay your own bills.

Chapter
Eight

CREATING A SYSTEM FOR MONTHLY AMORTIZATION SCHEDULES

Most spreadsheet amortization schedules are easy to generate. But since typical schedules take too much professional time to create and lack information that a business needs, they are not very useful within a business.

Figure 8-1 shows a Monthly Amortization Schedule designed to be a useful business tool. Let's see why it differs from the typical amortization schedule.

ADVANTAGES OF THE SCHEDULE

The main advantage of this schedule is that it's automated. Once the spreadsheet has been set up as described in this chapter, a new schedule can be generated in about two minutes. You simply enter the facts about the loan—interest rate, term, name of lender, and so on—and the 1-2-3 macro creates the schedule for you. Another macro prints it.

When you read the column headings of this schedule, you will see several unusual features. Public accountants insist that businesses report short-term liabilities separately from long-term liabilities. Beginning in cells E233 and F233, this schedule shows the monthly balances in each of these categories. Also, in cells G234..J234 the schedule shows the four General Ledger Account numbers that should be used each month when a check is written (cash, short-term liabilities, long-term liabilities, and interest).

	B	C	D	E	F	G	H	I	J	K	L
225					A C M E	C O R P O R A T I O N					
226						**********************************					
227					First National Bank and Auction Co.,	Loan #345-87324-26					
228											
229		Int Rate		# Months		Loan Amount		Payment			1st Pmt Due
230		12.25%		30		$100,000.00		$3,886.62			29-Jan-84
231											
232											
233			Total	Ending Bal	Ending Bal	Credit	Debit	Debit	Debit		Balance
234			Balance	G/L #2420	G/L #2720	G/L #1001	G/L #2420	G/L #2720	G/L #8201		G/L #2495
235	Pmt#	Date Due	Remaining	S/T Liab	L/T Liab	Cash	S/T Liab	L/T Liab	Interest		Acrd Int
236											
237	0	29-Dec-83	$100,000.00	$36,387.50	$63,612.50						$65.55
238	1	29-Jan-84	$97,134.21	$36,758.95	$60,375.26	$3,886.62	($371.45)	$3,237.24	$1,020.83		$63.67
239	2	29-Feb-84	$94,239.17	$37,134.20	$57,104.97	$3,886.62	($375.25)	$3,270.29	$991.58		$61.77
240	3	29-Mar-84	$91,314.58	$37,513.28	$53,801.30	$3,886.62	($379.08)	$3,303.67	$962.03		$59.85
241	4	29-Apr-84	$88,360.13	$37,896.23	$50,463.90	$3,886.62	($382.95)	$3,337.40	$932.17		$57.92
242	5	29-May-84	$85,375.52	$38,283.09	$47,092.43	$3,886.62	($386.86)	$3,371.47	$902.01		$55.96
243											
244				Fiscal Year Total		$19,433.10	($1,895.59)	$16,520.07	$4,808.62		
245											
246	6	29-Jun-84	$82,360.44	$38,673.90	$43,686.54	$3,886.62	($390.81)	$3,405.89	$871.54		$53.99
247	7	29-Jul-84	$79,314.58	$39,068.69	$40,245.89	$3,886.62	($394.79)	$3,440.65	$840.76		$51.99
248	8	29-Aug-84	$76,237.63	$39,467.52	$36,770.11	$3,886.62	($398.83)	$3,475.78	$809.67		$49.97
249	9	29-Sep-84	$73,129.27	$39,870.41	$33,258.86	$3,886.62	($402.89)	$3,511.25	$778.26		$47.93
250	10	29-Oct-84	$69,989.18	$40,277.43	$29,711.75	$3,886.62	($407.02)	$3,547.11	$746.53		$45.88
251	11	29-Nov-84	$66,817.03	$40,688.59	$26,128.44	$3,886.62	($411.16)	$3,583.31	$714.47		$43.80
252	12	29-Dec-84	$63,612.50	$41,103.95	$22,508.55	$3,886.62	($415.36)	$3,619.89	$682.09		$41.70
253	13	29-Jan-85	$60,375.26	$41,523.56	$18,851.70	$3,886.62	($419.61)	$3,656.85	$649.38		$39.57
254	14	28-Feb-85	$57,104.97	$41,947.44	$15,157.53	$3,886.62	($423.88)	$3,694.17	$616.33		$37.43

255	15	29-Mar-85	$53,801.30	$42,375.66	$11,425.64	$3,886.62	($428.22)	$3,731.89	$582.95	$35.27
256	16	29-Apr-85	$50,463.90	$42,808.24	$7,655.66	$3,886.62	($432.58)	$3,769.98	$549.22	$33.08
257	17	29-May-85	$47,092.43	$43,245.24	$3,847.19	$3,886.62	($437.00)	$3,808.47	$515.15	$30.87
258										
259				Fiscal Year Total		$46,639.44	($4,962.15)	$43,245.24	$8,356.35	
260										
261	18	29-Jun-85	$43,686.54	$43,686.54	$0.00	$3,886.62	($441.30)	$3,847.19	$480.73	$28.64
262	19	29-Jul-85	$40,245.89	$40,245.89	$0.00	$3,886.62	$3,440.65	$0.00	$445.97	$26.38
263	20	29-Aug-85	$36,770.11	$36,770.11	$0.00	$3,886.62	$3,475.78	$0.00	$410.84	$24.10
264	21	29-Sep-85	$33,258.86	$33,258.86	$0.00	$3,886.62	$3,511.25	$0.00	$375.37	$21.80
265	22	29-Oct-85	$29,711.75	$29,711.75	$0.00	$3,886.62	$3,547.11	$0.00	$339.51	$19.48
266	23	29-Nov-85	$26,128.44	$26,128.44	$0.00	$3,886.62	$3,583.31	$0.00	$303.31	$17.13
267	24	29-Dec-85	$22,508.55	$22,508.55	$0.00	$3,886.62	$3,619.89	$0.00	$266.73	$14.75
268	25	29-Jan-86	$18,851.70	$18,851.70	$0.00	$3,886.62	$3,656.85	$0.00	$229.77	$12.36
269	26	28-Feb-86	$15,157.53	$15,157.53	$0.00	$3,886.62	$3,694.17	$0.00	$192.45	$9.94
270	27	29-Mar-86	$11,425.64	$11,425.64	$0.00	$3,886.62	$3,731.89	$0.00	$154.73	$7.49
271	28	29-Apr-86	$7,655.66	$7,655.66	$0.00	$3,886.62	$3,769.98	$0.00	$116.64	$5.02
272	29	29-May-86	$3,847.19	$3,847.19	$0.00	$3,886.62	$3,808.47	$0.00	$78.15	$2.52
273										
274				Fiscal Year Total		$46,639.44	$39,398.05	$3,847.19	$3,394.20	
275										
276	30	29-Jun-86	$0.00	$0.00	$0.00	$3,886.46	$3,847.19	$0.00	$39.27	$0.00
277										
278				Fiscal Year Total		$3,886.46	$3,847.19	$0.00	$39.27	
279										
280										
281										
282				Grand Total		$116,598.44	$36,387.50	$63,612.50	$16,598.44	

Figure 8-1. A monthly amortization schedule

At the bottom of the figure, you will find grand totals of these four columns. These let you check the schedule's accuracy: total cash payments (cell G282) should equal the amount of the loan (G230) plus total interest (J282); and total debits in the two liability accounts (H282 and I282) should equal the respective initial balances (E237 and F237).

This schedule offers an additional convenience. At the end of each month, Accounting should record the interest that has accrued since the payment was due earlier in the month. The last column (L) of this figure shows the balance that should appear each month in this accrued interest account.

The totals shown for each fiscal year are another convenience. Not only do they make it easier to reconcile year-end financial statements, but they make the schedule easier to read by dividing it into sections.

To use the system to generate a schedule like Figure 8-1, we begin by entering information about the loan. Next we select a macro that generates the schedule, which it does in two steps: (1) it erases the range that will contain the schedule and then copies the new schedule down the range, and (2) it inserts and calculates the Fiscal Year Totals and the Grand Total. Finally, when we select the PRINT macro, 1-2-3 defines the print range and prints the schedule.

The following pages explain how to create this system. (Remember, you can purchase a disk set that includes this and all other major templates discussed in this book.)

BEGIN THE AMORTIZATION SCHEDULE

Start with a blank spreadsheet. Issue the /**W**orksheet **G**lobal **R**ecalculation **M**anual command and enter the name of your spreadsheet (I called mine AMORT) in A1.

Next, set the Global column width at 15 and then set these column widths:

Column	*Width*
A	9
B	4
C	13
E	14

Column	*Width*
H	14
J	14
K	1
L	11

These widths should allow you to amortize loans of up to $9 million or so.

Enter Information About Our Company

Figure 8-2 shows three screens of information. The first accepts information about our company; the second accepts information about the loan; and the third calculates some information that the schedule will need. We construct these screens in order.

Enter **UPDATE** in C1. Use /**R**ange **N**ame **L**abel **D**own to assign this range name to cell C2. Enter the information you see in rows 2 through 21. When cell C2 is the top left cell of your display, this information will fill your screen. Assign the range names: with the cell pointer on C8, use /**R**ange **N**ame **L**abel **R**ight to assign the name COMPANY to D8; with the cell pointer on G14, use /**R**ange **N**ame **L**abel **L**eft and then highlight the short column of names through G19.

Enter Information About the Loan

Enter the information that is shown in rows 22 through 41 of Figure 8-2. Format cells F32 and F39, the cells with the Loan Amount and with the Payment Amount, as Currency with two decimal places. Format F33, the cell with the interest rate, as Percent with two decimal places.

If you wish to calculate the monthly payment amount to be used by the schedule, leave cell F39, Payment Amount, blank or equal to zero. If you are creating a schedule for a current loan, put the actual payment amount in this cell.

As you did in the previous screen, assign range names to the lender's name and to the labels in column G, rows 32 through 39.

Create the Calculations Screen

Enter the information shown in rows 42 through 61 of Figure 8-2. As before, assign the range names shown in column G to the cells in column F.

```
        C               D               E               F               G
 1   UPDATE
 2                  ================================================
 3                  ENTER THE FOLLOWING INFORMATION ABOUT OUR COMPANY.
 4 =====================================================================
 5
 6 Range Name    Our Company Name
 7 ----------------------------------------------------------
 8 COMPANY         A C M E   C O R P O R A T I O N
 9 =====================================================================
10
11 Enter the following numbers:                  Number          Range Name
12 ---------------------------------------------------------------------
13 General Ledger Account Numbers for:
14   Cash                                                  1001 CASH
15   Long Term Debt Due Within One Year                    2420 STLIAB
16   Long Term Debt Due In More Than One Year              2720 LTLIAB
17   Interest Costs                                        8201 INTAMT
18   Liability for Accrued Interest                        2495 INTLIAB
19 Our fiscal year ends on what month?                        5 FYEAR
20
21 =====================================================================
22                  ==============================================
23                   ENTER THE FOLLOWING INFORMATION ABOUT THE LOAN.
24 =====================================================================
25 Range Name    The Lender's Name and Loan Number
26 ----------------------------------------------------------
27 LENDER        First National Bank and Auction Co., Loan #345-87324-26
28 =====================================================================
29
30 Enter the following numbers:                  Number          Range Name
31 ---------------------------------------------------------------------
32 Loan amount to amortize.                          $100,000.00 LOAN
33 Yearly interest rate.                                  12.25%INT
34 Length of Loan in months.                                 30 TERM
35 Payment Number of next payment.                            1 START_NO
36 Month first payment is due.                                1 MONTH
37 Day first payment is due.                                 29 DAY
38 Year first payment is due.                                84 YEAR
39 Payment amount (leave blank to calculate).                    EPMT
40
41 =====================================================================
42                               ==============
43                                CALCULATIONS
44 =====================================================================
45
46
47
48 Calculation of periodic payment.                   $3,886.62 CPMT
49 Payment amount to use in schedule.                 $3,886.62 PMT
50 End of Loan Date Month                             31-Dec-83 EDATE
51 Calculated Loan Date                               29-Dec-83 DATE
52 Monthly Interest Rate                                  1.02%MINT
53 Months from 1st pmt to end of fiscal year.                 4 FYEND
54 Interest is accrued for x% of the month.                  6%MOP
55
56
57
58
59
60
61 =====================================================================
```

Figure 8-2. Three screens of information

The formulas for these cells are as follows:

Cell F48 This calculation of our monthly loan payment is simple. It uses the loan amount, the monthly interest rate, and the length of the loan in months.

F48: @PMT($LOAN,$INT/12,$TERM)

Cell F49 Cell F49 uses either of two amounts to calculate the amortization schedule. If our banker specifies a monthly payment amount, we enter this amount in EPMT, cell F39, and F49 uses it; otherwise, F49 uses F48, the calculated payment amount, CPMT.

F49: @IF($EPMT>0,@ROUND($EPMT,2),@ROUND($CPMT,2))

Cell F50 This formula gives the last day of the month in which we obtained our loan.

F50: @DATE($YEAR,$MONTH,1)−1

Cell F51 The Calculated Loan Date is the date one month prior to the first payment date. This and cell F50 are used to calculate the percentage in cell F54.

F51: @DATE($YEAR−($MONTH=1),$MONTH−1+12*($MONTH=1),
@MIN($DAY,@DAY($EDATE)))

Cell F52 The Monthly Interest Rate is simply the yearly interest rate divided by 12.

F52: +INT/12

Cell F53 This calculation finds the number of months from the first payment to the end of the fiscal year. The macros use this figure to determine where to calculate the Fiscal Year Totals.

F53: @IF($FYEAR−$MONTH>=0,$FYEAR−$MONTH,12+$FYEAR−$MONTH)

Cell F54 This formula gives the percentage of the month that remains after we first obtained our loan. It is used in the month-end interest accrual, column L.

F54: 1−@DAY($DATE)/@DAY($EDATE)

	A	B	C	D	E	F	G	H	I	J	K	L
225						ACME CORPORATION						
226						**********************************						
227					First National Bank and Auction Co., Loan #345-87324-26							
228												
229			Int Rate		# Months		Loan Amount		Payment			1st Pmt Due
230			12.25%		30		$100,000.00		$3,886.62			29-Jan-84
231												
232												
233				Total	Ending Bal	Ending Bal	Credit	Debit	Debit	Debit		Balance
234				Balance	G/L #2420	G/L #2720	G/L #1001	G/L #2420	G/L #2720	G/L #8201		G/L #2495
235	Line#	Pmt#	Date Due	Remaining	S/T Liab	L/T Liab	Cash	S/T Liab	L/T Liab	Interest		Acrd Int
236	START											
237	0	0	29-Dec-83	$100,000.00	$36,387.50	$63,612.50					|	$65.55
238	1	1	29-Jan-84	$97,134.21	$36,758.95	$60,375.26	$3,886.62	($371.45)	$3,237.24	$1,020.83	|	$63.67
239	2	2	29-Feb-84	$94,239.17	$37,134.20	$57,104.97	$3,886.62	($375.25)	$3,270.29	$991.58	|	$61.77
240	3	3	29-Mar-84	$91,314.58	$37,513.28	$53,801.30	$3,886.62	($379.08)	$3,303.67	$962.03	|	$59.85
241	4	4	29-Apr-84	$88,360.13	$37,896.23	$50,463.90	$3,886.62	($382.95)	$3,337.40	$932.17	|	$57.92
x x x x	x x x	x x x	x x x x x	x x x x x	x x x x x	x x x x x	x x x x x	x x x x x	x x x x x	x x x x x	x x	x x x x
263	26	26	28-Feb-86	$15,157.53	$15,157.53	$0.00	$3,886.62	$3,694.17	$0.00	$192.45	|	$9.93
264	27	27	29-Mar-86	$11,425.64	$11,425.64	$0.00	$3,886.62	$3,731.89	$0.00	$154.73	|	$7.49
265	28	28	29-Apr-86	$7,655.66	$7,655.66	$0.00	$3,886.62	$3,769.98	$0.00	$116.64	|	$5.02
266	29	29	29-May-86	$3,847.19	$3,847.19	$0.00	$3,886.62	$3,808.47	$0.00	$78.15	|	$2.52
267	30	30	29-Jun-86	$0.00	$0.00	$0.00	$3,886.46	$3,847.19	$0.00	$39.27	|	$0.00

Figure 8-3. Portions of the temporary amortization schedule

CREATE THE SCHEDULE

Figure 8-3 shows the top and bottom of a temporary amortization schedule that we will create. From this schedule we will extract several rows of formulas, putting them into a Resources section for the macros to use. Then, after we erase everything in this schedule but the headings, we will write several macros to create new schedules for us.

Set Up the Resources Section

The first lines in the Resources section, shown in Figure 8-4, will be used by Version 2 string formulas to maintain the company headings. These formulas extract the headings from the Update section (Figure 8-2) and center them in the report. To do this, the formulas need to be given the width of the report. The first part of the Resources section contains this information.

(If you are using Version 1A, you will maintain your headings using the Version 1A macros, which are described at the end of this chapter. Nevertheless, you should leave room in the Resources section for the rows used to calculate the cell width. Doing so will help you follow this explanation more easily and allow you to update your spreadsheet when you update your system to Version 2.)

Go to A62. Row 62 should be the next row below the Calculations screen. Enter **RESOURCES**. Use the repeating dash to underline the word in A63; then copy the underline from B63 to M63. Copy this line to the other rows shown in Figure 8-4.

Enter the formula **@CELL("WIDTH",B65..B65)** in B64. This returns the width of column B. Copy the formula from C64 through L64. Then enter **WIDTH** in A65. Use **/R**ange **N**ame **L**abel **R**ight to assign this name to B65. In B65 enter the formula **@SUM(B64..L64)**, which gives you the width of the entire report (the value 131 in the figure). Finally, fill in the other labels and numbers shown in Figure 8-4. These will be used later by our macros.

Enter Names in the Headings

This section shows the string formulas that Version 2 will need when it generates the company headings shown in Figure 8-3. We enter these headings beginning in row 225. Later, we will fill in most of the intervening blank space with macros.

```
      A    B      C          D          E          F          G          H          I          J     K    L         M
61                ==================================================
62 RESOURCES
63 ---------------------------------------------------------------------------------------------------------------------
64         4     13         15         14         15         15         14         15         14 *       11
65   WIDTH 131
66 ---------------------------------------------------------------------------------------------------------------------
67 TOP                                                                                                              CRIT
68
69 ---------------------------------------------------------------------------------------------------------------------
70 BOT
71
72 ---------------------------------------------------------------------------------------------------------------------
73 LINE1                                                  ----------------------------------------
74                              Fiscal Year Total                                                                      1
75 ---------------------------------------------------------------------------------------------------------------------
76 LINE2                                                  ----------------------------------------
77                              Grand Total
78 ---------------------------------------------------------------------------------------------------------------------
79 CRIT     CRIT    |
80            1     |
81 ---------------------------------------------------------------------------------------------------------------------
```

Figure 8-4 Top of the Resources section, awaiting string formulas for headings

Cell B225 This formula returns the company name centered in the report.

B225: @REPEAT(" ",($WIDTH−@LENGTH($COMPANY))/2)&$COMPANY

Cell B226 This formula underlines the company name with stars, using two more stars than the number of characters and spaces in the company name.

B226: @REPEAT(" ",($WIDTH−@LENGTH($COMPANY))/2−1)&
@REPEAT("*",@LENGTH($COMPANY)+2)

Cell B227 This formula returns the lender's name and loan number.

B227: @REPEAT(" ",($WIDTH−@LENGTH($LENDER))/2)&$LENDER

Cell B228 This formula uses equal signs to underline the lender's name and loan number.

B228: @REPEAT(" ",($WIDTH−@LENGTH($LENDER))/2)&
@REPEAT("=",@LENGTH($LENDER))

Enter the Reference Loan Information in the Heading

The information below the lender's name, in row 230—the Interest Rate, Number of Months, and so on—is for reference only. It isn't used in any calculations. Here are the formulas for row 230.

C230: +$INT
E230: +$TERM
G230: +LOAN
I230: +$PMT
L230: +C238

Version 2 users may also want to use the following string formula to underline this information and the column headings that follow. The advantage of using a string formula is that you can leave "gutters" between the underlines that readjust themselves when the column widths are changed and the spreadsheet recalculated. The formula for C231 is +" "&@REPEAT ("−",C$62−2). (Cell C62 is the cell in the Resources section that holds the width for column C.) Copy cell C231 as needed to the other cells that will serve as underlines.

Enter the Column Headings

Enter the column headings for rows 233 through 236 as illustrated in Figure 8-3.

Version 1A Users Use /**R**ange **N**ame **C**reate to assign the range names HEAD1 through HEAD7 to cells E234 through J234 and L234 respectively (skipping K234). Assign HEAD8 to F225 and HEAD9 to E227. The macro that will update these headings must use these range names. Also, enter repeating stars, *, in cells F226 through H226. And enter repeating equal signs, \=, in cells E228 through I228.

Version 2 Users Use the following formulas to generate the labels in cells E234 through J234 and in L234 (skipping K234).

```
E234:  +" G/L #"&@STRING($STLIAB,0)
F234:  +" G/L #"&@STRING($LTLIAB,0)
G234:  +" G/L #"&@STRING($CASH,0)
H234:  +" G/L #"&@STRING($STLIAB,0)
I234:  +" G/L #"&@STRING($LTLIAB,0)
J234:  +" G/L #"&@STRING($INTAMT,0)
L234:  +" G/L #"&@STRING($INTLIAB,0)
```

After you have entered **START** in A236, use /**R**ange **N**ame **L**abel **D**own to assign this range name to A237.

Finally use /**R**ange **N**ame **C**reate to define the range HEAD. Define it with dimensions of A225 through L236. Later, a macro will use this range to define the borders we will use to print the spreadsheet.

Create the Amortization Table

Use /**D**ata **F**ill to generate the numbers 0 through 30 in column A, beginning in cell A237. Format C237 and C238 as Date 1. Format D237 through L238 as Currency 2. Then enter the formulas listed in the following paragraphs.

Cells B237 and B238 At times you will want to start an amortization table in the middle of the repayment period, using an outstanding balance at that point. Column B allows you to do this. It adds the payment number at that point, the START_NO minus one, to the current line number, generating the new payment number. When the table starts from the first payment, the START_NO is equal to 1.

```
B237:  +START+$START_NO-1
B238:  +A238+$START_NO-1
```

Cell C237 This cell for Date Due is simple. It is equal to $DATE, the date one month before the first payment is due. This is assumed to be the date the loan was obtained.

```
C237:  +$DATE
```

Cell C238 The remaining cells in the Date Due column are more involved than the first cell because each successive date must fall on the proper day of the month. For example, if the first payment date is on the fifth of the month, the succeeding due dates must also be the fifth. And if the first payment date is on the thirty-first of the month, the remaining due dates must be adjusted for 30-day months and for February. Here's the formula.

```
C238:  @DATE(@YEAR(C237)+(@MONTH(C237)=12),
       @MONTH(C237)+1-12*(@MONTH(C237)=12),
       @MIN($DAY,@CHOOSE(@MONTH(C237)-1,28+(@MOD(@YEAR(C237),12)=0),
       31,30,31,30,31,31,30,31,30,31,31,31) ) )
```

Although the formula in C238 is displayed on four lines, you enter it on one line, of course. The first line of the formula generates the new year; the second line, the new month; and the last two lines, the new day. Let's look at this formula more closely.

On the first line, the new year is equal to the old year plus either a 1 or 0. If (@MONTH(C237)=12) is true—if the previous month was December—the expression evaluates as 1, increasing the value of the current year by one. But if (@MONTH(C237)=12) is false—if the previous month was not December—the expression evaluates as 0, leaving the value of the current year equal to that of the previous year.

On the second line, the new month is equal to the old month plus one minus a value. The value is equal to 0 if the old month is not December; it is equal to 12 if the old month is December. Thus, a new month of January is equal to 12+1−12.

The third line guards against our attempting to generate an inappropriate date, February 31, for instance. From two values—the assigned payment date ($DAY) and the number of days in the current month—it chooses the smaller value. The @CHOOSE function generates this number of days in the following manner.

If the previous month was February, the function looks in position number one (month two, for February, minus one) for the number of days in the new month. Position number zero is the formula beginning "28+(@MOD(@YEAR. Position number one, therefore, is the first value on the fourth line, 31. If the previous month was any month from March through December, the process is the same.

If the previous month was January, the function looks in position zero. The formula in this position adds a value to the number 28. The value is equal to 1 if January's year is evenly divisible by four, that is, if this is a leap year. Otherwise the value of 0 is added to 28.

Figure 8-1 demonstrates the effectiveness of this formula. Notice that for 1984, which is a leap year, February's ending date is 29, but for 1985 and 1986 it is 28.

Cells D237 and D238 The Total Balance Remaining in cell D237 is the original amount of the loan. Cell D238 is the remaining loan balance after the first payment; it is equal to the previous balance plus interest minus the payment.

D237: +$LOAN
D238: +D237*(1+$MINT)−$PMT

Cells E237 and E238 The Ending Balance in Short-Term Liabilities is equal to the Total Loan Remaining minus the Ending Balance of Long-Term Liabilities.

E237: @ROUND($D237−$F237,2)
E238: @ROUND($D238−$F238,2)

Cells F237 and F238 The Ending Balance in Long-Term Liabilities is equal to the Total Loan Remaining 12 months into the future.

F237: +D249
F238: +D250

Cell G238 Each month's Cash payment is equal to $PMT for all payments but the last. As shown in G267, the last payment will be a slightly different value because it must adjust for any inaccuracies in rounding that have accumulated during the months of the loan. The formula for this final payment will be discussed in the next section.

G238: +$PMT

Cell H238 This change in the Short-Term Liability is equal to last period's Short-Term Liability minus this period's Short-Term Liability. Until the last 12 months of the loan, this change will increase the balance of the Short-Term Liability.

H238: +E237−E238

Cell I238 This change in the Long-Term Liability is equal to the rounded values of last period's Long-Term Liability minus this period's Long-Term Liability.

I238: @ROUND(F237,2)−@ROUND(F238,2)

Cell J238 This month's Interest is equal to this month's payment minus the changes in Short-Term and Long-Term Liabilities.

J238: +G238−H238−I238

Cell K237 The vertical lines in column K visually separate the final column (column L) from the previous four, which provide information when a check is written. Column L provides information for an accounting journal entry at the end of each month.

K237: '|

Cells L237 and L238 These cells report the interest that has accumulated from the due date until the end of the month. If, for example, the loan was first received on June 3, interest should accrue for 90% of the month (90%=1−(3/30)). This 90% would have been calculated in the Calculations section and have the range name MOP (for Month Percentage). The dollar amount of this month's interest is equal to 1 plus the month's interest rate taken to the MOP power, minus 1, and multiplied by the current loan amount outstanding.

L237: ((1+$MINT)^$MOP−1)*D237
L238: ((1+$MINT)^$MOP−1)*D238

Create the Last Row of the Amortization Table

When you have entered all of the previous formulas, /**C**opy B238..L238 to B239..B267. The numbers you generated in column A with the Data Fill command should end on row 267 also.

Next, enter the following amounts and formulas into the appropriate cells in row 267. Changing these cells as shown will ensure that your final payment is the amount necessary to reduce your loan to zero.

D267: 0
E267: 0
F267: 0
G267: @ROUND(D266*(1+$MINT),2)
H267: +E266
I267: 0
L267: 0

After you have entered these formulas and calculated twice, your numbers in row 267 should be the same as in Figure 8-3.

Copy Formulas to the Resources Section

When you have a working amortization schedule, the next step is to save your formulas in the Resources section (Figure 8-4). To save the first two rows of the schedule, /**C**opy B237..L238 to B67. To save the last row, /**C**opy B267..L267 to B70. Next, go to B67 and use /**R**ange **N**ame **C**reate to assign the range name TOP to B67..M68. Use the same command to assign the range name BOT to B70..L70.

When you look at these formulas in the Resources section, they won't make much sense. Some will show an ERR, and if you use Version 2, some may appear to have vanished altogether. But don't worry. If they remain undisturbed, they will work perfectly when we use them later.

You should be careful about one thing, however. Many of these formulas refer to rows above and below their own cells. If you insert or delete rows above row 82, you can throw these formulas off. But this shouldn't be a problem since you should have no reason to insert or delete rows in that area.

Erase Your Schedule

Now, after all the work we've been through, it is time to erase the schedule. But before you do, play it safe: store your current spreadsheet in a temporary file (call it TEMP1, for instance).

To erase your schedule, go to the range named START, cell A237, and then issue the /**R**ange **E**rase command. To specify the range to erase, press END and HOME. Then press ENTER. Next, issue the /**R**ange **F**ormat **R**eset command. Press END, HOME, and ENTER. Then, when you save this spreadsheet under the name AMORT or the name of your choice, 1-2-3 should treat row 235, the bottom row of your headings, as the bottom of the spreadsheet.

CREATE THE MACROS

Figures 8-5 through 8-7 show the macros that Version 2 will use to generate and print the amortization schedule. The macros are identified in column A of the figures, and notes explain what each cell entry does. Figures 8-8 and 8-9 show the modifications and additions that users of Version 1A must make to Figures 8-5 through 8-7. These modifications are needed because 1A uses macros to update the headings, a process for which Version 2 uses string formulas. In addition, you must eliminate a shortcut that Version 2 allows. Version 2 allows a command like {LEFT 3}, which is equivalent to {LEFT}{LEFT}{LEFT}. So, whenever you see such occurrences as {CALC 2} or {DOWN 4} in Figures 8-6 and 8-7, Version 1A users must substitute the appropriate number of individual commands.

Enter the Menu Macro

Figure 8-5 shows the menu that will control the amortization schedules. Since the overlap of the macro labels from column to column makes them largely unreadable, the figure shows the formulas for each cell in the menu.

The Update selection, beginning in cell B91, is the simplest macro. It sends the cell pointer to the Update section—shown in Figure 8-2—and then quits. In this section you enter the information that you wish about your company or a loan and then restart the macro.

Enter the Macro to Generate The Schedule

Figure 8-6 shows the GEN macro, which generates the amortization schedule, and the INSERT macro, which inserts the fiscal year subtotals. To the right of each row of the macro is an explanation of how the row works.

After you enter these macros and name them using /**R**ange **N**ame **L**abel **R**ight, you may want to test the GEN macro before using the INSERT macro. If you want to do so, do not enter row 113, the final row of the GEN

```
        A       B       C               D               E               F
88              Main menu for the Monthly Amortization Schedule.
89              -------------------------------------------------------------
90  \m          /XMmenu~/XQ
91  menu        UpdaGenerate    Print           Quit
92              UpdaGenerate the Calculate and pReturn to Ready mode.
93              {END/XCgen~     /XCprint~       /XQ
94              {GOT/XG\m~      /XG\m~
95              /X
96

A90: '\m
A91: 'menu

B90: '/XMmenu~/XQ
B91: 'Update
B92: 'Update loan information for the amortization schedule.
B93: '{END}{HOME}
B94: '{GOTO}update~
B95: '/XQ

C91: 'Generate
C92: 'Generate the amortization schedule.
C93: '/XCgen~
C94: '/XG\m~

D91: 'Print
D92: 'Calculate and print the amortization schedule.
D93: '/XCprint~
D94: '/XG\m~

E91: 'Quit
E92: 'Return to Ready mode.
E93: '/XQ
```

Figure 8-5. The MENU macro

macro. Omitting this row will let your macro end without an error message. Then, to test the macro, press ALT-M Generate. Before you evaluate the results of this test, calculate the spreadsheet twice.

Enter the Formulas Needed By the INSERT Macro

When the GEN macro appears to be working properly, enter **/XGinsert~** as shown in row 113. But before you can test this macro, you must complete the Resources section with the information this macro requires.

Go to G74 and enter **@SUM(G73..G61)**. This is the formula we will use to add the previous 12 months of Cash payments, giving us the Fiscal Year Totals. Copy this formula from G74 to H74..J74. (As before, don't be concerned if this formula evaluates as an error in the Resources section; it will work in the body of the schedule.) Use /**R**ange **N**ame **C**reate to assign the name LINE1 to cells B73..M74.

Go to B79 and use /**R**ange **N**ame **C**reate to assign the name CRIT to cells B79 and B80. Then go to G237 and use /**R**ange **N**ame **C**reate to assign the name DATA to cells G237 and H237. The INSERT macro will redefine the right boundary of this range (H237) to the lower right corner of the spreadsheet. But we must first create the range in order to satisfy the following formula.

Go to G77 and enter **@DSUM($DATA,0,$CRIT)**. When this formula is copied to the schedule, it will sum all values in the first column (the zero position) of the range named DATA that meet the criteria found in the range CRIT. That range specifies that the column headed by the word CRIT must have the value 1 in it. As you can see from Figure 8-4, column M of the schedule will always be headed by the word CRIT. And the value 1 will appear in column M whenever we copy LINE1, the Fiscal Year Total, to the schedule. In other words, the @DSUM formula in column G returns the sum of all the Fiscal Year Totals found in column G.

To calculate the other totals, copy G77 to H77..J77 and then edit the cells to replace 0 (zero) with the numbers 1, 2, and 3, respectively. When you are done, these four cells should have the following formulas:

G77: @DSUM($DATA,0,$CRIT)
H77: @DSUM($DATA,1,$CRIT)
I77: @DSUM($DATA,2,$CRIT)
J77: @DSUM($DATA,3,$CRIT)

Finally, use /**R**ange **N**ame **C**reate to assign the range name LINE2 to B76..K77.

Enter the Insert Macro

The bottom section of Figure 8-6 shows the macro that inserts the Fiscal Year Totals as needed and then calculates the Grand Totals for the schedule. Remember to use the /**R**ange **N**ame **L**abel **R**ight command on this macro's range names in column A before you attempt to use the macro.

```
          A        B        C                 D              E                   F                 G
 98                Generate the amortization table
 99                ----------------------------------------------------------------------------
100  gen           {GOTO}start~                           Go to range START.
101                /RE.{END}{HOME}{DOWN}~                 Erase previous amortization table.
102                /Ccalc1~calc1~                         Calculate parameters for building the table.
103                {RIGHT}/Ctop~~                         Copy range TOP to the table.
104                {LEFT}                                 Go back to START.
105                /DF{BS}.{END}{DOWN}~                   Data Fill column A for the number of
106                0~1~TERM~                                months equal to the TERM of the loan.
107                {DOWN}{RIGHT}                          Copy the second row of the table
108                /C.{END}{RIGHT}~                         down the remainder of the table.
109                {DOWN}.{LEFT}                                            "
110                {END}{DOWN}{RIGHT}~                                      "
111                {LEFT}{END}{DOWN}                      Move to the bottom of the table.
112                {RIGHT}/Cbot~~                         Copy range BOT to the last row of the table.
113                /XGinsert~                             Go to macro for inserting the Fiscal Years.
114
115
116
117
118
119                Insert the Fiscal Year Subtotals and Grand Total
120                ------------------------------------------------------------------
121  insert        {GOTO}start~                           Go to START.
122                {DOWN FYEND+2}                         Move to first month in next Fiscal Year.
123                /WIR{DOWN 2}~                          Insert 3 spaces.
124                {RIGHT}/Cline1~~                       Copy LINE1, Fiscal Year Total line, to this space.
125                {END}{RIGHT}{DOWN}                     Find subtotals for the remainder of current
126                @SUM({UP}.{END}{UP})~                    Fiscal Year.
127                /C~{RIGHT}.{RIGHT 2}~{UP}                                "
128  iump1         {DOWN 2}{END}{LEFT}{DOWN 13}           Move to first month of next Fiscal Year.
```

```
        A       B         C              D                E                 F               G

129             /RNChere~~                          If we are out of data, go to JUMP2.
130             /XIhere=0~/RNDhere~/XGjump2~                       "
131             /RNDhere~                           Delete range HERE.
132             /WIR{DOWN 2}~                       Insert 3 spaces.
133             {RIGHT}/Cline1~~                    Copy LINE1 to the schedule.
134             /XGjump1~                           Loop back to JUMP1.
135 jump2       {END}{UP}{DOWN}                     Go to first blank line below data.
136             {RIGHT}/Cline1~~                    Copy LINE1 to the schedule.
137             {END}{RIGHT}{DOWN}                  Calculate subtotals for the ending period.
138             @SUM({UP}.{END}{UP})~                              "
139             /C~{RIGHT}.{RIGHT 2}~                              "
140             /RNChere~~                          Define the DATA range for Grand Totals.
141             {GOTO}start~{RIGHT 6}                              "
142             /RNCdata~{BS}.{END}{HOME}~                         "
143             {GOTO}here~/RNDhere~                               "
144             {DOWN 3}{END}{LEFT}                 Copy LINE2, Grand Total, to bottom of table.
145             {RIGHT}/Cline2~~                                   "
146             {CALC 2}                            Calculate twice.
147             /XR                                 Return to menu.
```

Figure 8-6. The GEN and INSERT macros

```
         A      B          C              D              E                 F                G            H

149
150             Calc and Print
151             -----------------
152 print       {CALC 2}                         Calculate twice.
153             {GOTO}start~{RIGHT}              Move to first cell to be printed.
154             {RIGHT}/RNChere~~                Return to Menu if the table has not been generated.
155             /XIhere=0~/RNDhere~/XR                          "
156             /RNDhere~{LEFT}                                 "
157             /PPR{BS}.{DOWN}{END}{RIGHT 3}    Define range for printing, then print table.
158             {END}{DOWN}{LEFT 4}                             "
159             {END}{UP}{RIGHT 2}~                             "
160             OBRhead~QAGPPQ                   Set borders, align, print, formfeed, quit.
161             /XR                              Return to menu.
162
```

Figure 8-7. The macro for calculating and printing the schedule

Enter the Print Macro

Figure 8-7 shows the macro that calculates and prints the schedule. As with other print macros in this book, this one does not include a printer setup command for your own printer's compressed print feature. You must add this command to the PRINT macro.

Set your left margin at 0 (zero) and your right margin at 135. After you have printed your first amortization schedule, you may want to adjust these slightly to match your printer's characteristics. You may also want to reduce your top and bottom margins to 0.

After you have found the settings that give you the best results, be sure to save them by saving your spreadsheet.

If you use Version 2, you are ready to produce amortization schedules. Simply press ALT-M Update and then enter the information that is requested for your company and for a loan. Then press ALT-M Generate to generate the amortization schedule and Print to print it. However, if you use Version 1A, you have several more steps.

Enter the Macros for Version 1A Users

Figure 8-8 shows the modifications 1A users must make to the MENU and GEN macros. Two of these modifications use the macros shown in Figure 8-9. Figure 8-8 shows that one additional selection has been added to the MENU macro. Whenever you change your company information, use this macro selection to update the schedule's heading. The added row below row 112 of the GEN macro in Figure 8-8 simply copies the lender's name to HEAD9. The substitution in row 122 of the INSERT macro supplies the short macro FIND_FY for a command not available in Version 1A. Both COMP and FIND_FY are shown in Figure 8-9.

One additional change will improve the appearance of the company and lender names in your heading. Version 1A has no simple way to center these names. We can fake it, however, by entering the following two labels:

```
E9:   '======^==========
F28:  '=======^=========
```

Each caret (^) marks the approximate center point of the company and lender names when they are copied to the schedule. So after you've entered each name for the first time, insert the number of spaces necessary before each name to center it over the caret. This should also center the names in the schedule.

```
          A      B          C              D              E              F              G

88              Main menu for the Monthly Amortization Schedule--Version 1A.
89              ------------------------------------------------------------
90        \m    /XMmenu~/XQ
91        menu  UpdaGenerate      Print          Company        Quit
92              UpdaGenerate the Calculate and pUpdate informaReturn to Ready mode.
93              {END/XCgen~       /XCprint~      /XCcomp~       /XQ
94              {GOT/XG\m~        /XG\m~         /XG\m~
95              /XQ

      E91: 'Company
      E92: 'Update information about our company.
      E93: '/XCcomp~
      E94: '/XG\m~

      F91: 'Quit
      F92: 'Return to Ready mode.
      F93: '/XQ


      A     B          C              D              E              F              G              H


            (These are the last few lines of the GEN macro from Figure 8.6.)
            -----------------------------------------------------------------
111         {LEFT}{END}{DOWN}                   Move to the bottom of the table.
112         {RIGHT}/Cbot~~                      Copy range BOT to the last row of the table.
            /Clender~head9~                     *Transfer lender's name
113         /XGinsert~                          Go to macro for inserting the Fiscal Years.
```

```
        A        B          C              D              E               F               G              H
118
119              Insert the Fiscal Year Subtotals and Grand Total
120              ---------------------------------------------------------
121 insert       {GOTO}start~                       Go to START.
122              /XCfind fy~                        **Move to first month in next Fiscal Year.
123              /WIR{DOWN}{DOWN}~                  Insert 3 spaces.
```

*Insert a row at this point into the macro in Figure 8.6.
Then add this macro command.

**Substitute this macro command for the command in Figure 8.6.

Figure 8-8. The MENU and GEN macro modifications for Version 1A

```
          A         B      C           D           E                F              G              H

163                 Update company information
164                 ------------------------------
165  comp           {GOTO}head1~                   Copy account numbers to headings and
166                 /Cstliab~~                       insert "G/L #" before each number.
167                 {EDIT}{HOME}^G/L #~                            "
168                 {GOTO}head2~                                   "
169                 /Cltliab~~                                     "
170                 {EDIT}{HOME}^G/L #~                            "
171                 {GOTO}head3~                                   "
172                 /Ccash~~                                       "
173                 {EDIT}{HOME}^G/L #~                            "
174                 {GOTO}head4~                                   "
175                 /Cstliab~~                                     "
176                 {EDIT}{HOME}^G/L #~                            "
177                 {GOTO}head5~                                   "
178                 /Cltliab~~                                     "
179                 {EDIT}{HOME}^G/L #~                            "
180                 {GOTO}head6~                                   "
181                 /Cintamt~~                                     "
182                 {EDIT}{HOME}^G/L #~                            "
183                 {GOTO}head7~                                   "
184                 /Cintliab~~                                    "
185                 {EDIT}{HOME}^G/L #~                            "
186                 /Ccompany~head8~               Update company name.
187                 /XR                            Return
188
189
190
191
192                 Find first Fiscal Year for Version 1A
193                 -------------------------------------------
194  find_fy        {DOWN}                         Move down.
195                 /RNChere~~                     If this line number equals the number months to the
196                 /XIhere=fyend~/XGjump3~          end of the Fiscal Year, go to JUMP3.  Otherwise,
197                 /RNDhere~/XGfind_fy~             loop back to FIND_FY.
198  jump3          /RNDhere~{DOWN}{DOWN}          Move down two.
199                 /XR                            Return.
```

Figure 8-9. The COMP and FIND_FY macros, used by Version 1A MENU and Gen macros

Chapter
Nine

SUMMARIZING SALES AND CALCULATING VARIANCES

"Our sales increased this month, but our gross profits went down. How can that be?" This question is a difficult one to answer, for two reasons.

First, many accounting systems lack the level of detail required to analyze the sales data. If sales and cost of sales are summarized too compactly, the reasons for the poor performance will be lost within the summaries. But if there is too much detail, the data becomes overwhelming. Companies with relatively few products find that sales summarized by product provides the right amount of detail. As the number of products grows, however, companies often will summarize the sales by product line.

Second, even if the data is available, performing the analysis can be a complex process. To explain the decline in gross profits, we must compare this month's sales and costs to last month's sales and costs, calculate the variances, and analyze the results. This is a tedious process without help from a computer.

This chapter explains how to simplify both problems. First, it presents a simple method for finding subtotals in your data. This method is a general one that can be used in many different applications. Second, this chapter shows how to calculate the variances that will help us explain the strange performance of our gross profit margin.

FINDING SUBTOTALS IN YOUR DATA

Let's assume that when you load your monthly sales data into 1-2-3, it looks something like the Widget Corporation's data in Figure 9-1. That is,

	A	B	C	D	E	F
1	Widget Corporation, February Sales and Cost of Sales					
2	---					
3				Product		
4	Product	Sales	Cost	Line		
5	-------	-------	-------	-------		
6	85.1	212	119			
7	82901	56	23			
8	8200	122	22			
9	99.3	148	101			
10	85.6	300	176			
11	6600	12	4			
12	150.1	410	164			
13	1.1	230	127			
14	85.1	94	44			
15	85.1	113	61			
16	99.3	124	85			
17	82901	45	17			
18	150.6	1,298	585			
19	1.1	70	45			
20	8202	59	12			
21	85.6	338	142			
22	82901	74	29			
23		---------	---------			
24		3,705	1,756			

Figure 9-1. Illustration of Widget's monthly sales detail

it shows sales and costs by product but shows no information by product line. Let's also assume that our sales budgeting and analysis require that information be organized by product line. Before we can analyze sales performance, therefore, we must summarize sales by product line.

Create a Product Line Column

If the product numbers that we are to summarize had a consistent pattern, we could write a formula in the Product Line column in Figure 9-1 that makes use of that pattern. For example, suppose that we used the first digit of our product numbers to indicate the product line number. The following formula would return that first digit, whatever the length of the product number.

```
D6:  @INT(A6/10^@INT(@LOG(A6)-(A6<1))+.000000001)
```

This formula divides A6 by the power of ten necessary to "move" the decimal point to the right of the leftmost digit in A6; then it finds the integer value of the new number. If copied down column D in Figure 9-1, for example, column D would contain the product line numbers 8, 8, 8, 9, 8, 6, 1, and so on.

Or if our product line number were the first two digits to the right of the decimal place of the product number, the following formula would return this number.

D6: @INT(100*(A6−@INT(A6))+.0000000001)

But let's suppose that there is no consistent pattern that could tie our product number to our product line number. Figure 9-2 shows a table we can add to Figure 9-1 that contains each of our products and the product line number that we have assigned.

To use this table to fill in column D of 9-1, we assign the range name DATA to the two columns of numbers in Figure 9-2. Then we use an @VLOOKUP formula to look up the product number and find its product line number. When we do this, however, we must make sure that we ask the right questions of the table.

	A	B	C
26			
27		DATA	
28		----------	----------
29			Product
30		Product	Line
31		----------	----------
32		1.1	2
33		85.1	3
34		85.6	3
35		99.3	4
36		150.1	1
37		150.6	1
38		6600	2
39		8200	1
40		8202	1
41		82901	3

Figure 9-2. A reference table showing the product line number for each product

Remember that the @VLOOKUP formulas do not look for an exact match when they look up a number; they find the next greater value, and then back up one cell. But our @VLOOKUP formula must make sure that we have an exact match. The following formula, which we will add to Figure 9-1, finds that match

```
D6:  @IF(@VLOOKUP(A6,$DATA,0)=A6,@VLOOKUP(A6,$DATA,1),@NA)
```

If a match is found, this formula returns the product line number; otherwise it returns @NA, indicating that we have sold a product that isn't included in our DATA Table. Use this approach whenever you are using a lookup formula and expecting an exact match.

Create Subtotals by Product Line

The table at the bottom of Figure 9-3, from row 44 down, shows the Product Line Summary that we want. To generate this summary, we begin by sorting our Sales, using Product Line as the primary sort column (D) and Product as the secondary sort column (A). The range A6 through D22 shows the result of the sort.

Next, we generate the subtotals of Sales and Cost for each Product Line number. These are shown in columns F and H of Figure 9-3. Two columns are used to generate the Sales subtotals in column F. The formulas in row 6 are as follows:

```
E6:  @IF($D6=$D7,$E5+$B6,0)
F6:  @IF($D6<>$D7,$E5+$B6,0)
```

Column E is a scratch column that holds the running total for each Product Line number until the last row in the sequence is reached; then it evaluates to a zero. Column F is the subtotal column that we want. It is equal to zero until the last row in a sequence is reached, then it returns the subtotal for the sequence. Since column E is only a scratch column, its width is set to 1, leaving the column of stars that you see in the figure.

Version 2 users must take one precaution when using the formulas in columns E through H. Remember that Version 2 returns an ERR when a value is added to a label. So make sure that you do not include an underline in cells E5, E23, G5, or G23. If you do, your subtotals will evaluate as ERR.

The formulas for the Cost subtotals are virtually identical.

```
G6:  @IF($D6=$D7,$G5+$C6,0)
H6:  @IF($D6<>$D7,$G5+$C6,0)
```

```
       A            B          C          D     E      F      G      H
 1 Widget Corporation, February Sales and Cost of Sales
 2 ---------------------------------------------------------------------
 3                                    Product
 4  Product     Sales      Cost        Line          Sales         Cost
 5  -------    -------    -------    -------        -------      -------
 6    150.1       410        164          1 *          0 *          0
 7    150.6     1,298        585          1 *          0 *          0
 8     8200       122         22          1 *          0 *          0
 9     8202        59         12          1 *      1,889 *        783
10      1.1       230        127          2 *          0 *          0
11      1.1        70         45          2 *          0 *          0
12     6600        12          4          2 *        312 *        176
13     85.1        94         44          3 *          0 *          0
14     85.1       212        119          3 *          0 *          0
15     85.1       113         61          3 *          0 *          0
16     85.6       300        176          3 *          0 *          0
17     85.6       338        142          3 *          0 *          0
18    82901        56         23          3 *          0 *          0
19    82901        74         29          3 *          0 *          0
20    82901        45         17          3 *      1,232 *        611
21     99.3       148        101          4 *          0 *          0
22     99.3       124         85          4 *        272 *        186
23              ------------------               --------- ---------
24                3,705      1,756                  3,705       1,756
25
26
27                     DATA
28              ------------------
29                         Product
30               Product      Line
31              ------------------
32                   1.1         2
33                  85.1         3
34                  85.6         3
35                  99.3         4
36                 150.1         1
37                 150.6         1
38                  6600         2
39                  8200         1
40                  8202         1
41                 82901         3
42
43
44          Product Line Summary
45          ----------------------
46          PL#     Sales     Cost
47          ----------------------
48            1     1,889      783
49            2       312      176
50            3     1,232      611
51            4       272      186
52              ------------------
53                  3,705    1,756
```

Figure 9-3. Illustration of the data used to produce the Product Line Summary

Create a Product Line Summary

The table at the bottom of Figure 9-3, rows 44 through 53, shows the Product Line Summary that we are after. The formulas in this table look up the subtotals that we have just calculated. These subtotals are in the range LINES. Use /**R**ange **N**ame **C**reate to specify this range from D6 to H22.

The Product Line Summary Table uses a variation of the @VLOOKUP formula that we discussed earlier. The variation overcomes the fact that if the formula searches through a block of duplicate numbers, it returns information relating to the first number in the block. In Figure 9-3 we want to find information relating to the last value in the block. Here are the formulas in the table that do this.

```
B48:  @IF(@VLOOKUP($A48,$LINES,0)=$A48,@VLOOKUP($A48+.1,$LINES,2),0)
C48:  @IF(@VLOOKUP($A48,$LINES,0)=$A48,@VLOOKUP($A48+.1,$LINES,4),0)
```

Notice that in B48 we again check to see if we have an exact match. If not, the function returns a zero. If there have been sales for the product line, the function searches for a product line number of 0.1 more than the actual product line number. For example, when the product line number is 1, it searches for the value of 1.1. When it comes to the value 2, it backs up one row to the last occurrence of 1 in the table. Finally, the formula returns the data in column number 2 of this row. Since the formula views column D—the leftmost column in LINES—as column zero, it treats column F as column 2 and returns the value 1,889.

The formula in C48 works much like the formula in B48. In C48, however, the formula returns values found in column number 4 of LINES, or column H.

When B48 and C48 are copied to rows 49 through 51, the Sales subtotals are summarized as shown. Finally, @SUM formulas in B53 and C53 total the Product Line Summary. Since these totals equal those in row 24, we know that the summary includes all of our original sales.

ANALYZE THE SALES VARIANCES

Now that we have the information in the form in which we need it, we can deal with our financial questions.

Suppose that the five-line income statement for a different company, the Acme Corporation, looks something like Figure 9-4. This example compares Actual performance to Budgeted performance. (The following analysis would apply also to comparing this month's performance to last

```
                              A             B         C         D         E

 1
 2
 3
 4                                      Actual    Budget       Var     Var %
 5                                     --------  --------  --------  --------
 6 Sales                                    47        40         7       18%
 7 Cost of Sales                            28        19         9       47%
 8                                     --------  --------  --------
 9 Gross Profit                             19        21        -2      -10%
10
11 Operating Expenses                       18        18         0        0%
12                                     --------  --------  --------
13 Profit                                    1         3        -2      -67%
14
```

Figure 9-4. Illustration of a profit decline that needs analysis

month's performance.) We obviously have a problem: our sales are 18% over budget, but our profits are 67% under budget. Since our Operating Expenses are okay, the problem must lie in Cost of Sales.

Let's look at the data. Figure 9-5 shows our Actual and Budgeted performance for each of our products. (The following analysis would be the same for product line.) Somewhere in that data are the answers to our questions. But the answers aren't obvious, even though we have only four products to analyze.

We can get the answers to many of our questions if we calculate three variances: the Volume Variance, the Profit Margin Variance, and the Mix Variance.

The Volume Variance

The Volume Variance occurs when actual gross shipments of a product differ from budgeted shipments. If, for example, our actual shipments are 20% greater than budget, we would expect our gross profits to be 20% greater also. The Volume Variance represents the dollar value of this increase. We can therefore define the Volume Variance as

Volume Variance = (Variance in Shipment Dollars) * (Average Budgeted Gross Margin)

```
         A        B         C         D         E    F    G         H         I         J
 1
 2
 3
 4            -------------Actual-----  ---------   ------------Budgeted---   ---------
 5     Prod    Sales     Costs       Prof      Mrgn        Sales     Costs       Prof      Mrgn
 6  -----------------------------------------------    -------------------------------------------
 7        A       12         9          3       25%           4         3          1       25%
 8        B       10         3          7       70%          10         4          6       60%
 9        C        5         4          1       20%          10         8          2       20%
10        D       20        12          8       40%          16         4         12       75%
11            ------------------------------------    -------------------------------------------
12    TOTAL       47        28         19       40%          40        19         21       53%
13
```

Figure 9-5. A comparison of Acme's actual and budgeted sales for a month

The Profit Margin Variance

The Profit Margin Variance occurs when the actual profit margin for a product differs from the budgeted profit margin. There can be two reasons for this variance: (1) actual unit costs can differ from budgeted unit costs and (2) the actual sales price can differ from the budgeted sales price.

For example, suppose that our profit margin for a product was budgeted to be 60% of sales but was actually 55% of sales. The Profit Margin Variance for that product is calculated by multiplying our actual shipments by this 5% variance; in other words,

Profit Margin Variance = (Actual Shipment Dollars) * (Difference between Actual and Budgeted Product Profit Margins)

The Mix Variance

The Mix Variance arises because our company's profit margin is an average of the various product profit margins. The company gross profit will differ from budget when the various product profit margins combine in different proportions than we had budgeted.

For example, a proportional increase in the shipment of a product with a high profit margin will create a favorable Mix Variance: our profits improve.

The dollar amount of the Mix Variance for a particular product depends on two things. It depends, first, on the variance between actual sales and budgeted sales, and second, on the size of the difference between the product's budgeted profit margin and the budgeted company average. There will be no Mix Variance for a product if either actual sales of the product equal budgeted sales or the product's budgeted profit margin equals the company's budgeted average.

The size of the Mix Variance equals the product of these two differences:

Mix Variance = (Variance in Shipment Dollars) * (Budgeted Profit Margin of Product minus Average Profit Margin Budgeted for the company)

The Formulas for the Variances

The three variances just described can be expressed in the formulas that follow.

Volume Variance: (AS−BS)*($CBP/$CBS)
Profit Margin Variance: AS*((AP/AS)−(BP/BS))
Mix Variance: (AS−BS)*((BP/BS)−($CBP/$CBS))

where

AS = Actual Sales for a product.
AP = Actual gross Profits for a product.
BS = Budgeted Sales for a product.
BP = Budgeted gross Profits for a product.
CBS = Company Budgeted Sales.
CBP = Company Budgeted Profits.

Remember that in 1-2-3, $ designates an absolute cell reference.

Using the Formulas

Figure 9-6 has used these formulas to calculate the three variances. Notice that the range names for the formulas have also been inserted in rows 7 and 14 of the figure. The /Range Name Label Down command was used to label the top row of range names, and the /Range Name Label Up command was used to label the bottom row.

Let's see what these variances can tell us about Acme's miserable performance this month.

Product A: marketing did a great job with this product. Sales had been budgeted for $4.00, but marketing sold $12.00. If the profit margin on Product A had been equal to the company average, we would have had an increase of $4.20 (our Volume Variance) in our gross profit. Unfortunately, Product A has a low profit margin. Selling a large quantity of this product depressed our average profit margin, taking back $2.20 of our $4.20 gain. Perhaps marketing should apply their skills to a more profitable product.

Product B: we sold just what we said we would, and, happily, we maintained a better margin than we had predicted. This cost savings directly benefits our gross profit. Unfortunately, we can't tell whether margin has improved because costs have decreased or prices have increased. After all, nowhere are we tracking the number of units sold. More research is necessary here.

Product C: this product's performance is a mirror image of Product A's

	A	B	C	D	E	F	G	H	I	J	K	L	M	N	O
1															
2															
3															
4		Actual					Budgeted					Vol	Mrgn	Mix	Total
5	Prod	Sales	Costs	Prof	Mrgn		Sales	Costs	Prof	Mrgn		Var	Var	Var	Var
6															
7		AS		AP			BS		BP						
8	A	12	9	3	25%		4	3	1	25%		4.20	0.00	(2.20)	2.00
9	B	10	3	7	70%		10	4	6	60%		0.00	1.00	0.00	1.00
10	C	5	4	1	20%		10	8	2	20%		(2.63)	0.00	1.63	-1.00
11	D	20	12	8	40%		16	4	12	75%		2.10	(7.00)	0.90	-4.00
12															
13	TOTAL	47	28	19	40%		40	19	21	53%		3.68	(6.00)	0.32	-2.00
14							CBS		CBP						
15															
16															

Figure 9-6. Acme's actual and budgeted sales showing the addition of the variance calculations

performance. Our sales of this product were cut in half. On the average, this $5.00 decrease in sales would have decreased our gross profit by $2.63. But since our margins on this product are so poor, our gross profit was reduced by only $1.00.

Product D: Somebody goofed with this product. But without further research, we don't know who is responsible for the decline in our margins. One possibility is that manufacturing let the costs go crazy. More likely, though, marketing decided to lower the price to increase sales. "It's our most profitable item," someone said. "It can stand a little decrease." Unfortunately, marketing gave away more than they got.

In reviewing Acme's performance, we can see that if our margins had remained as budgeted, our added volume should have increased our gross profit by $3.68. And because of an improved mix, our costs would have been lower than expected, adding another $0.32 to our profits. Unfortunately, the major decrease in Product D's margin cost us $6.00, leaving us with a loss of $2.00 in gross profit for the month.

Chapter
Ten

BREAK-EVEN ANALYSIS

Whether you are making money or losing it, break-even analysis can provide valuable insight into the overall financial performance of your company or division.

Break-even analysis examines the relationship between total costs and total revenues as these amounts change from month to month. The break-even point is the sales volume at which a firm's total revenues will equal its total costs.

Generally, managers use two different approaches to break-even analysis. The better-known approach is the use of graphs. In its various forms, graphical break-even analysis provides an understandable picture of performance. Less well known are the various ways to use break-even formulas without graphs. We will discuss this latter approach first.

Neither approach in this chapter uses the Data Bank, which works well for financial reporting but is too inflexible for analysis.

AN ARITHMETIC APPROACH TO BREAK-EVEN ANALYSIS

As a young controller, I first used break-even analysis during pricing meetings. The formulas were simple enough to calculate in my head during the meeting. Suppose, for example, that marketing suggested that we cut prices, reducing our margins by 10%.

"Let's see," I'd say. "Today our variable costs are about sixty percent of sales, which leaves us forty cents out of every dollar to cover our fixed costs. Since fixed costs are running at $40,000 per month, we have a break-even point of $100,000 per month.

"Today, if we sell $150,000 per month, we get to keep the profits generated by that extra $50,000. Our profits at that level would therefore be about $20,000.

"Now, you want to cut our margins. You want us to have only thirty cents for each dollar of sales. This means we would have to sell $40,000 divided by thirty cents or more than $130,000 per month just to break even.

"To make a $20,000 profit, we would have to generate additional sales of about $70,000, for total monthly sales of $200,000. And these figures ignore the fact that we can't increase our volume that much without increasing our fixed costs.

"So which is easier to do: Sell $150,000 per month with a forty percent margin or $200,000 per month with a thirty percent margin?"

Unfortunately, the response to this brilliant analysis was frequently a blank stare and a mumbled, "What did you say?" I then had to review the arithmetic with them, using paper, pencil, and patience. Today, spreadsheets make it easier to communicate the effects of the break-even equation.

Charting Break-Even Performance

Figure 10-1 shows a chart that takes only about five minutes to create in 1-2-3 and can save hours of discussion and analysis. As you can see, it offers a sizable range of possible sales volumes and variable cost percentages and the approximate profit that would result from each combination. The chart shows that we would be at break even with sales at $100,000 per month and variable costs of 60%, we would have a profit of $20,000 if sales were $150,000 and variable costs remained at 60%, and so on.

This chart can be tremendously revealing to managers who have never considered the implications of fixed and variable costs in financial performance. For some, the chart will represent a manager's first easy opportunity to play "What if?" with sales and margins.

Many variations of Figure 10-1 are possible. You could divide the profits by sales to display profit margins rather than dollar profits. You could produce yearly versions, monthly versions with yearly sales, and so on. It all depends on what type of information your management is accustomed to dealing with.

The numbers beneath the column letters in Figure 10-1 show the width

	A	B	C	D	E	F	G	H	I
	9	9	9	9	9	9	9	9	9
1	Monthly Profits When Fixed Costs = $40,000 per month.								
2	[Profits = Sales * (1 - Variable Cost %) - Fixed Cost $]								
3	====================								
4		----------Variable Costs----------							
5	Sales	58%	60%	62%	64%	66%	68%	70%	72%
6	---------	--------	--------	--------	--------	--------	--------	--------	--------
7	$80,000	(6,400)	(8,000)	(9,600)	(11,200)	(12,800)	(14,400)	(16,000)	(17,600)
8	$90,000	(2,200)	(4,000)	(5,800)	(7,600)	(9,400)	(11,200)	(13,000)	(14,800)
9	$100,000	2,000	0	(2,000)	(4,000)	(6,000)	(8,000)	(10,000)	(12,000)
10	$110,000	6,200	4,000	1,800	(400)	(2,600)	(4,800)	(7,000)	(9,200)
11	$120,000	10,400	8,000	5,600	3,200	800	(1,600)	(4,000)	(6,400)
12	$130,000	14,600	12,000	9,400	6,800	4,200	1,600	(1,000)	(3,600)
13	$140,000	18,800	16,000	13,200	10,400	7,600	4,800	2,000	(800)
14	$150,000	23,000	20,000	17,000	14,000	11,000	8,000	5,000	2,000
15	$160,000	27,200	24,000	20,800	17,600	14,400	11,200	8,000	4,800
16	$170,000	31,400	28,000	24,600	21,200	17,800	14,400	11,000	7,600
17	$180,000	35,600	32,000	28,400	24,800	21,200	17,600	14,000	10,400
18	$190,000	39,800	36,000	32,200	28,400	24,600	20,800	17,000	13,200
19	$200,000	44,000	40,000	36,000	32,000	28,000	24,000	20,000	16,000
20	$210,000	48,200	44,000	39,800	35,600	31,400	27,200	23,000	18,800
21	$220,000	52,400	48,000	43,600	39,200	34,800	30,400	26,000	21,600
22	$230,000	56,600	52,000	47,400	42,800	38,200	33,600	29,000	24,400
23	$240,000	60,800	56,000	51,200	46,400	41,600	36,800	32,000	27,200
24	$250,000	65,000	60,000	55,000	50,000	45,000	40,000	35,000	30,000

Figure 10-1. A break-even chart showing monthly profits under various assumptions when Fixed Costs are $40,000 per month

of each column. This figure uses the default global column width of 9.

The cells A7, under Sales, and B5, under Variable Costs, are given values. The formula for Sales in A8 is 10000+A7, is formatted as Currency 0, and is then copied down the column. The formula for Variable Costs in C5 is .02+B5, and is formatted as Percent 0, and is then copied across the row. To change the range of sales or variable costs, just change the values in A7 or B5.

Cell B7 shows that we would lose approximately $6,400 if Sales were $80,000 (A7), Variable Costs were 58% (B5), and Fixed Costs were $40,000 (E1). The formula for B7 in Figure 10-1 is (1−B$5)*$A7−$E$1 and is formatted as Fixed 0. Pay particular attention to the placement of the dollar ($) signs. Properly placed, these absolute cell references will allow you to easily copy this formula across the row and then copy the row down the spreadsheet.

Break-Even Charts and Turnaround Analysis

The numbers displayed in a chart like Figure 10-1 will change according to what questions are being asked and what actions are being considered. Suppose that our company is facing hard times. Our sales have dropped to $100,000 per month, variable costs have risen to 62%, and fixed costs have increased to $43,000 per month. We can use the break-even chart to perform *turnaround* analysis: to ask a question such as, what cost-cutting measures can we undertake to change our $5,000 per month loss into a consistent profit?

Figure 10-2 shows a display that can serve as a working document to assist in the turnaround analysis. The summary lists of Fixed and Variable Costs in this figure are not used in the calculations; they simply document the firm's current costs. In actual use, of course, these costs would be supported by pages of detail.

The formula for the Fixed Costs in A18 of Figure 10-2 is 1000+A17. The Variable Cost formula in C15 is .02+B15.

The profit formula for B17 in Figure 10-2 is (1−B$15)*$D$1−$A17. As with the formula for Figure 10-1, you shouldn't have any problems if you pay careful attention to the relative and absolute cell references shown.

Notice that the profit formulas in both figures use a number from row 1. This number appears to be part of the label, but of course it is not. In both figures the labels before and after the number are entered in such a way that the entire line looks like a label.

	A	B	C	D	E	F	G	H	I
	9	9	9	9	9	9	9	9	9
1	Monthly Profits If Sales = $100,000 per month.								
2	[Profits = Sales * (1 - Variable Cost %) - Fixed Cost $]								
3									
4	Fixed Costs					Variable Costs			
5									
6	Fixed Mfg		$14,700			Variable Mfg		38%	
7	General & Admin		$12,300			Mfg Variances		5%	
8	Marketing & Sales		$8,000			Freight		8%	
9	R & D		$5,500			Sales Commissions		5%	
10	Interest		$2,500			Advertising Co-op		6%	
11									
12			$43,000					62%	
13									
14	Fixed				Variable Costs				
15	Costs	52%	54%	56%	58%	60%	62%	64%	66%
16									
17	$30,000	18,000	16,000	14,000	12,000	10,000	8,000	6,000	4,000
18	$31,000	17,000	15,000	13,000	11,000	9,000	7,000	5,000	3,000
19	$32,000	16,000	14,000	12,000	10,000	8,000	6,000	4,000	2,000
20	$33,000	15,000	13,000	11,000	9,000	7,000	5,000	3,000	1,000
21	$34,000	14,000	12,000	10,000	8,000	6,000	4,000	2,000	(0)
22	$35,000	13,000	11,000	9,000	7,000	5,000	3,000	1,000	(1,000)
23	$36,000	12,000	10,000	8,000	6,000	4,000	2,000	(0)	(2,000)
24	$37,000	11,000	9,000	7,000	5,000	3,000	1,000	(1,000)	(3,000)
25	$38,000	10,000	8,000	6,000	4,000	2,000	(0)	(2,000)	(4,000)
26	$39,000	9,000	7,000	5,000	3,000	1,000	(1,000)	(3,000)	(5,000)
27	$40,000	8,000	6,000	4,000	2,000	(0)	(2,000)	(4,000)	(6,000)
28	$41,000	7,000	5,000	3,000	1,000	(1,000)	(3,000)	(5,000)	(7,000)
29	$42,000	6,000	4,000	2,000	(0)	(2,000)	(4,000)	(6,000)	(8,000)
30	$43,000	5,000	3,000	1,000	(1,000)	(3,000)	(5,000)	(7,000)	(9,000)
31	$44,000	4,000	2,000	(0)	(2,000)	(4,000)	(6,000)	(8,000)	(10,000)
32	$45,000	3,000	1,000	(1,000)	(3,000)	(5,000)	(7,000)	(9,000)	(11,000)
33	$46,000	2,000	(0)	(2,000)	(4,000)	(6,000)	(8,000)	(10,000)	(12,000)
34	$47,000	1,000	(1,000)	(3,000)	(5,000)	(7,000)	(9,000)	(11,000)	(13,000)

Figure 10-2. A break-even chart showing monthly profits under various assumptions when sales are $100,000 per month

A Break-Even Management Analysis

Figure 10-3 shows another use of break-even arithmetic. In a business it is often easier to find excuses to spend money than to find excuses to save money. Figure 10-3 was therefore created for a single purpose: to report the costs and benefits that accrue from a small change in fixed and variable costs.

The section beneath the Break-Even Summary heading is the report itself. Actually, of course, this report would be treated as a rough draft; data probably would be extracted from it and included in a more extensive management report of monthly performance.

The goal of this report is to give corporate managers some rule-of-thumb numbers. Three numbers in Figure 10-3 are particularly relevant. With the cost structure shown, (1) each $1.00 increase in overhead must be

```
              A        B        C       D       E      F     G      H
             12        9        9       8       8      6     6      7

 1    Break-Even Summary
 2    ------------------------------------------------------------------
 3    Fixed Costs =          $40,000 per month.
 4    Variable Costs =           60%.
 5    Break-Even Point =    $100,000 sales per month.
 6    Current Sales =       $150,000 per month.
 7    Current Profit =       $20,000 per month.
 8
 9    Each $1.00 increase (or decrease) in fixed costs raises
10      (or lowers) our Break-Even Point by    $2.50 and changes
11      our current profits by $1.00.
12
13    Each 1% addition to variable costs raises our
14      Break-Even Point by  $2,564 and requires additional
15      sales of    $3,846 to maintain our current profit level.
16      As a percentage, Break-Even sales must increase by 2.56%
17      and current sales must also increase    2.56%.  With no sales
18      change our profits would decline by  $1,500 , or 1% of sales.
19
20    Each 1% reduction of variable costs lowers our
21      Break-Even Point by  $2,439 and allows decreased
22      sales of    $3,659 to maintain our current profit level.
23      As a percentage, Break-Even sales drop by     2.44% and current
24      sales may also decrease by     2.44%.  With no sales
25      change our profits would increase    $1,500 , or 1% of sales.
```

Figure 10-3. A management report that explains the implications of changes in a firm's Fixed and Variable Costs

"paid for" by a $2.50 increase in sales; (2) each 1% increase in variable costs raises our break-even point and our break-even sales level by 2.56% and (3) lowers our profits by $1,500.

The Formulas for the Break-Even Management Analysis

The column widths for Figure 10-3 are shown beneath the column letters. These widths show the compromises necessary to make each value in rows 9 through 25 appear as if it were part of the sentence and not a separate cell.

To create this figure, enter the following cells and then enter the labels as shown in Figure 10-3.

Cell C3 Enter the amount of your average Fixed Costs in this cell. Use /**R**ange **N**ame **C**reate to assign the name FIXED to this cell.

Cell C4 Enter your average Variable Cost percentage in this cell. Assign the name VARIABLE to this cell.

Cell C5 This cell contains the classic formula for the Break-Even Point. Assign the name BRKEVEN to this cell.

C5: (C0) +$FIXED/(1−$VARIABLE)

Cell C6 Enter the amount of your Current Sales in this cell. Assign the name SALES to this cell.

Cell C7 The calculated Current Profit in this cell is equal to the Variable Cost in dollars less the Fixed Costs. Assign the name PROFIT to this cell.

C7: (C0) +$SALES*(1−$VARIABLE)−$FIXED

Cell E10 The effect on the Break-Even Point of a $1 change in Fixed Costs is equal to that $1 amount divided by the percentage that we make on each dollar of sales.

E10: (C2) 1/(1−$VARIABLE)

Cell C14 This formula calculates the Break-Even Point using a Variable Cost that is 0.01 lower than the current Variable Cost. Then it subtracts the current Break-Even Point.

C14: (CO) ($FIXED)/(1−$VARIABLE−0.01)−$BRKEVEN

Cell B15 Following the approach used for the previous cell, this formula calculates the amount that Sales must increase to maintain Current Profit levels if Variable Costs increase by 1%.

B15: (CO) ($FIXED+$PROFIT)/(1−$VARIABLE−0.01)−$SALES

Cell G16 This cell merely recalculates cell C14 and then divides it by the current Break-Even Point.

G16: (P2) (($FIXED)/(1−$VARIABLE−0.01)−$BRKEVEN)/$BRKEVEN

Cell E17 This cell recalculates cell B15 and then divides it by current Sales.

E17: (P2) (($FIXED+$PROFIT)/(1−$VARIABLE−0.01)−$SALES)/$SALES

Cell E18 If Variable Costs increase by 1% of current Sales, the dollar amount of the decline in profits is equal to 1% of current Sales.

E18: (CO) 0.01*$SALES

Rows 21-25 The formulas in rows 21 through 25 are similar to those in rows 14-18, but the signs have been changed to calculate a reduction in Variable Costs instead of an increase.

C21: (CO) −($FIXED)/(1−$VARIABLE+0.01)+$BRKEVEN
B22: (CO) −$FIXED+$PROFIT)/(1−$VARIABLE+0.01)+$SALES
F23: (P2) (−($FIXED)/(1−$VARIABLE+0.01)+$BRKEVEN)/$SALES
D24: (P2) (−($FIXED+$PROFIT)/(1−$VARIABLE+0.01)+$SALES)/$SALES
E25: (CO) 0.01*$SALES

A GRAPHICAL APPROACH TO BREAK-EVEN ANALYSIS

The most popular tool of break-even analysis is the graph. It helps you see how well you are controlling your costs from month to month. A break-even graph is easy to create in 1-2-3. And if you are new to using 1-2-3 graphics, it is a good application with which to begin.

The Break-Even Graph Explained

Figure 10-4 shows a simple break-even graph. Its numerical labels identify the following points.

1. The horizontal axis measures the company's monthly sales in dollars.

2. The vertical axis shows monthly costs.

3. This horizontal line shows costs that don't vary with normal changes in sales volume. They are usually called fixed costs. (Over time and with large increases in volume, of course, no cost is "fixed.")

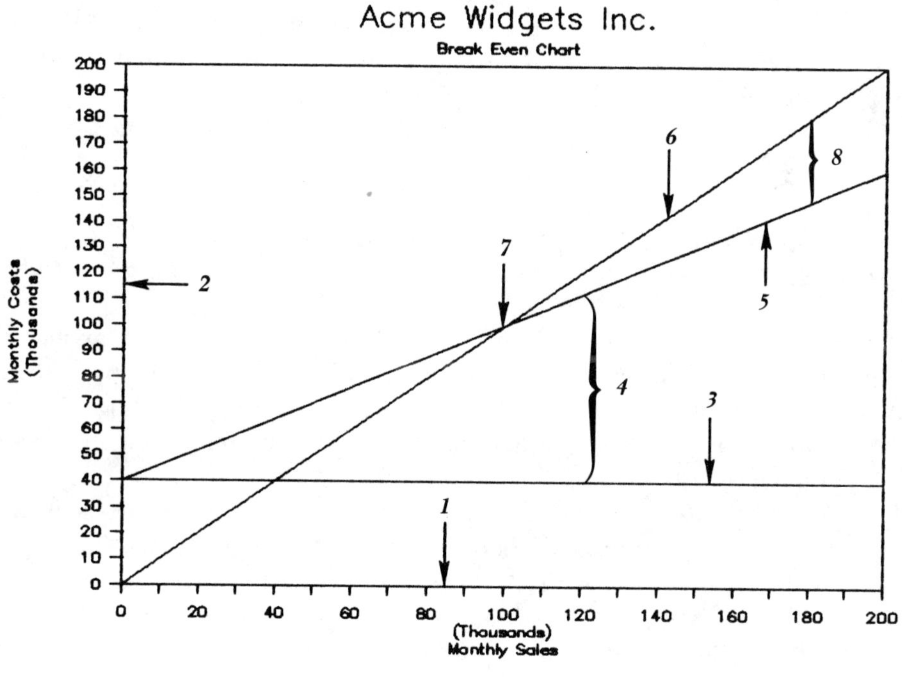

Figure 10-4. The elements of a break-even graph

4. This area reflects costs that vary as sales volume changes. If there are no sales, these variable costs are zero.

5. This is the total cost line. It is the sum of our total fixed and variable costs for any volume of sales that we expect to produce under our current operating structure.

6. You might call this line our goal line. It is the line where costs are equal to sales. Performance above this line produces losses; below it, profits. Our goal is to operate below this line, where the profits are.

7. This is our actual break-even point—the point at which our total cost line crosses the goal line. To the right of this point we expect our sales volume to be high enough so that income from sales exceeds total costs.

8. This area represents our profits. It is much like a boat's "freeboard"—the vertical distance between the waterline and the deck. The greater this distance, the less is the likelihood that water will slop over the edge and sink the boat. A company experiences a similar effect.The greater the area of this financial "freeboard," the more mistakes a firm can make and still be profitable.

How to Set Up the Break-Even Graph

Figure 10-5a graphs the break-even performance of Acme Widgets, Inc., over the past several months. Figure 10-5b shows the data used to produce this graph.

Columns B, C, and D in Figure 10-5b show actual performance data. Columns E, F, and G provide calculated data for graphing the lines showing the Fixed and Variable Costs in the break-even graph. These Graph Set-Up Values use the Fixed and Variable Cost parameters in G3 and G4 in their calculations.

Rows 13 and 20, the top and bottom data rows, are needed by the graph. To add additional months of performance to the data, insert new rows between these two rows. Cell B13 contains zero, the lowest value in the horizontal axis. Cell B20 contains the value 200,000, which was chosen as the greatest value to be graphed. The cells in columns E, F, and G contain the formulas to be described shortly. (To see why these top and bottom rows are needed, exclude them from your line assignments in step 2 of the procedure for setting up the graph. The lines in the graph will start in "midair" rather than at the vertical axis.)

For proper presentation in the graph, you must sort the X axis data (the Sales column) in ascending order. (This can cause the months to appear out of order.) When you perform this sort, select a DATA range of A14 through G19. Use a Primary-Key of B14 through B19.

The Formulas The following formulas are for row 14. Copy them as shown into the other rows of Figure 10-5b.

Sales:	Actual monthly Sales.	
Profit:	Actual monthly Profit.	
Total Costs:	Sales minus profit:	*D14:* +B14−C14
Variable Costs:	Sales times Variable Cost %:	*E14:* +B14*$G$3
Fixed Costs:	Amount estimated:	*F14:* $G$4
Ideal Total Costs:	Sum of Fixed and Variable Costs:	*G14:* +E14+F14

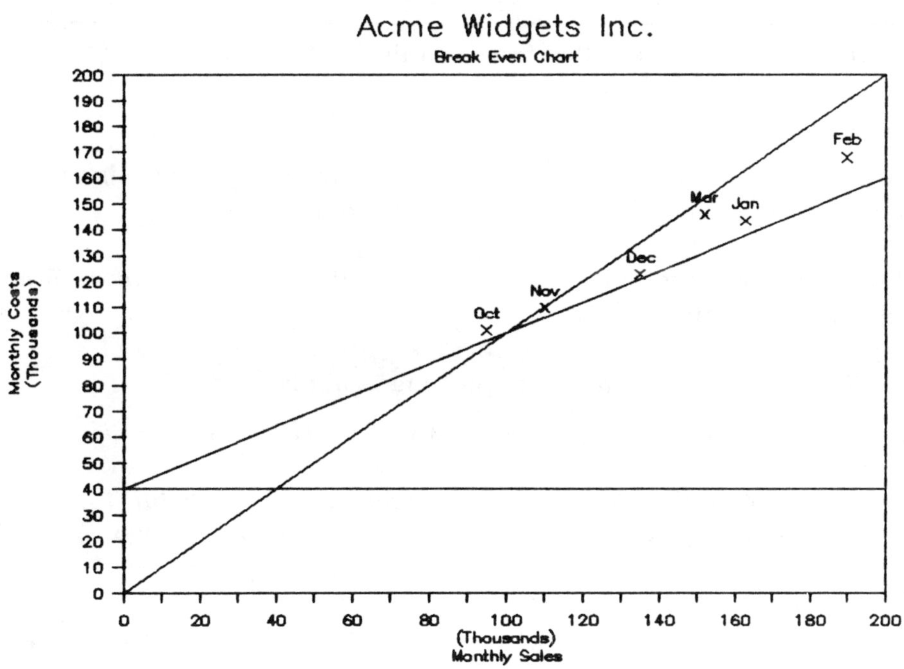

Figure 10-5a. A typical break-even graph

```
          A           B         C         D         E         F         G
         12           9         9         9         9         9         9

 1  Breakeven Data
 2  ======================
 3                                            Variable Cost % =          60%
 4                                            Fixed Cost Amt =      $40,000
 5
 6     Graph:      X,C                 E                  A           B
 7             ========================== ===========================
 8                    Actual Values              Graph Set-Up Values
 9  ---------- -------------------------- ---------------------------
10                                  Total       Var     Fixed     Ideal
11        Date      Sales    Profit   Costs     Costs     Costs Tot Csts
12  ---------- -------------------------- ---------------------------
13                      0                           0    40,000    40,000
14         Oct     95,000   (6,000) 101,000    57,000    40,000    97,000
15         Nov    110,000         0 110,000    66,000    40,000   106,000
16         Dec    135,000    12,000 123,000    81,000    40,000   121,000
17         Mar    152,000     6,000 146,000    91,200    40,000   131,200
18         Jan    163,000    19,500 143,500    97,800    40,000   137,800
19         Feb    190,000    22,000 168,000   114,000    40,000   154,000
20                200,000                     120,000    40,000   160,000
```

Figure 10-5b. The data that generated the graph in 10-5a

To format the data in Figure 10-5b, use /**R**ange **F**ormat ,0 (comma, zero). This produces commas in the display but no dollar signs.

The Graph The following steps will turn the data in Figure 10-5b into the graph in Figure 10-5a.

1. Enter the Graphics mode by pressing /**G**raph.

2. Assign the data to be graphed to the data set letters.

To Graph:	*Press:*	*Point From:*	*Point To:*
Horizontal axis	X	B13	B20
Fixed cost line	A	F13	F20
Total cost line	B	G13	G20
Goal line	C	B13	B20
Monthly actuals	E	D13	D20

In setting up your data, it's wise to document which letters you've assigned to which columns, as in Row 6 in Figure 10-5b.

3. Define the scale for the horizontal axis by selecting **O**ptions **S**cale **X**-Scale **M**anual **L**ower and setting the lower limit at 0. Then select **U**pper and set the upper limit at 200,000. Finally, return to the main Graph menu by selecting **Q**uit **Q**uit.

4. Define the scale for the vertical axis by following the preceding steps, but select the Y-Scale rather than the X-Scale.

5. Define the type of graph by selecting Type XY.

6. Define the graph format for lines by selecting **O**ptions **F**ormat **G**raph **L**ines **Q**uit **Q**uit. (You should now have returned to the main Graph menu.)

7. Define the graph format as symbols for each month's actual performance (column D, data set E) by selecting **O**ptions **F**ormat **E** **S**ymbols **Q**uit **Q**uit. (You should now have returned to the main Graph menu.)

8. Label each month's actual performance by selecting **O**ptions **D**ata-Labels **E**. Then point from A13 to A20, and choose **C**enter alignment. To return to the main Graph menu, select **Q**uit **Q**uit.

9. Title your graph by selecting **O**ptions **T**itles, and entering the titles as requested.

10. View the graph by selecting **V**iew.

Inserting Your Own Data in the Chart

Once you have the Acme break-even graph working successfully, you will probably want to substitute your own data in the chart, producing your own break-even analysis. You may face a new problem: most accounting systems don't classify costs by fixed and variable categories. You must perform your own analysis. When you do, many questions will occur to you.

Many costs are clearly variable, such as sales commissions, manufacturing labor, and the cost of material sold; and many costs are clearly fixed, such as rent, the president's salary, and, within limits, the telephone bill. But how do you classify some of the other costs?

Are marketing travel expenses fixed or variable? What about advertising expenses? Manufacturing variances are a function of goods produced, not sold, and of the skill of your manufacturing management. Fixed or variable? Many costs vary with planned production, not with actual sales. Are these costs of development and expansion fixed or variable—or neither?

There is another problem. You will probably find that there is a limited "relevant range" of time and volume during which your fixed costs will

```
             A                 B          C    D        E           F           G           H
             7                20          5    5       11          11          11          11

   1        GL                                       Fixed        June        June        June
   2     Acct #          Description     Fxd  Var     Alloc         Amt         Fxd         Var
   3     ------ -------------------- ---  ---  ---------- ---------- ---------- ----------
   4       3501 Cost of Sales--Matl          1             $31,546.78      $0.00 $31,546.78
   5       3502 Cost of Sales--Labr          1              $6,489.30      $0.00  $6,489.30
   6       3556 Scrap                        1              $5,478.90      $0.00  $5,478.90
   7       4101 Mfg Admin Labor       1                     $7,210.00  $7,210.00      $0.00
   8       4119 Equip Repair Labor              $2,200.00   $3,345.98  $2,200.00  $1,145.98
   9       4198 Mfg Overtime                 1              $3,844.84      $0.00  $3,844.84
  10       4236 Mfg Office Supplies   1                       $478.12    $478.12      $0.00
  11


         Formulas
         --------------------------------
           G4:   @IF(E4=0,C4*F4,E4)
           H4:   +F4-G4
```

Figure 10-6. A spreadsheet that can help classify Fixed and Variable Costs

remain fixed and your variable costs will vary as expected. Fixed costs don't stay fixed when it is time for the pesident's pay increase.

Unfortunately, there are no easy answers to these questions. I make the best division I can of the fixed and variable accounts, which usually means that I must examine each general ledger account number one at a time.

Creating a Spreadsheet to Separate Fixed From Variable Costs

Figure 10-6 shows one way that spreadsheets can simplify and document your assignment of costs to the fixed and variable categories. Here you generally would make the assignment by putting a 1 in the appropriate Fixed or Variable column. Then, each month, you insert the current month's expenses and let the spreadsheet calculate your fixed and variable expenses.

Occasionally an account contains both fixed and variable charges. This is true for Equipment Repair Labor in the figure, for example. We know that Joe, the general plant handyman, earns $2,200 per month. The remaining charges to this account are caused by wear and tear created by production volume. The formulas shown in the figure assign Joe's salary to the Fixed column and the remaining charges to the Variable column.

After examining several months of data, I calculate an average fixed cost and an average variable cost as a percent of sales. Next, I create the chart, plot recent performance, create the graph, and see what it looks like. If the graph doesn't make sense, I reconsider and readjust my estimates. The spreadsheets make this approach easy.

Regression Analysis With The Break-Even Graph

When you plot points on a graph by hand, it is easy to draw a line through them with a ruler. But to draw the line in 1-2-3, you must use regression analysis. However, making this extra effort rewards you with additional information.

Figures 10-7a and 10-7b illustrate the approach. Although the break-even graphs of Figures 10-7a and 10-5a plot nearly the same monthly performance, 1-2-3 has used least squares regression to calculate the total cost line in Figure 10-7a. (Chapter 14 explains least squares regression in greater detail; it also explains how to use the Regression command available to users of Version 2.)

Take the following steps to create Figures 10-7a and 10-7b.

1. Begin with the spreadsheet and graph assignments shown in Figure 10-5b.

2. Create the column H, Sales Times Total Costs, shown in Figure 10-7b. Enter the following formula in H14 and then copy it down the column through row 19 as shown in the figure.

H14: +B14*D14

3. Use /**R**ange **N**ame **C**reate to create the ranges X, Y, and XY as shown in Figure 10-7b.

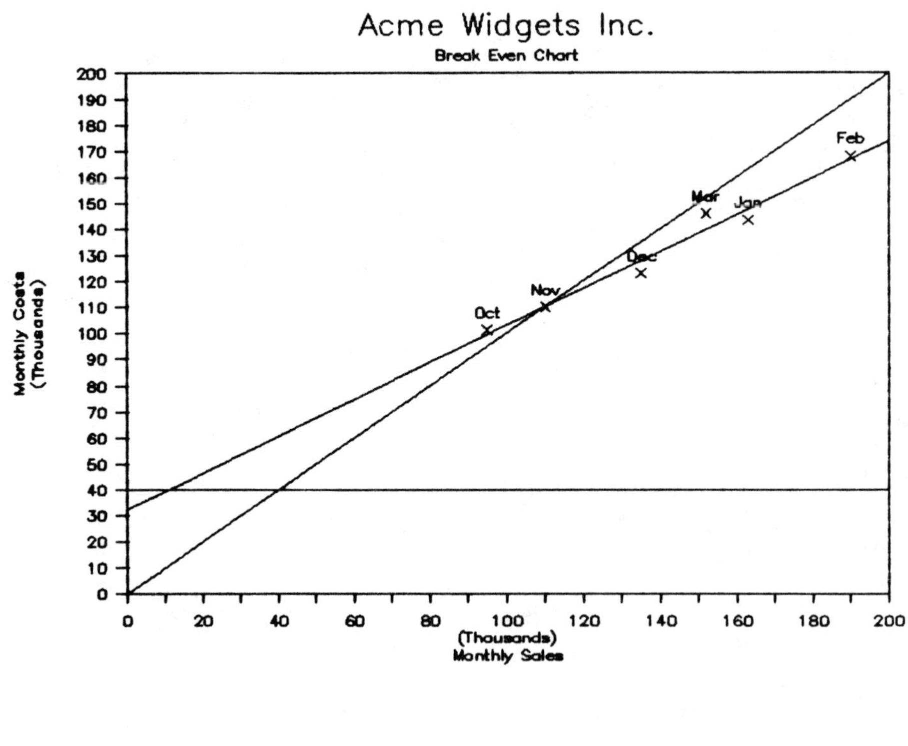

Figure 10-7a. A break-even graph using least squares regression

4. Set the column widths for columns L and M as shown in the figure; then enter the headings for columns K through M and the variable names in column K as shown.

5. Assign these variables in column K as range names for the cells in column L by using the /**R**ange **N**ame **L**abel **R**ight command.

6. Format cells L-6 through L-14 by using /**R**ange **F**ormat **T**ext; then enter the formulas as shown for column L. To display the value calculated for cell L6, enter **+L6** in cell M6. Copy M6 to cells M7, M10, and M13. Format M10 as Percent 0 and M13 as Currency 0.

	A	B	C	D	E	F	G	H	I	J
	12	9	9	9	9	9	9	13	11	9
1	Breakeven Data									
2	====================									
3					Variable Cost % =		60%			
4					Fixed Cost Amt =		$40,000			
5	Regression:	X		Y				XY		
6	Graph:	X,C		E		A			B	
7		=========================			=========================			=========================		
8		Actual Values			Graph Set-Up Values			Used for Regression		
9	----------	--------------------------			-------------------------			-------------------------		
10				Total	Var	Fixed	Ideal	Sales Times	Regr	
11	Date	Sales	Profit	Costs	Costs	Costs	Tot Csts	Total Costs	Tot Csts	
12	-----------	--------	--------	--------	--------	--------	--------	-----------	----------	
13		0			0	40,000	40,000		32,189	
14	Oct	95,000	(6,000)	101,000	57,000	40,000	97,000	9595000000	99,461	
15	Nov	110,000	0	110,000	66,000	40,000	106,000	12100000000	110,083	
16	Dec	135,000	12,000	123,000	81,000	40,000	121,000	16605000000	127,786	
17	Mar	152,000	6,000	146,000	91,200	40,000	131,200	22192000000	139,824	
18	Jan	163,000	19,500	143,500	97,800	40,000	137,800	23390500000	147,614	
19	Feb	190,000	22,000	168,000	114,000	40,000	154,000	31920000000	166,733	
20		200,000			120,000	40,000	160,000		173,814	

X Y XY

	K	L	M	N	O	P	Q
	9	31	11	9	9	9	9
1	Regression Formulas						
2	==						
3	Name of						
4	Variable	Formula	Value	Explanation			
5	--------	----------------------------	----------	------------------------------------			
6	N	@COUNT(X)	6	Number of months graphed			
7	Sxy	@SUM(XY)-N*@AVG(X)*@AVG(Y)	4332916667	Sum of			
8				(Each Sale - Average Sales)*			
9				(Each Cost - Average Costs)			
10	B	+SXY/(@VAR(X)*N)	70.81%	The slope of regression equation			
11				Y = A + B*X. This is our			
12				calculated Variable Cost %.			
13	A	@AVG(Y)-B*@AVG(X)	$32,188.65	The Y intercept of the regression			
14				equation. This is our calculated			
15				monthly Fixed Cost amount.			

Figure 10-7b. The data and formulas that generated the graph in 10-7a

7. Enter the following formula in I13 to create the Regression Total Costs column; then copy I13 down the column as shown in the figure.

I13: `$A+$B*B13`

8. To graph the Regression Costs data:

a. Make sure that the B in row 6 is in column I, above the heading Regr Tot Csts. This helps you document what is happening in your graph.

b. Enter the Graphics menu by selecting **/G**raph.

c. To specify the data for the Total Costs Regression line, select **B** and define the range by pointing from I13 to I20.

d. To view the graph, select **V**iew.

The Break-Even Graph From Regression Explained

Look again at Figure 10-7a. We plotted the points from regression and then drew the new total cost line. But this line intersected the vertical axis at a point below our previously calculated fixed cost line. In fact, as shown in column M of Figure 10-7b, the regression equation has calculated that Acme's fixed costs are lower ($32,188.65 versus $40,000) and its variable costs higher (70.81% versus 60%) than we had thought. What created these discrepancies?

Two answers are possible. First, it may be that Acme's fixed costs are indeed lower and their variable costs higher than was estimated in Figures 10-5a and 10-5b. But the second answer is more likely.

Look again at Figure 10-5a. Notice that the greater the sales, the farther from the total cost line Acme performs. This could well mean that Acme is failing to manage its increased volume profitably.

Perhaps Acme's sales force offered price discounts to book those greater sales. Perhaps their manufacturing manager had to increase overtime, hire marginal workers, and pay premium prices for hard-to-get material. Perhaps the controller had to hire new clerks just to keep track of all this activity.

Also, look at March's performance. When sales declined from February's peak, costs didn't decline proportionately. In January and February Acme apparently added some costs that it failed to eliminate in March. In other words, Acme is performing in a common but dangerous fashion: Acme's costs are becoming variable upward but fixed downward.

What should Acme do? Lay people off? Cut spending? Change pricing? Or should Acme accept its new cost structure and push harder to increase sales?

The break-even chart does not answer these questions. The fundamental value of the chart is that it helps managers to raise these questions in the first place.

Chapter
Eleven

FORECASTING FINANCIAL DISTRESS WITH Z SCORES

In the first half of this decade the average number of business bankruptcies per year was more than double that of the 1970s. And the percentage of U.S. businesses that failed each year has increased by more than half. By any measure, business failures have surged in the 1980s.

Will your major customer be among these failures? Your most critical vendor? Your high-flying stock market investment? You or your own employer?

If you had some warning that a bankruptcy was impending, you could protect yourself. But how can you predict which businesses will probably go bankrupt and which will probably not?

Roughly 20 years ago, Edward I. Altman set out to answer this question. Altman, a financial economist at New York University's Graduate School of Business, analyzed a sample of both bankrupt and healthy manufacturing firms. Combining traditional financial ratio analysis with a statistical technique called multiple discriminant analysis (MDA), he developed a model for predicting the likelihood that a firm would go bankrupt.

In Altman's model five financial ratios are combined in a specific way (described in this chapter) to produce a single number. This number, called the Z Score, is a general measure of corporate financial health. Altman developed the Z Score for publicly traded manufacturing firms. Later he developed a modified version for private manufacturing firms and a second modification for use by all businesses.[1]

BACKGROUND ON THE Z SCORE MODELS

In the next section we discuss how to calculate the three versions of the Z Score. Before we do so, a closer look at how the models were derived will help clarify what it is we will be calculating.

How the Z Score Model Was Created

In 1966 Altman selected a sample of 66 corporations, 33 of which had filed for bankruptcy between 1946 and 1965, and 33 of which were randomly selected from those still in existence in 1966. The asset size of all corporations ranged from $1 million to $26 million.

Altman calculated 22 common financial ratios for all 66 corporations. (For the bankrupt firms, he used the financial statements issued one year prior to bankruptcy.) His goal was to choose a small number of these ratios that could best distinguish between a bankrupt firm and a healthy firm.

To make his selection Altman used the statistical technique of multiple discriminant analysis. This approach shows which characteristics in which proportions can best be used for determining to which of several categories a subject belongs: bankrupt versus nonbankrupt, male versus female, Democrat versus Republican, and so on.

The advantage to MDA is that many characteristics can be combined into a single score. A low score implies membership in one group, a high score implies membership in the other group, and a middling score causes uncertainty as to which group the subject belongs.

Altman called this single score of corporate health the Z Score. A sufficiently high Z Score implies that the firm is financially healthy. A sufficiently low Z Score implies that the firm is near bankruptcy. A middling score puts the firm into an area of uncertainty Altman calls the "gray" area.

Finally, to test the model, Altman calculated the Z Scores for new groups of bankrupt and nonbankrupt firms. For the non-bankrupt firms,

---

[1] These three Z Scores and many other performance-monitoring ratios are discussed in a book by Edward I. Altman: *Corporate Financial Distress*, New York: Wiley-Interscience, 1983.

however, he chose corporations that had reported deficits during the recession of 1958 or of 1961. Two thirds of these firms had reported at least two years of deficits between 1958 and 1961. His goal, of course, was to discover how well the Z Score model could distinguish between sick firms and the terminally ill.

Altman found that about 95% of the bankrupt firms were correctly classified as bankrupt. And roughly 80% of the sick, nonbankrupt firms were correctly classified as nonbankrupt. Of the misclassified nonbankrupt firms, the scores of nearly three fourths of these fell into the gray area.

Modified Versions of the Z Score

The Z Score is calculated by multiplying each of five financial ratios by an appropriate coefficient and then summing the results. Under the heading Z Public Manufacturing, Figure 11-1 shows the values of the coefficients used to calculate the Z Score. These values result from Altman's regression equation. The values used in the Z Score ratios can be explained as follows:

- *Working Capital* is equal to current assets minus current liabilities.
- *Total Assets* is the total of the assets section of the balance sheet.
- *Retained Earnings* is found in the equity section of the balance sheet.
- *EBIT (Earnings Before Interest and Taxes)* includes the income or loss from operations and from any unusual or extraordinary items but not the tax effects of these items. It can be calculated as follows: find net income; add back any income tax expenses and subtract any income tax benefits; then add back any interest expenses.
- *Market Value of Equity* is the total value of all shares of common and preferred stock. The dates these values are chosen need not correspond exactly with the dates of the financial statements to which the market value is compared.
- *Net Worth* is also known as shareholders' equity or, simply, equity. It is equal to Total Assets minus Total Liabilities.
- *Book Value of Total Liabilities* is the sum of all current and long-term liabilities from the balance sheet.
- *Sales* includes other income normally categorized as revenues in the firm's income statement.

Summary of Z Score Models

Variable	Coefficients: Z Public Mfg	Coefficients: Z1 Private Mfg	Coefficients: Z2 General Use	Mean Values: Bankrupt	Mean Values: Nonbankrupt
X1 = Working Capital / Total Assets	1.200	0.717	6.560	(0.061)	0.414
X2 = Retained Earnings / Total Assets	1.400	0.847	3.260	(0.626)	0.355
X3 = EBIT / Total Assets	3.300	3.107	6.720	(0.318)	0.154
X4 = Mkt Value of Equity / Total Liabilities	0.600			0.401	2.477

X4A = Net Worth / Total Liabilities		0.420	1.050	0.494	2.684
X5 = Sales / Total Assets	1.000	0.998		1.503	1.939

Cutoff Values	Z	Z1	Z2
Safe if greater than:	2.99	2.90	2.60
Bankrupt if less than:	1.81	1.23	1.10

Mean Scores			
Nonbankrupt	5.02	4.14	7.70
Bankrupt	(0.29)	0.15	(4.06)

Figure 11-1. A summary of the three Z Score models

Use balance sheet figures from the *end* of the reporting period for all Z Score calculations.

Two of the ratios used by the Z Score have tended to limit the usefulness of this calculation, however. One is the Market Value of Equity divided by Total Liabilities, variable X4. Obviously, if a firm is not publicly traded, its equity has no market value. So it cannot use the Z Score.

The other problem ratio is Assets Turnover, variable X5, which is calculated by dividing Sales for the year by the value of Total Assets at the end of the year. This ratio varies significantly by industry. Jewelry stores, for example, have a low asset turnover while grocery stores have a high turnover. Manufacturing firms have a turnover between these extremes. But since the Z Score expects a value that is common to manufacturing, it could be biased in such a way that a healthy jewelry store looks sick and a sickly grocery store looks healthy. Therefore, only industries with normal turnovers similar to that of manufacturing can use the Z Score.

To deal with these problems, Altman went back to his original sample of 66 publicly traded manufacturers and calculated two modified versions of the Z Score. To make the Z Score applicable to private firms, he substituted variable X4A, the Net Worth of the firm, for variable X4, the Market Value of Equity. He calls this first modification of the Z Score the private-firm version or the Z′ (Z prime) version. We will call it the Z1 Score.

The second modification of the Z Score also uses variable X4A but eliminates Assets Turnover, variable X5, altogether. This omissions allows nonmanufacturers to calculate a version of the Z Score. Altman calls this the four-variable model or Z″ (Z double prime). We will call it the Z2 Score.

Figure 11-1 shows the values of the coefficients for the Z1 and Z2 Scores. The figure also shows related information about the bankrupt and nonbankrupt firms that Altman studied. We will discuss this information shortly.

What Does the Z Score Mean?

The Z Score is not intended to predict when a firm will file a formal declaration of bankruptcy in a federal district court. It is instead a measure of how closely a firm resembles other firms that have filed for bankruptcy. It is a measure of corporate financial distress, a measure of *economic* bankruptcy.

How accurately does the Z Score measure economic bankruptcy? The original model has drawn several statistical objections over the years. The model uses unadjusted accounting data; it uses data from relatively small firms; and it uses data that today is nearly 40 years old. And yet, despite these concerns, the original Z Score model is the best-known and most widely used measure of its kind. It isn't a perfect measure, but many users have found it useful.

The reliability of the modified models, however, is open to some question. Both models use data from the original sample of publicly traded manufacturing firms to provide clues to the health of private firms and nonmanufacturers. And neither of the modified models has been tested rigorously.

When you analyze publicly traded manufacturers, therefore, use the original Z Score. When the Z Score doesn't apply, Altman's experience shows that Z2 is a more reliable guide than Z1. All three models, however, seem to properly show the *trends* in a firm's financial health, even though the value of the score itself may at times be questionable.

The Z Score model is a tool that can complement your other analytical tools. Seldom, however, should you use the Z Score as your only means of analysis.

HOW TO SET UP A Z SCORE SPREADSHEET

Many different spreadsheet formats can be used to calculate a Z Score. Figures 11-2 and 11-3 show one convenient format. Figure 11-2 shows the recent ten-year financial history and Z Scores of the International Harvester Company. Figure 11-3 covers the same period and shows similar information for the Hewlett-Packard Company.

To build Figure 11-2, enter the headings and descriptions as shown, go to the Range Name column, enter the names, and then "turn them on" by using the /**R**ange **N**ame **L**abel **R**ight command. (Be sure to put brackets around X1 and X5 as shown; the brackets differentiate a range name of, say, [X1] from a cell name of X1.)

Next, enter the financial data shown in Figure 11-2. The source for this information was the annual reports for the years shown. Use a global format of ,0 (comma zero).

The formulas for the ratios X1 through X5 are

D23: +WC/TA
D24: +RE/TA
D25: +EBIT/TA
D26: +MKV/TL
D27: +NW/TL
D28: +SALES/TA

	A	B	C	D	E	F	G	H	I	J	K	L	M
1	Z SCORE HISTORY TABLE												
2	International Harvester												
3	================================												
4		Graph	Range										
5	Description	Name	Name	1975	1976	1977	1978	1979	1980	1981	1982	1983	1984
6	-------------------------------	------	------	------	------	------	------	------	------	------	------	------	------
7	Current Assets		CA	2,353	2,273	2,324	2,649	3,266	3,427	2,672	1,656	1,388	1,412
8	Property & Equipment			658	710	771	890	1,039	1,277	1,361	966	837	716
9	Other Assets			523	592	693	777	942	1,139	1,313	1,077	1,138	1,121
10	Total Assets		TA	3,533	3,575	3,788	4,316	5,247	5,843	5,346	3,699	3,362	3,249
11	Current Liabilities		CL	1,126	1,042	1,048	1,439	1,873	2,433	1,808	1,135	1,367	1,257
12	Long Term Liabilities			938	923	926	933	948	1,327	1,985	2,015	1,289	1,238
13	Other Liabilities			25	47	80	69	227	187	71	515	464	452
14	Total Liabilities		TL	2,089	2,012	2,054	2,441	3,048	3,947	3,864	3,665	3,119	2,947
15	Stock			601	615	641	664	694	872	882	1,112	1,730	1,839
16	Retained Earnings		RE	843	948	1,093	1,212	1,505	1,024	600	(1,078)	(1,487)	(1,537)
17	Net Worth		NW	1,444	1,563	1,734	1,876	2,199	1,896	1,482	34	243	302
18	Liabilities + Net Worth			3,533	3,575	3,788	4,317	5,247	5,843	5,346	3,699	3,362	3,249
19	Working Capital		WC	1,227	1,231	1,276	1,210	1,393	994	864	521	22	155
20	Sales		SALES	5,246	5,537	6,003	6,698	8,426	6,000	7,018	4,322	3,600	4,861
21	EBIT		EBIT	289	434	494	466	719	(402)	(16)	(1,274)	(231)	120

22	Market Value			MKV	622	845	821	1,001	1,122	1,147	376	151	835	575
23	Working Capital/Total Assets			[X1]	0.35	0.34	0.34	0.28	0.27	0.17	0.16	0.14	0.01	0.05
24	Retained Earnings/Total Assets			[X2]	0.24	0.27	0.29	0.28	0.29	0.18	0.11	(0.29)	(0.44)	(0.47)
25	EBIT/Total Assets			[X3]	0.08	0.12	0.13	0.11	0.14	(0.07)	(0.00)	(0.34)	(0.07)	0.04
26	Market Value of Equity/Tot Liab			[X4]	0.30	0.42	0.40	0.41	0.37	0.29	0.10	0.04	0.27	0.20
27	Net Worth/Total Liabilities			[X4A]	0.69	0.78	0.84	0.77	0.72	0.48	0.38	0.01	0.08	0.10
28	Sales/Total Assets			[X5]	1.48	1.55	1.58	1.55	1.61	1.03	1.31	1.17	1.07	1.50
29	Z Score		A		2.68	2.99	3.06	2.88	3.00	1.42	1.71	(0.18)	0.39	1.13
30	Gray Top	Z	D		2.99	2.99	2.99	2.99	2.99	2.99	2.99	2.99	2.99	2.99
31	Gray Bottom	Z	F		1.81	1.81	1.81	1.81	1.81	1.81	1.81	1.81	1.81	1.81
32	Z1 Score		B		2.48	2.72	2.83	2.65	2.76	1.28	1.67	(0.05)	0.52	1.28
33	Gray Top	Z1			2.90	2.90	2.90	2.90	2.90	2.90	2.90	2.90	2.90	2.90
34	Gray Bottom	Z1			1.23	1.23	1.23	1.23	1.23	1.23	1.23	1.23	1.23	1.23
35	Z2 Score		C		4.33	4.76	4.91	4.29	4.36	1.73	1.81	(2.33)	(1.78)	(0.87)
36	Gray Top	Z2			2.60	2.60	2.60	2.60	2.60	2.60	2.60	2.60	2.60	2.60
37	Gray Bottom	Z2			1.10	1.10	1.10	1.10	1.10	1.10	1.10	1.10	1.10	1.10
38	YEAR		X		75	76	77	78	79	80	81	82	83	84
39			DL A											Z
40			DL B											Z1
41			DL C											Z2
42			DL D		TOP									
43			DL F		BOT									

Figure 11-2. A ten-year financial history, and the Z Scores, for the International Harvester Company

	A	B	C	D	E	F	G	H	I	J	K	L	M
1	Z SCORE HISTORY TABLE												
2	Hewlett-Packard												
3	================================												
4		Graph	Range										
5	Description	Name	Name	1975	1976	1977	1978	1979	1980	1981	1982	1983	1984
6	------------------------------	------	------	------	------	------	------	------	------	------	------	------	------
7	Current Assets		CA	499	597	752	952	1,269	1,491	1,705	2,215	2,632	3,201
8	Property & Equipment			251	315	378	476	591	789	979	1,171	1,431	1,868
9	Other Assets			18	21	28	34	40	57	74	84	98	84
10	Total Assets		TA	768	933	1,158	1,462	1,900	2,337	2,758	3,470	4,161	5,153
11	Current Liabilities		CL	179	223	292	415	599	691	704	863	920	1,322
12	Long Term Liabilities			5	7	12	10	15	29	26	39	71	81
13	Other Liabilities			23	26	30	35	51	70	108	219	283	205
14	Total Liabilities		TL	207	256	334	460	665	790	838	1,121	1,274	1,608
15	Stock			166	200	236	276	326	393	481	587	733	775
16	Retained Earnings		RE	395	477	588	726	909	1,154	1,439	1,762	2,154	2,770
17	Net Worth		NW	561	677	824	1,002	1,235	1,547	1,920	2,349	2,887	3,545
18	Liabilities + Net Worth			768	933	1,158	1,462	1,900	2,337	2,758	3,470	4,161	5,153
19	Working Capital		WC	320	374	460	537	670	800	1,001	1,352	1,712	1,879
20	Sales		SALES	990	1,124	1,374	1,751	2,361	3,099	3,578	4,254	4,710	6,044
21	EBIT		EBIT	151	165	233	302	398	523	580	676	728	860

22	Market Value			MKV	2,612	2,357	2,000	2,218	3,107	4,410	5,048	7,731	8,868	9,291
23	Working Capital/Total Assets			[X1]	0.42	0.40	0.40	0.37	0.35	0.34	0.36	0.39	0.41	0.36
24	Retained Earnings/Total Assets			[X2]	0.51	0.51	0.51	0.50	0.48	0.49	0.52	0.51	0.52	0.54
25	EBIT/Total Assets			[X3]	0.20	0.18	0.20	0.21	0.21	0.22	0.21	0.19	0.17	0.17
26	Market Value of Equity/Tot Liab			[X4]	12.64	9.21	5.99	4.82	4.67	5.58	6.02	6.90	6.96	5.78
27	New Worth/Total Liabilities			[X4A]	2.71	2.64	2.47	2.18	1.86	1.96	2.29	2.10	2.27	2.20
28	Sales/Total Assets			[X5]	1.29	1.20	1.19	1.20	1.24	1.33	1.30	1.23	1.13	1.17
29	Z Score		A		10.74	8.51	6.63	5.91	5.83	6.52	6.77	7.19	7.10	6.38
30	Gray Top	Z	D		2.99	2.99	2.99	2.99	2.99	2.99	2.99	2.99	2.99	2.99
31	Gray Bottom	Z	F		1.81	1.81	1.81	1.81	1.81	1.81	1.81	1.81	1.81	1.81
32	Z1 Score		B		3.77	3.58	3.56	3.44	3.33	3.50	3.61	3.42	3.36	3.33
33	Gray Top	Z1			2.90	2.90	2.90	2.90	2.90	2.90	2.90	2.90	2.90	2.90
34	Gray Bottom	Z1			1.23	1.23	1.23	1.23	1.23	1.23	1.23	1.23	1.23	1.23
35	Z2 Score		C		8.58	8.26	8.21	7.70	7.23	7.42	7.90	7.72	7.94	7.58
36	Gray Top	Z2			2.60	2.60	2.60	2.60	2.60	2.60	2.60	2.60	2.60	2.60
37	Gray Bottom	Z2			1.10	1.10	1.10	1.10	1.10	1.10	1.10	1.10	1.10	1.10
38	YEAR		X		75	76	77	78	79	80	81	82	83	84
39			DL A											Z
40			DL B											Z1
41			DL C											Z2
42			DL D	Top										
43			DL F	Bot										

Figure 11-3. A ten-year financial history, and the Z Scores, for the Hewlett-Packard Company

The Z Score formulas use the coefficients shown in Figure 11-1. The formulas are

D29: 1.2*[X1]+1.4*[X2]+3.3*[X3]+.6*[X4]+[X5]
D32: .717*[X1]+.847*[X2]+3.107*[X3]+.42*[X4A]+.998*[X5]
D35: 6.56*[X1]+3.26*[X2]+6.72*[X3]+1.05*[X4A]

Graphing the Z Scores requires that other data be added. Enter the data for the top and bottom of each gray area, rows 30 and 31, 33 and 34, 36 and 37. Enter the numbers for the YEAR as shown in row 38. Finally, enter the labels that we will use as graph Data-Labels in rows 39-43.

M39: (3 blank leading spaces) Z
M40: (1 leading space) Z1
M41: (1 leading space) Z2
D42: TOP (4 trailing spaces)
D43: BOT (4 trailing spaces)

When you have finished entering the data for International Harvester, save the spreadsheet to disk. Then, to enter Hewlett-Packard's data as shown in Figure 11-3, erase IH's data in memory, substitute the data for HP, and then save the HP data to disk under another name.

Once both sets of data have been entered and the Z Scores calculated, the next step is to draw pictures of the data.

HOW TO CREATE A Z SCORE GRAPH

Let's begin by graphing data for the IH Z Score as shown at the top of Figure 11-4. Follow the same approach to produce the HP Z Score graph shown in the bottom of that figure. Here are the steps.

1. Type /**G**raph.
2. Assign the data to be graphed to the data range letters.

To Graph	*Choose*	*Assign the Range*
Horizontal axis (Year)	X	D38..M38
Z Scores	A	D29..M29
Top of gray area	D	D30..M30
Bottom of gray area	F	D31..M31

In setting up your data, it's wise to document which data range letters you assign to which columns, as in column B of Figure 11-2.

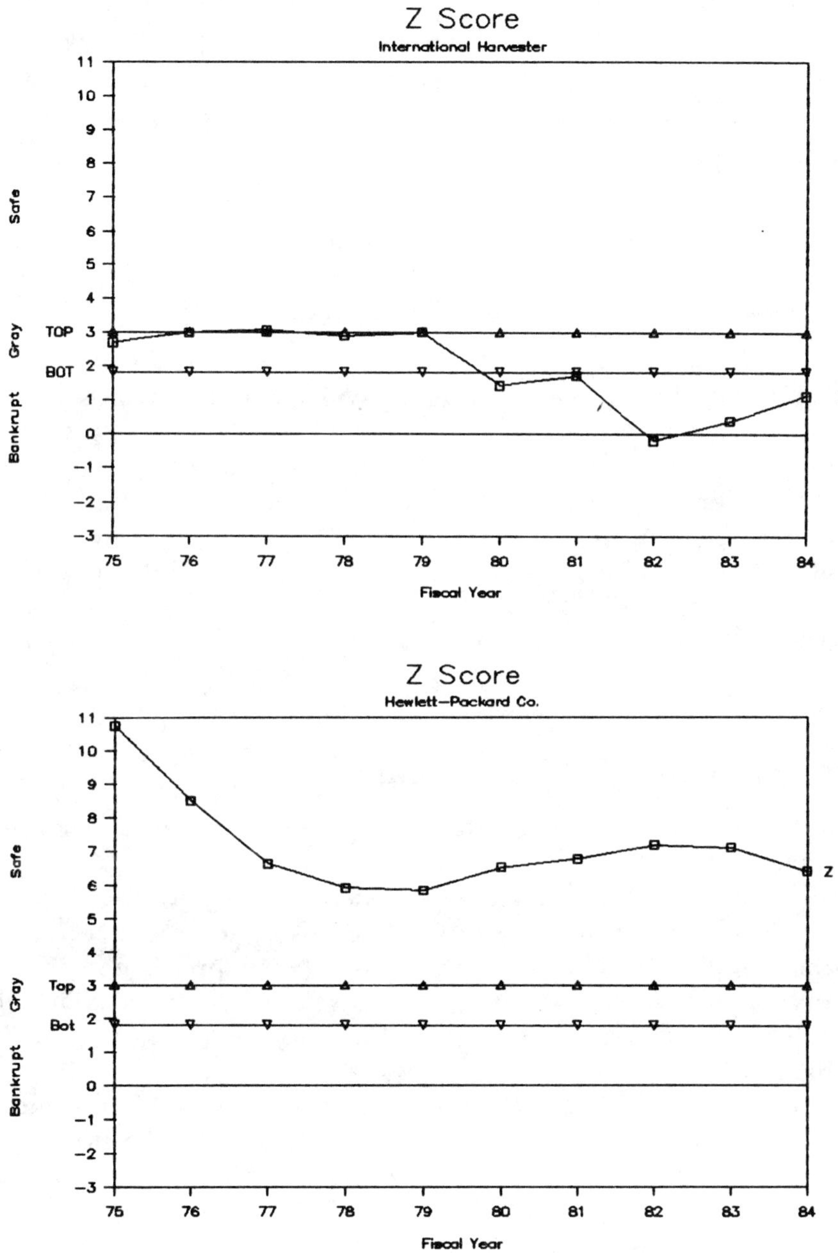

Figure 11-4. A graph of the Z Scores for Hewlett-Packard and for International Harvester

3. Now define the scale for the horizontal axis by selecting **O**ptions **S**cale **X**-Scale **M**anual **L**ower and set the lower limit at 75. Then select **U**pper, set the upper limit at 84, and select **Q**uit **Q**uit. You should now be in the main Graph menu.

4. Define the scale for the vertical axis by selecting **O**ptions **S**cale **Y**-Scale **M**anual **L**ower and set the lower limit at −3. Then select **U**pper, set the upper limit at 11, and select **Q**uit.

5. Title your graph by selecting **T**itles **F**irst and entering **Z Score**. Then select **T**itles **S**econd and enter **International Harvester**. To title the Y axis as shown, type **Bankrupt** (4 spaces) **Gray** (13 spaces) **Safe** (6 spaces) and then press ENTER.

6. Assign the labels for the graph lines by selecting **D**ata-Labels and then

To Label	*Choose*	*Assign the Range*	*Align*
Z Score line	A	D39..M39	Right
Top of gray area	D	D42	Left
Bottom of gray area	F	D43	Left

7. View the graph by selecting **Q**uit **V**iew.

8. Press **Q**uit to return to the Ready mode. Then save your spreadsheet.

How to Interpret the Z Score Results

Figure 11-4 makes it clear that HP is in better shape than IH. What else do these graphs tell us?

HP's Z Score, high in the safe zone, reflects its historically healthy performance. Consistent safe performance like this indicates that a firm will probably not go bankrupt in the near future. (Such a prediction assumes, of course, that a major problem doesn't arrive out of the blue; a multibillion dollar lawsuit or a major uninsured loss, for example, could sink the healthiest of firms.)

But the HP Z Score *has* shown a downward trend. Is this a dangerous trend? It all depends. On the one hand, an unusually high Z Score (above 8 or 9) might mean that a firm is missing opportunities for development and expansion. If so, HP's falling Z Score may be good, because it could indicate that the firm has begun to act on new opportunities for growth. But on the other hand, a falling Z Score could serve as an early warning of problems to come.

In either case, it is instructive to watch the value of a falling Z Score. HP's lowest score of 5.83 is still comfortably above 5.02, the value shown in Figure 11-1 as the average score for nonbankrupt firms. And HP's score is significantly above 2.99, the value shown as the top of the dangerous gray area.

Not so International Harvester. In Figure 11-4 we see that IH bounced around the top part of the gray area during the years 1975 through 1979. Then IH went downhill. The gray area is where the scores of the "better-performing" bankrupt firms overlap the scores of the worst-performing nonbankrupt firms. Here's one way to think about the gray area: if your company's Z Score falls within this area, remember that firms scoring higher than yours have already gone bankrupt.

If you find that your own firm is in the gray area, you may wonder which ratios have hurt your score the most. Figure 11-1 shows the Mean Value of each ratio for both bankrupt and nonbankrupt firms. When we compare these values to IH's ratios in 1980, we see that two ratios were particulary low. The ratio of Sales to Total Assets (cell I28 in Figure 11-2) was 1.03. This is far below the value of 1.503 shown in Figure 11-1 for the average bankrupt firm. Also, the ratio of Market Value of Equity to Total Liabilities (cell I26) is quite low, but it is higher than it will be again over the next several years.

How has IH survived? The data in Figure 11-2 tells us much. IH has survived since 1980 by selling $1 billion worth of stock and by disposing of more than $2.5 billion in assets. This cash was used to reduce total debt by $1 billion and to fund $2.5 billion in cumulative losses.

At this point IH's EBIT (Earnings Before Interest and Taxes) is positive, its Z Score is rising, and some analysts are predicting profitability. International Harvester might just make it.

Add the Other Z Score Versions

Someone once said that a person with one watch always knows what time it is, but someone with more than one watch is never quite sure. Calculating different versions of the Z Score produces a similar effect.

To see what I mean, retrieve your IH spreadsheet. Type /**G**raph. Then assign the graph ranges **B** and **C** to rows 32 and 35, respectively, just as you assigned the graph range A to row 29. Then assign the Data-Label ranges for **B** and **C** in row 40 and 41, just as you did for A in row 40.

When you view this graph, shown at the top of Figure 11-5, you will see that the Z1 line follows the Z line very closely. (In fact, this is why we inserted extra spaces in front of the Z in cell M39; the spaces kept the Z and the Z1 from printing on top of each other.) And the Z2 line behaves in an interesting way. Though it shows higher highs and lower lows, it generally agrees with the other two lines.

When you add the Z1 and Z2 lines to the HP graph, as shown at the bottom of Figure 11-5, you will see that the various Z Score graphs contradict themselves. HP's Z2 line gives a favorable report of HP's performance, roughly equivalent to the firm's Z line. But look at the firm's Z1 line.

The Z1 line shows that HP's performance has hovered just above the gray area during the past ten years. (True, we are comparing the Z1 line to the Z Score gray area, but the difference between the two sets of gray areas is not too significant.) The Z1 Score, of course, here gives an overly negative appraisal of HP's financial performance. But notice that although the *level* shown for the Z1 Score is too low, the flat *trend* that the graph shows is essentially correct. HP's financial health has not varied significantly during the period shown.

APPLICATIONS FOR THE Z SCORE

Over the years, business people have used the Z Score for many different applications. These have tended to fall into the following seven categories:

1. Credit analysis: Banks have used the Z Score to help assess whether to accept or reject a loan application. Nonfinancial institutions have used the scores to assist in trade credit decisions.

2. Investment analysis: Obviously, if a firm is headed for financial distress, investors would prefer to know that fact. Also, improving Z Scores can act as an early indicator of a turnaround.

3. Auditing analysis: The Z Score has helped public accountants assess whether an audit client will continue as a going concern.

4. Legal analysis: Those who invest other people's money tend to get sued if the investment goes sour. Depending on the score, Z Score analysis could help either side of the argument.

5. Merger analysis: By analyzing recent trends in the Z Score of a possible acquisition, a buyer can get an additional view of the direction in which the prospect is heading. Also, of course, the Z Score can help to assess how the merger would affect an acquiring firm's own financial health.

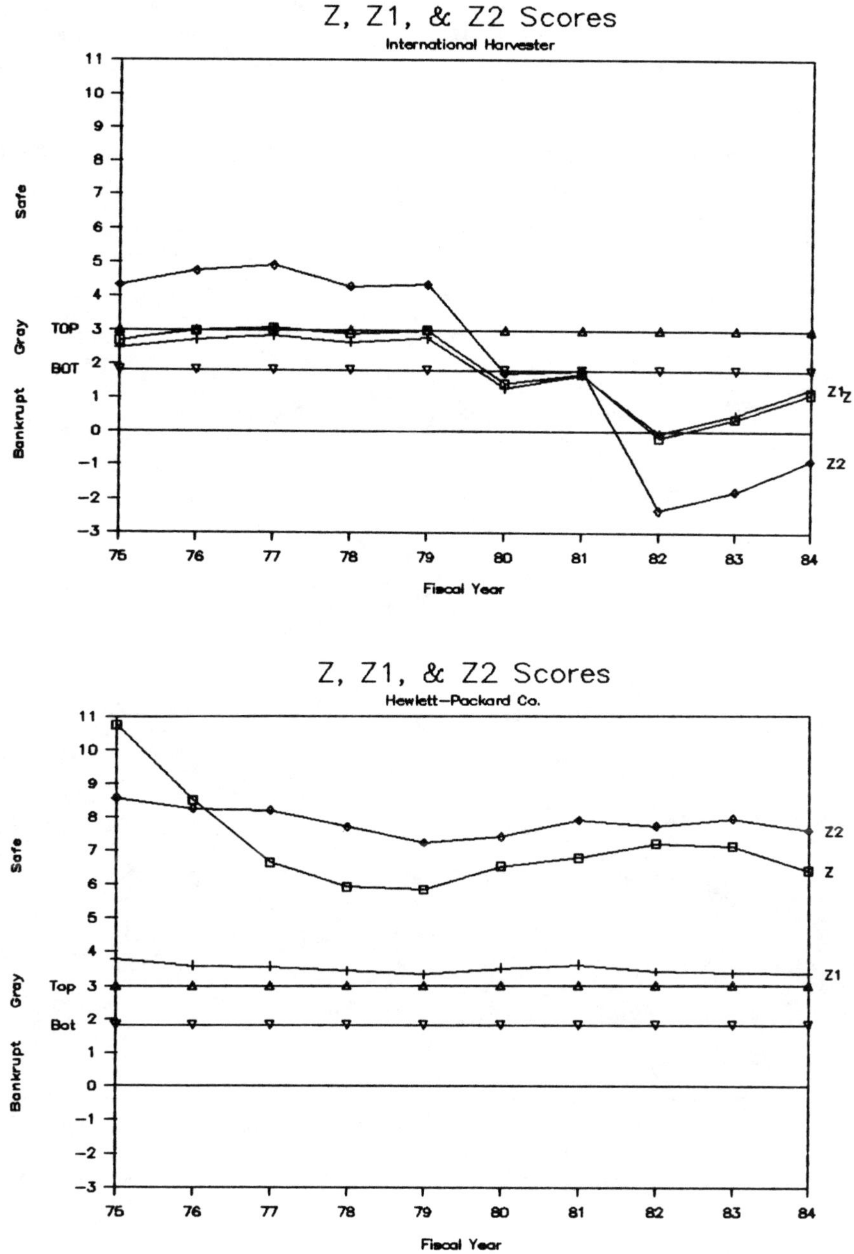

Figure 11-5. A graph of the Z, Z1, and Z2 Scores for Hewlett-Packard and for International Harvester

6. Turnaround management: Z Score analysis can help to guide turnaround decisions. For example, many managers would hesitate to sell assets at a book loss to pay off debt. But they might think differently if they knew that such a sale could raise the firm's Z Score significantly, and, in fact, improve its chances of survival.[2]

7. Managment reporting and control: The Z Score is one of the few statistics that can summarize a firm's own general performance; profit and loss, asset management, working capital management, stock performance—all are summarized in one Z Score calculation. A growing number of firms, therefore, include the Z Score in their internal management reports. (Chapter 13 shows how to use the Data Bank to report monthly Z Scores.)

---

[2] Jim La Fleur, CEO of GTI Corporation, San Diego, California, credits the Z Score as a major help in GTI's turnaround. For more information, see Altman and La Fleur's article "Managing a Return to Financial Health," in the *Journal of Business Strategy*, Volume 2, Number 1, Summer 1981. Pepperdine University's *Management Insights*, Winter 1984, has reprinted the *JBS* article and included an interview with La Fleur.

Chapter
Twelve

ACHIEVING GROWTH THROUGH PERFORMANCE: THE SUSTAINABLE GROWTH EQUATION[1]

Back in 1957, David Packard spoke to a meeting of the Institute of Radio Engineers (now the IEEE, the Institute of Electrical and Electronics Engineers). But the president of Hewlett-Packard didn't talk about electronics. He talked about managerial finance. "We have grown from a sales level of $2.3 million in 1950 to a level of $28 million this year. And we have accomplished this growth without any outside capital.

"In the last few years you have seen hundreds of small businesses acquired by larger businesses because they need capital for growth. Many firms, large and small, are issuing additional stock, and using many other financial devices to provide the money for growth in this industry.

"Since we have achieved a reasonable rate of growth without using these devices, I thought you might be interested in hearing how we do it."[2]

The audience *was* interested. Over the previous seven years HP had grown at an annual rate of 43% while maintaining firm control of its

[1] Reprinted with permission of *Management Accounting*. Chapter adapted from the author's article "Managing the Financial Demands of Growth," December 1981.

[2] All quotes attributed to David Packard are taken from the transcript of his speech "Growth From Performance," presented on April 24, 1957, to the Seventh Region Institute of Radio Engineers Conference.

finances. If HP had developed a formula that would help others to match that performance in their own businesses, the engineers were eager to learn what that formula was.

The formula that Packard described is generally known as the sustainable growth formula. Let's look at it in greater detail.

SUSTAINABLE GROWTH

The sustainable growth rate (g*), is the annual percentage increase in sales that a firm can maintain while keeping its capital structure in balance. If a firm grows at a faster rate than g*, it will be forced to increase its debt ratio, decrease dividends, sell additional stock, or engage in more drastic measures to finance its growth. If a firm grows at a slower rate than g*, it strengthens its capital structure. It can reduce its debt ratio, increase its dividends, increase its investments, and so on.

By calculating g*, a manager is calculating a firm's financial ability to grow through performance. This calculation needs to be put in proper perspective, however. As Packard told his audience, "In spending most of my time talking about the financial aspects of growth, I do not mean to imply that these are in any sense determining. The other things you do determine how fast you grow, provided you have the financial resources."

The Advantages of Using the Sustainable Growth Rate

Calculating g* is not a substitute for doing detailed financial analysis, but it does have several distinct advantages.[3]

1. It provides a benchmark against which internally generated projections can be compared. Projected growth rates that differ significantly from g* indicate that changes may be needed in the company's financial structure, forecasting process, or both.

---

[3] Several of the attractions listed for calculating the affordable growth rate, and many ideas on the subject, were suggested to the author by Robert C. Higgins, Associate Dean and Professor of Finance, University of Washington. See particularly his "Sustainable Growth: New Tool in Bank Lending," *The Journal of Commercial Bank Lending*, June 1977; "Sustainable Growth Under Inflation," *Financial Management*, Autumn 1981; and Chapter 5 of his book *Analysis for Financial Management*, (Homewood, Ill: Richard D. Irwin, Inc., 1984).

2. The sustainable growth rate is easy to calculate. It can usually be calculated in seconds in one's head. And the more complete substantial growth formulas can be easily manipulated in a 1-2-3 spreadsheet.

3. The g* focuses on the key operating and financial variables that affect a company's growth. This calculation allows managers to quickly relate the effect of changes in these variables to changes in the firm's financial ability to grow.

4. The formula provides a means of communicating the effect of the actions of lower-level managers on overall company performance. For example, a brief discussion of sustainable growth can demonstrate to a purchasing supervisor how the high inventory levels for which he or she is responsible directly affect the firm's growth rate and profitability, and ultimately influence the price of the firm's stock.

DEFINING THE SUSTAINABLE GROWTH RATE

The calculation of g* is based on the following two assumptions:

1. A firm's sales normally can grow only about as fast as its assets. For example, if there is the market potential for sales to increase at a 40% yearly rate, assets must also grow at about 40%. (This is equivalent to assuming that the firm's assets turnover ratio—sales divided by assets—will remain constant.)

2. The company has a target debt-to-equity ratio that is approved by the firm's lenders. This assumption implies that as stockholders' equity grows, debt can grow at the same rate, thereby maintaining a constant debt-to-equity ratio.

The sustainable growth rate can be determined easily by considering the effect of these assumptions on a company that wishes to increase its sales at a 30% rate over the next several years. If sales are to grow by 30%, assets must also grow at the same rate (assumption 1). Because the balance sheet must balance, total debt and equity must grow by 30% also. Lenders will allow debt to grow by 30% if equity increases by that amount (asumption 2). Therefore, the growth rate of a firm's sales depends upon the growth rate of its equity. The sustainable growth rate, (g*), is therefore *equal to the annual percentage increase in a firm's stockholders' equity section of its balance sheet.*

CALCULATING THE SUSTAINABLE GROWTH RATE: THE GROWTH EQUATION

Several factors can cause equity to grow. The most common source is the earnings retained after the payment of dividends. Among other sources are the issuance of common stock, income from equity investments, and other income.

The sustainable growth calculations, however, assume that retained earnings is the *only* source of equity growth, principally because the sustainable growth equation was derived to help management monitor and control operating performance. The other sources of equity are either irrelevant to operations or become necessary when management control is ineffective.

So if we assume that retained earnings is the only source of equity growth, the sustainable growth rate is

$$g* = \frac{\text{Earnings After Dividends}}{\text{Beginning Stockholders' Equity}}$$

$$= \frac{\text{Earnings After Dividends}}{\text{Earnings}} \times \frac{\text{Earnings}}{\text{Beginning Stockholders' Equity}}$$

$$= \text{Earnings Retention Ratio} \times \text{Return on Equity}$$

$$= bR$$

Here b is the firm's earnings retention ratio and R is the Return on Equity (ROE).

As a brief example of how the sustainable growth equation works, consider a company with a 30% ROE that pays out 20% of its earnings in dividends. The retention ratio (b), is 80% (1−20%); that is, it keeps 80% of its earnings. The firm's sustainable growth rate is therefore equal to 80%×30% =24%.

Notice, in the formula, that the stockholders' equity figure at the *beginning* of the period is used to calculate the ROE. When you use balance sheet data in these equations, always use data from the beginning of the period. (This is equivalent, of course, to using data from the year-end balance sheet of the previous period.) The reason for using data at the beginning of the period is that the sustainable growth equations compare "what you started with" (the balance sheet) with "what you did with it" (the income statement).

Hewlett-Packard and the Growth Equation

Nearly 30 years have passed since David Packard spoke to the engineers about his philosophy of matching growth with performance, and Figure 12-1 shows that the formula still works for HP.

	A	B	C	D	E	F	G	H	I	J	K	L
1	Hewlett-Packard											
2	Sustainable Growth Calculation											
3	Using the Growth Equation											
4	==================================											
5												
6		Compound										
7	Description	Growth Rate	1975	1976	1977	1978	1979	1980	1981	1982	1983	1984
8	-------------------------	----------	------	------	------	------	------	------	------	------	------	------
9	Total Assets	24%	768	933	1,158	1,462	1,900	2,337	2,758	3,470	4,161	5,153
10	Total Liabilities	26%	207	256	334	460	665	790	838	1,121	1,274	1,608
11	Common Stock & Capital	19%	166	200	236	276	326	393	481	587	733	775
12	Retained Earnings	24%	395	477	588	726	909	1,154	1,439	1,762	2,154	2,770
13	Net Worth	23%	561	677	824	1,002	1,235	1,547	1,920	2,349	2,887	3,545
14	Sales	22%	990	1,124	1,374	1,751	2,361	3,099	3,578	4,254	4,710	6,044
15	Dividends	24%	7	8	11	14	21	24	27	30	41	49
16	Net Earnings	26%	84	90	122	152	204	269	312	353	433	665
17												
18												
19												
20	Sustainable Growth	Average										
21	-------------------------	----------										
22	Earnings Retention Ratio	91%		91%	91%	91%	90%	91%	91%	92%	91%	93%
23	Return on Equity	19%		16%	18%	18%	20%	22%	20%	18%	18%	23%
24		----------		------	------	------	------	------	------	------	------	------
25	Sustainable Growth Rate	18%		15%	16%	17%	18%	20%	18%	17%	17%	21%
26												
27	Net Stock Transactions	5%		6%	5%	5%	5%	5%	6%	6%	6%	1%
28		----------		------	------	------	------	------	------	------	------	------
29	Yearly Growth of Net Worth	23%		21%	22%	22%	23%	25%	24%	22%	23%	23%
30												
31												
32	Yearly Growth Rate of Sales	22%		14%	22%	27%	35%	31%	15%	19%	11%	28%
33												

```
B9: (P0) (L9/C9)^(1/@COUNT(D9..L9))-1
D22: (P0) 1-(D15/D16)
D23: (P0) +D16/C13
D24: +" "&@REPEAT("-",@CELL("WIDTH",D23..D23)-1)
D25: (P0) +D23*D22
D27: (P0) (D11-C11)/C13
D28: +" "&@REPEAT("-",@CELL("WIDTH",D27..D27)-1)
D29: (P0) +D27+D25
D32: (P0) +D14/C14-1
```

Figure 12-1. Calculation of Hewlett-Packard's sustainable growth rate using the growth equation

As you can see, the compound growth rates for all major balance sheet and income statement categories B9 through B16, are roughly equal: 23-24%. HP's capital structure has stayed in balance.

The Sustainable Growth Rate is calculated in row 25. It is the product of the Earnings Retention Ratio (row 22) and the Return on Equity ratio (row 23). The formulas for these simple calculations are shown at the bottom of Figure 12-1. The Sustainable Growth Rate shows a slight variation from year to year, growing from 15% to 21%. We will discuss the reason for this increase when we apply the strategic equation to these figures.

Net Stock Transactions (row 27) have added another 5% to Average equity growth. Most of these transactions involve the sale of HP stock through employee stock purchase plans. (In 1984 the firm purchased HP stock to meet the needs of these plans, which is why Net Stock Transactions contributed only 1% that year.) These Stock Transactions pose a minor definitional problem for us. We could take the view that HP's sustainable growth rate consistently falls about 5% below its sales growth rate, "forcing" the firm to sell additional stock each year. In fact, however, employees have purchased HP stock regularly since the firm was founded, and these purchases have been such a reliable component of equity growth that HP's effective Sustainable Growth Rate, or Yearly Growth of Net Worth (B29) is the sum of these two amounts (B25 and B27), or 23%.

CALCULATING THE STRATEGIC EQUATION

The growth equation ($g* = bR$) calculates a firm's sustainable growth rate from information about dividend payment policies and ROE performance. This formula, however, offers little insight for those who wish to understand or improve upon that rate. The *strategic equation* provides some insight.

$$g* = \text{Earnings Retention Ratio} \times \text{Leverage} \times \text{Net Profit Margin} \times \text{Asset Turnover}$$

The strategic equation provides a valuable conceptual framework for decision making and control. It is the equation that Packard described in his speech and that HP still uses internally to guide its growth.

As a tool for decision making, the equation allows a manager to test how growth would be affected by proposed changes in the company's capital structure, marketing policies, dividend policy, and so on. As a means of control, it serves as a benchmark for performance and helps to communicate to employees the reasons for that benchmark.

The strategic equation is an expansion of the growth equation.

$$
\begin{aligned}
g* &= b \times R \\
&= b \times \frac{\text{Earnings}}{\text{Equity}} \\
&= b \times \frac{\text{Assets}}{\text{Equity}} \times \frac{\text{Earnings}}{\text{Assets}} \\
&= b \times \frac{\text{Equity + Debt}}{\text{Equity}} \times \frac{\text{Earnings}}{\text{Sales}} \times \frac{\text{Sales}}{\text{Assets}} \\
&= \underbrace{b}_{(a)} \times \underbrace{\left(1 + \frac{\text{Debt}}{\text{Equity}}\right)}_{(b)} \times \underbrace{\frac{\text{Earnings}}{\text{Sales}}}_{(c)} \times \underbrace{\frac{\text{Sales}}{\text{Assets}}}_{(d)}
\end{aligned}
$$

The equation combines two different types of components. Earnings retention and leverage, (a) and (b), are *decisions.* Net profit margin and asset turnover, (c) and (d), are *results.* The decision components can be described as policy statements reflecting management's attitude toward the risks and opportunities it expects in the future. The results components reflect the outcomes of managerial action. They reflect performance.

Operating performance, as expressed in this equation, is composed of both income performance (net profit margin) and asset performance (asset turnover).

Net profit margin indicates the market competitiveness of the firm, its manufacturing efficiency, its ability to manage its marketing and administrative costs, and its ability to achieve economies of scale.

Asset turnover measures the ability of assets to produce sales. As David Packard told the engineers, it measures the ability of the sales group to sell its products to paying customers, the efficiency with which manufacturing uses its fixed assets, and the ability of the purchasing group to deliver raw material to the plant when it is needed and not before.

The overall measure of operating performance is Return on Assets (ROA). It is equal to the product of the profit margin and the turnover.

Substituting the ROA for these two ratios produces a modified form of the strategic equation.

$$g* = b \times \left(1 + \frac{\text{Debt}}{\text{Equity}}\right) \times \text{ROA}$$

Because both the retention ratio and leverage tend to be relatively constant over time, it is sometimes convenient to treat their actual values as a constant in the strategic equation. Since this one number summarizes the decision components of the equation, I call this value the decision multiplier.

To illustrate its use, Hewlett-Packard has maintained a retention ratio of about 90% and a debt-to-equity ratio of about 45% over the past ten years. Its decision multiplier is therefore equal to about 1.31 (1.45 × 90%). The firm could therefore express its sustainable growth rate as:

$$g* = 1.31 \times \text{ROA}$$

This formulation emphasizes the importance of the ROA to a firm's financial ability to grow. Growth depends upon operating performance. The ROA reflects that performance.

Hewlett-Packard and the Strategic Equation

Figure 12-2 shows how to calculate HP's sustainable growth rate by using the strategic equation. As you would expect, the Sustainable Growth Rates shown in row 33 of Figure 12-2 are the same rates as shown in row 25 of Figure 12-1.

Row 30 of Figure 12-2 shows that HP has produced a remarkably consistent operating performance during the period shown. Only in 1984, when the firm received a one-time benefit from changing tax laws, has HP's Return on Assets varied by more than a point from its 13% average.

With the exception of 1984, the Leverage ratio (row 23) has accounted for the variability we noticed earlier in the sustainable growth rate. A slight increase in the debt-to-equity ratio during the late 1970s and early 1980s has created the disproportionate increase. This conclusion would not have been obvious if we had depended only upon the growth equation.

	A	B	C	D	E	F	G	H	I	J	K	L
1	Hewlett-Packard											
2	Sustainable Growth Calculation											
3	Using the Strategic Equation											
4												
5												
6		Compound										
7	Description	Growth Rate	1975	1976	1977	1978	1979	1980	1981	1982	1983	1984
8												
9	Total Assets	24%	768	933	1,158	1,462	1,900	2,337	2,758	3,470	4,161	5,153
10	Total Liabilities	26%	207	256	334	460	665	790	838	1,121	1,274	1,608
11	Common Stock & Capital	19%	166	200	236	276	326	393	481	587	733	775
12	Retained Earnings	24%	395	477	588	726	909	1,154	1,439	1,762	2,154	2,770
13	Net Worth	23%	561	677	824	1,002	1,235	1,547	1,920	2,349	2,887	3,545
14	Sales	22%	990	1,124	1,374	1,751	2,361	3,099	3,578	4,254	4,710	6,044
15	Dividends	24%	7	8	11	14	21	24	27	30	41	49
16	Net Earnings	26%	84	90	122	152	204	269	312	353	433	665
17												
18												
19												
20	Sustainable Growth	Average										
21												
22	Earnings Retention Ratio	91%		91%	91%	91%	90%	91%	91%	92%	91%	93%
23	Leverage (1 + Debt/Equity)	145%		137%	138%	141%	146%	154%	151%	144%	148%	144%
24												
25	Decision Multiplier	1.32		1.25	1.25	1.28	1.31	1.40	1.38	1.31	1.34	1.34
26												
27	Profit Margin	9%		8%	9%	9%	9%	9%	9%	8%	9%	11%
28	Asset Turnover	1.5		1.5	1.5	1.5	1.6	1.6	1.5	1.5	1.4	1.5
29												
30	Return On Assets	13%		12%	13%	13%	14%	14%	13%	13%	12%	16%
31												
32												
33	Sustainable Growth Rate	18%		15%	16%	17%	18%	20%	18%	17%	17%	21%
34												

```
D22: (P0) 1-(D15/D16)
D23: (P0) 1+C10/C13
D25: (F2) +D23*D22
D27: (P0) +D16/D14
D28: (F1) +D14/C9
D30: (P0) +D27*D28
D33: (P0) +D30*D25
```

Figure 12-2. Calculation of Hewlett-Packard's sustainable growth rate using the strategic equation

THE FINANCIAL PLANNING EQUATION

As useful as the strategic equation is, it has several drawbacks. While the equation may give some idea of the multiplier effect of a leverage policy, it offers few hints about the wisdom of that policy. It can't illustrate, for example, the advantages (or the dangers) of increased leverage. Another drawback is that tax and interest charges are not explicitly specified in the equation, which makes it difficult to monitor the effects of operating performance as distinct from the effects of both changing tax laws and our own financing decisions.

The financial planning equation, which is derived in Appendix D, provides a framework that will help us deal with both of these concerns.

$$g* = \underbrace{b}_{(a)} \times \underbrace{(1 - \text{Tax Rate})}_{(b)} \times \left(\underbrace{\text{EOA}}_{(c)} + \underbrace{\frac{\text{Debt}}{\text{Equity}} \times (\text{EOA} - \text{Interest Rate})}_{(d)}\right)$$

Here EOA is the EBIT on Assets, defined as Earnings Before Interest and Taxes, divided by the Assets at the beginning of the period.

Although this equation appears to be more complex than the strategic equation, the idea that it expresses is really more straightforward. The financial planning equation says that the sustainable growth rate is equal to the sum of two rates, (c) and (d), which is reduced by two earnings retention ratios, (a) and (b).

The first rate, (c), is the EOA. It is the before-tax-and-interest return that the firm is earning on its assets as a result of operating performance. The second rate, (d), is the net benefit to the firm's return on equity from the use of debt. It is equal to the proportion of debt used by the firm times the spread between its benefits and costs. The sum of these two rates is reduced by the two earnings retention ratios; the first, (a), after dividends, and the second, (b), after taxes.

The Financial Planning Equation And Leverage Decisions

Figure 12-3 illustrates a simple spreadsheet that can be used to analyze the wisdom of our decisions about financial leverage. A company can grow faster by increasing its leverage ratio only if the contribution from debt, (d) in the previous equation, is expected to increase significantly. At the worst, after new debt is added, there must continue to be a large and positive spread between the EOA and the before-tax interest rate.

Two leverage alternatives are shown in the figure. Case 1 shows a firm that earns a before-tax EOA of 20%. It has an average interest rate of 12% and a debt-to-equity ratio of 100%. As shown in cells C23 and C25, these ratios earn the firm a Before-Tax ROE of 28% and generate a Sustainable Growth Rate of 13%.

Case 2 assumes that new debt is available that would raise the average interest rate of the firm to 14% and the debt-to-equity ratio to 200%. In average years the change would raise the contribution from debt to 12%, the before-tax ROE to 32%, and g∗ to 15%. This change would do these things if (and this is a big "if") the firm can maintain its current EOA at 20%.

The danger of using large amounts of debt is that debt magnifies the fluctuations in a firm's return on equity. Suppose that in bad years the firm is subject to a decrease of up to 8% in its EOA. If the firm begins with the debt structure of Case 1, it will perform as in column D. Its Before-Tax ROE will fall (C23 and D23) by 16% to 12%, and its Sustainable Growth

	A	B	C	D	E	F	G	H	I	J	K
1	Using the Strategic Equation										
2	To Analyze Leverage Options										
3	============================										
4											
5			------------Case 1---------------					------------Case 2---------------			
6			Avg	Bad	Amt of	Percent		Avg	Bad	Amt of	Percent
7	Assumptions:		Year	Year	Decline	Decline		Year	Year	Decline	Decline
8	----------------------------	----	-------	-------	-------	-------		-------	-------	-------	-------
9	Dividend Retention Ratio	DIV	80%	80%				80%	80%		
10	Tax Rate	TAX	40%	40%				40%	40%		
11	EBIT On Assets	EOA	20%	12%	-8%	-40%		20%	12%	-8%	-40%
12	Debt/Equity Ratio	LEV	100%	100%				200%	200%		
13	Interest Rate	INT	12%	12%				14%	14%		
14											
15											
16	Calculations										
17	----------------------------										
18	(a) Dividend Retention Ratio	[A]	80%	80%				80%	80%		
19	(b) Tax Retention Ratio	[B]	60%	60%				60%	60%		
20	(c) Operating Contribution	[C]	20%	12%	-8%	-40%		20%	12%	-8%	-40%
21	(d) Debt Contribution	[D]	8%	0%	-8%	-100%		12%	-4%	-16%	-133%
22											
23	Before-Tax ROE, (c) + (d)		28%	12%	-16%	-57%		32%	8%	-24%	-75%
24											
25	Sustainable Growth Rate		13%	6%	-8%	-57%		15%	4%	-12%	-75%
26											

Formulas

```
C18: (P0) +DIV
C19: (P0) 1-TAX
C20: (P0) +EOA
C21: (P0) +LEV*(EOA-INT)
C23: (P0) +[C]+[D]
C25: (P0) +[A]*[B]*([C]+[D])
```

Figure 12-3. A spreadsheet that uses the financial planning equation to evaluate leverage decisions

Rate will fall (D25) to 6%. For both these ratios, a 40% decline in EOA creates a 57% decline in overall results.

But the decline is even more severe if the firm begins with the debt structure of Case 2. The same 40% decline in EOA causes a 75% decline in overall performance. And ominously, in Case 2 the EOA has fallen below the cost of debt. As a percentage, the firm is earning less on its assets than the interest it is paying to finance them.

The Financial Planning Equation And Operating Performance

We said earlier that the financial planning equation would help us monitor operating performance as distinct from the effects of interest and taxes. The ratio that reflects this operating performance is the EOA. In Chapter 13 we will create a report that helps us monitor the ratio easily.

Figure 12-4 presents a framework that illustrates just what we will be monitoring. (This chart is similar to one that the DuPont Corporation developed early in this century to manage its operating subsidiaries.) It quickly illustrates the components of this important ratio.

To illustrate how this framework can be used to improve a firm's ability to manage its growth, suppose that the Acme Corporation decides to implement an EOA improvement plan. Acme's management decides that its EOA, which averages 29%, must increase to about 35%.

Meeting this objective will be complicated by the fact that the firm has already undergone a massive effort to improve its operating margin (that is, its EBIT divided by total sales). Since Acme's management therefore believes that there is no practical way to increase their operating margin above its present level of 20%, an improvement in their EOA must come totally from an improvement in turnover. Figure 12.5 shows the situation that the firm's management faces.

Acme plans to manage this improvement by breaking the one measure of turnover into many detailed measures. Then, through the firm's management-by-objectives system, individuals throughout the company will commit to specific improvements in their own performance. Management will ensure that the sum of the detailed commitments will produce the desired turnover.

To begin this process, the Assets-to-Sales ratio is broken into its major components, as in the bottom half of Figure 12-5. Individuals are assigned to research these components and recommend ways to improve them. The Accounts Receivable section will serve as an illustration of this process.

The Accounts Receivable-to-Sales ratio of 17% is equivalent to a collection period of 62 days (.17×365). Since Acme's terms are net 30 days, significant improvements can be made.

Research reveals that there are four contributing factors to the long collection period.

1. Acme's major product has worked improperly on delivery. Customers have withheld payment until the problems have been solved.

2. Acme's marketing department has agreed unofficially to extended credit terms when salespeople felt that concessions would help to make a sale.

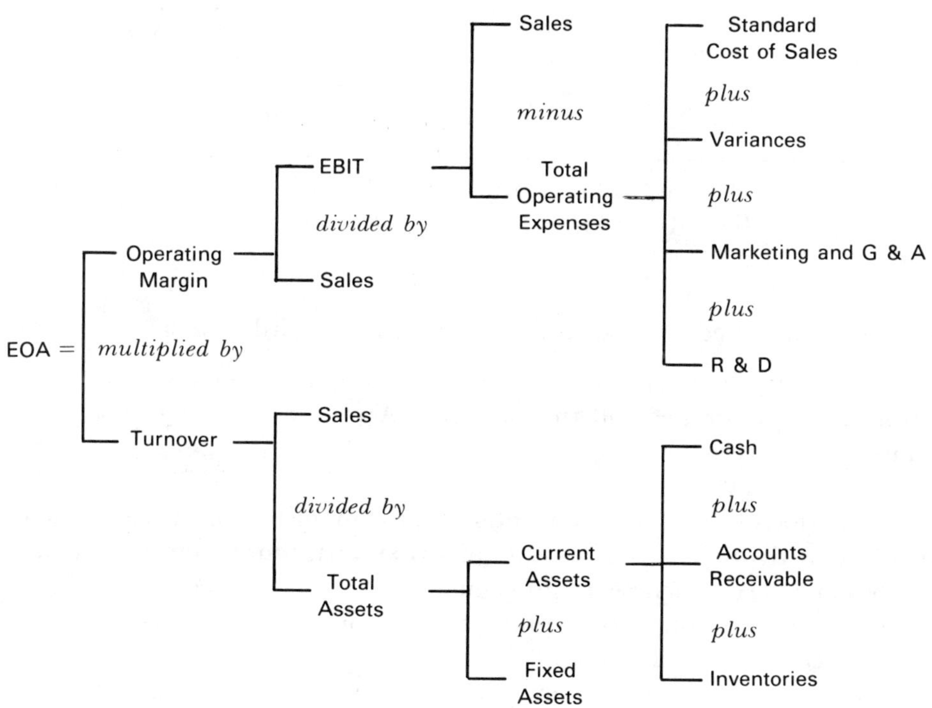

Figure 12-4. The components of the ratio EBIT on Assets (EOA)

Acme Corporation Financial Information

Ratios	Current	Required
EOA	29%	35%
Operating margin	20%	20%
Turnover	1.45 times	1.75 times
Assets-to-Sales	69%	57%

Assets-to-Sales Detail		
Cash	8%	?
Accounts Receivable	17%	?
Inventories	17%	?
Fixed Assets	23%	?
Other	4%	?
Total	69%	57%

Figure 12-5. How individual performance objectives can be set by dividing the turnover ratio into many detailed ratios

3. The firm's credit-checking methods are haphazard at best.

4. Frequently, there is a delay of several days between the time an order is shipped to a customer and the time that Acme's accounting department mails an invoice.

After a period of research and negotiation, the managers of the departments involved with these problems commit to specific improvements in their performance. When these improvements are implemented, management estimates that the collection period should drop to about 48 days, producing an Accounts Receivable-to-Sales ratio of 13% (48/365).

Acme managers examine their other assets in a similar manner. At times, however, the managers must make trade-offs in this process; for example, an improved credit-checking procedure may require increased administrative expenses. The DuPont framework, however, provides an approach for evaluating such trade-offs.

A FINAL NOTE

As he concluded his talk with the engineers, David Packard talked in a general way about the reasons for HP's success: "We have been able to achieve a fairly substantial rate of growth, first, by setting and adhering to some rather specific objectives, and second, by demanding a high level of performance from our management group, and, in fact, from all of our employees."

The sustainable growth rate model can serve as a valuable tool in this process of coordinating plans and performance. Viewed from the top down, the model provides the ability to translate overall growth and profitability objectives into many subsidiary objectives for individual supervisors. Viewed from the bottom up, the model allows those supervisors to calculate and understand the effect that their actual performances can have on the company as a whole.

Finally, the model can provide managers with new insight into the effect of their own decisions on the company's ability to grow.

Chapter
Thirteen

MANAGEMENT REPORTING WITH MINI GRAPHS

Diamond miners, they say, must move tons of dirt to find a single diamond. And in business, it seems, managers must read tons of reports to find a diamond of useful information. One way to help find the diamonds is to use graphs for management reporting. A quick glance at a graph often can tell a manager more than could a ten-page analysis using words and numbers.

Unfortunately, how these graphs are presented often creates problems. I know of one business that prints graphs one to a page, reproduces them on the office copier, binds them into volumes, and then distributes them to only those managers whose desks are strong enough to bear the weight of each report.

A small graph, however, can impart an amazing amount of information. The obvious way to deal with many pages of graphs, therefore, is to put many graphs on a single page. During the past several years, the *Harvard Business Review* has carried at least two articles demonstrating this approach.[1]

Until now, managers who wished to use a Mini Graph management reporting system experienced two problems when they tried to implement

---

[1] George B. Blake, "Graphic shorthand as an aid to managers," March-April 1978, page 6. Robert L. Janson, "Graphic indicators of operations," November-December 1980, page 164.

this approach. First, the data seldom was organized in a way that would allow the staff to generate multiple graphs easily; producing each graph became a major task. Second, there was no convenient way to print many small graphs on a single page.

The Data Bank solves the first problem, and this chapter will explain how to solve the second problem if you are using 1-2-3 Version 2. If you are using 1-2-3 Version 1A, however, there is no practical way to create these graphs.

THE MINI GRAPH REPORTING SYSTEM

Figure 13-1 shows a Mini Graph Management Report. This report, which uses the string features of Version 2, presents 18 graphs of ratios and data that one manager wishes to review monthly.

Both the manager and her staff see many advantages to the mini graph approach. One sheet of paper allows her to quickly review trends in important data. One glance at each small graph separates the dirt from the diamonds. The dirt is the trend she expects, the performance she understands. The diamonds are the questions, the problems, and data that need more research and explanation.

The staff also likes Mini Graphs. Once the staff created the Data Bank and the first Mini Graph report, the graphs have been easy to produce monthly and easy to update from time to time as old graphs are replaced by new ones.

Information in the Mini Graph

In general each graph is designated by a letter and a name, and each graph shows 13 months of data. (Using 13 months rather than 12 allows us to compare current performance to that of a year ago.)

Beneath the name of the graph, a number in parentheses indicates the magnitude of each graph symbol. In Figure 13-1, for example, graph A shows "(*=$5)": each symbol in this graph represents approximately $5 (or $5 thousand, or $5 million) of monthly sales.

```
                                           Mini Graph Management Report                             12-Jan-86

               [A]                 [B]                 [C]                 [D]                 [E]                 [F]
                           Rolling 12 Months                       Rolling 12 Months      Total Orders
          Monthly Sales     Cumulative Sales    Monthly Profits    Cumulative Profits  Booked Each Month      Order Backlog
        -----(*=$5)-----   ----(*=$38)-----   ----(*=$1.3)-----   ----(*=$12)-----   ----(*=$11)-----   ----(*=$41)-----
        $137  $186  $236   $1505 $1846 $2188  $9     $20    $32   $78   $187  $296   $139  $239  $339   $258  $624  $991
        |------|-------|   |------|-------|   |------|-------|    |------|-------|   |------|-------|   |------|-------|
Dec-84  *B                 **  B              *B***               B                  *B*                *   B
Jan-85  **B                ***  B             **** B              *B*                **B                *    B
Feb-85  **B                ***  B             *****   B           ***B               **B                **   B
Mar-85  ** B               **** B             *****    B          ****B              * B                **   B
Apr-85  ***B               ****  B            *****    B          *****B             **B*               **   B
May-85  *** B              *****  B           *****     B         ******B            ***B               ***   B
Jun-85  **** B             ****** B           **         B        ******  B          ***B*              ****  B
Jul-85  *****B             ******* B          *****       B       *******  B         ***B*****          ******B
Aug-85  ******B*           ******** B         ******       B      ********   B       ***B************** ******B**
Sep-85  ******B***         *********B         ********     B      ********    B      ****B**********    ******B*****
Oct-85  *******B***        **********B        *******       B     *********     B    ****B*******       *******B******
Nov-85  *******B********   ***********B*      *************   B   **********     B   ****B******        *******B*******
Dec-85  ********B*****     ************B**    ********        B   **********       B *****B*********    *******B*********

               [G]                 [H]                 [I]                 [J]                 [K]                 [L]
             Monthly        Tot Assets:  +A/R                       Month-to-Month    12-Mo Growth Rates:     12-Month
         Free Cash Flow    -Inv, *F/A, =Oth   Turnover of Assets    Gross Margin     Sales Minus Assets   EBIT On Assets
        -----(*=$6)-----   ----(*=$89)-----   ----(*=0.1)-----    ----(*=0.8%)----   ----(*=0.9%)----   ----(*=1.9%)----
        $-37 $0      $63   $0    $800 $1600   0      0.8    1.6   50%   58%   65%    -18%  -10%   -2%   11%   28%   45%
        |----|---------|   |------|-------|   |------|-------|    |------|-------|   |------|-------|   |------|-------|
Dec-84       |+            +++---*******      Times.Times.Time    *******B*              -----------|   *B**
Jan-85       |++           +++---******       Times.Times.Time    ******    B              ---------|   **B**
Feb-85       |++++         +++---******=      Times.Times.Times   *******     B                ----|   ****B*
Mar-85       |+++          ++---******=       Times.Times.Time    *****       B               -----|   *****B*
Apr-85       |++           +++---*******=     Times.Times.Time    *********    B              -----|   ******B
May-85       |++           +++---*******=     Times.Times.Time    ********     B                   |   *******B
Jun-85       |+++          +++---*******==    Times.Times.Time    *****        B               ----|   ********B
Jul-85       |++           +++---*******=     Times.Times.Time    *******      B                ---|   ********* B
Aug-85       |++           ++++---********=   Times.Times.Tim     *****        B              -----|   ********** B
Sep-85  -----|             +++++---********=  Times.Times.Ti      ********     B   -----------------|   *********** B
Oct-85       |+++++++++++  +++++---********=  Times.Times.Tim     ******       B       ------------|   ***********  B
Nov-85       |+            +++++---********=  Times.Times.Tim     *******       B        ----------|   ************   B
Dec-85       |++           +++++---********=  Times.Times.Tim     ******        B                -|   ************    B

               [M]                 [N]                 [O]                 [P]                 [Q]                 [R]
                           Sustainable Grth-*        Number              Monthly       Rolling 12-Month       Stock Price:
        Monthly Z Score    & 12-Mo Sls Grth-S   Of Employees      Sales Per Employee Earnings Per Share  Low, Close, High
        ----(*=0.2)-----   ----(*=2.7%)-----  ----(*=0.6)-----    ----(*=$0.1)----   ----(*=$0.4)----   ----(*=$1.9)----
        0       1.8    3   -15% 0%      33%   29    34      40    $4    $5     $6    $2     $6     $9   $30   $48   $65
        |--------|-----|   |---|----------|   |-----|--------|    |------|-------|   |-------|------|   |------|-------|
Dec-84  Gray.Gray.Gra      S    |******       ***                 ******B            *B                   ===X
Jan-85  Gray.Gray.Gray      S   |******       ********            ***B               **B                      =X=
Feb-85  Gray.Gray.Gray.      S  |*******      *****               ******B            ***B                   ====X==
Mar-85  Gray.Gray.Gray         S|*******      *******             ****  B            *****B                   ==X=
Apr-85  Gray.Gray.Gray          S*******      *******             *****  B           ***** B                    =X=
May-85  Gray.Gray.Gray          |*S******     ***                 ********* B        ****** B                    X=
Jun-85  Gray.Gray.Gray          |**S*****     ***                 ********** B       ******* B                  =X
Jul-85  Gray.Gray.Gray          |****S****    ***                 ************B      *******   B                 =X==
Aug-85  Gray.Gray.Gra           |*****S***    *******             **********B***     ********   B                 =X===
Sep-85  Gray.Gray.Gr            |*******S*    ***********         *******B***        *********   B                 =X=
Oct-85  Gray.Gray.Gra           |********S    *******             ***********B*****  *********     B                =X=
Nov-85  Gray.Gray.Gra           |********* S  *************       *******B********** **********     B                =X==
Dec-85  Gray.Gray.Gra           |*********  S ***************     *******B*******    ***********      B               X
```

Figure 13-1. A sample Mini Graph Management Report

One of the most critical elements of the graph appears next. This is the scale, the upper and lower bounds of the graph. In the figure most of these limits were produced automatically. But once you have the Mini Graph working, you will want to adjust these limits carefully to reduce distortions.

Graphs B and H in the figure illustrate the distortions that can occur. B shows how yearly sales have increased, while H shows how assets have increased. Which category has increased at a higher rate? At a glance, sales would appear to be growing more quickly. But when we examine the data, we find that sales have grown from $1,584 to $2,084, or 32%, and assets have grown from $1,124 to $1,524, or 36%. The scales deceive the eye.

One solution to this problem would be to lower B's left-hand limit. If we lower this amount too much, however, the difference between actual and budgeted performance disappears. But somewhere there is a compromise that best represents what the data means to you.

Another solution would be to add a third graph that reports the difference between these two important growth rates. Graph K is just such a graph. It shows, for example, that in December 1985 the yearly growth rate of sales was 4% less than the yearly growth rate of assets.

Let's see what the other graphs tell us.

Descriptions of the Graphs

The following is a brief description of each of the 18 graphs in Figure 13-1. When you first generate and distribute a Mini Graph report, you should include a similar description.

A. Monthly Sales: Reports the budgeted (B) and actual (*) sales for each month shown.

B. Cumulative Sales, Rolling 12 Months: For each of the 13 months shown, compares the total budgeted and actual sales for the most recent 12 months.

C. Monthly Profits: Reports the budgeted and actual profits for each month shown.

D. Cumulative Profits, Rolling 12 Months: For each of the 13 months shown, compares the total budgeted and actual profits for the most recent 12 months.

E. Total Orders Booked Each Month: Reports the budgeted and actual orders booked for each month shown.

F. Total Order Backlog: Shows the budgeted and actual order backlog for each month shown.

G. Monthly Free Cash Flow: Reports the cash that was generated by the business operations prior to financing transactions. Dividends, interest, and loan repayments are paid out of free cash flow. New debt and equity are raised to supplement free cash flow.

Monthly free cash flow is equal to income for the month, plus interest, plus depreciation and amortization, less the increase in total capital. The increase in total capital is equal to the increase in total assets less the increase in non-interest-bearing current liabilities such as accounts payable and accrued expenses.

H. Total Assets: Shows the total assets balance for each of the last 13 months as the sum of the major asset categories: accounts receivable, inventory, fixed assets, and other assets.

I. Turnover of Assets: For each month shown, reports the 12-month sales total divided by the beginning asset balance. For example, the graph of Dec-85 reports the sales for January 1985 through December 1985 divided by the total assets in December 1984.

J. Month-to-Month Gross Margin: Reports the gross margin (sales less cost of sales, divided by sales) for each month shown.

K. 12-Month Growth Rates: Sales Minus Assets: For each of the 13 months shown, divides the most recent 12 months of sales by the previous 12 months of sales, divides total assets by the total assets balance of 12 months ago, and then subtracts the asset percentage from the sales percentage. The result is the difference in the two figures' rate of growth.

L. 12-Month EBIT on Assets: For both the actual and budgeted figures, divides the EBIT for the most recent 12 months by the beginning total assets balance. This result can be compared to the firm's current rate of interest.

M. Monthly Z Score: Calculates the firm's Z Score for each month shown. If the score is less than 1.8, the graph shows "Dead"; if it is between 1.8 and 3, it shows "Gray"; and if it is greater than 3, it shows "Safe."

N. Substainable Growth and 12-Month Sales Growth: Shows the rolling 12-month sales growth rate (S), and the sustainable growth rate (g*) for the months shown. A sustainable growth rate greater than sales generally strengthens the firm's financial structure; a g* less than sales weakens the structure.

O. Number of Employees: Reports the number of employees on the payroll at the end of each month shown.

P. Monthly Sales per Employee: For both the budgeted and actual amounts, divides sales for the current month by the budgeted and actual number of employees.

Q. Rolling 12-Month Earnings per Share: Divides profits for the most recent 12 months by the number of shares outstanding at month end.

R. Stock Price: Low, Close, High: Shows the closing price for our stock at month end and the high and low values that were reached during the month.

HOW TO CREATE THE MINI GRAPH REPORT

The Mini Graph report has 18 data graphs representing 8 specific graph formats. The creation of each graph requires two additional sections: the data section extracts the necessary numbers and ratios from the Data Bank; using this data, the parameters section calculates the numbers and strings that the graph formulas require. Finally, the graph section produces our report.

Since there's a lot going on, our goal is to create the Mini Graph report without turning the whole effort into a full-time career. We will take the following four steps:

1. Set the stage. We'll load some data, discuss some system requirements, and write the macro that sets the column widths and prints the report. Then we'll build a framework to which we can attach our data. This framework will also allow us to Xtract and save the Mini Graph report easily.

2. Build the data section. We'll extract all necessary information from the Data Bank and calculate the ratios that the graphs will report.

3. Build the parameters section. We'll use data section information to generate the data needed by the graphs to generate the scales, to position each graph in the space available, and so on.

4. Build the graph section. We'll generate graphs as shown in the figure. We'll also discuss how to rearrange the graphs to meet the needs of your own business.

Before we get started, though, a warning. This chapter describes the most demanding of the Data Bank reports. Plan to spend most of the day creating your Mini Graphs. If you would rather not spend the time, you may want to order the disk set for the book, which includes the full Data Bank and reports, including the Mini Graph report shown in Figure 13-1.

Step One: Set the Stage

Many of the graphs in Figure 13-1 show both actual and budgeted performance. The data for these graphs is shown in Appendix A.

Add the Budget Data If you wish to include budgets in your Data Bank, add this information now. If you do not plan to include budgets in your Data Bank, your Mini Graphs could compare current performance to data from the previous year instead of comparing it to budgetary data.

If your computer does not have 640K of memory, you may want to postpone the reporting of budgets until you upgrade your computer. Including budgets in the Mini Graph report uses nearly all of that 640K.

Set the Columns Begin with a Data Bank that is empty of reports. Figure 13-2 shows the top left corner of the Mini Graph report we will add to the Data Bank. Rows 250 through 253 show the bottom of the DATA BANK macro section. You will find the discussion easier to follow if you insert the rows necessary at the bottom of your macro section to make the lines in your Data Bank match those in the figure.

Columns B and C, from row 254 down, hold the macro that will set column widths and print our report. Enter this macro as shown.

Notice that this macro contains three /Creport~report~ statements. These statements calculate the REPORT range three times. The first time loads the data section; the second loads the parameters section; and the third loads the graph section. The Version 2 macro command {RECALC-COL report} would have calculated the report in a similar way. However, when {RECALCCOL} and {RECALC} are calculating, no message is displayed in the 1-2-3 control panel. This lack of information can cause users to think that 1-2-3 has somehow "bombed." When the /Copy command is

```
         A                    B                       C
250 ------------------------------------------------------------
251
252 ------------------------------------------------------------
253 REPORT               REP_MAC               ---------------------
254           {GOTO}report~
255           /WCS9~                    A
256           {RIGHT}/WCS26~            B
257           {RIGHT}/WCS20~            C
258           {RIGHT}/WCS8~             D
259           {RIGHT}/WCS20~            E
260           {RIGHT}/WCS20~            F
261           {RIGHT}/WCS20~            G
262           {RIGHT}/WCS20~            H
263           {RIGHT}/WCS20~            I
264           {RIGHT}/WCS20~            J
265           {RIGHT}/WCR~              K
266           {RIGHT}/WCS22~            L
267           {RIGHT}/WCS9~             M
268           {RIGHT}/WCS9~             N
269           {RIGHT}/WCS9~             O
270           {RIGHT}/WCS9~             P
271           {RIGHT}/WCS9~             Q
272           {RIGHT}/WCS9~             R
273           /WGC12~
274           /Creport~report~
275           /Creport~report~
276           /Creport~report~/XQ
277           {GOTO}report~
278           {UP}{END}{RIGHT}
279           {DOWN}{DOWN}{END}
280           {LEFT}{END}{LEFT}
281           {END}{DOWN}
282           {END}{LEFT}{LEFT}
283           {DOWN}/PPR{BS}.
284           {UP}{RIGHT}
285           {END}{RIGHT}
286           {DOWN}{DOWN}
287           {END}{DOWN}{LEFT}~
288           OMR135~ML5~H
289           |Mini Graph Management Report|@|~
290           QAGOH{ESC}~QPQ
291           /XR
```

Figure 13-2. The macro that sets the columns and prints the Mini Graph report

used, on the other hand, the WAIT message lets us know that *something* is happening.

Also notice the /XQ statement in cell B276. When you load an unfinished report, you will want to set the column widths and calculate the report section before you resume construction. But you won't want to print anything yet. Inserting the /XQ command as shown allows you to do this. Remove this temporary command after you finish your report.

What if you want to use the *lower* part of the macro to print a report but don't want to set the columns? Simply go to A277 and enter ' **\X** (apostrophe \X). Then use **/R**ange **N**ame **L**abel **R**ight to assign the name \X to B277. Press ALT-X to run the lower part of your macro. However, make sure that you delete the \X range name before you save your Data Bank.

After you enter the macro shown in the figure, press ALT-M System Report to have the macro set your column widths and calculate the report.

Build the Framework Figure 13-3 uses the micro display to illustrate the entire Mini Graph. Although the detail is unreadable, the figure should give you a better idea of the direction in which we are heading. If you need a more detailed view of any section of this display, look ahead several pages

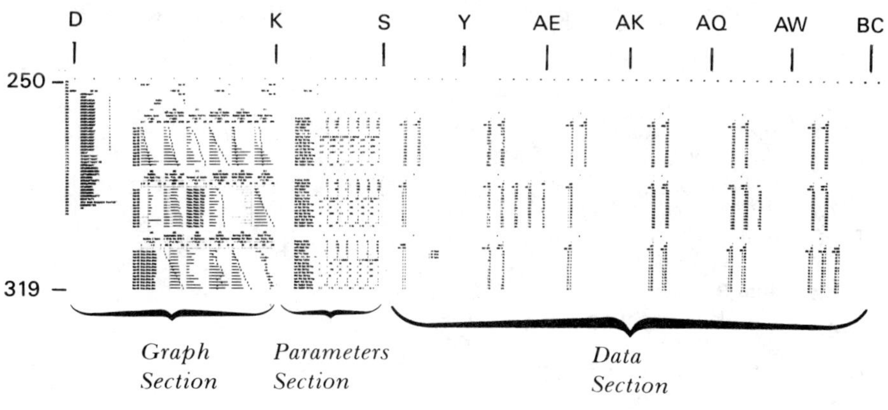

Figure 13-3. The complete spreadsheet that is loaded into the Data Bank to produce the Mini Graph Management Report

to the following figures: Figure 13-4 for the data section, Figure 13-7 for the parameters section, and Figure 13-9 for the graph section.

You will find it easier to insert the formulas to build these sections if we build a framework to hold them.

- *Set the system reference dates:* Copy MISC_DAT to FIRST_MO. This will load the date information that we need into the report area.
- *Create the dates for the graph:* Go to D265 and enter **+$FIRST_MO**. Format this cell and D266 as Date 3. In D266 enter **30+D265**. Copy this cell from D267 to D277. Then copy this column of dates, D265..D277, to D285 and to D305.
- *Enter the report boundary for the graph section:* Go to E258 and enter \=. Copy this underline from F258 to J258. Go to K255 and enter '| (apostrophe |). Copy this vertical line from K256 to K319. Then erase cell K259.
- *Enter the report width data:* The parameters section needs to know how wide each column in the graph section is. We need to calculate that width. So go to E256 and enter **^Width** (caret and Width). In F256 enter **@CELL("WIDTH",F255..F255)**. The parameters section also needs to know how much space (how wide a "gutter") to leave between each graph. So in E257 enter **^Gutter** (caret and "Gutter"). In F257 enter the value **2**.
- *Enter the parameter descriptions:* Enter the following labels in the cells shown.

L262: Display Width
L263: Right-Hand Num
L264: Left-hand Num
L265: Mid Number
L266: Mid Tic Point
L267: Type: 1=+, 0=+−, −1=−
L268: Scaling Factor
L269: Num String
L270: Len RH Num String
L271: LH Num String
L272: Len LH Num String
L273: Mid Num String
L274: Len Mid Num String
L275: Start Mid String
L276: One Symbol Equals
L277: One Symbol String

Copy this column to cells L282 and L302.

- *Enter the graph letter headings for the parameters section:* Go to M261 and enter \-. Copy this cell from N261 to R261. Copy M261..R261 to M281 and to M301. Enter **^A** in M260, **^B** in N260, and so on through **^F** in R260. Enter **^G** through **^L** in M280 through R280 and **^M** through **^R** in M300 through R300.
- *Enter the border between the parameters and data sections:* Go to S260 and enter '||| (apostrophe |||). Copy this cell from S261 to S317.
- *Enter the framework for the data section of the first graph:* Enter the following values and labels in the following cells.

T260: \-
T262: "*
T263: "ACT
T264: 100.01
U260: ^A
U262: "B
U263: "BUD
U264: 1100.01
V260: \-

Go to Y263 and enter '| (apostrophe |). Copy this cell from Y264 to Y277.

- *Enter the frameworks for the remaining graphs:* Here is a trick for copying this one frame to the rest of the section: /**C**opy from T260..AW277 to Z260; then /**C**opy from T260..BC299 to T280. If you have entered these commands exactly as shown, the entire framework will have been entered.

Here's what happens with the first /Copy command: 1-2-3 copies column T to column Z, column U to column AA, and so on, as you would expect. But when it is ready to copy from column Z, that column is no longer blank. Just a moment before, it was updated with data from column T. No matter. The data that is now in Z is copied to column AF, and so on. The command keeps copying what it has just created, from one column to the next, across the row. The approach works the same way when we copy down the column.

Unfortunately, each frame is labeled with **^A**. So change AA260 to a **^B**, AG260 to a **^C**, and so on through AY300, which will become an **^R**.

- *Enter the right boundary of the report:* In a way this is the most important step. The right boundary must be correct before the Data Bank macros can Xtract and save the report properly. Fortunately, it's an easy

	S	T	U	V	W	X	Y	Z	AA	AB	AC	AD	AE	AF	AG	AH	AI	AJ
250																		
251																		
252																		
253																		
254																		
255																		
256																		
257																		
258																		
259																		
260			A						B						C			
261																		
262		*	B					*	B					*	B			
263		ACT	BUD					ACT	BUD					ACT	BUD			
264		100.010	1100.01					800.010	1800.01					100.090	1100.09			
265		144	144					1584	1662					15	10			
266		147	147					1600	1676					14	16			
267		148	150					1620	1692					16	19			
268		148	153					1641	1710					15	20			
269		152	156					1666	1730					16	21			
270		155	159					1693	1752					15	22			
271		158	162					1720	1776					12	23			
272		166	165					1755	1802					15	24			
273		183	168					1804	1830					17	25			
274		190	171					1863	1860					19	26			
275		196	174					1925	1892					18	27			
276		225	177					2012	1926					26	29			
277		216	180					2084	1962					19	30			
278																		
279																		
280			G						H						I			
281																		
282		+	-						+	-	*	=						
283		AMT						TOT	AR	INV	F/A	OTH		AMT				
284		852.010						105.090	105.01	105.02	105.07			815.06				
285		5.0						1,124	258	242	582	42		1.41				
286		13.0						1,106	261	230	574	41		1.45				
287		24.0						1,093	245	236	566	46		1.48				
288		16.0						1,136	220	239	570	107		1.44				
289		12.0						1,156	223	247	592	94		1.44				
290		12.0						1,183	267	251	595	70		1.43				
291		17.0						1,248	234	255	621	138		1.38				
292		12.0						1,273	241	277	634	121		1.38				
293		13.0						1,341	331	271	688	51		1.35				
294		-35.0						1,474	425	290	706	53		1.26				
295		60.0						1,470	409	293	714	54		1.31				
296		3.0						1,519	413	292	753	61		1.32				
297		12.0						1,524	423	301	742	58		1.37				
298																		
299																		
300			M						N						O			
301																		
302								*	S					*				
303		SCORE						g*	SALES					AMT				
304		851.010						850.020	800.01					300.010				
305		2.1		-10 Dead.				15%	-14%					31.0				
306		2.3		1.81 Gray.				17%	-12%					34.0				
307		2.4		2.99 Safe.				19%	-9%					32.0				
308		2.4						20%	-5%					33.0				
309		2.4						21%	-2%					33.0				
310		2.4						22%	2%					31.0				
311		2.3						22%	6%					31.0				
312		2.3						24%	11%					31.0				
313		2.2						25%	14%					33.0				
314		2.0						24%	19%					36.0				
315		2.1						25%	25%					33.0				
316		2.1						26%	28%					37.0				
317		2.2						24%	32%					38.0				
318																		
319																		

	AL	AM	AR	AS	AT	AX	AY	AZ
260	D		E			F		
262	*	B	*	B		*	B	
263	ACT	BUD	ACT	BUD		ACT	BUD	
264	800.020	1800.02	400.010	1400.01		400.020	1400.02	
265	96	82	175	153		303	441	
266	109	94	163	156		319	450	
267	122	109	156	159		327	459	
268	129	124	153	162		332	468	
269	136	140	178	165		358	477	
270	146	156	181	168		384	486	
271	151	172	196	171		422	495	
272	162	189	239	174		495	504	
273	171	206	323	177		635	513	
274	179	224	290	180		735	522	
275	185	242	277	183		816	531	
276	198	262	258	186		849	540	
277	202	282	311	190		944	550	
280	J		K			L		
282	*	B	-	+		*	B	
283	COS	SALES	SALES	ASSETS	DIF	EBIT	ASSETS	
284	100.02	100.01	800.01	105.09		800.04	105.09	
285	58%	56%	86%	101%	-15%	18%	13%	
286	55%	58%	88%	102%	-14%	20%	15%	
287	56%	59%	91%	99%	-8%	22%	18%	
288	54%	59%	95%	104%	-10%	23%	20%	
289	57%	60%	98%	107%	-9%	25%	23%	
290	57%	60%	102%	105%	-2%	25%	24%	
291	54%	60%	106%	114%	-8%	27%	27%	
292	55%	60%	111%	116%	-5%	28%	30%	
293	54%	60%	114%	123%	-9%	30%	33%	
294	56%	60%	119%	136%	-17%	31%	35%	
295	55%	60%	123%	137%	-14%	32%	38%	
296	56%	60%	128%	140%	-12%	34%	40%	
297	55%	61%	132%	136%	-4%	34%	43%	
300	P		Q			R		
302	*	B	*	B		=	=	X
303	ACT	BUD	ACT	BUD		HI	LO	CLOSE
304	100.01	300.01	800.02	200.04		200.010	200.020	200.030
305	4.65	4.65	2.91	2.48		40.3	31.7	39.8
306	4.32	4.32	3.30	2.85		44.9	41.0	42.9
307	4.63	4.69	3.70	3.30		52.2	38.8	48.4
308	4.48	4.64	3.91	3.76		49.3	42.4	47.9
309	4.61	4.73	4.12	4.24		51.6	47.4	49.8
310	5.00	5.13	4.42	4.73		52.1	50.0	50.8
311	5.10	5.23	4.58	5.21		52.3	48.0	51.7
312	5.35	5.32	4.91	5.73		54.3	48.7	51.1
313	5.55	5.09	5.18	6.24		59.3	51.1	54.1
314	5.28	4.75	5.42	6.79		57.4	53.6	56.1
315	5.94	5.27	5.61	7.33		60.1	54.7	59.0
316	6.08	4.78	6.00	7.94		62.7	58.1	59.4
317	5.68	4.74	6.12	8.55		59.3	57.9	58.6

Figure 13-4. The Mini Graph data section

```
DB#s and Descriptions
=======================================

Actual
---------------------------------------
  100.01 Sales
  100.02 Cost of Goods Sold
  100.09 Net Earnings
  105.01 Accounts Receivable
  105.02 Inventories
  105.07 Net Prop, Plant, Equip
  105.09 Total Assets
  200.01 Stock Price, Monthly High
  200.02 Stock Price, Monthly Low
  200.03 Stock Price, Monthly Close
  200.04 Stock Shares Outstanding
  300.01 Employees, Number
  400.01 Orders Booked
  400.02 Order Backlog
  800.01 Sales, Last 12 Months
  800.02 Profits, Last 12 Months
  800.04 EBIT, Last 12 Months
  815.06 Sales/Tot Asts, [X5]
  850.02 Sustainable G/R, Cur
  851.01 Z Score
  852.01 Free Cash Flow

Budgets
---------------------------------------
 1100.01 Sales
 1100.02 Cost of Goods Sold
 1100.09 Net Earnings
 1105.09 Total Assets
 1300.01 Employees, Number
 1400.01 Orders Booked
 1400.02 Order Backlog
 1800.01 Sales, Last 12 Months
 1800.02 Profits, Last 12 Months
 1800.04 EBIT, Last 12 Months
```

Figure 13-5. The Data Bank numbers and descriptions used by the Mini Graph

step. Simply go to BC254, enter '| (apostrophe |), and copy this cell from BC255 to BC319. At its top, this line touches the horizontal line in row 253; at its bottom, it extends below the last row of the report. Now when you press ALT-M System Xtract, the Data Bank should save your report reliably.

Step Two: Build the Data Section

Figure 13-4 shows what the data section will look like when we have finished this step. Before we start to work on this section, let's see what it does.

Look at the data panel for graph A. Here we see column descriptions ACT (for actual) and BUD (for budget). These descriptions can be anything that you wish.

Above the words ACT and BUD are the two symbols used by the graph labeled "A" in the graph section. To change the symbols in graph A, you change the "*" or the "B" in these cells.

The numbers immediately below ACT and BUD are the Data Bank numbers for actual and budgeted sales. Figure 13-5 provides a list of all DB#s used in this chapter.

Figure 13-6 shows the data and formulas for all 18 graphs. After you have entered the material as shown for any graph, copy the @VLOOKUP formulas down 12 more rows. For graph A, for example, copy T265..U265 to T266..T277.

These @VLOOKUP formulas all do basically the same things: they look up the row specified by the DB# at the top of the column, and then return the data found by the offset number. The offset number is equal to $THIS_COL minus 14 plus an @COUNT formula.

$THIS_COL is the number of the column for the current month. (If the data for this month were in column Z, for example, $THIS_MO would be equal to 26.) Since the offset number begins its count from 0 (zero), not from 1, we must subtract 1 to find the representative offset number.

We subtract 12 more columns to find the offset number for the month one year before. And finally, we subtract 1 more and then add an @COUNT number. The @COUNT formula returns the value 1 for the first row, 2 for the second row, and so on, through the value 13 for the thirteenth row of formulas. To illustrate, the offset number for the current (thirteenth) month is equal to $THIS_COL−1−12−1+13.

Here's an easy way to add the @VLOOKUP formulas: enter the formula in T265, copy it to U265, and then copy these two formulas down the column as previously described.

Next, to enter the @VLOOKUP formulas for graph B, enter the proper DB#s in cells Z264 and AA264, copy the formula in U265 to Z265 and AA265, and then copy these formulas down the column. Continue this way across the row.

Next, go back to T265. Copy this formula to T285, edit the cell references in T285 to read as specified in Figure 13-6, and then copy this formula as required across the row. Do the same for the final row of formulas.

```
A         Monthly Sales
---------------------------------------------------------------------------
T262:  "*
T263:  "ACT
T264:  (F3) 100.01
T265:  (F0) @VLOOKUP(T$264,$DATA,$THIS_COL-14+@COUNT(T$265..T265))

U262:  "B
U263:  "BUD
U264:  1100.01
U265:  (F0) @VLOOKUP(U$264,$DATA,$THIS_COL-14+@COUNT(U$265..U265))

B         Rolling 12 Months Cumulative Sales
---------------------------------------------------------------------------
Z262:  "*
Z263:  "ACT
Z264:  (F3) 800.01
Z265:  (F0) @VLOOKUP(Z$264,$DATA,$THIS_COL-14+@COUNT(Z$265..Z265))

AA262:  "B
AA263:  "BUD
AA264:  1800.01
AA265:  (F0) @VLOOKUP(AA$264,$DATA,$THIS_COL-14+@COUNT(AA$265..AA265))

C         Monthly Profits
---------------------------------------------------------------------------
AF262:  "*
AF263:  "ACT
AF264:  (F3) 100.09
AF265:  (F0) @VLOOKUP(AF$264,$DATA,$THIS_COL-14+@COUNT(AF$265..AF265))

AG262:  "B
AG263:  "BUD
AG264:  1100.09
AG265:  (F0) @VLOOKUP(AG$264,$DATA,$THIS_COL-14+@COUNT(AG$265..AG265))

D         Rolling 12 Months Cumulative Profits
---------------------------------------------------------------------------
AL262:  "*
AL263:  "ACT
AL264:  (F3) 800.02
AL265:  (F0) @VLOOKUP(AL$264,$DATA,$THIS_COL-14+@COUNT(AL$265..AL265))

AM262:  "B
AM263:  "BUD
AM264:  1800.02
AM265:  (F0) @VLOOKUP(AM$264,$DATA,$THIS_COL-14+@COUNT(AM$265..AM265))

E         Total Orders Booked Each Month
---------------------------------------------------------------------------
AR262:  "*
AR263:  "ACT
AR264:  (F3) 400.01
AR265:  (F0) @VLOOKUP(AR$264,$DATA,$THIS_COL-14+@COUNT(AR$265..AR265))

AS262:  "B
AS263:  "BUD
AS264:  1400.01
AS265:  (F0) @VLOOKUP(AS$264,$DATA,$THIS_COL-14+@COUNT(AS$265..AS265))
```

Figure 13-6. The formulas used in the data section

```
F         Order Backlog
---------------------------------------------------------------------------------
AX262: "*
AX263: "ACT
AX264: (F3) 400.02
AX265: (F0) @VLOOKUP(AX$264,$DATA,$THIS_COL-14+@COUNT(AX$265..AX265))

AY262: "B
AY263: "BUD
AY264: 1400.02
AY265: (F0) @VLOOKUP(AY$264,$DATA,$THIS_COL-14+@COUNT(AY$265..AY265))


G         Monthly Free Cash Flow
---------------------------------------------------------------------------------
T282: "+
T283: "AMT
T284: (F3) 852.01
T285: (F1) @VLOOKUP(T$284,$DATA,$THIS_COL-14+@COUNT(T$285..T285))

U282: "-


H         Total Assets: +A/R, -INV, *F/A, =OTH
---------------------------------------------------------------------------------
Z283: "TOT
Z284: (F3) 105.09
Z285: (,0) @VLOOKUP(Z$284,$DATA,$THIS_COL-14+@COUNT(Z$285..Z285))

AA282: "+
AA283: "AR
AA284: 105.01
AA285: (,0) @VLOOKUP(AA$284,$DATA,$THIS_COL-14+@COUNT(AA$285..AA285))
AB282: "-
AB283: "INV
AB284: 105.02
AB285: (,0) @VLOOKUP(AB$284,$DATA,$THIS_COL-14+@COUNT(AB$285..AB285))

AC282: "*
AC283: "F/A
AC284: 105.07
AC285: (,0) @VLOOKUP(AC$284,$DATA,$THIS_COL-14+@COUNT(AC$285..AC285))

AD282: "=
AD283: "OTH
AD285: (,0) +Z285-@SUM(AA285..AC285)


I         Turnover of Assets
---------------------------------------------------------------------------------
AF283: "AMT
AF284: 815.06
AF285: (F2) @VLOOKUP(AF$284,$DATA,$THIS_COL-14+@COUNT(AF$285..AF285))


J         Month-to-Month Gross Margin
---------------------------------------------------------------------------------
AL282: "*
AL283: "COS
AL284: 100.02
AL285: (P0) 1-@VLOOKUP(AL$284,$DATA,$THIS_COL-14+@COUNT(AL$285..AL285))
             /@VLOOKUP(AM$284,$DATA,$THIS_COL-14+@COUNT(AL$285..AL285))
```

Figure 13-6. The formulas used in the data section (*continued*)

```
AM282: "B
AM283: "SALES
AM284: 100.01
AM285: (P0) 1-@VLOOKUP($AL$284+1000,$DATA,$THIS_COL-14+@COUNT(AM$285..AM285))
            /@VLOOKUP($AM$284+1000,$DATA,$THIS_COL-14+@COUNT(AM$285..AM285))


K          12-Month Growth Rates: Sales Minus Assets
------------------------------------------------------------------------------
AR282: "-
AR283: "SALES
AR284: 800.01
AR285: (P0) @VLOOKUP(AR$284,$DATA,$THIS_COL-14+@COUNT(AR$285..AR285))
            /@VLOOKUP(AR$284,$DATA,$THIS_COL-14+@COUNT(AR$285..AR285)-12)

AS282: "+
AS283: "ASSETS
AS284: 105.09
AS285: (P0) @VLOOKUP(AS$284,$DATA,$THIS_COL-14+@COUNT(AS$285..AS285))
            /@VLOOKUP(AS$284,$DATA,$THIS_COL-14+@COUNT(AS$285..AS285)-12)

AT283: "DIF
AT285: (P0) +AR285-AS285


L          12-Month EBIT On Assets
------------------------------------------------------------------------------
AX282: "*
AX283: "EBIT
AX284: 800.04
AX285: (P0) @VLOOKUP(AX$284,$DATA,$THIS_COL-14+@COUNT(AX$285..AX285))
            /@VLOOKUP(AY$284,$DATA,$THIS_COL-14+@COUNT(AX$285..AX285)-12)

AY282: "B
AY283: "ASSETS
AY284: 105.09
AY285: (P0) @VLOOKUP(AX$284+1000,$DATA,$THIS_COL-14+@COUNT(AY$285..AY285))
            /@VLOOKUP($AY$284+1000,$DATA,$THIS_COL-14+@COUNT(AY$285..AY285)-12)


M          Monthly Z Score
------------------------------------------------------------------------------
T303: "SCORE
T304: (F3) 851.01
T305: (F1) @VLOOKUP(T304,$DATA,$THIS_COL-14+@COUNT(T305..T305))

V305: -10
V306: 1.81
V307: 2.99

W305: 'Dead.
W306: 'Gray.
W307: 'Safe.


N          Sustainable Growth (*) and 12-Month Sales Growth (S)
------------------------------------------------------------------------------
Z302: "*
Z303: "g*
Z304: (F3) 850.02
Z305: (P0) @VLOOKUP(Z$304,$DATA,$THIS_COL-14+@COUNT(Z$305..Z305))

AA302: "S
AA303: "SALES
AA304: 800.01
AA305: (P0) @VLOOKUP(AA$304,$DATA,$THIS_COL-14+@COUNT(AA$305..AA305))
            /@VLOOKUP(AA$304,$DATA,$THIS_COL-14+@COUNT(AA$305..AA305)-12)-1
```

Figure 13-6. The formulas used in the data section (*continued*)

```
O         Number of Employees
--------------------------------------------------------------------------------
AF302: "*
AF303: "AMT
AF304: (F3) 300.01
AF305: (F1) @VLOOKUP(AF$304,$DATA,$THIS_COL-14+@COUNT(AF$305..AF305))

P         Monthly Sales Per Employee
--------------------------------------------------------------------------------
AL302: "*
AL303: "ACT
AL304: 100.01
AL305: (F2) @VLOOKUP(AL$304,$DATA,$THIS_COL-14+@COUNT(AL$305..AL305))
            /@VLOOKUP(AM$304,$DATA,$THIS_COL-14+@COUNT(AL$305..AL305))

AM302: "B
AM303: "BUD
AM304: 300.01
AM305: (F2) @VLOOKUP(AL$304+1000,$DATA,$THIS_COL-14+@COUNT(AM$305..AM305))
            /@VLOOKUP(AM$304+1000,$DATA,$THIS_COL-14+@COUNT(AM$305..AM305))

Q         Rolling 12-Month Earnings Per Share
--------------------------------------------------------------------------------
AR302: "*
AR303: "ACT
AR304: 800.02
AR305: (F2) @VLOOKUP(AR$304,$DATA,$THIS_COL-14+@COUNT(AR$305..AR305))
            /@VLOOKUP(AS$304,$DATA,$THIS_COL-14+@COUNT(AR$305..AR305))

AS302: "B
AS303: "BUD
AS304: 200.04
AS305: (F2) @VLOOKUP(AR$304+1000,$DATA,$THIS_COL-14+@COUNT(AS$305..AS305))
            /@VLOOKUP(AS$304,$DATA,$THIS_COL-14+@COUNT(AS$305..AS305))

R         Stock Price: Low, Close, High
--------------------------------------------------------------------------------
AX302: "=
AX303: "HI
AX304: (F3) 200.01
AX305: (F1) @VLOOKUP(AX$304,$DATA,$THIS_COL-14+@COUNT(AX$305..AX305))

AY302: "=
AY303: "LO
AY304: (F3) 200.02
AY305: (F1) @VLOOKUP(AY$304,$DATA,$THIS_COL-14+@COUNT(AY$305..AY305))

AZ302: "X
AZ303: "CLOSE
AZ304: (F3) 200.03
AZ305: (F1) @VLOOKUP(AZ$304,$DATA,$THIS_COL-14+@COUNT(AZ$305..AZ305))
```

Figure 13-6. The formulas used in the data section *(continued)*

Occasionally. you will have to make some alterations in the formulas. For example, graphs K and L require that you divide one @VLOOKUP formula by another while adding an extra −12 as shown in the figure. The

```
           K                L                 M        N        O        P        Q        R         S
250 ------------------------------------------------------------------------------------------------------
251                                   47
252 ------------------------------------------------------------------------------------------------------
253 ------------       THIS_COL           -------------------------------------------------------------
254                                   47
255 |
256 |
257 |
258 |
259
260 |                                     A        B        C        D        E        F     |||
261 |                                -------------------------------------------------------|||
262 |          Display Width               18       18       18       18       18       18 |||
263 |          Right-Hand Num             236     2188       32      296      339      991 |||
264 |          Left-Hand Num              137     1505        9       78      139      258 |||
265 |          Mid Number                 186     1846       20      187      239      624 |||
266 |          Mid Tic Point                9        9        9        9        9        9 |||
267 |          Type: 1=+, 0=+-, -1=-        1        1        1        1        1        1 |||
268 |          Scaling Factor       0.181818 0.026354 0.782608 0.082568     0.09 0.024556 |||
269 |          RH Num String        $236     $2188    $32      $296     $339     $991      |||
270 |          Len RH Num String            4        5        3        4        4        4 |||
271 |          LH Num String        $137     $1505    $9       $78      $139     $258      |||
272 |          Len LH Num String            4        5        2        3        4        4 |||
273 |          Mid Num String       $186     $1846    $20      $187     $239     $624      |||
274 |          Len Mid Num String           4        5        3        4        4        4 |||
275 |          Start Mid String             7        6        7        7        7        7 |||
276 |          One Symbol Equals            5       38      1.3       12       11       41 |||
277 |          One Symbol String    $5       $38      $1.3     $12      $11      $41       |||
278 |                                                                                     |||
279 |                                                                                     |||
280 |                                     G        H        I        J        K        L     |||
281 |                                -------------------------------------------------------|||
282 |          Display Width               18       18       18       18       18       18 |||
283 |          Right-Hand Num              63     1600      1.6      65%      -2%      45%|||
284 |          Left-Hand Num              -37        0        0      50%     -18%      11%|||
285 |          Mid Number                   0      800      0.8      58%     -10%      28%|||
```

```
      K              L                      M       N        O        P        Q        R         S
----------------------------------------------------------------------------------------------------
286 |          Mid Tic Point                     7        9        9       10        9         9 |||
287 |          Type: 1=+, 0=+-, -1=-             0        1        1        1       -1         1 |||
288 |          Scaling Factor                 0.18  0.01125    11.25      120    112.5  52.94117 |||
289 |          RH Num String              $63      $1600     1.6      65%     -2%      45%         |||
290 |          Len RH Num String                 3        5        3        3        3         3 |||
291 |          LH Num String              $-37     $0        0        50%     -18%     11%         |||
292 |          Len LH Num String                 4        2        1        3        4         3 |||
293 |          Mid Num String             $0       $800      0.8      58%     -10%     28%         |||
294 |          Len Mid Num String                2        4        3        3        4         3 |||
295 |          Start Mid String                  6        7        7        8        7         7 |||
296 |          One Symbol Equals                 6       89      0.1      0.8      0.9       1.9 |||
297 |          One Symbol String          $6       $89       0.1      0.8%     0.9%     1.9%        |||
298 |                                                                                             |||
299 |                                                                                             |||
300 |                                         M        N        O        P        Q        R       |||
301 |                                    --------------------------------------------------------|||
302 |          Display Width                    18       18       18       18       18        18 |||
303 |          Right-Hand Num                    3      33%       40        6        9        65 |||
304 |          Left-Hand Num                     0     -15%       29        4        2        30 |||
305 |          Mid Number                      1.8       0%       34        5        6        48 |||
306 |          Mid Tic Point                    11        6        8        9       10         9 |||
307 |          Type: 1=+, 0=+-, -1=-             1        0        1        1        1         1 |||
308 |          Scaling Factor                    6     37.5 1.636363        9 2.571428  0.514285 |||
309 |          RH Num String              3        33%       40       $6       $9       $65         |||
310 |          Len RH Num String                 1        3        2        2        2         3 |||
311 |          LH Num String              0        -15%      29       $4       $2       $30         |||
312 |          Len LH Num String                 1        4        2        2        2         3 |||
313 |          Mid Num String             1.8      0%        34       $5       $6       $48         |||
314 |          Len Mid Num String                3        2        2        2        2         3 |||
315 |          Start Mid String                  9        5        7        8        9         7 |||
316 |          One Symbol Equals               0.2      2.7      0.6      0.1      0.4       1.9 |||
317 |          One Symbol String          0.2      2.7%      0.6      $0.1     $0.4     $1.9        |||
318 |
319
```

Figure 13-7. The parameters section of the Mini Graph

−12 finds the balance sheet values, as required, at the *beginning* of each 12-month period.

And notice in graph J that one formula looks up the DB# plus 1,000. This formula finds our budget values. Notice in Figure 13-5, for example, that the DB#s for all budgeted amounts are exactly 1,000 more than the DB#s for the actual amounts.

Finally, you will have to add some extra formulas, as for graph H, or some extra values and labels, as for graph M. But nothing in this section is very sophisticated.

Step Three: Build the Parameters Section

Figure 13-7 shows the complete parameters section. Figure 13-8 shows the formulas you need to complete this section. The following discussion tells you how to enter these formulas. Figure 13-8 has 16 separate sections. Each section has one or several formulas in it. If only one formula is listed, copy it to the appropriate position for all 18 graphs. For example, copy M262 to N262..R262, to M282..R282, and to M302..R302.

If a section has more than one formula in it, copy the first formula in the list to the remaining positions, just as in the previous paragraph. (In all cases the first formula will be the formula for graph A.) Then go to the other cells for which this section of Figure 13-8 shows a formula and edit the formula to read as shown. Usually, only minor editing will be required. In most cases the formulas differ because of differences in format: one string formula may need a dollar sign; another formula may need a percentage sign, and so on.

You *will* have one additional editing job, however. Most of the formulas that calculate the Right-Hand Number and the Left-Hand Number of the graph do so by finding the @MAX and @MIN of the data being graphed. You must edit each such formula so that it looks at the proper range. Refer to Figure 13-4 to find the range designations to use for each graph.

A Description of the Parameters Section Formulas Let's take a brief look at each of the 16 types of formulas in Figure 13-8.

- *Display Width:* This is equal to the width of each column (found in E256) less the width of the gutter (found in E257). Strictly speaking, the Mini Graph that we are constructing doesn't need this formula repeated for each graph, as we are doing. We could have used but one formula. But using a separate Display Width value for each graph allows you to

```
Formulas for the Parameters Section
=======================================

  Display Width
  --------------------------------------------------------------------------
  M262: +$F$256-$F$257


  Right-Hand Number
  --------------------------------------------------------------------------
  M263: @ROUND(@MAX($T$265..$U$277)+0.05*@ABS(@MAX($T$265..$U$277)),0)
  O283: @ROUND(@MAX($AF$285..$AF$297)+0.05*@ABS(@MAX($AF$285..$AF$297)),1)
  P283: @ROUND(@MAX($AL$285..$AM$297)+0.07*@ABS(@MAX($AL$285..$AM$297)),2)
  Q283: @ROUND(@MAX($AT$285..$AT$297)+0.05*@ABS(@MAX($AT$285..$AT$297)),2)
  R283: @ROUND(@MAX($AX$285..$AY$297)+0.05*@ABS(@MAX($AX$285..$AY$297)),2)
  M303: @ROUND(@MAX($T305..$T317,3),0)
  N303: @ROUND(@MAX($Z$305..$AA$317)+0.05*@ABS(@MAX($Z$305..$AA$317)),2)


  Left-Hand Number
  --------------------------------------------------------------------------
  M264: @ROUND(@MIN($T$265..$U$277)-0.05*@ABS(@MIN($T$265..$U$277)),0)
  N284: 0
  O284: 0
  P284: @ROUND(@MIN($AL$285..$AM$297)-0.05*@ABS(@MIN($AL$285..$AM$297)),1)
  Q284: @ROUND(@MIN($AT$285..$AT$297)-0.05*@ABS(@MIN($AT$285..$AT$297)),2)
  R284: @ROUND(@MIN($AX$285..$AY$297)-0.1*@ABS(@MIN($AX$285..$AY$297)),2)
  M304: @ROUND(@MIN($T306..$T318,0),0)
  N304: @ROUND(@MIN($Z$305..$AA$317)-0.07*@ABS(@MIN($Z$305..$AA$317)),2)


  Middle Number
  --------------------------------------------------------------------------
  M265: @IF(M263*M264<0,0,@ROUND((M263+M264)/2,0))
  M305: 1.8
  N305: @IF(N303*N304<0,0,@ROUND((N303+N304)/2,2))


  Middle Tic Point
  --------------------------------------------------------------------------
  M266: @ROUND(((M265-M264)/(M263-M264))*M262,0)


  Graph Type: 1 = All + Values,  0 = + and - Values,  -1 = All - Values
  --------------------------------------------------------------------------
  M267: [W9] (M263>0)+(M264>=0)-1


  Scaling Factor
  --------------------------------------------------------------------------
  M268: +M262/(M263-M264)


  Right-Hand Number String
  --------------------------------------------------------------------------
  M269: +"$"&@STRING(M263,0)
  O289: @STRING(O283,1)
  P289: @STRING(100*P283,0)&"%"
  Q289: @STRING(100*Q283,0)&"%"
  R289: @STRING(100*R283,0)&"%"
```

Figure 13-8. The formulas used in the parameters section

```
M309: @STRING(M303,0)
N309: @STRING(N303*100,0)&"%"
O309: @STRING(O303,0)

Length of Right-Hand Number String
--------------------------------------------------------------------------
M270: @LENGTH(M269)

Left-Hand Number String
--------------------------------------------------------------------------
M271: +"$"&@STRING(M264,0)
O291: @STRING(O284,0)
P291: @STRING(100*P284,0)&"%"
Q291: @STRING(100*Q284,0)&"%"
R291: @STRING(100*R284,0)&"%"
M311: @STRING(M304,0)
N311: @STRING(N304*100,0)&"%"
O311: @STRING(O304,0)

Length of Left-Hand Number String
--------------------------------------------------------------------------
M272: @LENGTH(M271)

Middle Number String
--------------------------------------------------------------------------
M273: @IF((M262-M266<M270+2)#OR#(M266<M272+1),"","$"&@STRING(M265,0))
O293: @IF((O282-O286<O290+3)#OR#(O286<O292+1),"",@STRING(O285,1))
P293: @IF((P282-P286<P290+3)#OR#(P286<P292+1),"",@STRING(100*P285,0)&"%"
Q293: @IF((Q282-Q286<Q290+3)#OR#(Q286<Q292+1),"",@STRING(100*Q285,0)&"%"
R293: @IF((R282-R286<R290+3)#OR#(R286<R292+1),"",@STRING(100*R285,0)&"%"
M313: @IF((M302-M306<M310+3)#OR#(M306<M312+1),"",@STRING(M305,1))
N313: @IF((N302-N306<N310+3)#OR#(N306<N312+1),"",@STRING(100*N305,0)&"%"
O313: @IF((O302-O306<O310+3)#OR#(O306<O312+1),"",@STRING(O305,0))

Length of Middle Number String
--------------------------------------------------------------------------
M274: @LENGTH(M273)

Starting Position of Middle String
--------------------------------------------------------------------------
M275: +M266-@INT(M274/2+0.5)

One Symbol Equals Value
--------------------------------------------------------------------------
M276: @ROUND(1/M268,0)
O276: @ROUND(1/O268,1)
O296: @ROUND(1/O288,1)
P296: @ROUND(100/P288,1)
Q296: @ROUND(100/Q288,1)
R296: @ROUND(100/R288,1)
M316: @ROUND(1/M308,1)
N316: @ROUND(100/N308,1)
O316: @ROUND(1/O308,1)
P316: @ROUND(1/P308,1)
Q316: @ROUND(1/Q308,1)
R316: @ROUND(1/R308,1)
```

Figure 13-8. The formulas used in the parameters section (*continued*)

```
One Symbol String
----------------------------------------------------------------------
M277: +"$"&@STRING(M276,0)
O277: +"$"&@STRING(O276,1)
O297: @STRING(O296,1)
P297: @STRING(P296,1)&"%"
Q297: @STRING(Q296,1)&"%"
R297: @STRING(R296,1)&"%"
M317: @STRING(M316,1)
N317: @STRING(N316,1)&"%"
O317: @STRING(O316,1)
P317: +"$"&@STRING(P316,1)
Q317: +"$"&@STRING(Q316,1)
R317: +"$"&@STRING(R316,1)
```

Figure 13-8. The formulas used in the parameters section (*continued*)

vary the widths of your graphs later. You could, for example, erase graph I in Figure 13-1 and then make graph H twice as wide by changing the value of the Display Width for H to 38.

- *Right-Hand Number:* These formulas calculate the upper value limit of the graph. Generally, this number is equal to the maximum value in the range to be graphed plus an extra 5%. I added more in some cases, as in P283, to make the final graph look better. Feel free to substitute any value that you wish for proper scaling.
- *Left-Hand Number:* These formulas calculate the lower value of the graph. As before, feel free to substitute an actual value.
- *Middle Number:* This formula calculates the middle value of the graph. This value is calculated as zero if the upper and lower numbers have different signs. Notice that the middle number for the Z Score graph has the value 1.8. This is the value for the boundary between the "Dead" (near bankruptcy) values and the "Gray" values.
- *Middle Tic Point:* This is the character position where the middle tic point will lie in the graph.
- *Graph Type: 1=+, 0=+−, −1=−:* Some of the graph formulas need to know whether the data in the graph is all positive, mixed, or all negative. This set of formulas provides that information.
- *Scaling Factor:* This is the amount that we will multiply by each value to be graphed, producing the number of symbols required by the graph.

- *Right-Hand Number String:* The string value of the right-hand number on the graph scale.
- *Length of the Right-Hand Number String:* The number of characters in the string.
- *Left-Hand Number String:* The string value for the left-hand number of the graph scale.
- *Length of the Left-Hand Number String:* The number of characters in the string.
- *Middle Number String:* The string value for the middle number of the graph scale.
- *Length of the Middle Number String:* The number of characters in the string.
- *Starting Position of Middle String:* This is the starting position of the middle string when it is inserted into the graph scale.
- *One Symbol Equals Value:* These formulas calculate the values represented by one graph symbol.
- *One Symbol String:* This is the string representation of the previous value.

Step Four: Build the Graph Section

Figure 13-9 shows the full graph section; Figure 13-10 shows the graph formulas.

A Description of the Graph Section Formulas Figure 13-10 shows three heading and scale formulas and eight types of graph formulas. Let's take a closer look at each.

- *Cell E262:* Places the One Symbol String data from the parameters section, in the center of a line of dashes and surrounds it by "(*=" and ")".
- *Cell E263:* Begins with the left and right scale values, replaces the blank near the center of the cell with the middle scale value.
- *Cell E264:* Begins with a row of dashes with vertical lines at each end; replaces the appropriate character with the middle vertical line.

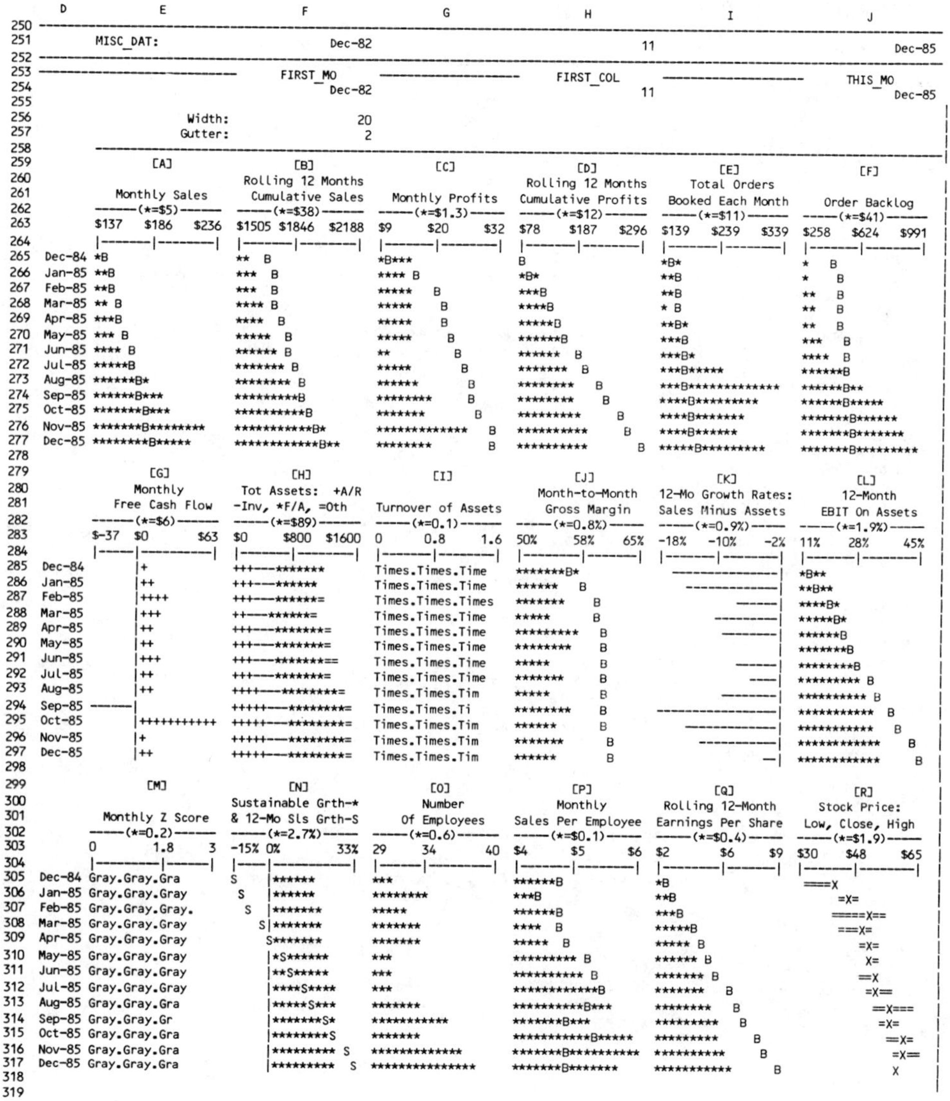

Figure 13-9. The graph section of the Mini Graph

```
Formulas for the Graph Section
=====================================

Heading and Scale Formulas
--------------------------------------------------------------------------------
E262: @REPLACE(@REPEAT("-",M262),(M262-@LENGTH(M277))/2-2,
               @LENGTH(M277)+4,"(*="&M277&")")

E263: @REPLACE(M271&@REPEAT(" ",M262-M270-M272)&M269,M275,M274,M273)

E264: @REPLACE("|"&@REPEAT("-",M262-2)&"|",@MAX(1,M266)-1,1,"|")

Graph Formulas
--------------------------------------------------------------------------------
E259: ^[A]
E261: ^Monthly Sales
E265: @REPLACE(@LEFT(@REPEAT($T$262,M$268*($T265-M$264)+0.5)
                     &@REPEAT(" ",M$262),M$262),
               M$268*($U265-M$264)+0.5,1,$U$262)


F259: ^[B]
F260: ^Rolling 12 Months
F261: ^Cumulative Sales
F265: @REPLACE(@LEFT(@REPEAT($Z$262,N$268*($Z265-N$264)+0.5)
                     &@REPEAT(" ",N$262),N$262),
               N$268*($AA265-N$264)+0.5,1,$AA$262)


G259: ^[C]
G261: ^Monthly Profits
G265: @REPLACE(@LEFT(@REPEAT($AF$262,O$268*($AF265-O$264)+0.5)
                     &@REPEAT(" ",O$262),O$262),
               O$268*($AG265-O$264)+0.5,1,$AG$262)


H259: ^[D]
H260: ^Rolling 12 Months
H261: ^Cumulative Profits
H265: @REPLACE(@LEFT(@REPEAT($AL$262,P$268*($AL265-P$264)+0.5)
                     &@REPEAT(" ",P$262),P$262),
               P$268*($AM265-P$264)+0.5,1,$AM$262)

I259: ^[E]
I260: ^Total Orders
I261: ^Booked Each Month
I265: @REPLACE(@LEFT(@REPEAT($AR$262,Q$268*($AR265-Q$264)+0.5)
                     &@REPEAT(" ",Q$262),Q$262),
               Q$268*($AS265-Q$264)+0.5,1,$AS$262)


J259: ^[F]
J261: ^Order Backlog
J265: @REPLACE(@LEFT(@REPEAT($AX$262,R$268*($AX265-R$264)+0.5)
                     &@REPEAT(" ",R$262),R$262),
               R$268*($AY265-R$264)+0.5,1,$AY$262)
```

Figure 13-10. The formulas used in the graph section

```
E279: ^[G]
E280: ^Monthly
E281: ^Free Cash Flow
E285: @REPEAT(" ",M$288*@ABS(M$284-@MIN(T285,0))-0.5)
      &@IF(T285>=0,"|","")
      &@REPEAT(@IF(T285<0,U$282,T$282),
               M$288*(@ABS(T285)-@CHOOSE(M$287+1,M$283,0,M$284))+0.5)
      &@IF(T285<0,"|","")


F279: ^[H]
F280: ^Tot Assets: +A/R
F281: '-Inv, *F/A, =Oth
F285: @REPEAT($AA$282,N$288*$AA285+0.5)&@REPEAT($AB$282,N$288*$AB285+0.5)
     &@REPEAT($AC$282,N$288*$AC285+0.5)&@REPEAT($AD$282,N$288*$AD285+0.5)


G279: ^[I]
G281: 'Turnover of Assets
G285: @LEFT(@REPEAT("Times.",5),$AF285*$O$288+0.5)


H279: ^[J]
H280: ^Month-to-Month
H281: ^Gross Margin
H285: @REPLACE(@LEFT(@REPEAT($AL$282,P$288*($AL285-P$284)+0.5)
                    &@REPEAT(" ",P$282),P$282),
               P$288*($AM285-P$284)+0.5,1,$AM$282)


I279: ^[K]
I280: ^12-Mo Growth Rates:
I281: 'Sales Minus Assets
I285: @REPEAT(" ",Q$288*@ABS(Q$284-@MIN(AT285,0))-0.5)
      &@IF(AT285>=0,"|","")
      &@REPEAT(@IF(AT285<0,AR$282,AS$282),
               Q$288*(@ABS(AT285)-@CHOOSE(Q$287+1,-Q$283,0,Q$284))+0.5)
      &@IF(AT285<0,"|","")


J279: ^[L]
J280: ^12-Month
J281: ^EBIT On Assets
J285: @REPLACE(@LEFT(@REPEAT($AX$282,R$288*($AX285-R$284)+0.5)
               &@REPEAT(" ",R$282),R$282),R$288*($AY285-R$284)+0.5,1,$AY$282)


E299: ^[M]
E301: ^Monthly Z Score
E305: @LEFT(@REPEAT(@VLOOKUP(T305,$V$305..$W$308,1),15),M$308*(T305-M$304)+0.5)


F299: ^[N]
F300: ^Sustainable Grth (*)
F301: ^& 12-Mo Sls Grth (S)
F305: @REPLACE(@REPEAT(" ",N308*@ABS(N304-@MIN(Z305,0))-0.5)
               &@IF(Z305>=0,"|","")
               &@REPEAT(Z302,N308*(@ABS(Z305)-@CHOOSE(N307+1,N303,0,N304))+0.5)
```

Figure 13-10. The formulas used in the graph section (*continued*)

```
                &@IF(Z305<0,"|","")
                &@REPEAT(" ",N302),
         N308*(AA305-N304)+0.5,1,AA302)


G299: ^[O]
G300: ^Number
G301: ^Of Employees
G305: @REPEAT($AF$302,(AF305-O$304)*O$308+0.5)


H299: ^[P]
H300: ^Monthly
H301: ^Sales Per Employee
H305: @REPLACE(@LEFT(@REPEAT($AL$302,P$308*($AL305-P$304)+0.5)
                       &@REPEAT(" ",P$302),P$302),P$308*($AM305-
                       P$304)+0.5,1,$AM$302)


I299: ^[Q]
I300: ^Rolling 12-Month
I301: ^Earnings Per Share
I305: @REPLACE(@LEFT(@REPEAT($AR$302,Q$308*($AR305-Q$304)+0.5)
                &@REPEAT(" ",Q$302),Q$302),Q$308*($AS305-Q$304)+0.5,1,$AS$302)


J299: ^[R]
J300: ^Stock Price:
J301: ^Low, Close, High
J305: @REPEAT(" ",($AY305-R$304)*R$308+0.5)
      &@REPEAT(AX$302,R$308*($AZ305-$AY305)+0.5)&AZ$302
      &@REPEAT(AX$302,R$308*($AX305-$AZ305)+0.5)
```

Figure 13-10. The formulas used in the graph section (*continued*)

After you've entered the formulas for the column headings and scales that are shown in Figure 13-10, you can copy them from graph to graph without modification.

- *Graphs A-F, J, L, P, and Q:* These graphs of actual and budgeted performance begin with the graph symbol repeated by a quantity equal to the scaled-down value to be graphed, plus 0.5. (Since only the integer value is used by @REPEAT formulas, adding 0.5 rounds the number of symbols to be graphed.) The formula adds a number of spaces equal to the Display Width and then takes the left most number of symbols and spaces equal to this width. Finally, the formula inserts the budget symbol into this string.

- *Graphs G and K:* These graphs automatically adjust themselves to the sign of the graph data (positive, negative, or mixed). It is the most flexible graph type we will discuss. The graph is the sum of four strings. The first is a string of spaces equal to the distance between the left-hand border and the first graph symbol. The second string, a vertical line, is added when the value being graphed is greater than or equal to zero.

The third string is the graph symbol. It repeats the plus sign if the value is positive and the minus sign if the value is negative. It repeats this sign by the scaled-down value of its length. The fourth string is equal to a vertical line if the value being graphed is less than zero.

- *Graph H:* This short formula is easy to enter. Each @REPEAT formula repeats the appropriate symbol by the scaled-down value to be graphed.
- *Graph I:* The @REPEAT function in this graph formula creates a supply of symbols. The @LEFT function selects the number of symbols equal to the scaled-down value to be graphed.
- *Graph M:* This graph is much like graph I. But unlike graph I, this function looks up the symbols to be used in the graph. As the value of the amount to be graphed changes, the graph symbol can change also.
- *Graph N:* This graph starts with the core of the graph formula for graphs G and K. This core, however, uses the same graph symbol, an * for both positive and negative values. Surrounding this core is a function that inserts an S in the proper location. S represents the actual sales growth rate for the previous 12 months.
- *Graph O:* This is the easiest graph in the figure. It illustrates the scaled-down value of the number of employees.
- *Graph R:* This graph of our Low, Close, and High stock prices is the sum of four strings. The first string is the distance between the left border and the Low value. The second string is the scaled-down value of the difference between the Close and the Low. The third string is an X. And the fourth string is the scaled-down value of the difference between the High and the Close.

WRAPPING UP

When you have finally created and saved your Mini Graph report, you have one very important step left: checking your work. As was said, many formulas are doing many things within this report. That leaves much room for error. So go back to your original data and calculate several data points on your calculator. Check first to see if your formulas in the data section have produced the proper amount. Then check to see if your graph properly reflects this amount. If not, make the changes where necessary.

HOW TO CHANGE THE MINI GRAPH TO REPORT YOUR OWN DATA

You will, of course, want to change the Mini Graph to reflect your own data. This shouldn't be too difficult.

After you've entered your data in the Data Bank, write an @VLOOKUP formula in the data section that will generate the proper data. Next, adjust the rounding values and string formats in the Parameters section to properly reflect this data.

If you wish to adjust the graph type, you have two ways to do this. First, you can enter its formula from Figure 13-10 into the first row of the graph you are updating. Next, edit this formula, adjusting the row and column designations as required. Finally, copy the formula down the remainder of the graph.

Alternatively, you can copy the formula from another of the graphs in your report. If possible, copy from another graph on the same row as the new graph. This will allow the cell references for the parameters section to adjust properly. If you must copy the formula from another row of your report, be sure to edit the formula and change the parameters section row numbers as required. In both cases, however, you will have to edit and adjust the cell references for the data section. Finally, copy the working graph formula down the remaining rows of the graph.

Making these adjustments may take quite a while the first time you try it. But after you go through this process several times you should be able to adjust all three sections and produce a new graph in about ten minutes.

Chapter Fourteen

USING TIME SERIES ANALYSIS FOR SALES FORECASTING

In most businesses sales are difficult to forecast accurately. The reasons for this difficulty aren't hard to find. We must cope with a fluctuating economy, changing tastes, changing prices, new competition, turnover in our sales and marketing staff, new customers replacing old customers, new products replacing old products, and so on. In the face of all this activity, if you or I could forecast sales with total accuracy, no firm could afford to hire us. We'd be making millions in Las Vegas or Atlantic City.

Unfortunately, one fact remains: businesses need accurate sales forecasts. And often you and I are expected to produce them. Most firms use one or both of two general approaches to generate forecasts. One approach is to have the sales and marketing department prepare the forecasts for management to revise and approve. We will examine this approach in Chapter 15. The other approach uses time series analysis.

SALES FORECASTING WITH TIME SERIES ANALYSIS

The purpose of time series analysis of sales is to find patterns in past sales data that we can use to predict future sales. As we find a pattern, we strip it away from the data, changing the shape of the data that remains. Then we look for new patterns and strip them away. We continue to strip away patterns until only unexplained fluctuations remain.

Generally, we will find four reasons for the sales fluctuations: seasonal fluctuations, overall trend, cyclical fluctuations, and unexplained events.

Seasonal Fluctuations

Most firms find that their sales vary with the seasons. Hot weather, summer vacations, the start of the school year, cool weather, Christmas, cold weather, the spring thaw, and the end of school—each can have its effect on a firm's orders and shipments.

If we graph these fluctuations from year to year, they might look something like this:

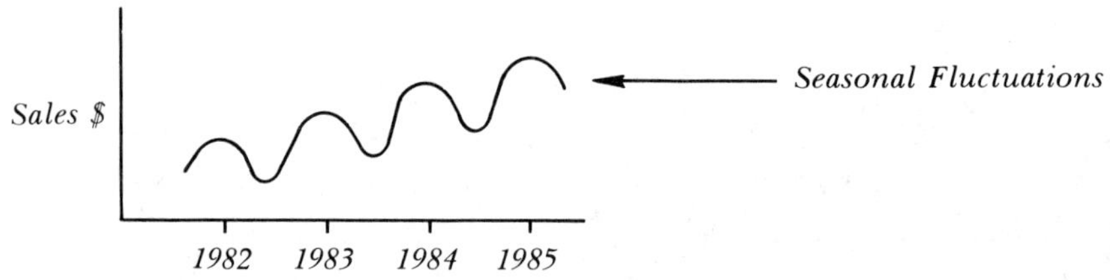

Overall Trend

Most firms find that their sales, however they may fluctuate, follow a general trend: up, down, or sideways. Even firms with the most unsophisticated methods of sales analysis have a general idea of what this trend is. The graph of this trend might look like this:

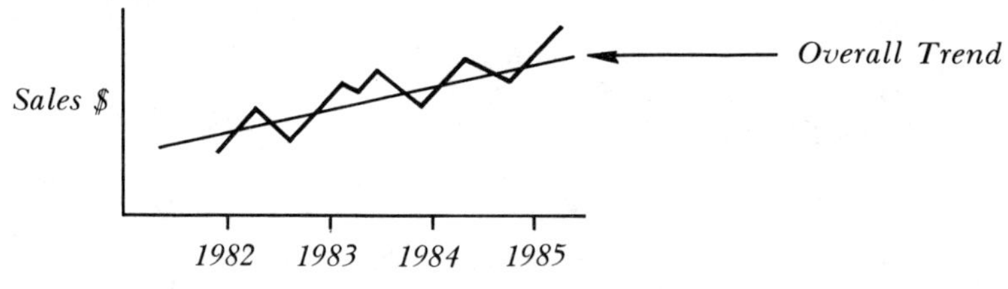

Cyclical Fluctuations

Most businesses are affected by the general business cycle. When the economy is booming, business is up; when the economy is down, business is down. These cyclical fluctuations may take several years to complete one cycle and could be graphed like this:

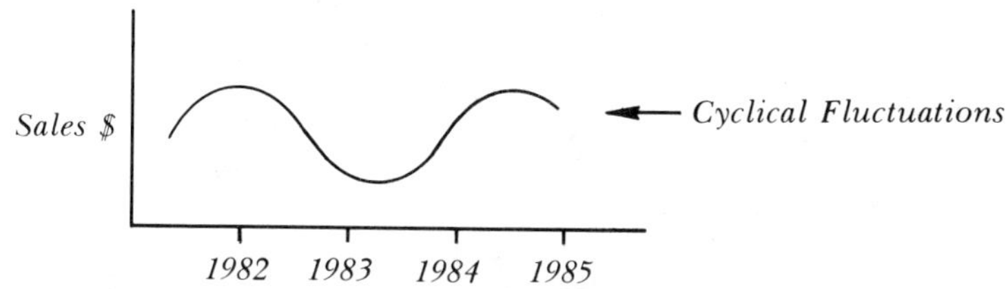

Unexplained Events

The world is full of surprises, some pleasant, some not. Some of these are random events, and some are events that would make sense if we better understood the way the world works. We try, of course, to explain past performance as well as we can, making this unexplained component as small as possible. If the unexplained events are random, as we assume they are, they balance themselves out over the long run.

The Combined Sales Forecast

When we combine all four components of our actual sales, they might look like this:

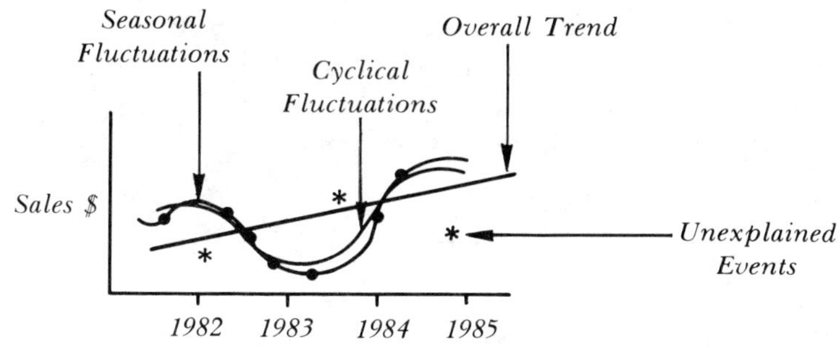

If we've done a good job of forecasting, our forecast will look much like this illustration. The difference, however, is that our forecast excludes the unexplained events.

The Prediction Model

After we have defined the various components of our sales behavior, we will build a forecast from them. For any one month, the formula for our predicted sales will be

$$P = S \times T \times C$$

where

P = the predicted sales value
S = the value of the seasonal component
T = the value of the trend component
C = the value of the cyclical component

If we use valid predictors, actual sales for any month will be equal to the predicted sales plus the value of a small unexplained component.

A Note About the Time Series Analysis Spreadsheet

Most of the spreadsheets that we have discussed in this book have been somewhat orderly. They generally have looked as though numbers were placed where they belonged. But the time series analysis spreadsheet that we create in this chapter won't look like that at all.

There are two reasons for this apparent disorder. First, the analysis that we will do is a creative effort—an exploration. We may find one pattern in our data; we may find half a dozen. And each pattern can take many forms. Soon, our spreadsheet may be littered with data. Second, our goal is to produce a forecast, not a spreadsheet. In a way the time series analysis spreadsheet is nothing but computerized scratch paper.

PREPARING THE DATA

Our goal in this chapter is to produce a forecast for the 1986 sales of the Widget Corporation. Figure 14-1 shows the data we'll use to produce this forecast: the firm's sales for the past four years.

When you enter these sales into your spreadsheet, the following macro should help:

```
\x {?}{DOWN}
   /xg \x~
```

Every time you enter a number and press ENTER, this macro will move the cell pointer to the next lower cell. If you make a mistake in data entry, simply move your cell pointer to the cell that needs correcting. When you get to the bottom of a column of data, move your cell pointer to the new column and continue. When you have finished with the macro, press CTRL-BREAK to stop it. Then delete the range name \x and erase the macro.

Using Data Bank Sales Data

When you do an actual forecast in the future, the source of your data will probably be the Data Bank or a similar file. An easy way to extract this data from such a file is to use the /File Xtract Values command, sending the data you need to a temporary file, say, TRASH. When you /**F**ile **R**etrieve **TRASH**, you will have only the selected data in your spreadsheet.

	A	B	C	D	E	F
2			Widget Corporation Sales			
3			============	============	============	============
4						
5			1982	1983	1984	1985
6						
7		Jan	$5,055	$3,994	$5,971	$5,649
8		Feb	$5,904	$4,326	$6,816	$7,188
9		Mar	$6,180	$5,176	$7,179	$7,837
10		Apr	$7,073	$5,900	$8,338	$8,631
11		May	$7,545	$7,485	$8,549	$9,805
12		Jun	$8,037	$8,034	$8,773	$9,760
13		Jul	$6,650	$6,431	$7,727	$7,921
14		Aug	$6,947	$7,215	$8,295	$9,094
15		Sep	$7,222	$7,744	$8,679	$9,413
16		Oct	$6,132	$8,017	$7,275	$8,755
17		Nov	$6,073	$7,685	$5,434	$8,069
18		Dec	$3,724	$4,950	$4,270	$5,174
19			------------	------------	------------	------------
20		Total	$76,542	$76,957	$87,306	$97,296

Figure 14-1. Widget's actual sales for the past four years

In the Data Bank the monthly sales data is in one row. To analyze these sales, we need to have the data in a column. Version 2 users can use the /Range Transpose command to copy the row of data to a convenient column. If you are using Version 1A, use /**D**ata **F**ill to place the numbers 1, 2, 3, and so on in the row immediately above the row of sales data in your TRASH spreadsheet. (Start with 1 and use 1 as the increment.) Then assign the range name DATA to both rows of data. In an empty cell below this data—in D30, for example—enter this formula:

```
@HLOOKUP(@COUNT($D$30..D30),$DATA,1)
```

This should return the value of the sales immediately below the value 1 that you added with the /Data Fill command. When you copy this formula down the column, each successive cell should return the succeeding sales amount from the DATA row. Finally, use /**F**ile **X**tract **V**alues to send this column to a temporary file. Call it TRASH again. When you /**F**ile **R**etrieve the TRASH file, you will have the column of sales values that you need.

THE SEASONAL COMPONENT

The /Graph command is an ideal tool for helping us to understand the nature of our data. To use it, simply press /**G**raph, assign the graph ranges that you want to view, and then select **V**iew. When you want to look at other data, use **R**eset **G**raph to wipe the slate clean. As with our spreadsheet, these graphs are much like scratch paper. We seldom bother with titles, legends, and such. However, the graphs in this chapter include some of these titles and legends to make the explanations easier to follow.

When you graph Widget's sales column, as in Figure 14-2, you will see that we have an interesting task ahead of us. When we look for patterns in the data, the most obvious one looks like a misshapen "M" and seems to repeat itself yearly. In other words, our sales seem to vary with the seasons. We can get a better view of this pattern if we assign the sales for each year to a different graph range. Figure 14-3 shows the results. This graph shows that although the sales level changes each year, the pattern of month-to-month variations remains about the same.

Calculate the Seasonal Ratio

If we remove this seasonal sales component, or pattern, from the sales data, we can find other patterns in the data. To remove this seasonal pattern, we must calculate how far above or below the yearly average each month falls.

We will average the individual variations for January, for February, and so on, to calculate a Seasonal Index we can use to eliminate the pattern.

Figure 14-4 shows the first few columns of the data analysis section of our spreadsheet. Columns A and B were filled in using the /Data Fill command. For column A, use a beginning value and increment of 1 and an ending value of 48. For column B, use a beginning value of @DATE(82,1,15), an increment of 365/12, and an ending value of 99999. Then format column B as Date (3).

Column C shows the sales figures rearranged from Figure 14-1. I copied the sales data from Figure 14-1 into a blank area of the spreadsheet, used the /Move command to turn the four short columns into one long column, and then moved this column to C39 as shown.

Column D calculates the ratio of the current month's sales divided by the 12-month moving average of the sales. Here's the formula for the value

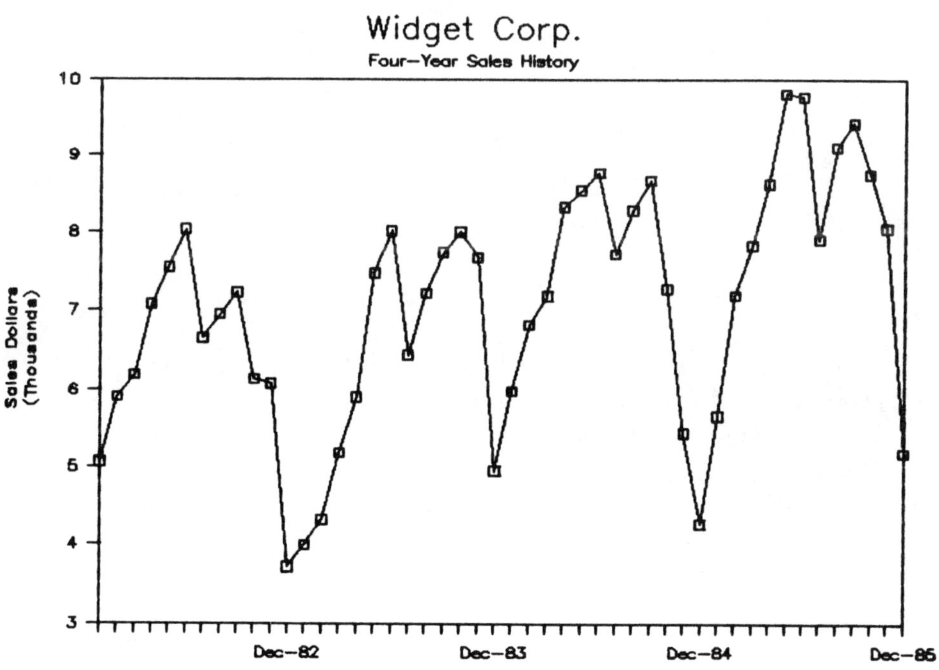

Figure 14-2. A graph of Widget's sales history

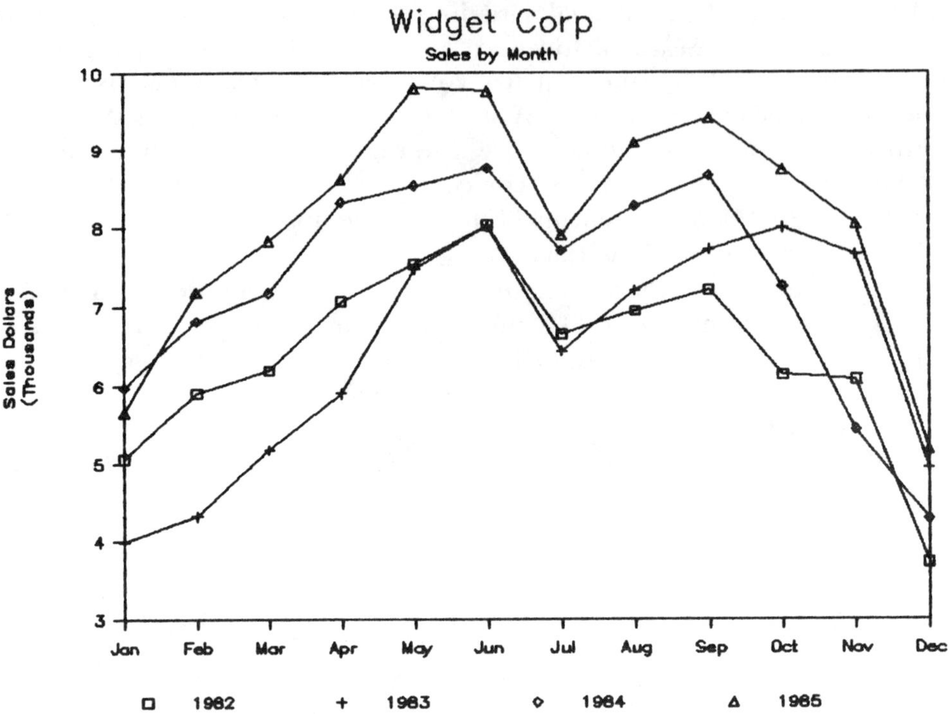

Figure 14-3. A graph showing the seasonal pattern of Widget's sales

located in D45:

D45: (F3) +C45/(@SUM(C39..C50,C40..C51)/24)

This formula, with its moving averages, needs some explanation. It divides the current sales by a "centered 12-month moving average." The formula for this centered average places the sales for the month being calculated at the center of the sales data used to calculate the average.

For example, suppose we want to find the centered moving average sales for July 1982. To do this, we could sum the sales for January through December 1982 and then divide by 12. But the 30 days at the center of this averaging period is the 30 days from June 16 through July 15.

Similarly, if we found the 12-month average for February 1982 through

	A	B	C	D	E	F
33					[S]	
34				Ratio:		
35				Sales to		
36			Actual	Moving	Seasonal	Deseasonalized
37	Sequence #	Month	Sales	Average	Index	Sales
38						
39	1	Jan-82	5,055		0.746	6,779
40	2	Feb-82	5,904		0.865	6,826
41	3	Mar-82	6,180		0.949	6,509
42	4	Apr-82	7,073		1.066	6,638
43	5	May-82	7,545		1.200	6,287
44	6	Jun-82	8,037		1.229	6,540
45	7	Jul-82	6,650	1.050	1.038	6,404
46	8	Aug-82	6,947	1.116	1.117	6,221
47	9	Sep-82	7,222	1.181	1.169	6,175
48	10	Oct-82	6,132	1.018	1.052	5,829
49	11	Nov-82	6,073	1.016	0.942	6,444
50	12	Dec-82	3,724	0.624	0.627	5,943
51	13	Jan-83	3,994	0.670	0.746	5,356
52	14	Feb-83	4,326	0.725	0.865	5,002
53	15	Mar-83	5,176	0.863	0.949	5,452
54	16	Apr-83	5,900	0.967	1.066	5,537
55	17	May-83	7,485	1.199	1.200	6,237
56	18	Jun-83	8,034	1.263	1.229	6,538
57	19	Jul-83	6,431	0.990	1.038	6,193
58	20	Aug-83	7,215	1.080	1.117	6,461
59	21	Sep-83	7,744	1.127	1.169	6,622
60	22	Oct-83	8,017	1.137	1.052	7,621
61	23	Nov-83	7,685	1.067	0.942	8,155
62	24	Dec-83	4,950	0.680	0.627	7,900
63	25	Jan-84	5,971	0.811	0.746	8,008
64	26	Feb-84	6,816	0.914	0.865	7,880
65	27	Mar-84	7,179	0.952	0.949	7,561
66	28	Apr-84	8,338	1.104	1.066	7,825
67	29	May-84	8,549	1.151	1.200	7,123
68	30	Jun-84	8,773	1.201	1.229	7,139
69	31	Jul-84	7,727	1.064	1.038	7,441
70	32	Aug-84	8,295	1.142	1.117	7,429
71	33	Sep-84	8,679	1.188	1.169	7,421
72	34	Oct-84	7,275	0.990	1.052	6,916
73	35	Nov-84	5,434	0.733	0.942	5,766
74	36	Dec-84	4,270	0.569	0.627	6,815
75	37	Jan-85	5,649	0.748	0.746	7,576
76	38	Feb-85	7,188	0.946	0.865	8,311
77	39	Mar-85	7,837	1.023	0.949	8,255
78	40	Apr-85	8,631	1.113	1.066	8,100
79	41	May-85	9,805	1.238	1.200	8,170
80	42	Jun-85	9,760	1.209	1.229	7,942
81	43	Jul-85	7,921		1.038	7,628
82	44	Aug-85	9,094		1.117	8,144
83	45	Sep-85	9,413		1.169	8,049
84	46	Oct-85	8,755		1.052	8,323
85	47	Nov-85	8,069		0.942	8,562
86	48	Dec-85	5,174		0.627	8,258

Figure 14-4. The spreadsheet columns necessary to extract Widget's Deseasonalized Sales data

January 1983, the center period would be July 16 through August 15. But if we average these two overlapping averages, we will have a center period equal to the month of July, just as we wanted. This calculation is the same as adding January through December and February through January and then dividing by 24—just as in the formula.

This ratio in column D shows how each month varies from the 12-month average. Now we need to find an average for January's variations, for February's variations, and so on.

Calculate the Seasonal Index

Once we find a satisfactory method of calculating an index of seasonal adjustments, we will use this method in two different ways. First, we will apply it to past data. This will eliminate seasonal variations in the data so that we can see more clearly the other components affecting our sales. Second, we will apply the method to our forecast.

We start by arranging the monthly variations in column D into sets of yearly columns, as shown in columns H through K of Figure 14-5. When the data is arranged as shown, it is easier to compare the variations from year to year and calculate an average seasonal index.

The formula shown in row 22 of Figure 14-5 uses the @INDEX function, and the numbers shown in row 1 and column G of the figure, to look up data from column D of Figure 14-4. Since this function is new to Version 2, let's take a closer look at it.

The format of this function is @INDEX(range,column,row). It returns the value of the cell in *range* at the intersection of the *column* and *row.* In H7 the range is defined as column D, from one row above the first row of monthly data to the last row of data. Since the @INDEX function begins with zero when it counts numbers and rows, the first (and only) column in the range is numbered zero. The row number to extract from column D is found by adding the number found in G7 to 12 times the number found in H1. If you insert the $ signs as shown in the formula, you can copy it from H7 to I7..K7 and from H7..K7 to H8..H18.

Version 1A users can substitute a similar formula:

H7: `(F3) @VLOOKUP($A$38__$D$86,3,$G7+12*H$1)`

There are two common methods we can use to produce an average index for each month of the year. If the seasonal variations appear to be changing from year to year, we could use a weighted average of the same month in each successive year. For example, the average index for each successive month might be equal to 60% of the actual ratio for the month one year previously, plus 30% of the ratio for the month two years previously, plus 10% of the ratio for the month three years previously. The faster the trend appears to be changing, the more heavily you would weight the more recent years.

If the pattern of seasonal variations is changing slowly, we can use a simple average of the recent variations for the same month over several years. This is what we've done in column L of Figure 14-5. The formula shown for L7 can be copied down column L as in the figure.

When you calculate this average for your own data, be sure that it does *not* include any zeros where data is missing. Columns H and K show these zeros. Including the zeros in the average would produce a false index, of course. The formula in L7 shows one way to exclude these zeros from your averages.

To produce the seasonal index as shown in column M, we simply scale column L's averages so they will sum to the value 12. The formula shown for M7 does this for us. Copy it down the column as shown in the figure.

Finally, transfer the Seasonal Index, column M of Figure 14-5, to column E, as shown in Figure 14-4. Version 2 users can do this by using the /Range Value command, copying the values to cell E39. Version 1A users can use /File Xtract Values command, extracting the index to a TRASH file, and then use /File Combine to combine the TRASH file to E39.

To copy this index down the rest of the row, /Copy from E39..E74 to E51. This approach will copy the 12-month index to the remaining 36 months.

Calculate the Column Of Deseasonalized Sales

Notice [S] above the Seasonal Index column of Figure 14-4. This marks the first of the three values that we will multiply to generate our sales forecast. To get the other two values, we must "deseasonalize" our sales.

The final column of Figure 14-4 shows these Deseasonalized Sales. The formula is easy; it divides Sales by the Seasonal Index:

F39: `+C39/E39`

Format this cell as ,0 (comma zero), and then copy it down the column as shown.

```
            G         H          I          J          K          L          M
 1                    0          1          2          3
 2
 3               Calculation of the Average Seasonal Index
 4               ==================================================================
 5                 1982       1983       1984       1985        AVG       INDEX
 6
 7            1   0.000      0.670      0.811      0.748      0.743      0.746
 8            2   0.000      0.725      0.914      0.946      0.862      0.865
 9            3   0.000      0.863      0.952      1.023      0.946      0.949
10            4   0.000      0.967      1.104      1.113      1.062      1.066
11            5   0.000      1.199      1.151      1.238      1.196      1.200
12            6   0.000      1.263      1.201      1.209      1.224      1.229
13            7   1.050      0.990      1.064      0.000      1.035      1.038
14            8   1.116      1.080      1.142      0.000      1.113      1.117
15            9   1.181      1.127      1.188      0.000      1.165      1.169
16           10   1.018      1.137      0.990      0.000      1.048      1.052
17           11   1.016      1.067      0.733      0.000      0.939      0.942
18           12   0.624      0.680      0.569      0.000      0.624      0.627
19               ------------------------------------------------------------------
20       Totals       6         12         12          6     11.957     12.000
21
22                 H7: (F3) @INDEX($D$38..$D$86,0,+$G7+12*H$1)
23                 L7: (F3) @IF(K7=0,@AVG(J7..H7),@AVG(K7..I7))
24                 M7: (F3) [W16] (12/$L$20)*L7
25                 H20: (,0) @SUM(H19..H7)
```

Figure 14-5. The table and formulas used to calculate Widget's Average Seasonal Index

THE TREND COMPONENT

Now that we've removed the seasonal component from our past sales, Figure 14-6 shows what our sales look like without it. This graph of column F of Figure 14-4 shows that our data changed considerably from the data graphed in Figure 14-2. Without the seasonal variations, other patterns begin to emerge. Notice that these Deseasonalized Sales appear to increase over the years. Let's look more closely at this trend.

Linear Regression

Linear regression is a statistical technique that allows us to answer several questions about the trend that we see in Figure 14-6.

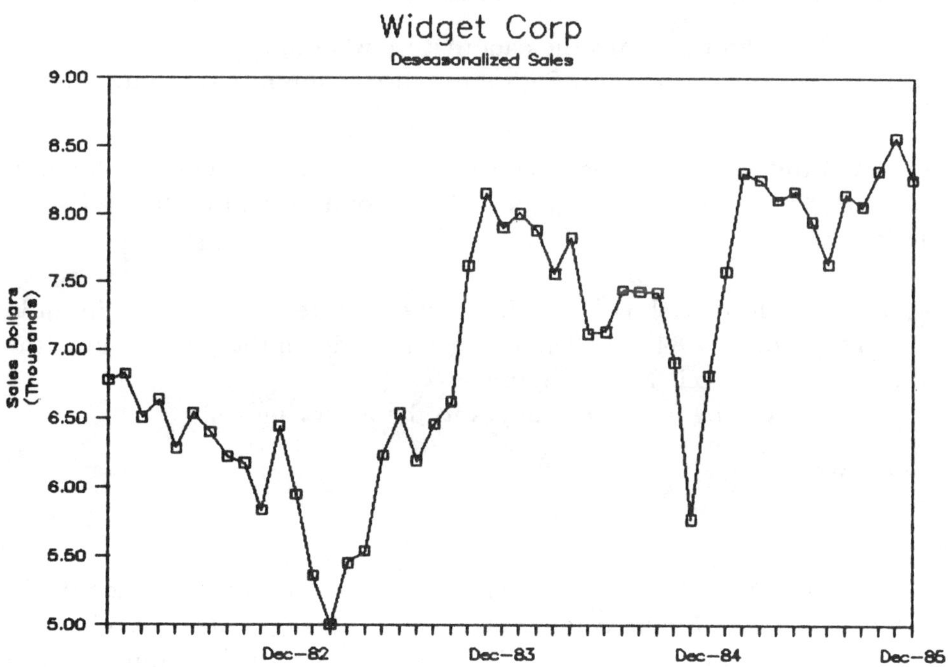

Figure 14-6. A graph of Widget's Deseasonalized Sales

1. How certain are we that there really is a trend in our sales? Has our eye been fooled?

2. What is the formula for the line that would illustrate the trend? This formula would allow 1-2-3 to draw the line in the graph, and it would tell us the approximate yearly growth rate of our sales.

3. On average, how far do actual sales tend to vary from the trend line? This would allow us to say that sales will grow to a certain size in the future, give or take some amount.

How to Calculate the Regression Statistics

To answer these questions about Figure 14-6, we need three columns of data:

1. The X column represents the passage of time. In this chapter our X column will always be column A of the spreadsheet.

2. The Y column contains the data that we wish to explain as a function of time. The graph shown in Figure 14-6 used column F of Figure 14-4 as the Y column.

3. An X times Y column is a scratch column and is shown in column N of Figure 14-7. Its only use is to provide the total found in cell N88 of that figure.

To create the data shown in column N of Figure 14-7, enter the formula shown in Figure 14-8 for N39 and then copy it down the column. Find the sum as shown in cell N88 of figure 14-7.

Next, assign the following ranges to the following cells:

```
A A39..A86
F F39..F86
H H39..H86
```

Then in cells M92 through M102 enter the labels shown for those cells in Figure 14-7. Use /**R**ange **N**ame **L**abel **R**ight to assign labels in cells M92 through M97 as range names for the cells to their right in column N. Use /**R**ange **N**ame **C**reate to assign the range names [B], [A], [R2], and SEE to cells N98 through N101, respectively. Then enter the formulas for column N as shown in Figure 14-8.

	M	N	O
34		Linear Regression Values	
35		============================	
36			
37		AxF	AxH
38			
39		6,779.182	1.149
40		13,651.995	2.294
41		19,527.899	3.255
42		26,550.661	4.389
43		31,432.936	5.155
44		39,241.316	6.385
45		44,829.596	7.236
46		49,771.340	7.971
47		55,578.111	8.833
48		58,294.403	9.193
49		70,885.431	11.093
50		71,321.026	11.077
51		69,631.785	10.733
52		70,021.971	10.713
53		81,777.026	12.419
54		88,589.793	13.354
55		106,022.104	15.866
56		117,680.005	17.483
57		117,673.114	17.356
58		129,228.521	18.924
59		139,055.581	20.219
60		167,671.511	24.208
61		187,556.763	26.890
62		189,602.083	26.994
63		200,190.376	28.305
64		204,890.919	28.772
65		204,161.339	28.474
66		219,094.570	30.350
67		206,570.837	28.424
68		214,174.484	29.273
69		230,684.143	31.321
70		237,716.000	32.064
71		244,899.227	32.817
72		235,145.477	31.305
73		201,812.796	26.694
74		245,333.604	32.243
75		280,304.077	36.604
76		315,799.506	40.979
77		321,929.105	41.512
78		323,990.891	41.516
79		334,955.527	42.655
80		333,578.041	42.217
81		328,014.926	41.259
82		358,343.615	44.799

Figure 14-7. The section of the spreadsheet used to calculate regression statistics

	M		N	O
83			362,196.591	45.006
84			382,858.855	47.287
85			402,419.108	49.406
86			396,364.111	48.373
87			-------------	-------------
88	Total XxY		8,737,802.279	1,174.845
89				
90			Y = Column F	Y = Column H
91				
92	NUM		48	48
93	XAV		24.5	24.5
94	YAV		7048.1638886	1.0002003567
95	SXX		9212	9212
96	SYY		41744861.848	0.425624756
97	SXY		449161.54635	-1.3901848906
98	Coef	[B]	48.758309418	-0.0001509102
99	Constant	[A]	5853.5853079	1.003897657
100	R-Squared	[R2]	0.52462403	0.0004929062
101	Std Er Est	SEE	656.81219923	0.0961673092
102	Std Er Coef		6.8432789897	0.0010019603

Figure 14-7. The section of the spreadsheet used to calculate regression statistics (*continued*)

An Explanation of the Regression Statistics

Most linear regression analysis uses a combination of the following six values:

1. NUM, the number of observations. In the formula for cell N92 (Figure 14-8), we use the @COUNT function to count this number of observations. Since we are analyzing four years of data, the number is equal to 48.

2. XAV, the average, or mean, of the X values. Here the X values are the sequence numbers in column A of Figure 14-4. This value is therefore equal to @AVG($A), as shown in cell N93 of Figure 14-8. (Remember that we have assigned the range name A to the range A39..A86. The $A in the @AVG formula refers to that range name.)

3. YAV, the average, or mean, of the Y values: The Y values consist of the column of data to be explained—in our case, Deseasonalized Sales, column

```
Linear Regression Formulas
=============================================

Column F  Statistics
---------------------------------------------
N39: (,3) +A39*F39
N88: (,3) @SUM(N87..N39)
N92: @COUNT(N86..N39)
N93: @AVG($A)
N94: @AVG($F)
N95: @VAR($A)*NUM
N96: @VAR($F)*NUM
N97: @SUM(N86..N39)-NUM*@AVG($A)*@AVG($F)
N98: +SXY/SXX
N99: +YAV-[B]*XAV
N100: +SXY^2/(SYY*SXX)
N101: @SQRT(((SYY*(1-[R2]))/(NUM-2)))
N102: +SEE/@SQRT(SXX)

Column H  Statistics
---------------------------------------------
O39: (,3) +A39*H39
O88: (,3) @SUM(O87..O39)
O92: @COUNT(O86..O39)
O93: @AVG($A)
O94: @AVG($H)
O95: @VAR($A)*O92
O96: @VAR($H)*O92
O97: @SUM(O86..O39)-O92*@AVG(A)*@AVG(H)
O98: +O97/O95
O99: +O94-O98*O93
O100: +O97^2/(O96*O95)
O101: @SQRT(((O96*(1-O100))/(O92-2)))
O102: +O101/@SQRT(O95)
```

Figure 14-8. The regression formulas in columns N and O that are used to calculate statistics about columns F and H, respectively

F in Figures 14-4 and 14-9. The formula for the YAV value in N94 of Figure 14-7 is shown in Figure 14-8 as @AVG($F).

4. SXX, the sum (S) of the squares of each X deviation from its mean (XX) (in other words, the sum of the squares of all the "give or take" amounts): 1-2-3 makes this calculation easy. Since the @VAR function is the mean value of these squared deviations, we simply multiply the @VAR value by the number of observations, NUM. This produces the sum that we

	F	G	H
33		[T]	
34			Econ Cycle &
35			Unexplained
36	Deseasonalized	Sales	Sales Ratio
37	Sales	Trend	(F/G)
38			
39	6,779	5,902	1.149
40	6,826	5,951	1.147
41	6,509	6,000	1.085
42	6,638	6,049	1.097
43	6,287	6,097	1.031
44	6,540	6,146	1.064
45	6,404	6,195	1.034
46	6,221	6,244	0.996
47	6,175	6,292	0.981
48	5,829	6,341	0.919
49	6,444	6,390	1.008
50	5,943	6,439	0.923
51	5,356	6,487	0.826
52	5,002	6,536	0.765
53	5,452	6,585	0.828
54	5,537	6,634	0.835
55	6,237	6,682	0.933
56	6,538	6,731	0.971
57	6,193	6,780	0.913
58	6,461	6,829	0.946
59	6,622	6,877	0.963
60	7,621	6,926	1.100
61	8,155	6,975	1.169
62	7,900	7,024	1.125
63	8,008	7,073	1.132
64	7,880	7,121	1.107
65	7,561	7,170	1.055
66	7,825	7,219	1.084
67	7,123	7,268	0.980
68	7,139	7,316	0.976
69	7,441	7,365	1.010
70	7,429	7,414	1.002
71	7,421	7,463	0.994
72	6,916	7,511	0.921
73	5,766	7,560	0.763
74	6,815	7,609	0.896
75	7,576	7,658	0.989
76	8,311	7,706	1.078
77	8,255	7,755	1.064
78	8,100	7,804	1.038

Figure 14-9. The columns that extract the Sales Trend from the Deseasonalized Sales

	F	G	H
79	8,170	7,853	1.040
80	7,942	7,901	1.005
81	7,628	7,950	0.959
82	8,144	7,999	1.018
83	8,049	8,048	1.000
84	8,323	8,096	1.028
85	8,562	8,145	1.051
86	8,258	8,194	1.008

Figure 14-9. The columns that extract the Sales Trend from the Deseasonalized Sales (*continued*)

need. The value for SXX is, therefore, equal to @VAR($A)*NUM (cell N95 in Figure 14-8). To summarize:

$$SXX = \Sigma (X_i - \overline{X})^2$$

$$@VAR\ (X\ data) = \frac{\Sigma (X_i - \overline{X})^2}{\text{number of observations}}$$

$$SXX = @VAR\ (X\ data) * (\text{number of observations})$$

5. SYY, the sum of the squares of each Y deviation from its mean: It is equal to @VAR($F)*NUM. To summarize:

$$SYY = \Sigma (Y_i - \overline{Y})^2$$

$$@VAR\ (Y\ data) = \frac{\Sigma (Y_i - \overline{Y})^2}{\text{number of observations}}$$

$$SYY = @VAR\ (Y\ data) * (\text{number of observations})$$

6. SXY, the sum of the cross products of the X and Y deviations. That is, it is the sum of each value of X minus the mean of X, times each value of Y minus the mean of Y. Unfortunately, 1-2-3 does not provide a function that allows us to calculate this sum directly.

Algebraically, the sum of these cross products is equal to the sum of the X and Y products less the number of observations times the product of the X and Y means:

$$\begin{aligned} SXY &= \Sigma\,(X_i - \overline{X})\,(Y_i - \overline{Y}) \\ &= \Sigma\,X_iY_i - n\overline{XY} \\ &= \text{@SUM (X-times-Y column)} - \\ &\quad \text{(number of observations)} * \text{@AVG (X data)} * \text{@AVG (Y data)} \end{aligned}$$

As shown in Figure 14-7, cell N88 provides the sum of the XY values. And the formula shown for N97 in Figure 14-8 returns the SXY value.

Finally, the remaining values that we will use are defined as follows:

Coefficient of regression:

$$B = \frac{SXY}{SXX} = [B]$$

Regression constant:

$$A = \overline{Y} - B \cdot \overline{X} = [A]$$

Coefficient of determination:

$$R^2 = \frac{SXY^2}{SXX \cdot SXY} = [R2]$$

Standard error of the estimate:

$$S = \sqrt{\frac{SYY\,(1 - R^2)}{n - 2}} = SEE$$

In this chapter we will not use one additional regression statistic, the standard error of the coefficient. The formula follows, however, because it is one of the statistics provided by the /Data Regression command in 1-2-3 Version 2:

Standard error of the coefficient:

$$S\,(B) = \frac{S}{\sqrt{SXX}}$$

Another Method: The /Data Regression Command (Version 2)

Many readers will be wondering by now why we haven't used 1-2-3's /Data Regression command, just referred to. After all, it's quick and easy. All we must do is define range A as the X range, range F as the Y range, any unused section of the spreadsheet as the output range, and then press **Go**.

Here's why I recommend that when you are doing linear regression you use the preceding formulas instead: the /Data Regression command produces numeric values. The regression formulas, on the other hand, are just that—formulas. Their results change as the data changes and the spreadsheet is recalculated. If you depend on the /Data Regression command, you might forget to issue it after the data has changed, and failing to do so could distort your entire analysis.

Nevertheless, the /Data Regression command is valuable for several applications. First, it is handy for quick analyses of data. Second, it is useful for checking the results of the formulas shown in Figure 14-8. And third, it is the only convenient method to use when you are doing multiple regression—regression with more than one column of X variables.

Calculate the Sales Trend

When we look at the regression statistics in Figure 14-7, we see that the regression of column F produces in cell N100 an R-Squared (coefficient of determination) of approximately 0.52. This means that 52% of the variance that we find in column F can be explained by the trend line.

Column G in Figure 14-9 shows this Sales Trend. The [T] above the column marks the second of the three columns we need for our forecast. The formula for each value in this column is easy. It is equal to the regression constant plus an X value times the regression coefficient, or:

```
G39:  +$[A]+$A39*$[B]
```

Format this cell as ,0 (comma zero) and copy G39 down the column.

Calculate the Ratio of Remaining Variations

The ratio of Deseasonalized Sales (column F) to the Sales Trend (column G) returns a ratio in column H that we have yet to explain. When we graph column H, we get Figure 14-10. There appears to be an indication of a cycle in this data.

THE CYCLE COMPONENT

Let's briefly review what we have done. First, we had four years of actual sales data from which we removed the seasonal fluctuations; then we removed the trends. Remaining in column H of Figure 14-9 is a ratio that

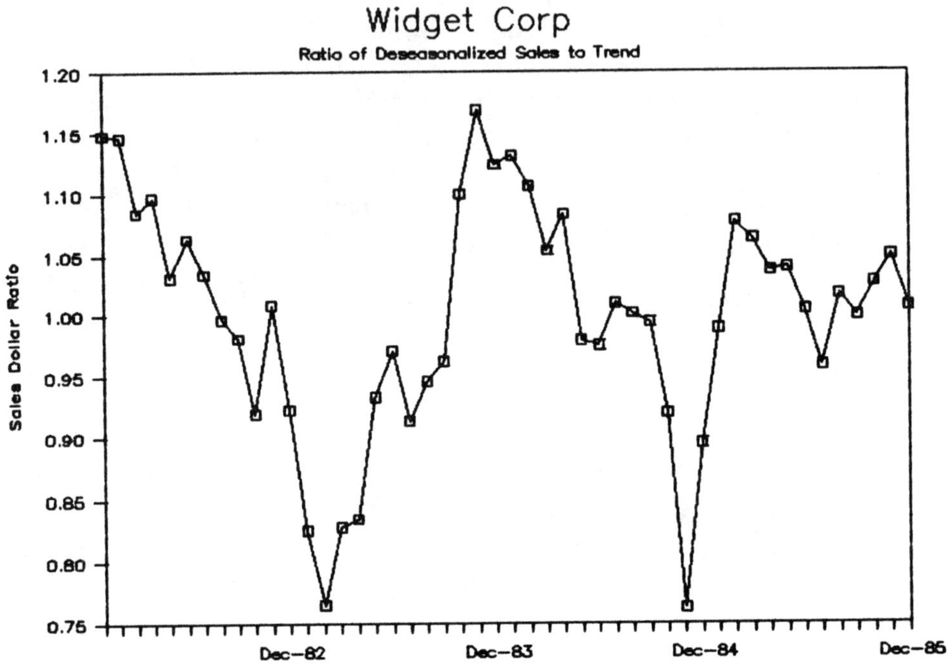

Figure 14-10. A graph of the Ratio of the Deseasonalized Sales to the Sales Trend, representing the sales activity yet to be explained

represents the economic cycle and unexplained variations in sales. So our final step is to remove this cycle from the data, leaving only the unexplained variations.

Figure 14-11 shows the spreadsheet columns we will use. Starting with column H, we will remove the Economic Cycle multiplier shown in column I. Column J is a scratch column that will help us find the best values for column I. Next we will calculate the Predicted Sales in column K and the Unexplained Sales in column L. Finally, we will calculate our sales forecast.

	H	I	J	K	L
33		[C]			
34	Econ Cycle &				
35	Unexplained		Absolute Value		
36	Sales Ratio	Economic	Of Unexplained	Predicted	Unexplained
37	(F/G)	Cycle	ABS(H-I)	Sales $	Sales $
38					
39	1.149	1.094	0.055	4,814	241
40	1.147	1.097	0.050	5,647	257
41	1.085	1.094	0.009	6,231	(51)
42	1.097	1.084	0.013	6,987	85
43	1.031	1.069	0.038	7,821	(275)
44	1.064	1.049	0.016	7,919	117
45	1.034	1.025	0.009	6,594	56
46	0.996	1.000	0.004	6,972	(25)
47	0.981	0.975	0.006	7,174	48
48	0.919	0.951	0.032	6,346	(214)
49	1.008	0.931	0.077	5,608	465
50	0.923	0.916	0.007	3,695	29
51	0.826	0.906	0.080	4,384	(390)
52	0.765	0.903	0.138	5,104	(778)
53	0.828	0.906	0.078	5,665	(489)
54	0.835	0.916	0.081	6,474	(574)
55	0.933	0.931	0.002	7,469	16
56	0.971	0.951	0.020	7,870	164
57	0.913	0.975	0.061	6,863	(432)
58	0.946	1.000	0.054	7,625	(410)
59	0.963	1.025	0.062	8,245	(501)
60	1.100	1.049	0.052	7,640	377
61	1.169	1.069	0.100	7,025	660
62	1.125	1.084	0.041	4,771	179
63	1.132	1.094	0.038	5,768	202
64	1.107	1.097	0.009	6,758	58
65	1.055	1.094	0.039	7,446	(267)
66	1.084	1.084	0.000	8,339	(1)
67	0.980	1.069	0.089	9,321	(772)
68	0.976	1.049	0.073	9,427	(654)
69	1.010	1.025	0.015	7,840	(113)
70	1.002	1.000	0.002	8,278	16
71	0.994	0.975	0.020	8,508	171
72	0.921	0.951	0.031	7,517	(242)
73	0.763	0.931	0.169	6,635	(1,201)
74	0.896	0.916	0.020	4,367	(96)
75	0.989	0.906	0.083	5,174	475
76	1.078	0.903	0.175	6,018	1,170
77	1.064	0.906	0.158	6,672	1,165
78	1.038	0.916	0.122	7,616	1,015
79	1.040	0.931	0.109	8,777	1,028
80	1.005	0.951	0.054	9,238	522
81	0.959	0.975	0.015	8,048	(127)
82	1.018	1.000	0.018	8,932	162
83	1.000	1.025	0.025	9,648	(235)
84	1.028	1.049	0.021	8,930	(175)
85	1.051	1.069	0.017	8,203	(134)
86	1.008	1.084	0.076	5,566	(392)
87			--------------		--------------
88		Total	2.46427	Total:	126

Figure 14-11. The columns that strip away the Economic Cycle and produce Widget's final values of Unexplained Sales

Sine Waves and Cosine Waves

The @SIN function and the @COS function produce graphs of the same wavy shape. But since the @COS function makes it easy to start a graph at the top of an economic cycle, we will use this function to produce our cyclic component. Figure 14-12 shows our first attempt at fitting this wavy line to our data.

To graph this line, we estimate how near the economic cycle was when our data started, how long the cycle has tended to last, and the degree to

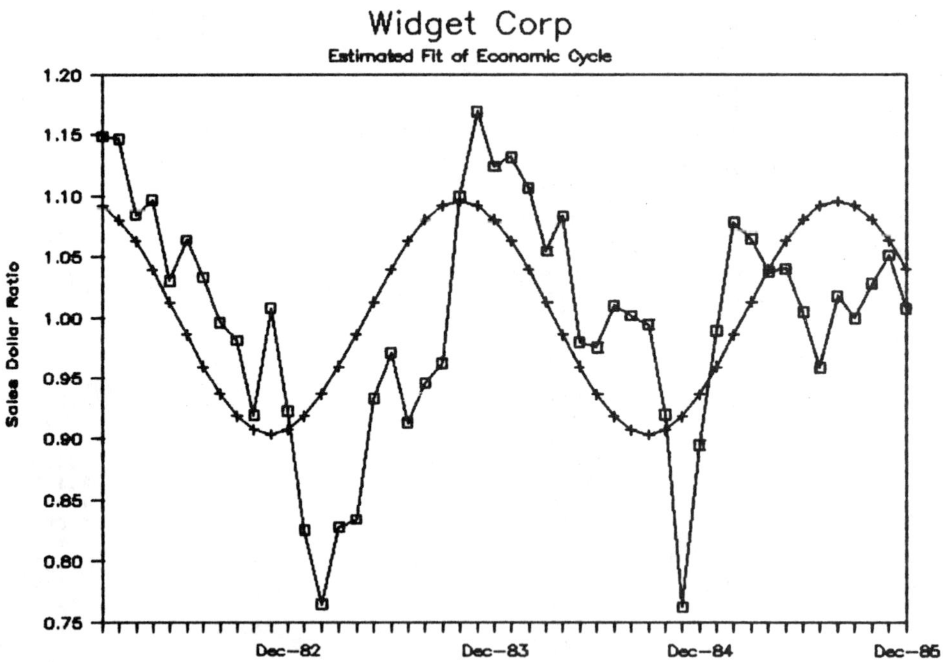

Figure 14-12. A graph of the Estimated Fit of the Economic Cycle to Widget's sales ratio in column H

which the cycle helps or hurts our sales on average. More specifically, we use the formula:

```
@COS((month number+offset)*(2/cycle life)*@PI)*height+central value
```

- The month number is provided by column A. The first month we wish to analyze is 1, the second month is 2, and so on.
- The offset is the number of months between the first month we are examining (month number 1) and the top of the business cycle. If the top of the business cycle was three months before month number 1, the offset is 3. If the top of the business cycle is five months after month number 1, the offset is equal to −5.
- The cycle life is the number of months from the top of one business cycle to the top of the next cycle.
- The height of the cycle is the approximate distance between the top of the cycle and its central value. Being approximately equal to the Standard Error of the Estimate of column H, the height is in effect the "give or take" value on each side of H's central value.
- The central value is the value for the ratio shown in column H that we would experience if the economic cycle had no effect on our sales. A quick glance at column H shows this value to be approximately equal to 1, as we would expect.

To begin, therefore, we need to calculate regression statistics for column H. This will give us the standard error of the estimate (the "give or take" amount) that we will use to estimate the height of the cycle.

Calculate the Regression Statistics For Column H

Enter and format the formula shown for cell O39 in Figure 14-8. Copy the formula down the column and total it, just as you did with column N. Copy the regression statistics in N92 through N102 to O92 through O102. Then edit the formulas in column O to read as shown in Figure 14-8. Your numbers should read as shown in Figure 14-7.

We need two numbers from the statistics in column O of Figure 14-7. The value of the constant of the regression equation, in cell O99, confirms for us that the central value is approximately 1. And also, the standard error of the estimate in cell O101 tells us that our values generally fall within 0.096, or 9.6%, of this amount.

Enter Estimated Values for The Economic Cycle

To estimate the economic cycle, we will need some constant values for the @COS formula. As shown in Figure 14-13, enter the labels **CENTER**, **OFFSET**, **LIFE**, and **HEIGHT** in cells G90, G91, G92, and G93, respectively. Use /**R**ange **N**ame **L**abel **R**ight to assign these as names for the cells to their right. Now we enter some initial values, in the following manner.

- We said that the CENTER value appears to be equal to 1; enter this in H90.
- We don't know what the OFFSET is yet; enter **0** for now.
- The LIFE of the business cycle varies; let's guess that it's 22 months.
- The HEIGHT will be approximately equal to the standard error of the estimate for column H; Figure 14-7 shows that this value is found in cell O101, so enter **+$O$101**.

Now, as shown in Figure 14-11, go to the top of your data columns and enter formulas in these two cells:

```
I39: @COS(($A39+$OFFSET)*(2/$LIFE)*@PI)*$HEIGHT+$CENTER
J39: @ABS(H39-I39)
```

Format both cells as Fixed (3) and copy them down the column of data. Next, go to the bottom of column J. Draw an underline and then @SUM the column.

Here's what we've done. In column I we have put our initial estimate of the effects of the economic cycle on our sales. In column J we have put the absolute value of the remaining sales variations that are not explained by the economic cycle. Our immediate goal is to find values for the economic cycle that will minimize the sum of these unexplained variations.

	G	H	I	J	K	L
84	8,096	1.028	1.049	0.021	8,930	(175)
85	8,145	1.051	1.069	0.017	8,203	(134)
86	8,194	1.008	1.084	0.076	5,566	(392)
87				-----------		-----------
88			Total	2.46427	Total:	126
89						
90	CENTER	1				
91	OFFSET	-2				
92	LIFE	24	Min		2.46427	
93	HEIGHT	9.71%				
94						
95			-----------	-----------	-----------	-----------
96	+$O$101		+J88	23	24	25
97	0.99		+G97*$G$96	2.50131	2.46467	2.70726
98	1.00		+G98*$G$96	2.50241	2.46430	2.70980
99	1.01		+G99*$G$96	2.50131	2.46427	2.71235
100	1.02		+G100*$G$96	2.50021	2.46556	2.71489
101	1.03		+G101*$G$96	2.49912	2.46685	2.71743
102			-----------	-----------	-----------	-----------

Figure 14-13. The section of the spreadsheet used to find the best fit for the Economic Cycle

Fit the Economic Cycle by Eye

Use the /**G**raph command to assign graph range A to the data in column H. Assign graph range B to the data in column I. Now **V**iew the graph.

Figure 14-12 is what your graph should show. This isn't a bad start for a first guess. Our curve seems shifted to the left slightly. And the actual cycle may be longer than 22 months. So, to shift the graph to the right, enter an OFFSET of −3 in cell H91 and then recalculate.

We know immediately that this adjustment has helped our fit, because the sum of the absolute values of our variations—column J's @SUM—has declined. And when we press /Graph View, the graph looks like a better fit.

The cycle still seems a little short, however. Let's extend its LIFE to 23 months. When we recalculate, we see that J's sum has declined. And the graph looks better.

We continue with this approach. The graph will suggest changes we could make that might improve the fit. Column J's total will tell us whether the suggestion was a good one.

Use a Data Table for the Final Fit

Soon we see that the CENTER is definitely equal to 1, and the OFFSET is equal to −2. But the cycle LIFE could be anywhere from 23 to 25 months, and the HEIGHT could be somewhat above or below the SEE. The Data Table helps us find the combination of cycle life and height that produces the lowest total for column J.

Figure 14-13 shows the Data Table set-up that produces our final values. Since G96 in this figure has been formatted as Text, we can see that it references cell O101, the standard error of the estimate. The cells below this cell contain suggested values that we will multiply by the SEE to find a HEIGHT value that might produce a better fit.

The Data Table itself is shown within the dashed lines, rows 95 and 102, in Figure 14-13. Cell I96 references column J's total. The formulas in I97 through I101 use the values in column G to calculate a range of specific HEIGHT values. And the values in J96, K96, and L96 are suggested cycle LIFE values.

To use the Data Table, enter your suggested multipliers of the SEE in cells G97 through G101, enter your suggestions for the cycle LIFE values in cells J96 through L96, and then issue the /**D**ata **T**able **2** command. Specify the **R**ange as I96..L101, input cell 1 as H93, and input cell 2 as H92. When you next press ENTER, and after a wait of several minutes, 1-2-3 will fill the

Data Table with the values shown in the figure. Each cell value represents what the total for column J would be if you used the HEIGHT value at the left of the cell in the table and the LIFE value at the top of the cell's column.

The easiest way to find the lowest value in the table is to enter in cell K92 the formula @MIN(J97..L101), the results of which are shown in K92. In Figure 14-13 the value shown for this minimum can be found in the table, in cell K99. It represents a LIFE of 24 months and a HEIGHT of 1.01 times the SEE. When we substitute the value 24 into H92 and the formula 1.01*$O$101 into H93, and then recalculate, the Total for column J will be equal to the minimum. Figure 14-14 shows a graph of the cycle that appears to best fit our data.

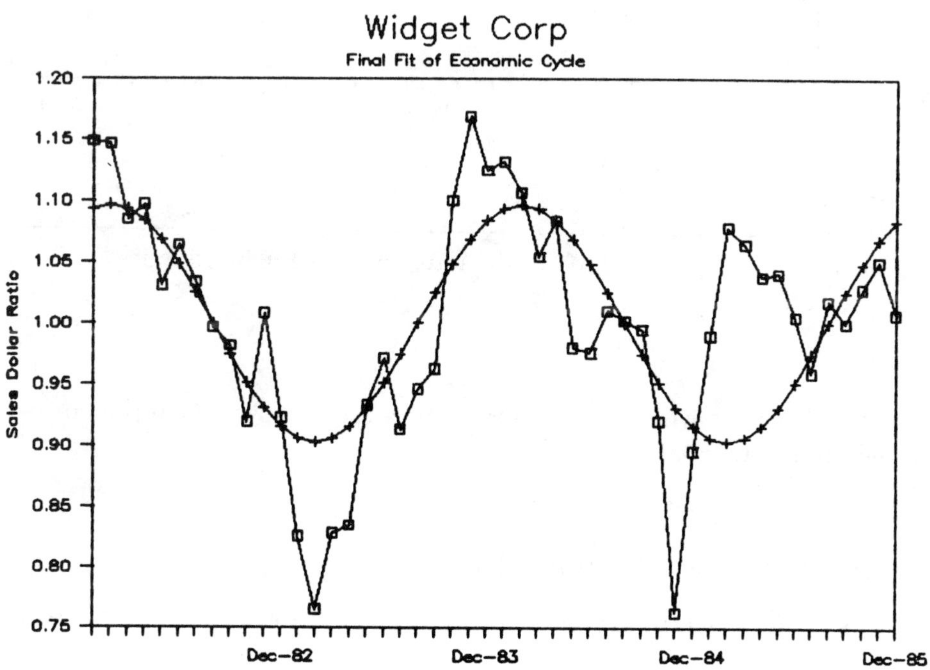

Figure 14-14. A graph of the Final Fit of the Economic Cycle to Widget's sales ratio in column H

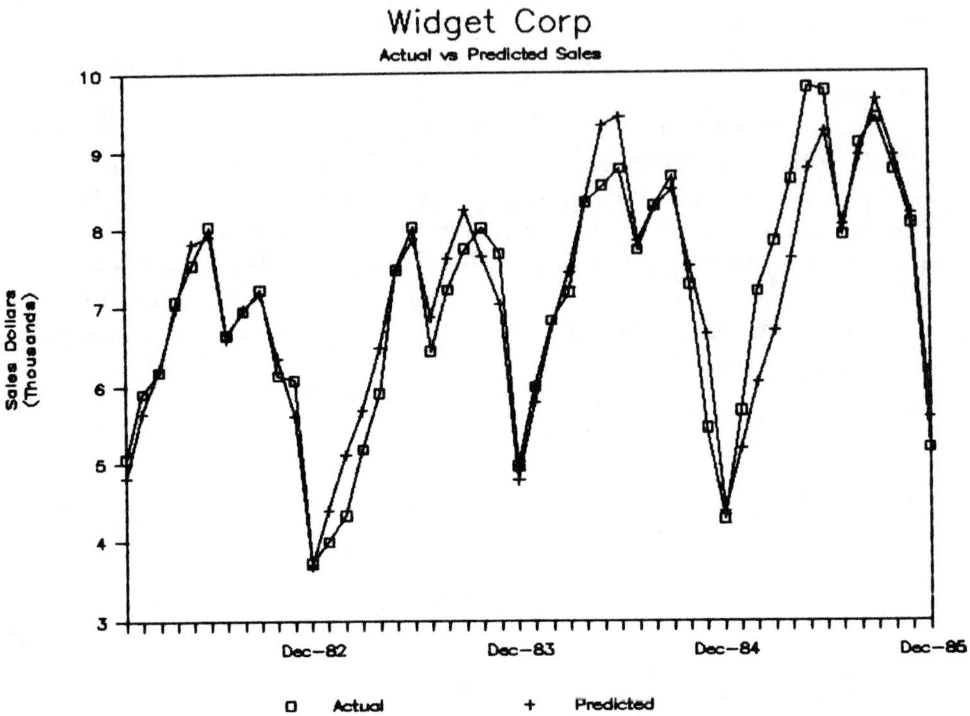

Figure 14-15. A graph of Widget's Actual Versus Predicted Sales

Now that we have found the best values for the Cycle Component, we are nearly to our goal.

Calculate the Predicted Sales Value

Go to K39, as shown in Figure 14-11, and enter the formula +E39*G39*I39. Format this formula as Currency (0) and copy it down the column.

This formula represents our reassembled sales data. It is the product of the seasonal component (column E), the trend component (column G) and the cycle component (column I). Column K ignores the sales variations that we have been unable to explain.

```
           N              O               P

 1
 2
 3       Sales        Predicted     Unexplained
 4      76,542          75,809              -1%
 5      76,957          79,136               3%
 6      87,306          90,206               3%
 7      97,296          92,824              -5%
 8
 9                  N4: (,0) @SUM(C39..C50)
10                  N5: (,0) @SUM(C51..C62)
11                  N6: (,0) @SUM(C63..C74)
12                  N7: (,0) @SUM(C75..C86)
13
14                  O4: (,0) @SUM(K39..K50)
15                  O5: (,0) @SUM(K51..K62)
16                  O6: (,0) @SUM(K63..K74)
17                  O7: (,0) @SUM(K75..K86)
18
19                  P4: (P0) +O4/N4-1
20                  P5: (P0) +O5/N5-1
21                  P6: (P0) +O6/N6-1
22                  P7: (P0) +O7/N7-1
```

Figure 14-16. An analysis of Widget's Actual and Predicted Sales for the years 1982-1985

Evaluate the Results

How well have we done? Let's look at the graph. Define the graph range A as our column of Actual Sales, column C. Define the graph range B as our column of Predicted Sales, column K. When we View the graph, we see Figure 14-15. This graph seems to say that we've done a good job of re-creating the mess that our actual sales represent.

Another measure of our success would be a comparison of actual sales and predicted sales for each of the four years. Figure 14-16 shows this comparison and the formulas used to produce the values. This comparison shows that over a four-year period, the yearly totals of our actual and predicted sales were fairly close. It is rather disturbing, however, that the largest error is in the most recent year. We'll see another indication of this problem shortly.

A third measure of our success is the actual value of our Unexplained

Sales, shown in column L of Figure 14-11. This column is equal to actual sales less predicted sales. Cell L39, for example, is equal to +C39−K39. The total of this column shows that over four years our forecast has been off by only $126. But when we add this column to our previous graph, we get a different perspective. Defining column L as graph range C, we get Figure 14-17. Notice that as time passes, the errors grow more extreme. Since our projections of total sales have been more reliable than our month-to-month projections, the seasonal variations must be changing more than we had thought. This trend creates some concern for next year's forecast.

If we were preparing an actual sales forecast, we would probably go back and use a weighted average to calculate a revised seasonal index. Although a new seasonal index would probably change the values of our

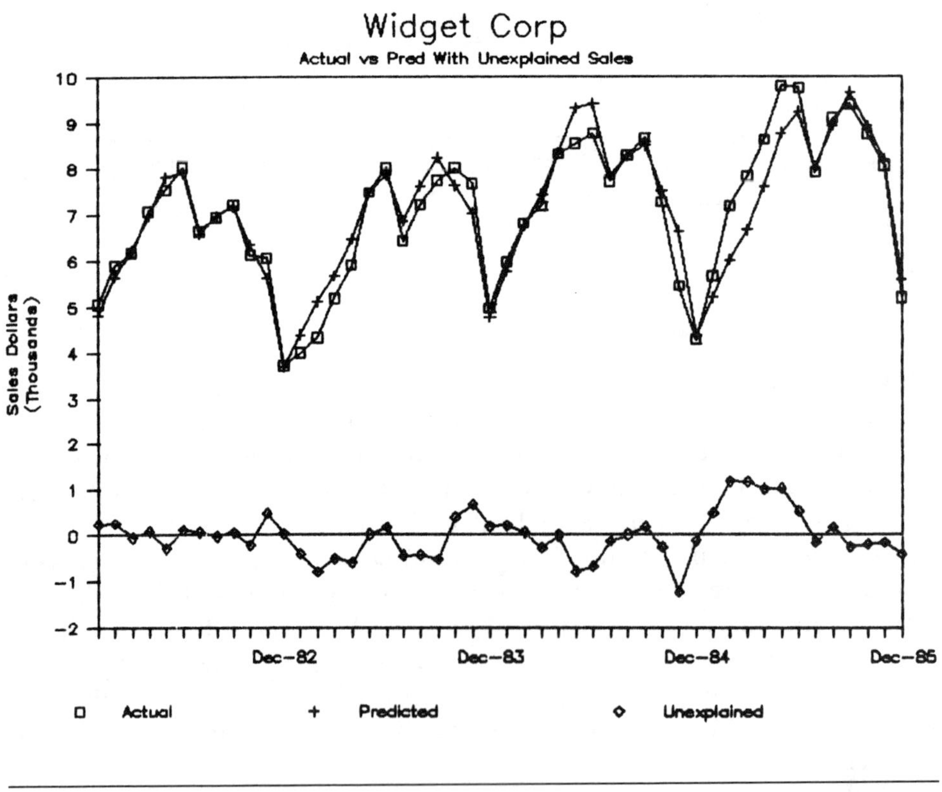

Figure 14-17. A graph of Widget's Actual, Predicted, and Unexplained Sales

trend and economic components slightly, our spreadsheet arrangement should help us recalculate these components quickly.

For now, however, let's assume that our prediction is accurate enough to produce a satisfactory sales forecast.

PRODUCE THE SALES FORECAST

With all the preparation behind us, producing the actual sales forecast is a breeze. Figure 14-18 illustrates the process. Here we have dropped one line below our columns of data to calculate the forecast. The Forecast itself is in column C, below our actual sales. This arrangement will allow us to easily graph our column of actual and forecasted sales.

As you can see from the labels and formulas beneath the columns, each cell of the sales forecast is the product of the Index, Trend, and Cycle components for the month.

When we graph this forecast, graphing the trend and cyclical values as well helps to explain our results. Figure 14-19 illustrates the columns of

	A	B	C	D	E	F
85	47	Nov-85	8,069		0.942	8,562
86	48	Dec-85	5,174		0.627	8,258
87						
88	49	Jan-86	6,723	0.746	8,243	1.094
89	50	Feb-86	7,868	0.865	8,291	1.097
90	51	Mar-86	8,661	0.949	8,340	1.094
91	52	Apr-86	9,691	1.066	8,389	1.084
92	53	May-86	10,822	1.200	8,438	1.069
93	54	Jun-86	10,935	1.229	8,487	1.049
94	55	Jul-86	9,086	1.038	8,535	1.025
95	56	Aug-86	9,585	1.117	8,584	1.000
96	57	Sep-86	9,842	1.169	8,633	0.975
97	58	Oct-86	8,689	1.052	8,682	0.951
98	59	Nov-86	7,662	0.942	8,730	0.931
99	60	Dec-86	5,038	0.627	8,779	0.916
100						
101			Forecast^	Index^	Trend^	Cycle^
102						

```
C88: (,0) +D88*E88*F88
D88: (F3) 0.7456652167
E88: (,0) +$[A]+A88*$[B]
F88: (F3) @COS((A88+$OFFSET)*(2/$LIFE)*@PI)*$HEIGHT+$CENTER
```

Figure 14-18. The section of the spreadsheet used to predict Widget's Sales Index, Trend, and Cycle for 1986

	Q	R
34	Values for Graphing	
35		
36	Sales	Cycle
37	Trend	& Trend
38	----------	----------
39	5902	6456
40	5951	6529
41	6000	6563
42	6049	6557
43	6097	6516
44	6146	6445
45	6195	6351
46	6244	6244
47	6292	6134
48	6341	6033
49	6390	5951
50	6439	5897
51	6487	5879
52	6536	5901
53	6585	5967
54	6634	6076
55	6682	6224
56	6731	6404
57	6780	6610
58	6829	6829
59	6878	7050
60	6926	7263
61	6975	7454
62	7024	7615
63	7073	7736
64	7121	7813
65	7170	7843
66	7219	7826
67	7268	7767
68	7316	7672
69	7365	7550
70	7414	7414
71	7463	7275
72	7511	7147
73	7560	7041
74	7609	6969
75	7658	6939
76	7706	6958
77	7755	7028
78	7804	7147
79	7853	7313
80	7901	7518

Figure 14-19. The columns holding the values for Sales Trend and Cycle Trend for the years 1982-1986

	Q	R
81	7950	7750
82	7999	7999
83	8048	8250
84	8096	8490
85	8145	8705
86	8194	8883
87		
88	8243	9016
89	8292	9097
90	8340	9123
91	8389	9095
92	8438	9017
93	8487	8899
94	8535	8750
95	8584	8584
96	8633	8416
97	8682	8260
98	8730	8131
99	8779	8041

Figure 14-19. The columns holding the values for Sales Trend and Cycle Trend for the years 1982-1986 (*continued*)

data we'll need. In Q39 enter **+G30**, which returns the value of the calculated sales trend. In R39 enter **+I39*G39**, which returns the dollar value of the cycle-adjusted trend. Copy these cells to rows 40 through 86 as shown in the figure.

Next, go to Q88 and enter the formula **+E88**, which returns the forecasted value of our future sales trend. In R88 enter **+F88*E88**, which returns the forecasted value of the future cycle-adjusted trend. Copy these formulas to rows 89 through 99 as shown.

Finally, assign the graph range **B** to Q39..Q99, the graph range C to R39..R99, and the graph range A to C39..C99. Figure 14-20 shows the graph that these data ranges generates.

The first four Ms that we see in Figure 14-20 are our actual sales over the past four years. The last M, to the right of the break in the graph, is our forecasted performance for next year. As you can see, we are predicting that sales will start strong next year and then deteriorate in the fall. We expect a deterioration because we expect the economy to take its periodic trip south.

Adjustments to the Sales Forecast

It was already mentioned that the seasonal index might need some adjustment. Before we complete this forecast, however, we need to ask how certain we are about the other two components, our sales trend and the economic cycle.

First, the coefficient of our regression equation (cell N98 in Figure 14-7) says that over the past four years our sales have grown about $49 per

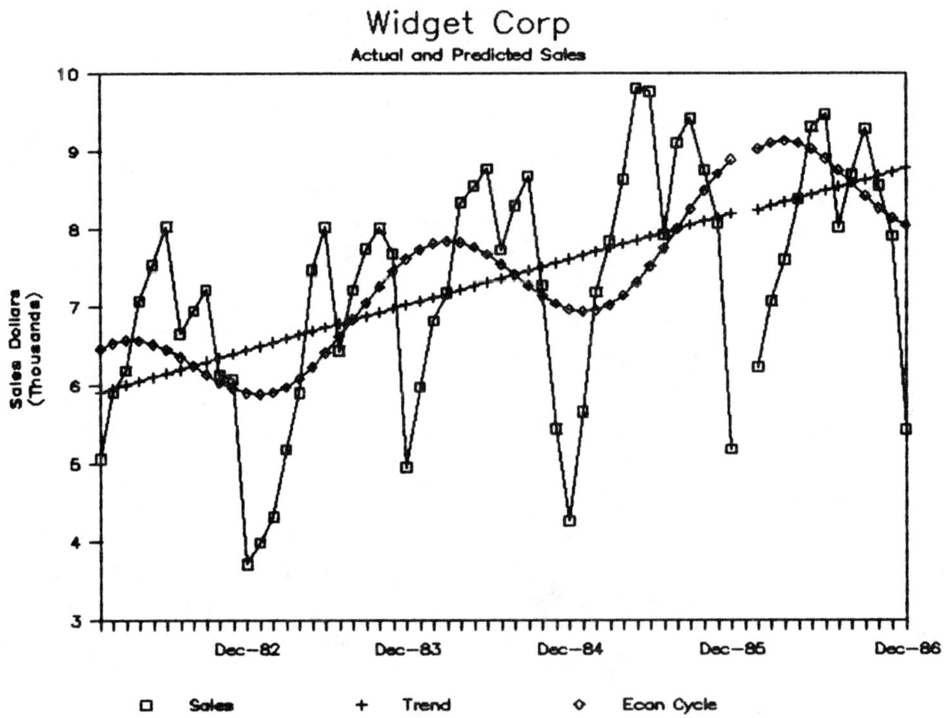

Figure 14-20. A graph of Widget's Actual and Predicted Sales, Trend, and Economic Cycle

month, give or take $7 (cell N102). Do we know of any fundamental changes in our industry that would cause us to use a different value to calculate our future trend line?

Second, we were careful to find the proper value for the life of the economic cycle. It wasn't 23 months, we decided, or 25, it was really 24 months. But looking ahead, what will it be? Will it be 15 months, or will it be 40 months?

In Figure 14-7, we found that the economic cycle increases or decreases our sales by about 9.6% (cell O101), over or under what we would otherwise expect. We therefore need solid reasons to justify the value for the cycle life that we use in our forecast. Of course, your concern about the accuracy of the number will be proportionate to how sensitive your sales are to the economic cycle. If they are significantly affected, you will want to be careful about your forecast number, but if your sales aren't greatly affected by the cycle, you will be less concerned about this number.

LIMITATIONS OF TIME SERIES ANALYSIS

There are several common objections to using time series analysis to forecast sales.

- First, such a forecast is based largely upon past performance. It ignores the effects of new people, new strategies, new markets, new competitors, and other changing conditions.
- Second, it is difficult to apply such a forecast method to sales of new products, which have no past sales to project into the future.
- Finally, many firms have a small number of large customers or a small number of large-volume sales. For these firms, the gain or loss of a handful of customers or orders can be the difference between success and failure. Under such circumstances statistical forecasting techniques simply don't apply.

Luckily, we have an alternative. People in marketing and sales are meeting with customers, planning promotions, and laying the groundwork for the new year. The next chapter discusses ways to assemble the forecasts of these people.

Chapter
Fifteen

SALES FORECASTING WITHOUT STATISTICS

Given the limitations of time series analysis, as described in the preceding chapter, it is often necessary to base a sales forecast on other methods. This chapter describes two general approaches. The first bases projections on the selling actions that the marketing department plans to take; the second uses the projections of the people who do the selling. Both approaches are easy to do, but difficult to do well.

ESTIMATING SALES FROM SELLING ACTIONS

The sales and marketing department must *do* something to generate sales. They must call on prospective customers, place ads where prospects will see them, capture retail shelf space, and so on. The amount of sales they generate is a function of the *quality* and *quantity* of these selling actions.

The quality of the selling action involves everything about the product and its presentation to a prospective customer: the price, the packaging, the reputation of the manufacturer, the seller's product knowledge, the quality of the promotional literature, the appeal of the product itself, and so on.

The quantity of selling actions means different things to different businesses. The number of selling actions could mean the number of telephone solicitations placed by a stockbroker, the number of feet of grocery shelves

```
      A  B      C      D       E      F      G      H      I      J         K         L       M         N
      3  6      6      6       7      6      6      6      6      6        11         6       8         9

 1
 2 Acme Computers:  Sales Rep Analysis
 3 ========================================
 4
 5 ASSUMPTIONS:                       RESULTS:
 6 Rep Selling Cost/Wk  $1,000        Rep Commissions/Month      $21,275
 7 Rep Sales Effort        100%       Rep Profits/Month          ($1,075)
 8 Sales Difficulty Fctr   2.5        Total Orders/Month              96
 9 Commission Rate           8%       Total Units/Month              287
10 Selling Price           $925       Total Sales/Month         $265,932
11 Average Order Qty          3
12
13               Avg   Avg            Avg   Avg   Avg    Avg   Avg      -----Averages for Our Firm---
14 Sls   #    Calls   Pres     #     Ords Calls  Pres    Cst   Cst        Pres Orders Profit    Profit
15 Rep Slrs    /Wk  /Call    Prin    /Wk  /Ord  /Ord  /Pres  /Ord         /WK   /WK  /Order       /Wk
16
17 A      8     30      3      17     80   3.0     9    $11  $100          42     2   ($28)     ($53)
18 B      6     20      2      13     80   1.5     3    $25   $75          18     2    $35       $85
19 C     12     25      4      30    100   3.0    12    $10  $120          40     1   ($78)    ($104)
20 D      9     30      3      22     75   3.6    11    $11  $120          37     1   ($78)    ($106)
21 E     20     25      3      20    200   2.5     8    $13  $100          75     4   ($28)    ($112)
22 F     11     30      4      18    150   2.2     9     $8   $73          73     3    $39      $129
23 G     16     35      3      18    175   3.2    10    $10   $91          93     4    ($7)     ($26)
24 H      4     25      3      23     45   2.2     7    $13   $89          13     1    ($0)      ($0)
25 I      7     35      3      21     80   3.1     9    $10   $88          35     2     $3        $5
26 J      9     30      3      22     85   3.2    10    $11  $106          37     2   ($43)     ($66)
27                                                                             ------          ---------
28                                                                                22             ($248)
```

```
G17: (F1) (B17*C17)/F17
H17: (F0) +G17*D17
I17: (C0) +$E$6/(C17*D17)
J17: (C0) +H17*I17
K17: (F0) [W11] ($E$7*B17*C17*D17)/E17
L17: (F0) +K17/(H17*$E$8)
M17: (C0) +$E$11*$E$10*$E$9-J17*$E$8
N17: (C0) [W9] +M17*L17

K6: (C0) [W11] (52/12)*$L$28*$E$9*$E$10*$E$11
K7: (C0) [W11] (52/12)*$N$28
K8: (,0) [W11] (52/12)*$L$28
K9: (,0) [W11] +$E$11*$K$8
K10: (C0) [W11] +$E$10*$K$9
```

Figure 15-1. A spreadsheet that estimates the monthly sales of a new product and the profitability of that product to a sales rep organization

captured and held by a manufacturer of laundry detergent, the number of quotes submitted by a consulting engineer, the number of retail stores visited by a manufacturer's sales representative, the number of catalogs distributed by a mail order merchandiser, and so on.

One common way to forecast sales, therefore, is to estimate the quantity of sales resulting from each selling action and then to estimate the number of selling actions. The following example illustrates this approach.

Projecting Sales From A Sales Rep Network

Several years ago I was associated with a startup company that designed and manufactured a microcomputer for the home and office. Let's call the company Acme Computers. Acme's marketing manager, Bob, assembled a nationwide network of ten regional organizations of manufacturer's representatives to sell this computer.

Bob used a two-step approach to forecast the sales that this network would generate. He first estimated the number of Acme computers that the sales reps could move in an average month, once they were trained. He next generated a forecast based on his product-introduction and sales-training schedule.

To execute the first step, Bob created a spreadsheet much like Figure 15-1. The spreadsheet does two things. First (in column N), it estimates how profitable the Acme computers will be to each rep organization. Estimating this profitability was important because Bob wanted to know how the reps viewed his product. If the reps could expect to make money from the product, Bob could expect to get his fair share of effort from the rep organization. If the reps could make a lot of money, Bob could expect to get better than his fair share of effort.

The second purpose of this spreadsheet was to estimate the potential sales (K9 and K10) that the network could produce under various assumptions. This allowed him to both evaluate the adequacy of his network and forecast his sales with some degree of confidence. Let's look at this spreadsheet more closely.

Building the Sales Rep Analysis Spreadsheet

The width of each column in the Sales Rep Analysis spreadsheet is shown at the top of the spreadsheet, beneath the column letters. The Assumptions section of this figure identifies certain categories of variables about which assumptions must be made.

- Rep's Selling Costs per Week: This is an estimate of the sales rep organization's average cost per salesperson per week. It includes both variable costs and overhead.
- Rep's Sales Effort: If a sales rep organization represents 20 lines of products, then theoretically each line will receive, on average, one-twentieth of the rep's time. In real life, however, reps have favorite lines. These lines might receive significantly more than the average share of time. The Rep Sales Effort percentage shows how much of Acme's theoretical time share Bob estimated that he would actually receive from the rep organization.
- Sales Difficulty Factor: On average, a sales person must make a certain number of sales presentations to receive one order. Pioneering products may take two or three times the number of presentations than would the average product. The Sales Difficulty Factor reflects Bob's estimate of how many times more presentations the Acme product would require to obtain an order than would the average product.
- Commission Rate: The percentage amount of each sale paid to the sales rep.
- Selling Price: The amount Acme Computer is paid for its computer.
- Average Order Quantity: The average number of units ordered on a purchase order.

Below the assumptions in Figure 15-1 are various facts and calculations about each rep organization. This information involves the total business of each rep firm, not the business that each firm may be doing with Acme:

- Column A: The name of the sales rep organization.
- Column B: The number of full-time sellers in each rep organization.
- Column C: The average number of sales calls each seller makes each week.
- Column D: The average number of sales presentations that each seller makes during each sales call, where each presentation is for a different principal. (A principal is a firm whose product the sales rep organization is contracted to sell.)

- Column E: The total number of principals that each rep organization represents.
- Column F: The average number of purchase orders that each rep organization receives each week for all products that the rep organization represents.
- Column G: The average number of sales calls that each rep makes to receive one order. As shown for G17 in the formula at the bottom of Figure 15-1, this average is equal to the total number of calls made by the rep organization during the week divided by the number of orders received each week.
- Column H: The average number of presentations made per order received is equal to the number of calls per order received times the number of presentations per call.
- Column I: The average cost per presentation is equal to the estimated selling cost per week divided by the number of presentations per week.
- Column J: The average cost per order is equal to the number of presentations per order times the cost per presentation.

The following columns use this information about each sales rep organization as a whole and apply it to the Acme Computers' product line.

- Column K: The number of presentations that Bob expected to receive each week. This is equal to the total number of presentations that each firm will make each week, divided by the number of principals. This share of the total is multiplied by the Rep Sales Effort that Bob expected to receive for the Acme products. (Strictly speaking, when each rep organization adds Acme as a principal, the number of principals should be increased by one. But all numbers in the range B17 through F26 are estimates of numbers that change frequently. Generally, therefore, little is to be gained by adjusting these numbers for the addition of Acme as a principal.)
- Column L: The number of purchase orders that Bob expected to receive each week is equal to the number of presentations divided by the number of presentations necessary to generate an order for the Acme product.
- Column M: The sales rep organization's profits per order received for Acme Computers is equal to the total commissions earned per order minus the estimated cost to obtain the order. Notice that this cost is

equal to the Average Cost per Order times the Sales Difficulty Factor. After all, if Acme's product requires 2.5 times more sales calls than the average order, each order should cost 2.5 times as much.

- Column N: The rep's profit per week for Acme's business is equal to the profit per order times the number of orders per week.

Finally, using all this information, Bob could calculate the results of his assumptions, in K6 through K10:

- The Rep Commissions per Month figure is the amount that he expected to pay. It is equal to the number of orders received per month times the commission cost per order.
- The Rep Profits per Month figure is equal to the number of weeks in a month times the profits received per week.
- The Total Number of Orders Received per Month figure is equal to the number of weeks in a month times the number of orders received in a week.
- The Total Number of Units Sold per Month figure is equal to the number of orders received per month times the average number of units sold per order.
- The Total Sales per Month figure is equal to the total number of units sold per month times the selling price per unit.

Using the Sales Rep Analysis Spreadsheet

The Assumptions and Results shown in Figure 15-1 gave Acme's marketing manager an approximate forecast of the early sales of the Acme computer. He wanted the Average Order Quantity to be three units. This number would allow the computer dealer to have "one to show, one to go, and one for service." That is, the dealer would have one unit to demonstrate, one unit to sell, and one unit for parts and testing if either of the other two needed service.

He estimated that selling this flashy but unknown computer would be two to three times more difficult than average. But because the sales reps were enthusiastic about the product, he thought Acme would get at least 100% of its proper share of the selling effort.

The 8% commission, although higher than Bob wanted to pay, was necessary to minimize the sales rep organization's early losses. (Yet he knew that *some* early losses are acceptable if a rep organization believes in a new product. When reps begin to make a lot of money with established products, manufacturers tend to fire the rep firm and use their own sales force to sell the product. Therefore, rep firms must continually develop new lines to represent.)

Bob knew that after several months of success, the product would be easier to sell and the Average Order Quantity would rise. Because of these improvements and because of how he negotiated the rep contracts, the commission rate could fall to 5%. Also, since Acme was using a promotional price on first orders, repeat orders should raise the average selling

```
Part A
=========
ASSUMPTIONS:                              RESULTS:
Rep Selling Cost/Wk   $1,000              Rep Commissions/Month        $22,760
Rep Sales Effort        100%              Rep Profits/Month               $411
Sales Difficulty Fctr      2              Total Orders/Month               120
Commission Rate           5%              Total Units/Month                479
Selling Price           $950              Total Sales/Month           $455,200
Average Order Qty          4

Part B
=========
ASSUMPTIONS:                              RESULTS:
Rep Selling Cost/Wk   $1,000              Rep Commissions/Month       $291,987
Rep Sales Effort        200%              Rep Profits/Month           $247,288
Sales Difficulty Fctr    0.8              Total Orders/Month               599
Commission Rate           5%              Total Units/Month              5,989
Selling Price           $975              Total Sales/Month         $5,839,731
Average Order Qty         10

Part C
=========
ASSUMPTIONS:                              RESULTS:
Rep Selling Cost/Wk   $1,000              Rep Commissions/Month           $886
Rep Sales Effort         25%              Rep Profits/Month            ($4,701)
Sales Difficulty Fctr      5              Total Orders/Month                12
Commission Rate           8%              Total Units/Month                 12
Selling Price           $925              Total Sales/Month            $11,081
Average Order Qty          1
```

Figure 15-2. An illustration of the results of three different sets of assumptions used in Figure 15-1

price. These improvements should produce the results shown in part A of Figure 15-2.

As time goes by and Bob takes the steps necessary to make the Acme Computer easier to sell, the rep organization should produce more and more orders. Eventually, if the assumptions hold true, part B shows that the network might achieve Acme sales of nearly $6 million per month.

For the reps to achieve these impressive sales, many assumptions must hold true. What if the assumptions are wrong? What if dealers, instead of buying three computers, refuse to buy more than one computer? And what if this minor sale is five times more difficult than the normal sale? The reps would probably become discouraged and expend less and less effort. Part C of Figure 15-2 shows that if these assumptions hold true, Acme's sales could drop to nearly zero. In other words, the assumptions *are* the forecast.

The Last Step: Produce A Sales Forecast

Once Bob understood what his network could do under various circumstances, he initiated step two of his sales forecast; he laid his plans for introducing the product and training the sales reps. Because he was working on a tight budget, Bob and his staff planned to introduce the product and train the reps one region at a time. This gradual introduction would allow him to add each new region to a solid foundation of sales success.

Figure 15-3 is the eight-month forecast that Bob generated from his plans. The width of each column is shown at the top of the figure, beneath the column letters. The formulas for column E—the first complete column of data in the spreadsheet—are shown in Table 15-1. To build the figure, copy the formulas, as required, across the rows. Let's look more closely at the forecast in Figure 15-3.

As shown in the Pricing section, Bob used two different prices. To induce dealers to try the Acme product, Bob offered a 40% discount on all first orders. Reorders were at a 35% discount.

The next three sections reflect Bob's assumptions about the various stages a new dealer would go through. New dealers, he hoped, would order three units. After a delay, most of the new dealers would reorder five units. After another delay, he thought, most of the remaining dealers would reorder about ten units periodically.

Row 14 shows the number of new dealers Bob expected that his rep organizations would sign. This number was based on Bob's product training and introduction schedule, on the capabilities of the sales reps, esti-

	A	B	C	D	E	F	G	H	I	J
	26	7	11	11	11	11	11	11	11	11
1	Acme Computers: Monthly Sales Forecast									
2	========================									
3			Mar-82	Apr-82	May-82	Jun-82	Jul-82	Aug-82	Sep-82	Oct-82
4			———	———	———	———	———	———	———	———
5	PRICING									
6	————————									
7	Retail Price	$1,495								
8	First Order Price	40%	$897	$897	$897	$897	$897	$897	$897	$897
9	Reorder Price	35%	$972	$972	$972	$972	$972	$972	$972	$972
10										
11	NEW DEALERS									
12	————————									
13	Average First Order	3 Units								
14	New Dealers Signed		10	20	40	75	100	125	125	125
15	Stocking Order Sales Qty		30	60	120	225	300	375	375	375
16	Stocking Order Sales $		$26,910	$53,820	$107,640	$201,825	$269,100	$336,375	$336,375	$336,375
17										
18	FIRST REORDER									
19	————————									
20	Reorder Delay		30 Days	60 Days	90 Days					
21	"		30%	60%	10%					
22	Fall Out	15%								
23	Average Qty Reordered	5 Units								
24	First Reorder Dealers		0	8	17	34	63	85	106	106
25	First Reorder Sales Qty		0	10	45	105	205	330	445	515
26	First Reorder Sales $		$0	$9,718	$43,729	$102,034	$199,209	$320,678	$432,429	$500,451
27										

	A	B	C	D	E	F	G	H	I	J
	26	7	11	11	11	11	11	11	11	11
28	CONTINUING DEALERS									
29	———————————									
30	Reorder Delay		30 Days	60 Days	90 Days					
31	"		70%	25%	5%					
32	2nd Reorder Fall-Out	10%								
33	Month-to-Month Fall Out	2%								
34	Average Qty Reordered	10 Units								
35	Continuing Dealers				7	22	52	107	181	272
36	Continuing Sales Quantity				40	170	420	890	1560	2410
37	Continuing Sales $				$38,870	$165,198	$408,135	$864,858	$1,515,930	$2,341,918
38										
39	TOTALS									
40	———————————									
41	Total Number of Orders		10	22	53	113	183	280	370	469
42	Total Quantity Sold		30	70	205	500	925	1595	2380	3300
43	Total Sales Dollars		$26,910	$63,538	$190,239	$469,056	$876,444	$1,521,910	$2,284,734	$3,178,744
44										

Figure 15-3. A forecast of the first eight months of sales of Acme's new product

First Order Price: 1 minus 40% discount, times retail price.

E8: (CO) (1−$B$8)*$B$7

Reorder Price: 1 minus 35% discount, times retail price.

E9: (CO) (1−$B$9)*$B$7

Stocking Order Sales Quantity: Units per dealer times number of new dealers.

E15: +$B$13*E14

Stocking Order Sales Dollars: Stocking Order Sales Quantity times First Order Price.

E16: (CO) +E15*E8

First Reorder Dealers: The dealers signed last month who we expect will reorder.

E24: @INT((1−$B$22)*D14)

First Reorder Sales Quantity: The number of dealers signed this month who we expect to reorder this month plus last month's dealers who should order in 30-60 days plus dealers from two months ago who should reorder in 60-90 days, all multiplied by the expected reorder quantity.

E25: @INT($C$21*E24+$D$21*D24+$E$21*C24)*$B$23

First Reorder Sales Dollars: Expected quantity times Reorder Price.

E26: (CO) +E25*E9

Continuing Dealers: Dealers remaining from last month plus newer dealers less 2nd Reorder Fall Out.

E35: @INT((1−$B$33)*D35+(1−$B$32)*D24)

Continuing Sales Quantity: Dealer orders after delays times expected reorder quantity.

E36: @INT($C$31*E35+$D$31*D35+$E$31*C35)*$B$34

Continuing Sales Dollars: Quantity times reorder price.

E37: (CO) +E36*E9

Total Number of Orders: Quantity ordered divided by average order size for each of the New Dealers, First Reorders, and Continuing Dealers.

E41: (E36/$B$34)+(E25/$B$23)+(E15/$B$13)

Table 15-1. The formulas in column E of Figure 15-3

Total Quantity Sold: Sum of subtotals in each category.

E42: +E36+E25+E15

Total Sales Dollars: Sum of subtotals in each category.

E43: (C0) +E37+E26+E16

Table 15-1. The formulas in column E of Figure 15-3 (*continued*)

mated in Figure 1511-1, and on his knowledge of the people involved.

Rows 21 and 22 allowed Bob to vary his assumptions about how quickly new dealers would reorder. The Fall Out percentage, shown in row 22, reflects Bob's assumptions about the percentage of dealers that would not reorder.

He thought that there might be additional fall out between the first and second reorders, as is shown in row 32. Row 33 shows the assumption that 2% of Acme's total dealership will fall out each month. Rows 30 and 31 reflect Bob's assumption that continuing dealers would reorder more quickly than would the newer dealers.

The Totals section shows the results of Bob's assumptions. Within eight months, Acme's sales should be quite substantial.

Advantages and Risks of Bob's Forecast

One advantage to building a forecast like Figure 15-3 is that it allows Bob to see the logical results of his plans and assumptions. It says: "*If* the rep organization performs as promised, *if* the product is as popular as we think, and *if* we can manufacture the product on time and to specification, then *maybe* our sales will be somewhat as shown."

Another advantage to this approach is that it helps Bob identify those things he needs to do to improve his chances of success. It forces him to monitor and increase the number of his sales rep network's selling actions each month. And it demonstrates how his efforts to make each selling action more successful affect his total sales.

But there are major risks associated with using this kind of forecast. One is that the spreadsheet could have an error in it. Somewhere the spreadsheet might add 2 plus 2 and get 22. Actions based on such a forecast could lead to disaster.

A second risk is that key assumptions could be missing. For example, all of Bob's forecasts and analyses that we have seen involved selling *to* computer dealers. But where are the plans to assist the dealers in selling computers to the end users? What selling actions are involved? How could Acme increase the quality and quantity of these selling actions? With this element missing, Bob was assuming that he could shove thousands of products through a plugged pipeline.

A third risk is that a key assumption could be wrong. In the case of Acme Computers, for example, Figure 15-1 assumes that the computer would be 2.5 times harder to sell than the average product. In fact the company on which this example is based found that its computer was ten times harder to sell. This experience devastated the rep network.[1] Actual results from the sales reps efforts were worse than shown in part C of Figure 15-2.

A fourth risk is illustrated by an insight that someone had years ago. Imagine the forecasts there would have been, the person said, if computers had been around in the 1850s. Given the growth rate of the population and the habits of the common mode of transportation, surely someone would have proved that by 1950 the world would be four feet deep in horse manure.

In other words, even if the initial assumptions are reasonable and the initial formulas are correct, the eventual results can still be far different. One reason is that inexperienced forecasters often forget to consider how the competition will react to sudden success. Even if the competition responds with an inferior product, their thrashing about in the marketplace can cause enough confusion to hurt your sales. And the competing product might well be superior to yours.

Another reason for poor forecasts is that we forget that few companies grow in a straight line. On the one hand growth causes problems that retard growth; on the other hand, problems and losses force solutions that can lead to higher profits and faster growth. Nothing stays the same.

---

[1] More than a decade ago, marketing researcher R. W. Wood set out to improve the way marketing managers like Bob could estimate the number of sales calls necessary to produce an order. Wood's research led to a series of tables that show what the number will probably be, and how others have improved that number. Richard M. White, Jr., reproduces these tables in his book *The Entrepreneur's Manual.* For more information about the tables, you can contact Richard White at Business Solutions, Inc., P.O. Box 28220, San Jose, CA 95159.

ANOTHER FORECASTING APPROACH: ASK THE SALES FORCE

One method that is used frequently to forecast sales is to poll the sales force. Technically, this method is not very sophisticated, but often it is the most accurate method available. Figures 15-4, 15-5, and 15-6 illustrate this approach.

Figure 15-4 shows a form that each member of the sales force uses to forecast the sales for his or her region. In this example, places are provided for Best Case and Worst Case forecasts as well. This information can be extremely useful if members of the sales force actually think about the forecasts that they generate.

Figure 15-5 shows the response from the Eastern Region. (The value 1 inserted below the region name East identifies the region to which the forecast belongs.) As often happens, this forecast includes estimates not only for the listed products but for new products as well. This is why blank lines were added to the original forecasting form. The information for the best and worst cases is probably of little value here, since little thought went into the numbers. (A quick test shows that each Best Case and Worst Case number is a fixed percentage of the Most Likely Case.)

Figure 15-6 shows the combined sales forecast for the Most Likely sales for all four regions. This forecast was generated using the /File Combine Add command. When you use this command, make sure of the following:

- In all files that you combine, data of the same type must be in the same place. That is, if sales for Needles are in row 12 of one spreadsheet, they must be in row 12 of every spreadsheet.
- Since the command will not add values to formulas, make sure that all data in the original spreadsheet is represented as numbers and not as formulas.
- When you issue the **/F**ile **C**ombine command, make sure that your cell pointer is in the place where you want to position the top left cell of the spreadsheet being combined. It is generally a good idea to make sure that this is cell A1.

Figure 15-6 shows why we identified the sales regions with a number 1. As we combine spreadsheets, the numbers serve as markers to indicate which regions we have added. In the figure we know that we have added each region only once, because each region has the number 1 beneath it.

```
Unit Sales Forecast--1987
==========================
Circle One:

Region:  East  West South North

Most Likely Units
====================
           Jan   Feb   Mar   Apr   May   Jun   Jul   Aug   Sep   Oct   Nov   Dec   Tot
          ----- ----- ----- ----- ----- ----- ----- ----- ----- ----- ----- ----- -----
Needles   _____ _____ _____ _____ _____ _____ _____ _____ _____ _____ _____ _____ _____
Pins      _____ _____ _____ _____ _____ _____ _____ _____ _____ _____ _____ _____ _____
EEPROMs   _____ _____ _____ _____ _____ _____ _____ _____ _____ _____ _____ _____ _____
________  _____ _____ _____ _____ _____ _____ _____ _____ _____ _____ _____ _____ _____


Best Case Units
====================
           Jan   Feb   Mar   Apr   May   Jun   Jul   Aug   Sep   Oct   Nov   Dec   Tot
          ----- ----- ----- ----- ----- ----- ----- ----- ----- ----- ----- ----- -----
Needles   _____ _____ _____ _____ _____ _____ _____ _____ _____ _____ _____ _____ _____
Pins      _____ _____ _____ _____ _____ _____ _____ _____ _____ _____ _____ _____ _____
EEPROMs   _____ _____ _____ _____ _____ _____ _____ _____ _____ _____ _____ _____ _____
________  _____ _____ _____ _____ _____ _____ _____ _____ _____ _____ _____ _____ _____


Worst Case Units
====================
           Jan   Feb   Mar   Apr   May   Jun   Jul   Aug   Sep   Oct   Nov   Dec   Tot
          ----- ----- ----- ----- ----- ----- ----- ----- ----- ----- ----- ----- -----
Needles   _____ _____ _____ _____ _____ _____ _____ _____ _____ _____ _____ _____ _____
Pins      _____ _____ _____ _____ _____ _____ _____ _____ _____ _____ _____ _____ _____
EEPROMs   _____ _____ _____ _____ _____ _____ _____ _____ _____ _____ _____ _____ _____
________  _____ _____ _____ _____ _____ _____ _____ _____ _____ _____ _____ _____ _____
```

Figure 15-4. An illustration of the form that salespeople can use to record their sales forecasts

```
Unit Sales Forecast--1987
==============================

Region:    East    West South   North
              1
```

Most Likely Units

	Jan	Feb	Mar	Apr	May	Jun	Jul	Aug	Sep	Oct	Nov	Dec	Tot
Needles	41	49	44	38	40	38	44	49	43	38	31	45	500
Pins	25	22	28	21	25	28	20	20	29	27	21	27	293
EEPROMs	227	280	254	246	229	222	263	247	230	271	240	272	2,981
Top Hats	59	104	64	102	52	89	71	57	65	62	108	89	922

Best Case Units

	Jan	Feb	Mar	Apr	May	Jun	Jul	Aug	Sep	Oct	Nov	Dec	Tot
Needles	49	59	53	46	48	46	53	59	52	46	37	54	602
Pins	30	26	34	25	30	34	24	24	35	32	25	32	351
EEPROMs	272	336	305	295	275	266	316	296	276	325	288	326	3,576
Top Hats	71	125	77	122	62	107	85	68	78	74	130	107	1,106

Worst Case Units

	Jan	Feb	Mar	Apr	May	Jun	Jul	Aug	Sep	Oct	Nov	Dec	Tot
Needles	37	44	40	35	36	35	40	44	39	35	28	41	454
Pins	23	20	26	19	23	26	18	18	26	24	19	24	266
EEPROMs	204	252	229	221	206	200	237	222	207	244	216	245	2,683
Top Hats	53	94	58	92	47	80	64	51	59	56	98	80	832

Figure 15-5. A spreadsheet with the sales forecast from the Eastern Region

```
           A         B       C       D       E       F       G       H       I       J       K       L       M        N
           9         7       7       7       7       7       7       7       7       7       7       7       7        8

 1 Unit Sales Forecast--1987
 2 ==============================
 3
 4
 5 Region:     East    West  South   North
 6                1       1       1       1
 7
 8 Most Likely Units
 9 =======================
10                Jan     Feb     Mar     Apr     May     Jun     Jul     Aug     Sep     Oct     Nov     Dec      Tot
11              -----   -----   -----   -----   -----   -----   -----   -----   -----   -----   -----   -----    -----
12 Needles        178     202     155     183     166     176     183     180     178     228     198     189    2,216
13 Pins           129     113     116     112     119     107     123      98     110     111     129     115    1,382
14 EEPROMs      1,139   1,170     981   1,026   1,160   1,187   1,086   1,051   1,334   1,062   1,111   1,103   13,410
15 Top Hats       436     392     429     446     330     365     341     266     318     475     332     375    4,505
16
17
18 Prices
19 =========
20 Needles       0.69    0.69    0.69    0.69    0.69    0.72    0.72    0.72    0.72    0.72    0.72    0.72
21 Pins          1.23    1.23    1.23    1.23    1.23    1.28    1.28    1.28    1.28    1.28    1.28    1.28
22 EEPROMs      17.57   17.57   15.00   15.00   15.00   15.00   11.95   11.95   11.95    8.88    8.88    8.88
23 Top Hats      4.58    4.58    4.58    2.79    2.79    2.79    2.79    2.79    2.79    6.95    6.95    6.95
24
25
26 Sales Dollars
27 ===============
28 Needles        123     139     107     126     115     127     132     130     128     164     143     136    1,570
29 Pins           159     139     143     138     146     137     157     125     141     142     165     147    1,739
30 EEPROMs     20,012  20,557  14,715  15,390  17,400  17,805  12,978  12,559  15,941   9,431   9,866   9,795  176,449
31 Top Hats     1,997   1,795   1,965   1,244     921   1,018     951     742     887   3,301   2,307   2,606   19,734
32            -------------------------------------------------------------------------------------------------------
33 Total       22,291  22,630  16,930  16,898  18,582  19,087  14,218  13,556  17,097  13,038  12,481  12,684  199,492
34

        B28: (,0) @ROUND(B20*B12,0)
        B33: (,0) @SUM(B32..B28)
        C20: (F2) +B20
        N12: (,0) [W8] @SUM(M12..B12)
        N33: (,0) [W8] @IF(@SUM(N32..N28)<>@SUM(M33..B33),@ERR,@SUM(N32..N28))
```

Figure 15-6. An illustration of the combined sales forecasts of all four regions

The Prices section allows prices to change during the period. To build this section, begin by inserting prices for each product for January. Then, in C20, enter the formula shown at the bottom of the figure. When you copy this formula throughout the section, January's prices will be repeated throughout the year. Then it is a simple matter to enter new prices where necessary. When you recalculate the spreadsheet, these will be repeated in later months, until the price is changed again.

Each formula in the Sales Dollars section is simply the appropriate price times the appropriate quantity, rounded to the nearest dollar. One such cell entry can be copied throughout.

Cell N33 "foots and cross-foots" the data. That is, it makes sure that the sum of the monthly totals equals the sum of the product totals. If this is not true, if, in other words, we have entered an incorrect @SUM formula, cell N33 returns an ERR.

The controller, by the way, could use this spreadsheet to forecast the cost of goods sold. All he or she must do is substitute product costs for the prices and then recalculate.

Risks and Limitations Of Polling the Sales Force

Forecasting sales from sales force polls presents problems, just as the other approaches do. These problems arise because the goals and attitudes of the people in the field differ from those of the forecaster at the home office; specifically:

- Time spent on forecasting is time spent not selling. To many salespeople, this means it is wasted time. "Which do you want?" sellers have asked me, "Sales? Or forecasts?"
- The home office tends to turn forecasts into quotas. Often, therefore, salespeople will "sandbag," forecasting fewer sales than they really think they'll make.
- On the other hand, salespeople are eternally optimistic. Their forecasts, therefore, are frequently too high to be believed. Firms fail when those unbelievable forecasts *are* believed.
- Often, the timing of orders isn't critical to a salesperson. After all, today's order may not be shipped for months. And the commission check may

not arrive until several months after that. So even when the forecast for a year is accurate, the month-to-month forecasts can be way off.

- In startup companies, salespeople have been known to forecast, and to sell, only the quantity that they think the factory can produce. "Our reputation is all we have," they'll say. "If the factory can't ship, we are the ones who suffer." This tendency can really become a problem if the factory, in turn, limits itself to producing only what the manufacturing people think the sales force can sell.
- Many people, salespeople among them, tend to believe that all trends last. When managers fail to take the broader perspective, planning for reverses, forecasts can produce some nasty surprises.

As I said, sales forecasts are simple but not easy. The most successful forecasts result from extensive research, common sense, careful planning, and minimum greed.

Chapter
Sixteen

FORECASTING CASH FLOW AND OTHER FINANCIALS

Cash is to a business what a stay of execution is to a condemned man. Cash gives a business time—time to live, to grow, to find more cash before time runs out. This is why the cash flow forecast is so important. It tells management how much time remains to find more time.

Cash flow forecasts are important even if your firm has plenty of cash. The more you know about your future cash flow, the easier it will be to plan ways to invest that cash.

The cash flow forecast is the most difficult forecast to prepare accurately. It depends, after all, on the accuracy of most of our other forecasts and assumptions. If our projections of sales or costs are wrong, if our customers pay us more slowly than we think they will, if we buy more inventory than we plan, if interest rates go crazy, if one of dozens of other surprises occur—then our cash flow forecast will probably be wrong.

Since the cash flow forecast depends so much on these other forecasts, it is a common practice to prepare the forecasts of the income statement, the balance sheet, and cash flows all in one spreadsheet. In this way each forecast has the information it needs from the other forecasts, each uses the same set of assumptions, and each helps to document the calculations on which the other forecasts were based.

This chapter explains how to create this spreadsheet and how to adjust it to meet the requirements of your own business. The spreadsheet consists of three basic sections: assumptions, projections, and reconciliations.

Along the way we'll look at ways to make the assumptions you plug into this spreadsheet more reliable.

BEGIN THE SPREADSHEET

Begin by setting the global format to Currency (2) and the recalculation mode to manual. The global column width will vary, depending on how large your numbers are. The sample spreadsheet uses a global column width of 8. To leave room for the time shown in cell B4 of Figure 16-1, set the width of column B to 9. Enter the name of your spreadsheet in A1.

Enter the Heading

Figure 16-1 shows the first section of a forecast for the 1987 calendar year. This spreadsheet holds our assumptions about the year, using these to forecast the income statement, balance sheet, and cash flow. Because of space limitations, the months May through October have been omitted from the figure.

The date and time cells in A4 and B4 both hold the function @NOW. Cell A4, however, has been formatted as Date (2) and B4 has been formatted as Date (7). (Version 1A uses the @TODAY function to provide the date; the time function isn't available.) In financial forecasting the date and time message becomes important, because you will be generating and printing many different versions of your projections. Without a date and time indication, it is often difficult to keep the printouts of your projections straight.

When you print this figure, use the command /**P**rint **P**rinter **O**ptions **B**order **R**ows to designate the range A4..U5 as the top border of the spreadsheet. (Start the print range with row 6.) Using this border command will cause the rows with the date, time, and title to be printed at the top of each page, as shown in Figures 16-1 through 16-9.

Months and Underlines

To enter the border in row 6, enter \= in cell A6 and copy the cell across the spreadsheet. Enter the names of the months as shown in row 7 and center them with the /**R**ange **L**abel **C**enter command. Then enter \= in A8 and copy this cell from B8 to F8.

If you have Version 1A, you have two choices for drawing the lines beneath each month in row 8. You may enter \= in G8, which will produce

	A	D	G	H	I	J	Q	R	S	T	U
4	11-Jan 05:29 PM										
5	PROJECTED FINANCIAL PERFORMANCE, 1987										
6											
7	SALES & COLLECTIONS		Jan	Feb	Mar	Apr	Nov	Dec			
8											
9	Detailed Sales Forecast		$1,000	$1,000	$1,000	$1,000	$1,000	$1,000			
10	Adjustment to Sales Forecast		100%	100%	100%	100%	100%	100%			
11											
12	Total Sales Forecasted		$1,000	$1,000	$1,000	$1,000	$1,000	$1,000			
13											
14		Cash	7%	7%	7%	7%	7%	7%			
15	Collections	30 Days	48%	48%	48%	48%	48%	48%			
16	Schedule	60 Days	32%	32%	32%	32%	32%	32%			
17		90 Days	13%	13%	13%	13%	13%	13%			
18											
19			100%	100%	100%	100%	100%	100%			
20											
21	Collections of Current Receivables		$1,000	$1,000	$500						
22	Collections of New Sales		$70	$550	$870	$1,000	$1,000	$1,000			
23											
24	Total Collections		$1,070	$1,550	$1,370	$1,000	$1,000	$1,000			

Figure 16-1. The Sales and Collections section of a financial forecast spreadsheet

a solid underline, or you may enter a space and seven = signs, which will produce the underlines as shown in the figure. (When you use this method, however, you will have to add more = signs if you expand the width of the column.) Then copy G8 across the remainder of the row.

If you use Version 2, enter the following label and formula:

C1: WIDTH
C2: @CELL("WIDTH",C1..C1)

Put your cell pointer on C1 and use /**R**ange **N**ame **L**abel **D**own to assign the name WIDTH to C2. Then enter the following formula:

F8: @REPEAT("=",$WIDTH-1)

Copying this formula across the row produces the underline sections shown beneath each month. When you expand the column width and recalculate, these underlines will expand also, leaving one space between each section.

The single underlines within the figures use \- instead of the string formulas, however. This is because the @SUM range can include cells using \- but returns an ERR when the range includes a string formula. We want to include the underline in the @SUM range because this allows us to insert additional rows of data into the range by inserting the new data above the underline. If the @SUM range did not include this underline, the new data would *appear* to be in the range but would actually be below the @SUM range.

The Page Break

Compare Figures 16-1 and 16-2. Notice that row 25 is missing. This row uses a feature that is new to Version 2 but poorly documented: the | (the vertical bar). Similar to a label alignment symbol, this bar can be used in three different ways:

- To force a page break. This feature was used in row 25 by entering |:: (vertical bar, colon, colon) in A25. If you issue the /**W**orksheet **P**age command, 1-2-3 will insert a row where the cell pointer is and then insert these symbols for you.
- To embed printer commands in a spreadsheet. As explained on page 106 in the reference manual for Version 2 (but not found in its index), you can change from boldface to compressed print, to underline, and so on

	A–D		E–F	G	H	I	J	Q	R	S	T	U
4	11-Jan 05:29 PM											
5	PROJECTED FINANCIAL PERFORMANCE, 1987											
26												
27	MATERIAL COSTS & PURCHASES			Jan	Feb	Mar	Apr	Nov	Dec			
28												
29	Material Cost of Goods Sold											
30	Per Bill of Materials			$350	$350	$350	$350	$350	$350	$350	$350	$350
31	Sales Adjustment			100%	100%	100%	100%	100%	100%	100%	100%	100%
32												
33	Adjusted Material Cost of Sales			$350	$350	$350	$350	$350	$350	$350	$350	$350
34	Material Waste & Scrap, + Hedge		10%									
35												
36	Net Material Cost of Sales			$385	$385	$385	$385	$385	$385	$385	$385	$385
37	Material Requirements for Purchasing			$385	$385	$385	$385	$385	$385	$385	$385	$385
38												
39	Inventory	Current		30%	30%	30%	30%	30%	30%	30%	30%	30%
40	Purchasing	30 Days in Advance		40%	40%	40%	40%	40%	40%	40%	40%	40%
41	Schedule	60 Days in Advance		25%	25%	25%	25%	25%	25%	25%	25%	25%
42		90 Days in Advance		5%	5%	5%	5%	5%	5%	5%	5%	5%
43												
44				100%	100%	100%	100%	100%	100%	100%	100%	100%
45												
46												
47	Total Inventory Purchases			$385	$385	$385	$385	$385	$385			
48												
49		Cash		20%	20%	20%	20%	20%	20%			
50	Payment	30 Days		60%	60%	60%	60%	60%	60%			
51	Schedule	60 Days		15%	15%	15%	15%	15%	15%			
52		90 Days		5%	5%	5%	5%	5%	5%			
53												
54				100%	100%	100%	100%	100%	100%			
55												
56	Payment of Current Payables			$700	$550	$400	$100					
57	Payment of New Purchases			$77	$308	$366	$385	$385	$385			
58												
59	Total Payment of Purchases			$777	$858	$766	$485	$385	$385			

Figure 16-2. The Material Costs and Purchases forecast section

from within your spreadsheet. You do this by entering || (two vertical bars) and then your normal printer setup string. For example, on some printers, || \015 will print everything that follows as compressed print; using || \018 will return those printers to standard print.

- To suppress the printing of rows. Whenever a cell on the left-hand border of a print range begins with a |, 1-2-3 will skip the entire row that the cell is in when it prints the spreadsheet. This allows you to add documentation and comments to the body of a spreadsheet, knowing they won't appear when the spreadsheet is printed.

Therefore, when you have finished entering the data shown in Figure 16-1, enter |:: in A25.

THE ASSUMPTIONS

Wherever possible, we want to make our assumptions obvious and easy to understand. One way to do this is to group them into logical sections as shown in Figures 16-1 through 16-5. The first of these sections details our sales forecast and expected receivables collections.

Before looking at this section, let's be clear about what we are doing and what we are not doing . We are creating a template that will hold our assumptions. We are not yet generating the actual assumptions themselves. The data used in Figures 16-1 through 16-9 will be meaningless, but it will help us to find and correct errors in our formulas. At the end of this chapter we will briefly discuss how to add real data to this forecast and how to check it.

Sales and Collections

Row 9 of Figure 16-1 shows the final line from our detailed sales forecast (Chapters 14 and 15 discuss ways to generate this number.) Only the final line is used because the forecast will usually result from an analysis too extensive to be included in this spreadsheet. To load that final line, we gave it the range name TOTAL in the original forecast. Then, in this spreadsheet, we used /File Combine Range to combine the range TOTAL into row 9 as shown.

Row 10 adds some flexibility to the sales projections. This multiplier allows you to analyze "what if" assumptions about your sales without having to disturb the data from the original sales forecast. In the figure the value 1 (or 100%) has been copied throughout the row. At present, therefore, the multiplier has no effect on the data.

Row 12 shows the sales figures we will use in our forecast. Each month's forecast is simply the product of the multiplier and the detailed sales forecast. For example, the formula in G12 is +G10*G9.

Rows 14 through 19 hold our assumptions about how quickly our customers will pay. Column G shows how we expect to collect January's sales, column H shows how we expect to collect February's sales, and so on. We use the reports discussed in Chapter 3 to guide us in choosing realistic percentages. Notice that this section allows these ratios to change monthly. This allows you to alter your collection expectations during the year. The only restriction is that each column of percentages should add to 100% as shown. (A line for bad debts could be inserted below row 17, however.)

Row 21 shows us when, over the next several months, we expect to collect the accounts receivable balance that now exists. (Remember that "today" for the figure is January 11, 1987, and that the accounts receivable balance for December 1986 is the most recent month-end balance.) This row is necessary because the collection schedule for the current balance often will be totally different from the schedule that we are assuming for the forecast. This is because the current balance always seems to contain exceptions that we assume will not exist in the future.

Row 22 shows our forecast for the Collections of New Sales. The formulas for the first four data columns of that row are

```
G22:  +G14*G12
H22:  +H14*H12+G15*G12
I22:  +I14*I12+H15*H12+G16*G12
J22:  +J14*J12+I15*I12+H16*H12+G17*G12
```

These formulas calculate the collections for each month by multiplying the sales of previous months by the appropriate percentages in rows 14 through 17. But since row 21 contains the collections forecast for the current accounts receivable, sales data has not been entered for the months prior to the beginning of the forecast. This is why each formula is longer than the one before it; there is no data for the early formulas to use. Finally, the formula in J22 is a complete formula. It can be copied across the rest of the row.

Row 24, Total Collections, is simply the sum of rows 21 through 23. Cell G24, for example, is @SUM(G23..G21).

Material Costs and Purchases

Row 30 in Figure 16-2 is found by using a separate spreadsheet to multiply our detailed unit shipment forecast by the materials cost for each product.

As we did with row 9 of Figure 16-1, we combined the TOTAL from that separate spreadsheet into row 30.

Notice that in columns S through U, Figure 16-2 shows three additional months of activity beyond the end of our forecast. This information will be used by row 47 to calculate inventory purchases near the end of the forecast. Those additional months, remember, are months for which detailed projections probably have not been made. This lack of data is hardly ever a problem, though. Any reasonable assumption about the volumes in those added months will usually produce satisfactory numbers for the forecast. In the figure, for example, the December number is simply repeated for January. That is, the formula in cell S30 is +R30.

Row 31 is the percentage used to adjust cost of sales by the same assumptions about volume we used to adjust sales. Cell G31, for example, is simply +G10.

Row 33 shows total cost of sales using this sales adjustment, much as row 12 shows adjusted sales. The formula in G33 is +G31*G30.

Row 36 uses the percentage in E34 to calculate total projected cost of sales. This percentage takes two factors into account. First, some of what we buy will be damaged or become obsolete before we can use it in our products. Second, actual cost of goods sold is often different from our projected costs. The percentage in E34 allows us to test our assumptions about the sum of these factors. The formula in G36 that uses this factor is (1+$E$34)*G33.

In many companies the purchasing department uses an official production schedule and information about the quantity of parts in inventory to calculate the quantity of parts to buy. This production schedule is based on a sales forecast that frequently is not very accurate. If the production schedule isn't updated often, what purchasing buys may have little relationship to what marketing sells.

This is why row 37 is shown. Although the numbers are the same in this figure, row 36 shows the cost of goods that are actually sold; row 37 shows the cost of goods that purchasing thinks will be sold. The difference between the two calculations is caused by row 31, the Sales Adjustment. Row 36 includes the adjustment; row 37 does not. In other words, the formula in G37 is (1+$E$34)*G30.

A well-run company works to keep the values in rows 36 and 37 close together. After all, if row 37 continually exceeds row 36 (if purchasing attempts to buy what marketing doesn't sell) then the firm will soon be awash in inventory; and if row 37 is less than row 36, the firm will soon run short of inventory. If the distinction between rows 36 and 37 is not a problem in your company, change the formula in G37 to +G36.

Rows 39 through 43 project the percentages of the current month's requirements that will be delivered during the current month and 30, 60, and 90 days in advance. The earlier that inventory is delivered, of course, the larger will be our inventory balance with respect to sales.

Row 47 projects total inventory purchases each month. Each value in this row is equal to the cost of current sales that should be purchased currently, plus next month's cost of sales that should be purchased one month early, plus cost of sales in two months that should be purchased two months early, and so on. The formula for G47 is

G47: +G39*G37+H40*H37+I41*I37+J42*J37

This formula is similar to the formulas in row 22 that calculate accounts receivable collections. Unlike row 22, however, we use but one formula in row 47 because we have provided all the data needed by this forward-looking formula. We needed four formulas in row 22 because early sales data was unavailable for that backward-looking formula.

Rows 49 through 53 show the percentage of each month's purchases that we expect to pay in the current month and in each month in the future. Chapter 5 explains how to track past payment history to serve as a guide for making this estimate.

New and fast-growing firms should be careful to project reasonably short payment schedules in this section. New firms must frequently buy on COD terms, and fast growing firms continually reach credit limits set by their vendors. Since vendors often hesitate to raise the limits, fast-growing firms must pay invoices early so that vendors will ship more product. Often, therefore, fast growing firms will pay the average invoice in well under 30 days.

Row 56 is much like row 21. It shows the schedule we expect to follow in paying the current accounts payable balance.

Row 57 is much like row 22. Its formulas are

G57: +G49*G47
H57: +H49*H47+G50*G47
I57: +I49*I47+H50*H47+G51*G47
J57: +J49*J47+I50*I47+H51*H47+G52*G47

Copy the final formula (J57) down the remainder of the row.

Row 59 is the sum of the two payment schedules. Cell G58 is simply @SUM(G58..G56). As always, this cell is copied down the row.

Labor and Overhead

Figure 16-3 combines Labor and Overhead Expenses in one display. These categories are often displayed separately, because the payment schedule for labor and payroll taxes differs significantly from the payment schedule for other overhead expenses. Figure 16-3, however, reflects the assumption that overhead spending is forecasted and budgeted in detail and that only the total spending figures are conveniently available. Rows 64 through 68 show the totals from this detailed analysis. They were combined into the spreadsheet much as were rows 9 and 30. Sales Commissions (row 69) and Advertising Co-op expenses (row 70) have been listed separately, because both expenses are directly related to monthly sales. The formula in G69, for example, is +$D69*G$12. Inserting the dollar signs as shown allows this formula to be copied to the remaining cells in rows 69 and 70.

Rows 74 through 78 show the expected payment schedules for this section. Since labor is included in these expenses, the percentage of cash payments is significantly greater than the payment schedule for accounts payable.

Row 80, which is similar to row 57, contains the formulas for total payments of expenses. The schedule for current liabilities is excluded, because overhead expenses were included in the schedule of current payables shown in row 56. The formulas are

G80: +G74*G72
H80: +H74*H72+G75*G72
I80: +I74*I72+H75*H72+G76*G72

As before, the final formula (I80) can be copied down the rest of the row.

Capital Budget

Row 85 in Figure 16-4 displays the total from our detailed capital equipment budget. Rows 87 through 93 show the estimated payment schedules for the capital equipment. The schedule reflects the fact that capital equipment purchases often require payments both in advance of delivery and after delivery.

Often, the payments for capital equipment can vary significantly from item to item, making it difficult to estimate an average payment schedule.

	A	B	C	D	E	F	G	H	I	J	Q	R	S	T	U
4	11-Jan 05:29 PM														
5	PROJECTED FINANCIAL PERFORMANCE, 1987														
61															
62	LABOR AND OVERHEAD EXPENSES						Jan	Feb	Mar	Apr	Nov	Dec			
63															
64	Manufacturing Overhead						$100	$100	$100	$100	$100	$100			
65	Direct Labor						$100	$100	$100	$100	$100	$100			
66	Research and Development						$100	$100	$100	$100	$100	$100			
67	General & Administrative						$100	$100	$100	$100	$100	$100			
68	Marketing & Sales--Fixed						$100	$100	$100	$100	$100	$100			
69	Sales Commissions			5%			$50	$50	$50	$50	$50	$50			
70	Advertising Co-op			5%			$50	$50	$50	$50	$50	$50			
71															
72	Total Expenses						$600	$600	$600	$600	$600	$600			
73															
74	Payment		Cash				60%	60%	60%	60%	60%	60%			
75	Schedule		30 Days				35%	35%	35%	35%	35%	35%			
76			60 Days				5%	5%	5%	5%	5%	5%			
77															
78							100%	100%	100%	100%	100%	100%			
79															
80	Total Payment of Expenses						$360	$570	$600	$600	$600	$600			

Figure 16-3. The Labor and Overhead Expenses forecast section

```
      A         B         C         D         E         F         G         H         I         J           Q         R         S         T         U
 4  11-Jan 05:29 PM
 5 PROJECTED FINANCIAL PERFORMANCE, 1987
82 ==========================================================================||================
83 CAPITAL BUDGET                                         Jan       Feb       Mar       Apr  ||   Nov       Dec
84 ============================================= ======= ======= ======= ======= ||======= =======
85 Purchase of Fixed Assets                              $100      $100      $100      $100  ||   $100      $100      $100      $100
86                                                                                         ||
87                    60 Days in Advance                   20%       20%       20%       20%||    20%       20%       20%       20%
88 Payments           30 Days in Advance                   10%       10%       10%       10%||    10%       10%       10%       10%
89 Schedule           On Receipt                           30%       30%       30%       30%||    30%       30%       30%       30%
90                    30 Days After Receipt                30%       30%       30%       30%||    30%       30%       30%       30%
91                    60 Days After Receipt                10%       10%       10%       10%||    10%       10%       10%       10%
92                                                ------------------------------------------||------------------------------------
93                                                        100%      100%      100%      100%||   100%      100%      100%      100%
94                                                                                         ||
95 Payments for Fixed Assets                              $60       $90      $100      $100  ||   $100      $100
96                                                                                         ||
97 Depreciable Life of Assets            60 Months                                         ||
```

Figure 16-4. The Capital Budget forecast section

In such cases we would calculate the payments schedule in the same spreadsheets we used to calculate our detailed capital budgets. Then, after combining the capital equipment purchases into row 85, we would combine the payments schedule into row 95.

In Figure 16-4, however, row 95 uses the payments schedules shown in rows 87 through 93. Since part of the formula in row 95 uses data from previous months, the first few cells are restricted—much like the schedule in row 22 of Figure 16-1. But since part of the formula in row 95 uses data from future months, we must add data as shown to cells S85 and T85—much like we added data in columns S, T, and U in Figure 16-2. Here are the formulas.

G95: +G89*G85+H88*H85+I87*I85
H95: +H89*H85+I88*I85+J87*J85+G90*G85
I95: +I89*I85+J88*J85+K87*K85+H90*H85+G91*G85

Copy I95 down the remainder of the row.

Finally, cell E97 contains the number of months that both the projected income statement and the projected balance sheet use to calculate their straight-line depreciation schedules.

Financing Transactions

Row 103 in Figure 16-5 shows the interest rate that we expect to pay each month for short-term debt. Assigning a rate for each month allows us to show the changes that we expect in these rates during the year.

Cells E104 and E105 hold the upper and lower limits of our cash balances. If the cash balance drops below the value in E104, the template will borrow enough cash to bring the balance to this value. If the cash balance exceeds the value in E105, the template will repay enough of the loan to bring the cash balance back to that value. If the balance of the short term loan is zero, the cash balance will grow without restriction.

Row 108 carries Interest information about our long-term loan. Cell E108 shows the interest rate of this loan. The dollar amounts of the interest costs are shown beginning in G108. The formula for the interest cost is

G108: ($E$108/12)*F178

This formula multiplies the monthly interest cost by the amount of the loan (which we will put in cell F178 of the projected balance sheet) that was outstanding at the end of the previous month. Copy this formula across the row.

```
        A        B        C        D        E        F        G        H        I        J          Q        R        S        T        U
  4  11-Jan 05:29 PM
  5 PROJECTED FINANCIAL PERFORMANCE, 1987
 99 ==============================================================================||===============
100 FINANCING TRANSACTIONS                                Jan     Feb     Mar     Apr ||    Nov     Dec
101 ============================================= ======= ======= ======= ======= ||======= =======
102 Short-Term Loan                                                                 ||
103   Interest Rate                                       18%     18%     18%     18%||    18%     18%
104   Borrow If Cash Is Less Than        $25                                        ||
105   Repay If Cash Exceeds              $75                                        ||
106                                                                                  ||
107 Long-Term Loan                                                                  ||
108   Interest                            12%             $18     $17     $17     $16 ||    $12     $11
109   Principal                                           $59     $60     $60     $61 ||    $65     $66
110                                                 --------------------------------||----------------
111   Tctal Loan Payment                 $77              $77     $77     $77     $77 ||    $77     $77
112                                                                                  ||
113 Equity Transactions                                                              ||
114   Stock Sales (Purchase)                             $300      $0    $225      $0 ||     $0      $0
115   Dividend Payments                                   $10     $10     $10     $10 ||    $10     $10
116                                                                                  ||
117 ==============================================================================||===============
118 INCOME TAXES                                          Jar     Feb     Mar     Apr ||    Nov     Dec
119 ============================================= ======= ======= ======= ======= ||======= =======
120 Income Tax Rate                  40%                                            ||
121                                                                                  ||
122 Quarterly Income Tax Payments                        $200                   ($54)||
```

Figure 16-5. The Financing Transactions forecast section

Row 109 contains the amount of our long-term loan payment that reduces the principal each month. This amount is equal to the Total Loan Payment, which is shown in E111, less the monthly interest cost. The formula for G109, for example, is +$E$111−G108.

Cell E111 contains the amount of the monthly payment necessary to amortize our long term loan. The other values in row 111 simply demonstrate that the sum of the interest costs and the principal reductions do in fact equal the amount in E111. The formula in G111, for example, is @SUM(G110..G108).

Row 114 shows the amounts that we expect to receive in the future from the sale of stock.

Row 115 shows the amounts that we expect to pay in dividends. Most firms that pay dividends pay them quarterly. This Figure shows monthly dividends to ensure that the formulas handle dividend payments properly. Later we will insert the dividend schedule that we actually expect to pay.

Income Taxes

Every firm will have its unique set of tax assumptions. The assumptions at the bottom of Figure 16-5 do little more than acknowledge that taxes exist. Cell D120 contains the Income Tax Rate. The numbers in cells G122 and J122 reflect the assumption that on the first month of each quarter, we will pay the taxes accrued during the previous quarter. The formula in G122 is +F172. (Row 172 in Figure 16-7 will contain Income Taxes Payable.) Your own set of tax assumptions will probably be much more complete.

THE INCOME STATEMENT

The Income Statement (Figure 16-6) is the first financial statement that we will generate on the basis of the assumptions entered in Figures 16-1 through 16-5. Look at each formula shown in column G of Figure 16-6.

Sales per month is equal to our total sales forecasted in Figure 16-1.

G127: +G12

Cost of Sales is equal to direct labor plus manufacturing overhead plus materials cost of sales. This calculation assumes that the amount of manufacturing overhead in inventory remains constant from month to month. This simplifying assumption usually is adequate for most purposes. The formula follows.

	A B C D E F	G	H	I	J	Q	R	S	T	U
4	11-Jan 05:29 PM									
5	PROJECTED FINANCIAL PERFORMANCE, 1987									
124	==	=======	=======	=======	=======	=======	=======			
125	INCOME STATEMENT	Jan	Feb	Mar	Apr	Nov	Dec			
126	==	=======	=======	=======	=======	=======	=======			
127	Sales	$1,000	$1,000	$1,000	$1,000	$1,000	$1,000			
128	Cost of Sales	$585	$585	$585	$585	$585	$585			
129		-------	-------	-------	-------	-------	-------			
130	Gross Profit	$415	$415	$415	$415	$415	$415			
131										
132	Research and Development	$100	$100	$100	$100	$100	$100			
133	General & Administrative	$100	$100	$100	$100	$100	$100			
134	Depreciation	$33	$34	$36	$38	$49	$51			
135	Marketing & Sales	$200	$200	$200	$200	$200	$200			
136		-------	-------	-------	-------	-------	-------			
137	Total Operating Expenses	$433	$434	$436	$438	$449	$451			
138										
139	Operating Profit	($18)	($19)	($21)	($23)	($34)	($36)			
140										
141	Interest Expenses	$26	$26	$26	$25	$39	$41			
142		-------	-------	-------	-------	-------	-------			
143	Profits Before Taxes	($43)	($45)	($47)	($48)	($73)	($77)			
144										
145	Provision for Income Taxes	($17)	($18)	($19)	($19)	($29)	($31)			
146		-------	-------	-------	-------	-------	-------			
147	Net Profit After Taxes	($26)	($27)	($28)	($29)	($44)	($46)			

Figure 16-6. The Income Statement forecast section

G128: +G65+G64+G36

Gross Profit is equal to Sales minus cost.

G130: +G127–G128

Research and Development costs and General and Administrative costs are simply those from Figure 16-3.

G132: +G66
G133: +G67

Depreciation costs are equal to the Fixed Assets costs we will put in row 160 (in the balance sheet) divided by the depreciable life in E97.

G134: +G160/$E$97

Marketing costs are equal to the sum of the three rows of costs shown in Figure 16-3.

G135: @SUM(G68..G70)

Total Operating Expenses are equal to the sum of the operating expenses.

G137: @SUM(G136..G132)

Operating Profit is equal to Gross Profit less Total Operating Expenses.

G139: +G130–G137

Interest Expenses are equal to this month's short-term interest rate times last month's ending short-term loan balance (a balance we will put into row 171 of the balance sheet) plus the calculated amount of this month's interest cost for long term loans.

G141: (G103/12)*F171+G108

Profits Before Taxes are equal to Operating Profit less Interest Expenses.

G143: +G139–G141

The Provision for Income Taxes is equal to Profits Before Taxes times our tax rate.

G145: +$D$120*G143

Net Profit After Taxes is equal to Profits Before Taxes less taxes.

G147: +G143−G145

THE BALANCE SHEET

The Balance Sheet for each month is equal to the amounts for the previous month plus changes. Since the projection must then begin with the actual balance sheet, Column F in Figure 16-7 is the month of December 1986.

As shown in the following formula, cash is equal to the previous Cash balance (row 153), plus Total Collections (row 24), minus Payments for Inventory Purchases (row 59), minus Payments for Overhead Expenses (row 80), minus Payments for Fixed Assets (row 95), minus Tax Payments (row 122), minus Long-Term Loan Payments (row 111), minus Short-Term Loan Interest Payments (rows 103 and 171), plus the amount of new Short-Term Loans we will calculate in Figure 16-8 (row 216), minus Dividend Payments (row 115), plus Stock Sales (row 114).

G153: +F153+G24−G59−G80−G95−G122−G111−(G103/12)*F171+G216
−G115+G114

Accounts Receivable is equal to last month's balance less collections plus sales.

G154: +F154−G24+G12

Inventory is equal to beginning inventory plus purchases less the cost of sales.

G155: +F155+G47−G36

Other Current Assets is usually too small to worry much about. The formula beginning in column H simply increases the Other Current Assets projection by the percentage increase in sales. (Since we don't track sales for December, column G repeats the balance in column F.) You will see that our forecast for Other Current Liabilities increases by the same dollar amount as Other Current Assets. The changes in these accounts must match to keep the Balance Sheet in balance.

G156: +F156
H156: (H12/G12)*G156

Total Current Assets are equal to the sum of the foregoing accounts.

	A B C D E	F	G	H	I	J	Q	R	S	T	U
4	11-Jan 05:29 PM										
5	PROJECTED FINANCIAL PERFORMANCE, 1987										
149	==========										
150	BALANCE SHEET	Dec	Jan	Feb	Mar	Apr	Nov	Dec			
151	==========	=======	=======	=======	=======	=======	=======	=======			
152	Assets										
153	Cash	$100	$25	$25	$58	$25	$25	$25			
154	Accounts Receivable	$2,500	$2,430	$1,880	$1,510	$1,510	$1,510	$1,510			
155	Inventory	$2,000	$2,000	$2,000	$2,000	$2,000	$2,000	$2,000			
156	Other Current Assets	$250	$250	$250	$250	$250	$250	$250			
157		-------	-------	-------	-------	-------	-------	-------			
158	Total Current Assets	$4,850	$4,705	$4,155	$3,818	$3,785	$3,785	$3,785			
159											
160	Fixed Assets	$1,850	$1,950	$2,050	$2,150	$2,250	$2,950	$3,050			
161	Accumulated Depreciation	$600	$633	$667	$703	$740	$1,049	$1,100			
162		-------	-------	-------	-------	-------	-------	-------			
163	Net Fixed Assets	$1,250	$1,318	$1,383	$1,448	$1,510	$1,901	$1,950			
164											
165	Other Noncurrent Assets	$200	$200	$200	$200	$200	$200	$200			
166											
167	Total Assets	$6,300	$6,223	$5,738	$5,466	$5,495	$5,886	$5,935			
168											
169	Liabilities & Equity										
170	Accounts Payable	$1,750	$1,598	$1,155	$774	$674	$674	$674			
171	Notes Payable	$500	$547	$610	$610	$804	$2,009	$2,212			
172	Income Taxes Payable	$200	($17)	($35)	($54)	($19)	($57)	($88)			
173	Fxd Assets Payable	$25	$65	$75	$75	$75	$75	$75			
174	Other Current Liabilities	$25	$25	$25	$25	$25	$25	$25			
175		-------	-------	-------	-------	-------	-------	-------			
176	Total Current Liabilities	$2,500	$2,217	$1,830	$1,430	$1,559	$2,726	$2,898			
177											
178	Loans Payable	$1,800	$1,741	$1,681	$1,621	$1,560	$1,118	$1,052			
179		-------	-------	-------	-------	-------	-------	-------			
180	Total Liabilities	$4,300	$3,958	$3,511	$3,051	$3,119	$3,844	$3,949			
181											
182	Common Stock	$750	$1,050	$1,050	$1,275	$1,275	$1,275	$1,275			
183	Retained Earnings	$1,250	$1,214	$1,177	$1,139	$1,101	$767	$711			
184		-------	-------	-------	-------	-------	-------	-------			
185	Net Worth	$2,000	$2,264	$2,227	$2,414	$2,376	$2,042	$1,986			
186											
187	Total Liabilities & Equity	$6,300	$6,223	$5,738	$5,466	$5,495	$5,886	$5,935			
188											
189											
190	Error (Assets less Liabilities & Equity)	$0	$0	$0	$0	$0	$0	$0			

Figure 16-7. The Balance Sheet forecast section

G158: @SUM(G157..G153)

The new Fixed Assets balance is equal to the old balance plus additions.

G160: +F160+G85

The new Accumulated Depreciation balance is equal to the old balance plus depreciation expense.

G161: +F161+G134

Net Fixed Assets is equal to assets minus depreciation.

G163: +G160−G161

Other Noncurrent Assets is unchanged during the forecast. If your firm has a similar account—perhaps for intangible assets—you may want to enter your own assumption at this point. (Figure 16-9 demonstrates how you can do this with confidence.)

G165: +F165

The Total Assets balance is equal to the sum of appropriate asset balances.

G167: @SUM(G165..G163,G158)

Accounts Payable is equal to its previous balance, plus inventory purchases, less inventory payments, plus overhead expense purchases, less overhead expense payments.

G170: +F170+G47−G59+G72−G80

Notes Payable is equal to the previous balance plus the new loans amount that we will calculate in row 216 of Figure 16-8.

G171: +F171+G216

Income Taxes Payable is equal to the previous balance plus new provisions for taxes less tax payments.

G172: +F172+G145−G122

The Fixed Assets Payable balance is tracked separately from the Accounts Payable balance because in some companies, this balance is quite large and varies considerably from month to month. If it were included

```
      A         B        C        D        E        F        G        H        I        J        Q        R        S        T        U
  4  11-Jan 05:29 PM
  5 PROJECTED FINANCIAL PERFORMANCE, 1987
192 ====================================================================||===============
193 CASH FLOW SUMMARY                              Jan      Feb      Mar      Apr  ||   Nov      Dec
194 ============================================= ======= ======= ======= ======= ||======= =======
195 Collection of Receivables                    $1,070  $1,550  $1,370  $1,000  || $1,000  $1,000
196                                                                               ||
197 Cash Disbursements                                                            ||
198   Payment of Inventory Purchases               $777    $858    $766    $485  ||   $385    $385
199   Payment of Operating Expenses                $360    $570    $600    $600  ||   $600    $600
200   Payment of Capital Purchases                  $60     $90    $100    $100  ||   $100    $100
201   Short-Term Debt Service                        $8      $8      $9      $9  ||    $27     $30
202   Long-Term Debt Service                        $77     $77     $77     $77  ||    $77     $77
203   Dividend Payments                             $10     $10     $10     $10  ||    $10     $10
204   Income Tax Payments                          $200      $0      $0    ($54) ||     $0      $0
205   Other                                                                       ||
206                                              --------------------------------||---------------
207 Total Cash Disbursements                     $1,492  $1,613  $1,562  $1,227  || $1,199  $1,202
208                                              --------------------------------||---------------
209 Total Cash Generated By Operations           ($422)   ($63)  ($192)  ($227)  || ($199)  ($202)
210                                                                               ||
211 Beginning Cash Balance                         $100     $25     $25     $58  ||    $25     $25
212                                              --------------------------------||---------------
213 Cash Balance Before Financing                ($322)   ($38)  ($167)  ($169)  || ($174)  ($177)
214                                                                               ||
215 Stock Sales (Purchases)                        $300      $0    $225      $0  ||     $0      $0
216 Borrow (Repay) Short Term                       $47     $63      $0    $194  ||   $199    $202
217                                              --------------------------------||---------------
218 Ending Cash Balance                             $25     $25     $58     $25  ||    $25     $25
219                                                                               ||
220 Cumulative Cash Flow, Net of Stock Sales     ($122)  ($185)  ($152)  ($379)  ||($1,584)($1,787)
221                                                                               ||
```

Figure 16-8. The Cash Flow forecast section

with the Accounts Payable balance, it would raise unnecessary questions about the behavior of that account.

G173: +F173+G85−G95

The balance in Other Current Liabilities is equal to the beginning balance plus the change in Other Current Assets. This formula reflects our assumption that Other Current Assets and Liabilities will grow by the same dollar amount each month.

G174: +F174+G156−F156

The Total Current Liabilities balance is equal to the sum of the foregoing liability accounts.

G176: @SUM(G175..G170)

The Loans Payable Balance is equal to the previous balance less the amount of reduction in the principal.

G178: +F178−G109

The Total Liabilities balance is equal to Current Liabilities plus Loans Payable.

G180: @SUM(G179..G175)

Common Stock is equal to the previous balance plus Stock Sales.

G182: +F182+G114

Retained Earnings is equal to its previous balance plus Profits After Taxes minus Dividends.

G183: +F183+G147−G115

Net Worth is equal to the sum of the equity section.

G185: @SUM(G184..G182)

The balance in Total Liabilities and Equity is equal to

G187: +G185+G180

When you first create the Balance Sheet, you will make errors that will keep it from balancing. Row 190 finds the amount of this error each month by subtracting Total Liabilities and Equity from Total Assets. (This calculation is so convenient that I leave it in my cash flow spreadsheet.) As described early in the chapter, Version 2 users can suppress the printing of this row by inserting a | (vertical bar) as the first character in cell A190.

G190: @ROUND(G167−G187,0)

THE CASH FLOW SUMMARY

Fundamentally, the Cash Flow Summary (Figure 16-8) is simply an explanation of the formula we used in row 153 of the Balance Sheet to calculate the change in the cash balance. As was described earlier, the change in cash flow is a function of the following items.

Collection of Receivables:

G195: +G24

Payment of Inventory Purchases:

G198: +G59

Payment of Operating Expenses:

G199: +G80

Payment of Capital Purchases:

G200: +G95

Short-Term Debt Service:

G201: (G103/12)*F171

Long-Term Debt Service:

G202: +G111

Dividend Payments:

G203: +G115

Income Tax Payments:

G204: +G122

Total Cash Disbursements equals the sum of the previous disbursements.

G207: @SUM(G206..E196)

Total Cash Generated by Operations is equal to collections less disbursements.

G209: +G195−G207

Beginning Cash Balance is equal to last month's ending balance.

G211: +F153

Cash Balance Before Financing is equal to the sum of the previous two items.

G213: @SUM(G212..G208)

Stock Sales are

G215: +G114

The formula for the amount of the short-term loan we wish to borrow or repay is

```
G216:  −@IF((G213+G215)>$E$105,@MIN((G213+G215)−$E$105,F171),
                                @MIN((G213+G215)−$E$104,0))
```

This formula begins by summing Cash Balance Before Financing and Stock Sales (G213+G215), and comparing this balance with the amount of the upper limit we've entered in cell E105. If the amount on hand (G213+G215) is greater than the limit in E105, we may want to repay part of the loan; otherwise, we may need to borrow money.

If we are going to repay part of the loan, we will repay an amount equal to the amount on hand (G213+G215) less the upper limit (E105). But if this amount available for repayment exceeds the total amount we owe (F171), we will pay only the amount we owe.

If we need to borrow money, it will be an amount equal to the cash balance on hand (G213+G215) less the amount of the lower limit (E104) if this difference is less than zero. Otherwise, we won't borrow anything.

The negative sign at the front of the formula in G216 switches the signs of the amount we will borrow or repay. As shown in the description of row 216 in Figure 16-8, an amount to repay is displayed as a negative amount; an amount to borrow is displayed as a positive amount.

The Ending Cash Balance is equal to the cash balance before financing plus stock sales and new loans.

G218: +G213+G215+G216

Finally, Cumulative Cash Flow, Net of Stock Sales is equal to the previous balance, plus total cash generated by operations this month, plus stock sales this month. The template assumes that the entire amount of negative cash flow will be covered by short-term debt. And it assumes that the entire amount of positive cash flow will be kept as cash that does not bear interest.

Of course, when negative or positive cash flow is large, neither assumption is valid. Large negative cash flow must be corrected, and large positive cash flow must be invested. Row 220 therefore highlights the projected cash flow problems for which management must find satisfactory solutions.

G220: +F220+G209+G215

ADDING YOUR OWN ASSUMPTIONS

Many of the assumptions used to create this template will not be correct for your own business. You will want to change them. This quickly creates a problem, of course: How do you change the formulas without putting the balance sheet out of balance?

Figure 16-9 shows a reconciliation that will help you keep your balance sheet in balance as you change assumptions. This section details every transaction that will occur during the first month of the forecast. Let's take a closer look at it.

Column F shows the beginning balance sheet. Column G shows January's ending balance sheet. Each number in column G (other than column subtotals) is equal to the December figure plus the sum of all the transactions shown for the row in columns H through Z. For example, the formula for cell G229 is +F229+@SUM(H229..Z229).

The zeros in column Z mark the end of the @SUM range. Inserting additional columns to the left of this column will allow you to add transactions to the display while keeping them within the @SUM range.

The numbers for each transaction are simply a repeat of numbers used earlier in the spreadsheet but, occasionally, with a different sign. For each transaction shown for columns H through X, Table 16-1 provides a brief explanation and the formulas.

Rows 265 through 267 show numbers that all will equal zero when the balance sheet is in balance. Row 265 returns the value of the assets in this reconciliation minus the value of the liabilities and equity. Cell G265, for example, is +G243−G263. Row 266 subtracts the reconciliation assets from the assets calculated in Figure 16-7. Cell G266 is +G167−G243. Row 267

	A B C D E	F	G	H	I	J	K	L	M	N	O	P	Q	R	S	T	U	V	W	X	Y	Z
4	11-Jan 05:29 PM																					
5	PROJECTED FINANCIAL PERFORMANCE, 1987																					
223																						
224	RECONCILIATION OF CHANGES TO THE PROJECTED BALANCE SHEET																					
225																						
226						Op	Inv	A/R	A/P	Pay		Cap	Tax	Tax	Stock	Div	ST-Loan	LT-Loan	ST-Loan	Other		END
227		Begin	End	Sales	COS	Exp	Purch	Collect	Pmt	Assets	Depr	Purch	Pmt	Liab	Sale	Pmt	Borrow	Pmt	Intrst	Cur A&L		COLUMN
228	Assets																					
229	Cash	$100	$25					$1,070	($1,137)	($60)			($200)		$300	($10)	$47	($77)	($8)			0
230	Accounts Receivable	$2,500	$2,430	$1,000				($1,070)														0
231	Inventory	$2,000	$2,000		($385)		$385															0
232	Other Current Assets	$250	$250																	$0		0
233																						0
234	Total Current Assets	$4,850	$4,705																			0
235																						0
236	Fixed Assets	$1,850	$1,950									$100										0
237	Accumulated Depreciation	$600	$633								$33											0
238																						0
239	Net Fixed Assets	$1,250	$1,318																			0
240																						0
241	Other Non-Current Assets	$200	$200																			0
242																						0
243	Total Assets	$6,300	$6,223																			0
244																						0
245	Liabilities & Equity																					0
246	Accounts Payable	$1,750	$1,598			$600	$385		($1,137)													0
247	Notes Payable	$500	$547														$47					0
248	Income Taxes Payable	$200	($17)										($200)	($17)								0
249	Fxd Assets Payable	$25	$65							($60)		$100										0
250	Other Current Liabilities	$25	$25																	$0		0
251																						0
252	Total Current Liabilities	$2,500	$2,217																			0
253																						0
254	Loans Payable	$1,800	$1,741															($59)				0
255																						0
256	Total Liabilities	$4,300	$3,958																			0
257																						0
258	Common Stock	$750	$1,050												$300							0
259	Retained Earnings	$1,250	$1,214	$1,000	($385)	($600)					($33)			$17		($10)		($18)	($8)			0
260																						0
261	Net Worth	$2,000	$2,264																			0
262																						0
263	Total Liabilities & Assets	$6,300	$6,223																			
264																						
265	Error: Assets - Liabilities	$0	($0)																			
266	Error: B/S Assets - Detail	$0	$0																			
267	Error: B/S Liabilities - Detail	$0	$0																			

Figure 16-9. The Reconciliation of Charges to the Projected Balance Sheet section

Sales: Increase accounts receivable; increase retained earnings.

H230: +G12
H259: +G12

Cost of Sales: Decrease inventory; decrease retained earnings.

I231: −G36
I259: −G36

Operating Expenses: Increase accounts payable; decrease retained earnings.

J246: +G72
J259: −G72

Inventory Purchases: Increase inventory; increase accounts payable.

K231: +G47
K246: +G47

Accounts Receivable Collections: Increase cash; decrease accounts receivable.

L229: +G24
L246: −G24

Accounts Payable Payments: Decrease cash; decrease accounts payable.

M229: −G59−G80
M246: −G80−G59

Pay for Fixed Assets: Decrease cash; decrease fixed assets payable.

N229: −G95
N249: −G95

Book Depreciation: Increase accumulated depreciation; decrease retained earnings.

0237: +G134
0259: −G134

Capital Purchases: Increase fixed assets; increase fixed assets payable.

P236: +G85
P249: +G85

Table 16-1. Formulas used for the transactions in Figure 16-9

Tax Payment: Decrease cash; decrease income taxes payable.

Q229: −G122
Q248: −G122

Book Tax Liability: Increase the tax liability; decrease retained earnings. (In Figure 16-9, the loss caused the tax liability to decrease.)

R248: +G145
R259: −G145

Stock Sale: Increase cash; increase common stock.

S229: +G114
S258: +G114

Dividend Payment: Decrease cash; decrease retained earnings.

T229: −G115
T259: −G115

Short-Term Loan Borrowing: Increase cash; increase notes payable. (In the figure, we repaid part of the loan.)

U229: +G216
U247: +G216

Long-Term Loan Payment: Decrease cash; decrease loans payable by the principal amount; decrease retained earnings by the interest amount.

V229: −G111
V254: −G109
V259: −G108

Short-Term Loan Interest: Decrease cash; decrease retained earnings.

W229: −(G103/12)*F171
W259: −(G103/12)*F171

Other Current Assets and Liabilities: Increase other current assets; increase other current liabilities.

X232: (H12/G12)*F156−F156
X250: +X232

Table 16-1. Formulas used for the transactions in Figure 16-9 (*continued*)

subtracts the reconciliation assets and liabilities from the comparable figure in Figure 16-7. Cell G267 is +G187−G263.

Using the Reconciliation of Changes In the Balance Sheet

Generally, I use the reconciliation to solve two different problems when I create my cash flow forecast. The first problem is that the cash flow projection never balances when I first create it. That is, the assets minus the liabilities, as shown in row 190 of Figure 16-7, always seems to equal some amount other than zero. I use the reconciliation to find my errors.

I do this by carefully entering all the transactions that my cash flow is trying to reflect. As I do this, I make sure that each new column of data leaves cell G265 with a value of zero. When I am done, the formulas for each line of the balance sheet in Figure 16-7 should refer to the same cells as the comparable line of Figure 16-9. Also, the income statement in Figure 16-6 should refer to the same cells as does the row 259 (Retained Earnings) in Figure 16-9.

In short, with two different versions of the same report, it is easy to find and correct my errors.

The second contribution this report makes is to serve as a guide when I'm making changes to the cash flow. To illustrate, suppose we wish to add an assumption about bad debts, as was mentioned in the discussion of Figure 16-1.

We would begin by adding the necessary rows to our Sales and Collections section to hold our assumptions about bad debt losses. Then we would go to column Y of the Reconciliation section and show the double effect of bad debts. The first effect is to reduce receivables; the second effect is to reduce retained earnings. Finally, we would update the formula in the balance sheet that calculates receivables and add a line to the income statement that would reflect bad debts. When we are done with the changes, the new values in January's balance sheet as calculated by the reconciliation should equal the values calculated in the Balance Sheet section, which begins in row 150.

DOUBLE-CHECK YOUR SPREADSHEET

After you have entered everything and the numbers balance, double-check your figures. We have entered constant sales, cost of sales, and operating expenses. Most of the other numbers should therefore be the same for the entire period. Are they? If not, why?

Do some numbers drop off in the last month or two of the forecast? If so, the formulas may need additional numbers beyond the end of the forecast, as in rows 30 through 37 in Figure 16-2.

Next, change your data. Show your sales and expenses increasing by, say, 20% per month. After you recalculate, is your balance sheet still in balance? Are your subtotals increasing as quickly as you would expect? If any number in any row of numbers remains unchanged, is the lack of change reasonable?

Change your data again. Show your sales and cost of sales decreasing during the year. Does your model respond properly to losses? Particularly, is the tax treatment for your losses appropriate?

Finally, enter real data and proper assumptions; then calculate and print a forecast. Using a hand calculator and a pencil, check your numbers. This step is boring and usually fails to find an error, but perform it anyway. You would hate to run out of cash because your forecast was based on an incorrect formula.

Appendix A

THE DATA AND FORMULAS FOR THE DATA BANK

The figures in this appendix list the data contained in the Data Bank described in Chapters 1 and 2 and used in the creation of reports in this book. If you do not intend to purchase the disk set available for this book (see the Introduction), you must enter this data if you wish to assure the accuracy of your reports by comparing them with those shown in Chapters 3, 5, 6, and 13.

In Figure A-1, the Statement of Monthly Income, only values are shown for subtotals like "Earnings Before Interest and Taxes." You may wish to substitute simple formulas that calculate these values. This also applies to the Balance Sheet, shown in Figure A-2.

In Figure A-3, Agings for Accounts Receivable and for Accounts Payable, notice that the sums of both sets of agings equal the appropriate balance sheet totals for accounts receivable or accounts payable.

Several of the categories that appear in Figure A-4, Miscellaneous accounting and nonaccounting data, (such as "Employees, Voluntary Quit" and "Total Payroll") are not discussed in this book. These categories illustrate the kinds of additional information that can be maintained and reported by the Data Bank.

Figure A-5, Ratios and Running Totals, presents values for the first 12 months; Table A-1 presents formulas for the remaining months. Many of the formulas calculate a running total of the first 12 months of data. Therefore, within the first 12 months, only values, not formulas, can be used.

A	B	K	L	M	N	O	P	Q	R	S	T
	Description	Dec-82	Jan-83	Feb-83	Mar-83	Apr-83	May-83	Jun-83	Jul-83	Aug-83	Sep-83
100.010	Sales	153	158	164	167	167	167	165	162	146	139
100.020	Cost of Goods Sold	73	80	81	85	81	81	81	83	75	73
100.030	Research & Development	16	16	16	16	16	16	16	16	16	16
100.040	Marketing	24	23	23	26	27	25	26	27	28	28
100.050	General & Admin	20	19	22	24	23	25	24	25	24	22
100.055	Gain (Loss) on Sale of F/A	0	0	0	0	0	0	0	0	0	0
100.060	Erngs Before Int & Taxes	20	20	22	16	20	20	18	11	3	0
100.070	Interest	2	2	2	2	2	2	2	2	2	2
100.080	Provision for Taxes	8	8	9	6	8	8	7	4	0	-1
100.090	Net Earnings	10	10	11	8	10	10	9	5	1	-1

A	B	U	V	W	X	Y	Z	AA	AB	AC	AD
	Description	Oct-83	Nov-83	Dec-83	Jan-84	Feb-84	Mar-84	Apr-84	May-84	Jun-84	Jul-84
100.010	Sales	136	132	132	131	128	127	127	128	131	131
100.020	Cost of Goods Sold	72	72	64	65	61	61	59	65	64	68
100.030	Research & Development	16	16	16	16	16	16	16	16	16	16
100.040	Marketing	26	25	26	26	25	17	18	19	19	20
100.050	General & Admin	21	20	19	20	19	16	15	17	18	17
100.055	Gain (Loss) on Sale of F/A	0	0	0	0	0	0	0	0	0	0
100.060	Erngs Before Int & Taxes	1	-1	7	4	7	17	19	11	14	10
100.070	Interest	2	2	1	2	2	2	2	2	2	2
100.080	Provision for Taxes	0	-1	3	1	2	7	8	4	5	4
100.090	Net Earnings	-1	-2	3	1	3	8	9	5	7	4

A	B	AE	AF	AG	AH	AI	AJ	AK	AL	AM	AN
	Description	Aug-84	Sep-84	Oct-84	Nov-84	Dec-84	Jan-85	Feb-85	Mar-85	Apr-85	May-85
100.010	Sales	134	131	134	138	144	147	148	148	152	155
100.020	Cost of Goods Sold	67	59	58	59	61	66	65	68	65	67
100.030	Research & Development	16	16	16	16	16	16	16	16	16	16
100.040	Marketing	20	18	20	20	21	22	21	20	21	22
100.050	General & Admin	16	16	17	18	17	17	16	16	19	22
100.055	Gain (Loss) on Sale of F/A	2	0	0	0	0	0	0	0	0	0
100.060	Erngs Before Int & Taxes	17	22	23	25	29	26	30	28	31	28
100.070	Interest	2	2	2	1	1	1	1	1	1	1
100.080	Provision for Taxes	7	9	9	11	13	11	13	12	14	12
100.090	Net Earnings	8	11	12	13	15	14	16	15	16	15

A	B	AO	AP	AQ	AR	AS	AT	AU
	Description	Jun-85	Jul-85	Aug-85	Sep-85	Oct-85	Nov-85	Dec-85
100.010	Sales	158	166	183	190	196	225	216
100.020	Cost of Goods Sold	72	74	84	83	89	100	98
100.030	Research & Development	16	16	19	19	20	23	23
100.040	Marketing	25	25	25	27	27	27	32
100.050	General & Admin	23	23	24	25	26	26	28
100.055	Gain (Loss) on Sale of F/A	0	0	1	0	0	0	0
100.060	Erngs Before Int & Taxes	22	28	32	36	34	49	35
100.070	Interest	1	1	1	1	1	1	1
100.080	Provision for Taxes	9	12	14	16	15	22	15
100.090	Net Earnings	12	15	17	19	18	26	19

Figure A-1. Statement of monthly income

A	B Description	K Dec-82	L Jan-83	M Feb-83	N Mar-83	O Apr-83	P May-83	Q Jun-83	R Jul-83	S Aug-83	T Sep-83
105.005	Cash	31	32	33	33	33	33	33	32	29	28
105.010	Accounts Receivable	295	317	302	329	340	350	335	351	339	315
105.020	Inventories	248	242	253	251	240	249	246	237	236	232
105.030	Other Current Assets	9	8	9	10	8	7	9	9	8	7
105.040	Total Current Assets	583	599	597	623	621	639	623	629	612	582
105.050	Property, Plant, Equip	575	595	595	626	626	626	644	649	649	688
105.060	Accum Depreciation	56	62	68	70	77	84	91	98	105	112
105.070	Net Prop, Plant, Equip	519	533	527	556	549	542	553	551	544	576
105.080	Other Assets	5	15	17	5	5	5	5	5	4	4
105.090	Total Assets	1107	1147	1141	1184	1175	1186	1181	1185	1160	1162
105.100	Notes Payable	24	45	38	55	76	74	62	70	60	43
105.110	Accounts Payable	169	172	155	176	139	142	148	155	169	210
105.120	Payroll Taxes & Benefits	27	30	30	31	30	30	30	31	28	27
105.130	Other Accrued Liab	76	78	80	80	81	82	78	69	67	66
105.140	Total Current Liab	296	325	303	342	326	328	318	325	324	346
105.150	Deferred Income Taxes	152	155	162	162	161	162	162	156	134	119
105.160	Long Term Debt	128	126	124	122	120	118	116	114	111	109
105.170	Total Liabilities	576	606	589	626	607	608	596	595	569	574
105.180	Stock	300	300	300	300	300	300	300	300	300	300
105.190	Retained Earnings	231	241	252	258	268	278	285	290	291	288
105.200	Net Worth	531	541	552	558	568	578	585	590	591	588
105.210	Total Liab & Equity	1107	1147	1141	1184	1175	1186	1181	1185	1160	1162

A	B Description	U Oct-83	V Nov-83	W Dec-83	X Jan-84	Y Feb-84	Z Mar-84	AA Apr-84	AB May-84	AC Jun-84	AD Jul-84
105.005	Cash	27	26	26	26	26	25	25	26	26	26
105.010	Accounts Receivable	281	256	261	255	256	252	243	252	236	247
105.020	Inventories	231	220	230	217	220	219	225	235	227	224
105.030	Other Current Assets	7	5	6	6	7	6	6	6	6	8
105.040	Total Current Assets	546	507	523	504	509	502	499	519	495	505
105.050	Property, Plant, Equip	688	705	715	715	737	737	737	777	777	777
105.060	Accum Depreciation	119	126	133	140	147	155	163	171	179	187
105.070	Net Prop, Plant, Equip	569	579	582	575	590	582	574	606	598	590
105.080	Other Assets	4	4	4	4	4	4	4	4	4	4
105.090	Total Assets	1119	1090	1109	1083	1103	1088	1077	1129	1097	1099
105.100	Notes Payable	42	20	54	75	90	92	84	78	54	74
105.110	Accounts Payable	185	185	186	152	180	166	156	212	195	182
105.120	Payroll Taxes & Benefits	27	27	24	24	23	23	22	24	24	25
105.130	Other Accrued Liab	66	65	63	64	62	61	63	62	70	65
105.140	Total Current Liab	320	297	327	315	355	342	325	376	343	346
105.150	Deferred Income Taxes	105	103	93	80	60	54	53	52	50	47
105.160	Long Term Debt	107	105	103	101	98	96	94	91	89	87
105.170	Total Liabilities	532	505	523	496	513	492	472	519	482	480
105.180	Stock	300	300	300	300	300	300	300	300	300	300
105.190	Retained Earnings	287	285	286	287	290	296	305	310	315	319
105.200	Net Worth	587	585	586	587	590	596	605	610	615	619
105.210	Total Liab & Equity	1119	1090	1109	1083	1103	1088	1077	1129	1097	1099

Figure A-2. Balance sheet

A	B	K	L	M	N	O	P	Q	R	S	T
	Description	Dec-82	Jan-83	Feb-83	Mar-83	Apr-83	May-83	Jun-83	Jul-83	Aug-83	Sep-83
110.010	Receivables, 30 Days	146	152	156	161	161	160	159	155	141	133
110.020	Receivables, 60 Days	91	98	99	103	110	104	107	111	106	98
110.030	Receivables, 90 Days	43	36	46	40	51	51	46	45	55	50
110.040	Receivables, Over 90 Days	15	31	1	25	18	35	23	40	37	34
115.010	Payables, 30 Days	111	101	97	123	81	92	110	92	87	130
115.020	Payables, 60 Days	42	55	41	40	48	35	33	55	50	48
115.030	Payables, 90 Days	16	16	17	13	10	15	5	5	20	15
115.040	Payables, Over 90 Days	0	0	0	0	0	0	0	3	12	17

A	B	U	V	W	X	Y	Z	AA	AB	AC	AD
	Description	Oct-83	Nov-83	Dec-83	Jan-84	Feb-84	Mar-84	Apr-84	May-84	Jun-84	Jul-84
110.010	Receivables, 30 Days	130	126	127	124	123	120	122	122	124	133
110.020	Receivables, 60 Days	83	78	88	77	78	82	80	78	72	75
110.030	Receivables, 90 Days	55	37	35	38	35	27	40	34	31	19
110.040	Receivables, Over 90 Days	13	15	11	16	20	23	1	18	9	20
115.010	Payables, 30 Days	88	93	101	72	99	67	73	124	64	79
115.020	Payables, 60 Days	67	48	51	56	47	64	42	42	81	40
115.030	Payables, 90 Days	12	22	8	9	14	9	15	10	10	20
115.040	Payables, Over 90 Days	18	22	26	15	20	26	26	36	40	43

A	B	AE	AF	AG	AH	AI	AJ	AK	AL	AM	AN
	Description	Aug-84	Sep-84	Oct-84	Nov-84	Dec-84	Jan-85	Feb-85	Mar-85	Apr-85	May-85
110.010	Receivables, 30 Days	129	126	128	131	137	135	139	131	142	153
110.020	Receivables, 60 Days	83	72	77	81	76	75	73	68	53	75
110.030	Receivables, 90 Days	29	30	19	21	33	26	14	17	24	22
110.040	Receivables, Over 90 Days	0	14	9	0	12	25	19	4	4	17
115.010	Payables, 30 Days	84	77	70	90	86	66	74	91	84	82
115.020	Payables, 60 Days	40	48	48	51	67	59	30	44	50	36
115.030	Payables, 90 Days	9	13	15	14	14	15	13	8	9	13
115.040	Payables, Over 90 Days	48	49	51	41	29	15	15	10	5	15

A	B	AO	AP	AQ	AR	AS	AT	AU
	Description	Jun-85	Jul-85	Aug-85	Sep-85	Oct-85	Nov-85	Dec-85
110.010	Receivables, 30 Days	140	156	180	188	191	222	211
110.020	Receivables, 60 Days	82	50	111	152	135	123	121
110.030	Receivables, 90 Days	5	24	17	53	64	15	53
110.040	Receivables, Over 90 Days	7	11	23	32	19	53	38
115.010	Payables, 30 Days	115	100	148	144	100	163	115
115.020	Payables, 60 Days	45	58	51	107	103	68	122
115.030	Payables, 90 Days	15	28	21	20	60	50	9
115.040	Payables, Over 90 Days	20	15	18	24	30	18	22

Figure A-3. Agings for accounts receivable and for accounts payable

A	B	K	L	M	N	O	P	Q	R	S	T
	Description	Dec-82	Jan-83	Feb-83	Mar-83	Apr-83	May-83	Jun-83	Jul-83	Aug-83	Sep-83
120.010	Depreciation Expense	6	6	6	6	7	7	7	7	7	7
199.010	Dividends Paid	2	0	0	2	0	0	2	0	0	2
199.020	Purchases of Inventory, AP	87	74	92	83	70	90	78	74	74	69
199.022	Purchases, Expenses, AP	25	21	19	18	30	24	20	22	19	28
199.023	Purch of Fixed Assets	16	20	0	35	0	0	18	5	0	39
199.029	Total Purchases, AP	128	115	111	136	100	114	116	101	93	136
199.030	Accounts Payable Paid	101	112	128	115	137	111	110	94	79	95
199.040	AR Collected	124	136	179	140	156	157	180	146	158	163
199.060	Disp of Fxd Asts--Bk Val	0	0	0	4	0	0	0	0	0	0
199.070	Disp of Fxd Asts--Depr	0	0	0	4	0	0	0	0	0	0
199.080	Disp of Fxd Asts--Sales	0	0	0	0	0	0	0	0	0	0
200.010	Stock Price, Monthly High	34.5	33.0	33.3	33.4	31.9	33.7	38.3	35.1	29.5	27.4
200.020	Stock Price, Monthly Low	33.0	32.0	32.4	31.3	29.9	31.4	27.9	26.3	22.8	22.0
200.030	Stock Price, Monthly Close	33.4	32.4	33.1	32.6	30.9	32.3	32.4	28.8	25.7	24.6
200.040	Stock Shares Outstanding	33	33	33	33	33	33	33	33	33	33
300.010	Employees, Number	31	31	33	34	33	35	33	31	31	33
300.020	Employees, Vol Quit	0	1	2	1	2	0	1	1	0	2
300.100	Total Payroll	65	65	69	71	69	74	69	65	65	69
400.010	Orders Booked	203	194	203	187	165	162	135	124	54	102
400.020	Order Backlog	371	407	446	466	464	459	429	391	299	262

A	B	U	V	W	X	Y	Z	AA	AB	AC	AD
	Description	Oct-83	Nov-83	Dec-83	Jan-84	Feb-84	Mar-84	Apr-84	May-84	Jun-84	Jul-84
120.010	Depreciation Expense	7	7	7	7	7	8	8	8	8	8
199.010	Dividends Paid	0	0	2	0	0	2	0	0	2	0
199.020	Purchases of Inventory, AP	71	61	74	52	64	60	65	75	56	65
199.022	Purchases, Expenses, AP	24	19	27	26	19	13	15	16	16	19
199.023	Purch of Fixed Assets	0	17	10	0	22	0	0	40	0	0
199.029	Total Purchases, AP	95	97	111	78	105	73	80	131	72	84
199.030	Accounts Payable Paid	120	97	110	112	77	87	90	75	89	97
199.040	AR Collected	170	157	127	137	127	131	136	119	147	120
199.060	Disp of Fxd Asts--Bk Val	0	0	0	0	0	0	0	0	0	0
199.070	Disp of Fxd Asts--Depr	0	0	0	0	0	0	0	0	0	0
199.080	Disp of Fxd Asts--Sales	0	0	0	0	0	0	0	0	0	0
200.010	Stock Price, Monthly High	24.7	26.1	24.6	24.2	24.8	28.3	27.2	26.5	27.9	27.6
200.020	Stock Price, Monthly Low	22.8	23.7	23.9	23.5	22.5	24.5	24.8	23.7	22.0	20.0
200.030	Stock Price, Monthly Close	23.6	25.5	24.0	23.5	24.6	26.0	25.8	25.2	24.2	26.4
200.040	Stock Shares Outstanding	33	33	33	33	33	33	33	33	33	33
300.010	Employees, Number	32	32	32	32	31	31	32	31	32	32
300.020	Employees, Vol Quit	1	0	0	0	0	0	2	2	1	0
300.100	Total Payroll	67	67	67	67	65	65	67	65	67	67
400.010	Orders Booked	121	114	130	125	116	123	130	133	145	131
400.020	Order Backlog	247	229	227	221	209	205	208	213	227	227

A	B Description	AE Aug-84	AF Sep-84	AG Oct-84	AH Nov-84	AI Dec-84	AJ Jan-85	AK Feb-85	AL Mar-85	AM Apr-85	AN May-85
120.010	Depreciation Expense	8	8	8	8	8	8	8	8	8	9
199.010	Dividends Paid	0	2	0	0	3	0	0	4	0	0
199.020	Purchases of Inventory, AP	61	69	62	54	76	54	71	71	73	71
199.022	Purchases, Expenses, AP	21	15	15	16	16	22	18	18	23	23
199.023	Purch of Fixed Assets	10	0	0	25	0	0	0	12	30	12
199.029	Total Purchases, AP	92	84	77	95	92	76	89	101	126	106
199.030	Accounts Payable Paid	93	78	80	83	92	117	112	80	131	108
199.040	AR Collected	140	130	143	138	119	144	164	173	149	111
199.060	Disp of Fxd Asts--Bk Val	22	0	0	0	0	0	0	0	0	0
199.070	Disp of Fxd Asts--Depr	19	0	0	0	0	0	0	0	0	0
199.080	Disp of Fxd Asts--Sales	5	0	0	0	0	0	0	0	0	0
200.010	Stock Price, Monthly High	31.9	32.5	38.7	45.6	40.3	44.9	52.2	49.3	51.6	52.1
200.020	Stock Price, Monthly Low	23.7	20.7	33.1	31.9	31.7	41.0	38.8	42.4	47.4	50.0
200.030	Stock Price, Monthly Close	28.3	31.6	35.8	38.2	39.8	42.9	48.4	47.9	49.8	50.8
200.040	Stock Shares Outstanding	33	33	33	33	33	33	33	33	33	33
300.010	Employees, Number	32	31	33	32	31	34	32	33	33	31
300.020	Employees, Vol Quit	0	0	0	0	2	0	0	2	0	2
300.100	Total Payroll	67	65	69	67	65	71	67	69	69	65
400.010	Orders Booked	146	123	152	161	175	163	156	153	178	181
400.020	Order Backlog	239	231	249	272	303	319	327	332	358	384

A	B Description	AO Jun-85	AP Jul-85	AQ Aug-85	AR Sep-85	AS Oct-85	AT Nov-85	AU Dec-85
120.010	Depreciation Expense	9	9	9	10	10	10	11
199.010	Dividends Paid	4	0	0	15	0	0	15
199.020	Purchases of Inventory, AP	76	96	78	102	92	99	107
199.022	Purchases, Expenses, AP	20	21	19	31	25	33	37
199.023	Purch of Fixed Assets	35	22	63	28	18	49	0
199.029	Total Purchases, AP	131	139	160	161	135	181	144
199.030	Accounts Payable Paid	82	133	123	104	137	175	175
199.040	AR Collected	191	159	93	96	212	221	206
199.060	Disp of Fxd Asts--Bk Val	0	0	7	0	0	0	0
199.070	Disp of Fxd Asts--Depr	0	0	7	0	0	0	0
199.080	Disp of Fxd Asts--Sales	0	0	1	0	0	0	0
200.010	Stock Price, Monthly High	52.3	54.3	59.3	57.4	60.1	62.7	59.3
200.020	Stock Price, Monthly Low	48.0	48.7	51.1	53.6	54.7	58.1	57.9
200.030	Stock Price, Monthly Close	51.7	51.1	54.1	56.1	59.0	59.4	58.6
200.040	Stock Shares Outstanding	33	33	33	33	33	33	33
300.010	Employees, Number	31	31	33	36	33	37	38
300.020	Employees, Vol Quit	2	1	1	2	2	3	0
300.100	Total Payroll	65	65	69	76	69	78	80
400.010	Orders Booked	196	239	323	290	277	258	311
400.020	Order Backlog	422	495	635	735	816	849	944

Figure A-4. Miscellaneous accounting and nonaccounting data

A	B	K	L	M	N	O	P	Q	R	S	T	U	V
	Description	Dec-82	Jan-83	Feb-83	Mar-83	Apr-83	May-83	Jun-83	Jul-83	Aug-83	Sep-83	Oct-83	Nov-83
800.010	Sales, Last 12 Months	1593	1645	1700	1754	1797	1834	1862	1884	1889	1887	1874	1856
800.020	Profits, Last 12 Months	103	105	110	110	109	110	110	106	91	81	71	70
800.030	Dividends, Last 12 Months	6	6	6	6	6	6	6	6	6	6	6	8
800.040	EBIT, Last 12 Months	208	212	223	225	226	229	231	226	202	185	167	150
810.010	Return on Assets, Cur	9%	9%	10%	9%	9%	9%	9%	9%	8%	7%	6%	6%
810.020	Profit Margin	6%	6%	6%	6%	6%	6%	6%	6%	5%	4%	4%	4%
810.030	Months of Inventory	3.4	3.0	3.1	3.0	3.0	3.1	3.0	2.9	3.1	3.2	3.2	3.1
810.040	Working Capital	287	274	294	281	295	311	305	304	288	236	226	210
810.120	Return on Equity	19%	19%	20%	20%	19%	19%	19%	18%	15%	14%	12%	12%
815.010	Wrk Cap/Tot Assets, [X1]	0.26	0.24	0.26	0.24	0.25	0.26	0.26	0.26	0.25	0.20	0.20	0.19
815.020	Ret Erngs/Tot Asts, [X2]	0.21	0.21	0.22	0.22	0.23	0.23	0.24	0.24	0.25	0.25	0.26	0.26
815.030	EBIT/Tot Asts, [X3]	0.19	0.18	0.20	0.19	0.19	0.19	0.20	0.19	0.17	0.16	0.15	0.14
815.040	Mkt Val Eqty/T Liab, [X4]	1.91	1.76	1.85	1.72	1.68	1.75	1.79	1.60	1.49	1.41	1.46	1.67
815.050	NW/Tot Liab, [X4A]	0.92	0.89	0.94	0.89	0.94	0.95	0.98	0.99	1.04	1.02	1.10	1.16
815.060	Sales/Tot Asts, [X5]	1.44	1.43	1.49	1.48	1.53	1.55	1.58	1.59	1.63	1.62	1.67	1.70
815.062	Assets/Sales	0.69	0.70	0.67	0.68	0.65	0.65	0.63	0.63	0.61	0.62	0.60	0.59
850.010	Sustainable Growth Rate	22%	22%	23%	23%	22%	22%	22%	20%	17%	15%	12%	12%
851.010	Z Score	2.05	2.01	2.11	2.06	2.13	2.18	2.21	2.21	2.22	2.13	2.18	2.20
851.020	Z1 Score	2.77	2.73	2.86	2.80	2.89	2.93	2.98	2.99	2.99	2.90	2.96	2.97
851.030	Z2 Score	4.61	4.43	4.71	4.48	4.67	4.78	4.83	4.80	4.71	4.29	4.32	4.26
852.010	Free Cash Flow	18	-11	17	-5	-10	13	25	3	22	30	12	33
900.010	DATE	Dec-82	Jan-83	Feb-83	Mar-83	Apr-83	May-83	Jun-83	Jul-83	Aug-83	Sep-83	Oct-83	Nov-83

Figure A-5. Ratios and running totals

800.010	Sales, Last 12 Months Last 12 months of sales. *AU65:* @SUM(AJ5..AU5)
800.020	Profits, Last 12 Months Last 12 months of profits. *AU66:* @SUM(AU14..AJ14)
800.030	Dividends, Last 12 Months Last 12 months of dividends. *AU67:* @SUM(AU46..AJ46)
800.040	EBIT, Last 12 Months Last 12 months of earnings before interest and taxes. *AU68:* @SUM(AU11..AJ11)
810.010	Return on Assets, Cur Profits for the last 12 months divided by this month's total assets. *AU69:* (P0) +AU66/AU24
810.020	Profit Margin Profits for the last 12 months divided by sales for the last 12 months. *AU70:* (P0) +AU66/AU65
810.030	Months of Inventory This month's inventory divided by this month's cost of goods sold. *AU71:* (F1) +AU17/AU6
810.040	Working Capital This month's total current assets minus this month's total current liabilities. *AU72:* +AU19−AU29
810.120	Return on Equity Last 12 months' earnings divided by beginning net worth. *AU73:* (P0) @SUM(AU14..AJ14)/AI35
815.010	Wrk Cap/Tot Assets, [X1] This month's working capital divided by this month's total assets. *AU74:* (F2) +AU72/AU24
815.020	Ret Erngs/Tot Asts, [X2] This month's retained earnings divided by this month's total assets. *AU75:* (F2) +AU34/AU24
815.030	EBIT/Tot Asts, [X3] This month's EBIT divided by this month's total assets. *AU76:* (F2) +AU68/AU24

Table A-1. Ratios, Running Totals, and Miscellaneous Formulas Maintained in the Data Section of the Data Bank

815.040	Mkt Val Eqty/T Liab, [X4] This month's number of shares of stock outstanding times stock price divided by total liabilities. *AU77:* (F2) (AU59*AU58)/AU32
815.050	NW/Tot Liab, [X4A] This month's net worth divided by total liabilities. *AU78:* (F2) +AU35/AU32
815.060	Sales/Tot Asts, [X5] The last 12 months' sales divided by this month's total assets. *AU79:* (F2) +AU65/AU24
815.062	Assets/Sales This month's total assets divided by the last 12 months' sales. *AU80:* (F2) +AU24/AU65
850.010	Sustainable Growth Rate See Chapter 12. This month's net worth divided by last year's net worth, minus one. *AU81:* (P0) +AU35/AI35−1
851.010	Z Score See Chapter 11 for definition. *AU82:* (F2) 1.2*AU74+1.4*AU75+3.3*AU76+0.06*AU77+AU79
851.020	Z1 Score See Chapter 11 for definition. *AU83:* (F2) 0.717*AU74+0.847*AU75+3.107*AU76+0.42*AU78 +0.998*AU79
851.030	Z2 Score See Chapter 11 for definition. *AU84:* (F2) 6.56*AU74+3.26*AU75+6.72*AU76+1.05*AU78
852.010	Free Cash Flow See Chapter 6 for definition. *AU85:* +AU14+AU12+AU45−(AU24−@SUM(AU26...AU28) −AU30)+(AT24−@SUM(AT26...AT28)−AT30)

Table A-1. Ratios, Running Totals, and Miscellaneous Formulas Maintained in the Data Section of the Data Bank (*continued*)

900.010	DATE The current month and year. *AU86:* (D3) +AU4
9999.010	Error? Assets=Liab If assets do not equal liabilities plus equity, return an ERR. *AU152:* @IF(AU24=AU36,0,@ERR)
9999.020	Error? AR=Aging If accounts receivable doesn't equal the sum of this month's aging, return an ERR. *AU153:* @IF(AU98=@SUM(AU119..AU122),0,@ERR)

Table A-1. Ratios, Running Totals, and Miscellaneous Formulas Maintained in the Data Section of the Data Bank (*continued*)

Formulas are shown for the *last* month of the Data Bank. Copy them to the left as needed.

Figures A-6 through A-9 deal with budgets: Budgeted Income Statements, Budget Balance Sheet, Budgeted Agings of Accounts Receivable and Payable, and Budgeted and Forecasted Miscellaneous Data. In all of these, notice that the Data Bank number (DB#) for all budgets is equal to the number for the actual data, plus 1,000.

Finally, in Figure A-10, Values of the Formulas for Ratios and Running Totals, note that the formulas for these calculations are equivalent to the formulas for the actual data. Once the budgets were set, however, these formulas were converted to the values shown. This conversion saves memory and recalculation time.

A	B	K	L	M	N	O	P	Q	R	S	T
	Description	Dec-82	Jan-83	Feb-83	Mar-83	Apr-83	May-83	Jun-83	Jul-83	Aug-83	Sep-83
1100.010	Sales	153	155	157	159	161	163	165	167	169	171
1100.020	Cost of Goods Sold	73	74	75	76	77	78	79	80	81	82
1100.030	Research & Development	16	16	16	16	16	16	16	16	16	16
1100.040	Marketing	24	24	24	24	24	24	24	24	24	24
1100.050	General & Admin	20	20	20	20	20	20	20	20	20	20
1100.055	Other (Income) & Expenses	0	0	0	0	0	0	0	0	0	0
1100.060	Erngs Before Int & Taxes	20	21	22	23	24	25	26	27	28	29
1100.070	Interest	2	2	2	2	2	3	3	2	2	2
1100.080	Provision for Taxes	8	9	9	9	10	10	10	11	12	12
1100.090	Net Earnings	10	10	11	12	12	12	13	14	14	15

A	B	U	V	W	X	Y	Z	AA	AB	AC	AD
	Description	Oct-83	Nov-83	Dec-83	Jan-84	Feb-84	Mar-84	Apr-84	May-84	Jun-84	Jul-84
1100.010	Sales	173	175	177	133	134	135	136	137	138	139
1100.020	Cost of Goods Sold	83	84	85	64	64	64	64	64	64	64
1100.030	Research & Development	16	16	16	16	16	16	16	16	16	16
1100.040	Marketing	24	24	24	26	26	26	26	26	26	26
1100.050	General & Admin	20	20	20	19	19	19	19	19	19	19
1100.055	Other (Income) & Expenses	0	0	0	0	0	0	0	0	0	0
1100.060	Erngs Before Int & Taxes	30	31	32	8	9	10	11	12	13	14
1100.070	Interest	1	1	1	1	1	1	1	1	1	1
1100.080	Provision for Taxes	13	14	14	3	4	4	5	5	5	6
1100.090	Net Earnings	16	16	17	4	4	5	5	6	7	7

A	B	AE	AF	AG	AH	AI	AJ	AK	AL	AM	AN
	Description	Aug-84	Sep-84	Oct-84	Nov-84	Dec-84	Jan-85	Feb-85	Mar-85	Apr-85	May-85
1100.010	Sales	140	141	142	143	144	147	150	153	156	159
1100.020	Cost of Goods Sold	64	64	64	64	64	62	61	62	63	64
1100.030	Research & Development	16	16	16	16	16	16	16	16	16	16
1100.040	Marketing	26	26	26	26	26	21	21	21	21	21
1100.050	General & Admin	19	19	19	19	19	17	17	17	17	17
1100.055	Other (Income) & Expenses	0	0	0	0	0	0	0	0	0	0
1100.060	Erngs Before Int & Taxes	15	16	17	18	19	31	35	37	39	41
1100.070	Interest	1	1	1	1	1	1	1	1	1	1
1100.080	Provision for Taxes	6	7	7	8	8	14	15	16	17	18
1100.090	Net Earnings	8	8	9	9	10	16	19	20	21	22

A	B	AO	AP	AQ	AR	AS	AT	AU
	Description	Jun-85	Jul-85	Aug-85	Sep-85	Oct-85	Nov-85	Dec-85
1100.010	Sales	162	165	168	171	174	177	180
1100.020	Cost of Goods Sold	65	66	67	68	69	70	71
1100.030	Research & Development	16	16	16	16	16	16	16
1100.040	Marketing	21	21	21	21	21	21	21
1100.050	General & Admin	17	17	17	17	17	17	17
1100.055	Other (Income) & Expenses	0	0	0	0	0	0	0
1100.060	Erngs Before Int & Taxes	43	45	47	49	51	53	55
1100.070	Interest	1	1	1	1	1	0	0
1100.080	Provision for Taxes	19	20	21	22	23	24	25
1100.090	Net Earnings	23	24	25	26	27	29	30

Figure A-6. Budgeted income statements

A	B	K	L	M	N	O	P	Q	R	S	T
		Dec-82	Jan-83	Feb-83	Mar-83	Apr-83	May-83	Jun-83	Jul-83	Aug-83	Sep-83
1100.100	Cash	31	31	31	32	32	33	33	33	34	34
1105.010	Accounts Receivable	295	317	302	329	340	350	335	351	339	315
1105.020	Inventories	248	248	265	272	265	277	276	270	263	250
1105.030	Other Current Assets	9	8	9	10	8	7	9	9	8	7
1105.040	Total Current Assets	583	604	607	643	645	667	653	663	644	606
1105.050	Property, Plant, Equip	575	595	595	626	626	626	644	649	649	688
1105.060	Accum Depreciation	56	62	68	70	77	84	91	98	105	112
1105.070	Net Prop, Plant, Equip	519	533	527	556	549	542	553	551	544	576
1105.080	Other Assets	5	15	17	5	5	5	5	5	4	4
1105.090	Total Assets	1107	1152	1151	1204	1199	1214	1211	1219	1192	1186
1105.100	Notes Payable	24	50	48	71	94	94	81	84	59	19
1105.110	Accounts Payable	169	172	155	176	139	142	148	155	169	210
1105.120	Payroll Taxes & Benefits	27	30	30	31	30	30	30	31	28	27
1105.130	Other Accrued Liab	76	78	80	80	81	82	78	69	67	66
1105.140	Total Current Liab	296	330	313	358	344	348	337	339	323	322
1105.150	Deferred Income Taxes	152	155	162	162	161	162	162	156	134	119
1105.160	Long Term Debt	128	126	124	122	120	118	116	114	111	109
1105.170	Total Liabilities	576	611	599	642	625	628	615	609	568	550
1105.180	Stock	300	300	300	300	300	300	300	300	300	300
1105.190	Retained Earnings	231	241	252	262	274	286	296	310	324	336
1105.200	Net Worth	531	541	552	562	574	586	596	610	624	636
1105.210	Total Liab & Equity	1107	1152	1151	1204	1199	1214	1211	1219	1192	1186

A	B	U	V	W	X	Y	Z	AA	AB	AC	AD
		Oct-83	Nov-83	Dec-83	Jan-84	Feb-84	Mar-84	Apr-84	May-84	Jun-84	Jul-84
1100.100	Cash	43	219	239	224	147	144	149	153	173	150
1105.010	Accounts Receivable	281	256	261	255	256	252	243	252	236	247
1105.020	Inventories	238	215	204	192	192	188	189	200	192	193
1105.030	Other Current Assets	7	5	6	6	7	6	6	6	6	8
1105.040	Total Current Assets	569	695	710	677	602	590	587	611	607	598
1105.050	Property, Plant, Equip	688	705	715	715	737	737	737	777	777	777
1105.060	Accum Depreciation	119	126	133	140	147	155	163	171	179	187
1105.070	Net Prop, Plant, Equip	569	579	582	575	590	582	574	606	598	590
1105.080	Other Assets	4	4	4	4	4	4	4	4	4	4
1105.090	Total Assets	1142	1278	1296	1256	1196	1176	1165	1221	1209	1192
1105.100	Notes Payable	0	0	0	0	0	0	0	0	0	0
1105.110	Accounts Payable	185	185	186	152	180	166	156	212	195	182
1105.120	Payroll Taxes & Benefits	27	27	24	24	23	23	22	24	24	25
1105.130	Other Accrued Liab	66	65	63	64	62	61	63	62	70	65
1105.140	Total Current Liab	278	277	273	240	265	250	241	298	289	272
1105.150	Deferred Income Taxes	105	228	239	230	144	140	135	131	127	122
1105.160	Long Term Debt	107	105	103	101	98	96	94	91	89	87
1105.170	Total Liabilities	490	610	615	571	507	486	470	520	505	481
1105.180	Stock	300	300	300	300	300	300	300	300	300	300
1105.190	Retained Earnings	352	368	381	385	389	390	395	401	404	411
1105.200	Net Worth	652	668	681	685	689	690	695	701	704	711
1105.210	Total Liab & Equity	1142	1278	1296	1256	1196	1176	1165	1221	1209	1192

Figure A-7. Budget balance sheet

A	B	AE	AF	AG	AH	AI	AJ	AK	AL	AM	AN
		Aug-84	Sep-84	Oct-84	Nov-84	Dec-84	Jan-85	Feb-85	Mar-85	Apr-85	May-85
1100.100	Cash	160	166	186	195	168	149	153	207	197	177
1105.010	Accounts Receivable	241	242	233	233	258	261	245	220	223	267
1105.020	Inventories	190	195	193	183	195	187	197	206	216	223
1105.030	Other Current Assets	7	6	5	6	9	8	9	6	7	8
1105.040	Total Current Assets	598	609	617	617	630	605	604	639	643	675
1105.050	Property, Plant, Equip	765	765	765	790	790	790	790	802	832	844
1105.060	Accum Depreciation	176	184	192	200	208	216	224	232	240	249
1105.070	Net Prop, Plant, Equip	589	581	573	590	582	574	566	570	592	595
1105.080	Other Assets	4	4	4	4	4	4	4	4	5	5
1105.090	Total Assets	1191	1194	1194	1211	1216	1183	1174	1213	1240	1275
1105.100	Notes Payable	0	0	0	0	0	0	0	0	0	0
1105.110	Accounts Payable	181	187	184	196	196	155	132	153	148	146
1105.120	Payroll Taxes & Benefits	25	22	21	22	23	24	24	25	24	25
1105.130	Other Accrued Liab	64	66	67	70	74	73	70	73	75	78
1105.140	Total Current Liab	270	275	272	288	293	252	226	251	247	249
1105.150	Deferred Income Taxes	118	114	110	105	101	96	96	97	110	123
1105.160	Long Term Debt	84	82	80	77	75	72	70	67	64	62
1105.170	Total Liabilities	472	471	462	470	469	420	392	415	421	434
1105.180	Stock	300	300	300	300	300	300	300	300	300	300
1105.190	Retained Earnings	419	423	432	441	447	463	482	498	519	541
1105.200	Net Worth	719	723	732	741	747	763	782	798	819	841
1105.210	Total Liab & Equity	1191	1194	1194	1211	1216	1183	1174	1213	1240	1275

A	B	AO	AP	AQ	AR	AS	AT	AU
		Jun-85	Jul-85	Aug-85	Sep-85	Oct-85	Nov-85	Dec-85
1100.100	Cash	257	254	181	117	157	135	103
1105.010	Accounts Receivable	234	241	331	425	409	413	423
1105.020	Inventories	234	264	275	309	332	361	397
1105.030	Other Current Assets	8	8	9	9	9	9	9
1105.040	Total Current Assets	733	767	796	860	907	918	932
1105.050	Property, Plant, Equip	879	901	957	985	1003	1052	1052
1105.060	Accum Depreciation	258	267	269	279	289	299	310
1105.070	Net Prop, Plant, Equip	621	634	688	706	714	753	742
1105.080	Other Assets	5	5	5	6	6	7	6
1105.090	Total Assets	1359	1406	1489	1572	1627	1678	1680
1105.100	Notes Payable	0	0	0	0	0	0	0
1105.110	Accounts Payable	195	201	238	295	293	299	268
1105.120	Payroll Taxes & Benefits	27	27	31	31	33	37	36
1105.130	Other Accrued Liab	82	87	92	94	109	106	111
1105.140	Total Current Liab	304	315	361	420	435	442	415
1105.150	Deferred Income Taxes	137	151	166	182	198	215	232
1105.160	Long Term Debt	59	57	54	51	48	46	43
1105.170	Total Liabilities	500	523	581	653	681	703	690
1105.180	Stock	300	300	300	300	300	300	300
1105.190	Retained Earnings	559	583	608	619	646	675	690
1105.200	Net Worth	859	883	908	919	946	975	990
1105.210	Total Liab & Equity	1359	1406	1489	1572	1627	1678	1680

Figure A-7. Budget balance sheet (*continued*)

A	B	K	L	M	N	O	P	Q	R	S	T
		Dec-82	Jan-83	Feb-83	Mar-83	Apr-83	May-83	Jun-83	Jul-83	Aug-83	Sep-83
1110.010	Receivables, 30 Days	146	152	156	161	161	160	159	155	141	133
1110.020	Receivables, 60 Days	91	98	99	103	110	104	107	111	106	98
1110.030	Receivables, 90 Days	43	36	46	40	51	51	46	45	55	50
1110.040	Receivables, Over 90 Days	15	31	1	25	18	35	23	40	37	34
1115.010	Payables, 30 Days	111	101	97	123	81	92	110	92	87	130
1115.020	Payables, 60 Days	42	55	41	40	48	35	33	55	50	48
1115.030	Payables, 90 Days	16	16	17	13	10	15	5	5	20	15
1115.040	Payables, Over 90 Days	0	0	0	0	0	0	0	3	12	17

A	B	U	V	W	X	Y	Z	AA	AB	AC	AD
		Oct-83	Nov-83	Dec-83	Jan-84	Feb-84	Mar-84	Apr-84	May-84	Jun-84	Jul-84
1110.010	Receivables, 30 Days	130	126	127	124	123	120	122	122	124	133
1110.020	Receivables, 60 Days	83	78	88	77	78	82	80	78	72	75
1110.030	Receivables, 90 Days	55	37	35	38	35	27	40	34	31	19
1110.040	Receivables, Over 90 Days	13	15	11	16	20	23	1	18	9	20
1115.010	Payables, 30 Days	88	93	101	72	99	67	73	124	64	79
1115.020	Payables, 60 Days	67	48	51	56	47	64	42	42	81	40
1115.030	Payables, 90 Days	12	22	8	9	14	9	15	10	10	20
1115.040	Payables, Over 90 Days	18	22	26	15	20	26	26	36	40	43

A	B	AE	AF	AG	AH	AI	AJ	AK	AL	AM	AN
		Aug-84	Sep-84	Oct-84	Nov-84	Dec-84	Jan-85	Feb-85	Mar-85	Apr-85	May-85
1110.010	Receivables, 30 Days	129	126	128	131	137	135	139	131	142	153
1110.020	Receivables, 60 Days	83	72	77	81	76	75	73	68	53	75
1110.030	Receivables, 90 Days	29	30	19	21	33	26	14	17	24	22
1110.040	Receivables, Over 90 Days	0	14	9	0	12	25	19	4	4	17
1115.010	Payables, 30 Days	84	77	70	90	86	66	74	91	84	82
1115.020	Payables, 60 Days	40	48	48	51	67	59	30	44	50	36
1115.030	Payables, 90 Days	9	13	15	14	14	15	13	8	9	13
1115.040	Payables, Over 90 Days	48	49	51	41	29	15	15	10	5	15

A	B	AO	AP	AQ	AR	AS	AT	AU
		Jun-85	Jul-85	Aug-85	Sep-85	Oct-85	Nov-85	Dec-85
1110.010	Receivables, 30 Days	140	156	180	188	191	222	211
1110.020	Receivables, 60 Days	82	50	111	152	135	123	121
1110.030	Receivables, 90 Days	5	24	17	53	64	15	53
1110.040	Receivables, Over 90 Days	7	11	23	32	19	53	38
1115.010	Payables, 30 Days	115	100	148	144	100	163	115
1115.020	Payables, 60 Days	45	58	51	107	103	68	122
1115.030	Payables, 90 Days	15	28	21	20	60	50	9
1115.040	Payables, Over 90 Days	20	15	18	24	30	18	22

Figure A-8. Budgeted agings of accounts receivable and payable

A	B	K	L	M	N	O	P	Q	R	S	T
		Dec-82	Jan-83	Feb-83	Mar-83	Apr-83	May-83	Jun-83	Jul-83	Aug-83	Sep-83
1120.010	Depreciation Expense	6	6	6	6	7	7	7	7	7	7
1199.010	Dividends Paid	2	0	0	2	0	0	3	0	0	3
1199.020	Purchases of Inventory, AP	87	74	92	83	70	90	78	74	74	69
1199.022	Purchases, Expenses, AP	25	21	19	18	30	24	20	22	19	28
1199.023	Purch of Fixed Assets	16	20	0	35	0	0	18	5	0	39
1199.029	Total Purchases, AP	128	115	111	136	100	114	116	101	93	136
1199.030	Accounts Payable Paid	101	112	128	115	137	111	110	94	79	95
1199.040	AR Collected	124	133	172	132	150	153	180	151	181	195
1199.060	Disp of Fxd Asts—Bk Val	0	0	0	4	0	0	0	0	0	0
1199.070	Disp of Fxd Asts—Depr	0	0	0	4	0	0	0	0	0	0
1199.080	Disp of Fxd Asts—Sales	0	0	0	0	0	0	0	0	0	0
1200.010	Stock Price, Monthly High	34.5	33.0	33.3	33.4	31.9	33.7	38.3	35.1	29.5	27.4
1200.020	Stock Price, Monthly Low	33.0	32.0	32.4	31.3	29.9	31.4	27.9	26.3	22.8	22.0
1200.030	Stock Price, Monthly Close	33.4	32.4	33.1	32.6	30.9	32.3	32.4	28.8	25.7	24.6
1200.040	Stock Shares Outstanding	33	33	33	33	33	33	33	33	33	33
1300.010	Employees, Number	31	31	33	34	33	35	33	31	31	33
1300.020	Employees, Vol Quity	0	1	2	1	2	0	1	1	0	2
1300.100	Total Payroll	65	65	69	71	69	74	69	65	65	69
1400.010	Orders Booked	203	255	163	165	167	169	171	173	175	177
1400.020	Order Backlog	371	471	477	483	489	495	501	507	513	519

A	B	U	V	W	X	Y	Z	AA	AB	AC	AD
		Oct-83	Nov-83	Dec-83	Jan-84	Feb-84	Mar-84	Apr-84	May-84	Jun-84	Jul-84
1120.010	Depreciation Expense	7	7	7	7	7	8	8	8	8	8
1199.010	Dividends Paid	0	0	4	0	0	4	0	0	4	0
1199.020	Purchases of Inventory, AP	71	61	74	52	64	60	65	75	56	65
1199.022	Purchases, Expenses, AP	24	19	27	26	19	13	15	16	16	19
1199.023	Purch of Fixed Assets	0	17	10	0	22	0	0	40	0	0
1199.029	Total Purchases, AP	95	97	111	78	105	73	80	131	72	84
1199.030	Accounts Payable Paid	120	97	110	112	77	87	90	75	89	97
1199.040	AR Collected	207	200	172	139	133	139	145	128	154	128
1199.060	Disp of Fxd Asts—Bk Val	0	0	0	0	0	0	0	0	0	0
1199.070	Disp of Fxd Asts—Depr	0	0	0	0	0	0	0	0	0	0
1199.080	Disp of Fxd Asts—Sales	0	0	0	0	0	0	0	0	0	0
1200.010	Stock Price, Monthly High	24.7	26.1	24.6	24.2	24.8	28.3	27.2	26.5	27.9	27.6
1200.020	Stock Price, Monthly Low	22.8	23.7	23.9	23.5	22.5	24.5	24.8	23.7	22.0	20.0
1200.030	Stock Price, Monthly Close	23.6	25.5	24.0	23.5	24.6	26.0	25.8	25.2	24.2	26.4
1200.040	Stock Shares Outstanding	33	33	33	33	33	33	33	33	33	33
1300.010	Employees, Number	32	32	32	32	31	31	32	31	32	32
1300.020	Employees, Vol Quity	1	0	0	0	0	0	2	2	1	0
1300.100	Total Payroll	67	67	67	67	65	65	67	65	67	67
1400.010	Orders Booked	179	181	45	136	137	138	139	140	141	142
1400.020	Order Backlog	525	531	399	402	405	408	411	414	417	420

Figure A-9. Budgeted and forecasted miscellaneous data

A	B	AE	AF	AG	AH	AI	AJ	AK	AL	AM	AN
		Aug-84	Sep-84	Oct-84	Nov-84	Dec-84	Jan-85	Feb-85	Mar-85	Apr-85	May-85
1120.010	Depreciation Expense	8	8	8	8	8	8	8	8	8	9
1199.010	Dividends Paid	0	4	0	0	4	0	0	4	0	0
1199.020	Purchases of Inventory, AP	61	69	62	54	76	54	71	71	73	71
1199.022	Purchases, Expenses, AP	21	15	15	16	16	22	18	18	23	23
1199.023	Purch of Fixed Assets	10	0	0	25	0	0	0	12	30	12
1199.029	Total Purchases, AP	92	84	77	95	92	76	89	101	126	106
1199.030	Accounts Payable Paid	93	78	80	83	92	117	112	80	131	108
1199.040	AR Collected	146	140	151	143	119	144	166	178	153	115
1199.060	Disp of Fxd Asts—Bk Val	22	0	0	0	0	0	0	0	0	0
1199.070	Disp of Fxd Asts—Depr	19	0	0	0	0	0	0	0	0	0
1199.080	Disp of Fxd Asts—Sales	5	0	0	0	0	0	0	0	0	0
1200.010	Stock Price, Monthly High	31.9	32.5	38.7	45.6	40.3	44.9	52.2	49.3	51.6	52.1
1200.020	Stock Price, Monthly Low	23.7	20.7	33.1	31.9	31.7	41.0	38.8	42.4	47.4	50.0
1200.030	Stock Price, Monthly Close	28.3	31.6	35.8	38.2	39.8	42.9	48.4	47.9	49.8	50.8
1200.040	Stock Shares Outstanding	33	33	33	33	33	33	33	33	33	33
1300.010	Employees, Number	32	31	33	32	31	34	32	33	33	31
1300.020	Employees, Vol Quity	0	0	0	0	2	0	0	2	0	2
1300.100	Total Payroll	67	65	69	67	65	71	67	69	69	65
1400.010	Orders Booked	143	144	145	146	153	156	159	162	165	168
1400.020	Order Backlog	423	426	429	432	441	450	459	468	477	486

A	B	AO	AP	AQ	AR	AS	AT	AU
		Jun-85	Jul-85	Aug-85	Sep-85	Oct-85	Nov-85	Dec-85
1120.010	Depreciation Expense	9	9	9	10	10	10	11
1199.010	Dividends Paid	5	0	0	15	0	0	15
1199.020	Purchases of Inventory, AP	76	96	78	102	92	99	107
1199.022	Purchases, Expenses, AP	20	21	19	31	25	33	37
1199.023	Purch of Fixed Assets	35	22	63	28	18	49	0
1199.029	Total Purchases, AP	131	139	160	161	135	181	144
1199.030	Accounts Payable Paid	82	133	123	104	137	175	175
1199.040	AR Collected	195	158	78	77	190	173	170
1199.060	Disp of Fxd Asts—Bk Val	0	0	7	0	0	0	0
1199.070	Disp of Fxd Asts—Depr	0	0	7	0	0	0	0
1199.080	Disp of Fxd Asts—Sales	0	0	1	0	0	0	0
1200.010	Stock Price, Monthly High	52.3	54.3	59.3	57.4	60.1	62.7	59.3
1200.020	Stock Price, Monthly Low	48.0	48.7	51.1	53.6	54.7	58.1	57.9
1200.030	Stock Price, Monthly Close	51.7	51.1	54.1	56.1	59.0	59.4	58.6
1200.040	Stock Shares Outstanding	33	33	33	33	33	33	33
1300.010	Employees, Number	31	31	33	36	33	37	38
1300.020	Employees, Vol Quity	2	1	1	2	2	3	0
1300.100	Total Payroll	65	65	69	76	69	78	80
1400.010	Orders Booked	171	174	177	180	183	186	190
1400.020	Order Backlog	495	504	513	522	531	540	550

Figure A-9. Budgeted and forecasted miscellaneous data (*continued*)

A	B		K	L	M	N	O	P	Q	R	S
	Description	Dec-82	Jan-83	Feb-83	Mar-83	Apr-83	May-83	Jun-83	Jul-83	Aug-83	Sep-83
1800.010	Sales, Last 12 Months	1593	1645	1700	1754	1797	1834	1862	1884	1889	1887
1800.020	Profits, Last 12 Months	103	105	110	110	109	110	110	106	91	81
1800.030	Dividends, Last 12 Months	6	6	6	6	6	6	6	6	6	6
1800.040	EBIT, Last 12 Months	208	212	223	225	226	229	231	226	202	185
1810.010	Return on Assets, Cur	9%	9%	10%	9%	9%	9%	9%	9%	8%	7%

A	B	U	V	W	X	Y	Z	AA	AB	AC	AD
	Description	Oct-83	Nov-83	Dec-83	Jan-84	Feb-84	Mar-84	Apr-84	May-84	Jun-84	Jul-84
1800.010	Sales, Last 12 Months	1874	1968	1992	1970	1947	1923	1898	1872	1845	1817
1800.020	Profits, Last 12 Months	71	155	162	156	149	142	135	129	123	116
1800.030	Dividends, Last 12 Months	6	10	12	12	12	14	14	14	15	15
1800.040	EBIT, Last 12 Months	167	306	318	305	292	279	266	253	240	227
1810.010	Return on Assets, Cur	6%	12%	13%	12%	12%	12%	12%	11%	10%	10%

A	B	AE	AF	AG	AH	AI	AJ	AK	AL	AM	AN
	Description	Aug-84	Sep-84	Oct-84	Nov-84	Dec-84	Jan-85	Feb-85	Mar-85	Apr-85	May-85
1800.010	Sales, Last 12 Months	1788	1758	1727	1695	1662	1676	1692	1710	1730	1752
1800.020	Profits, Last 12 Months	110	103	96	89	82	94	109	124	140	156
1800.030	Dividends, Last 12 Months	15	16	16	16	16	16	16	16	16	16
1800.040	EBIT, Last 12 Months	214	201	188	175	162	185	211	238	266	295
1810.010	Return on Assets, Cur	9%	9%	8%	7%	7%	8%	9%	10%	11%	12%

A	B	AO	AP	AQ	AR	AS	AT	AU
	Description	Jun-85	Jul-85	Aug-85	Sep-85	Oct-85	Nov-85	Dec-85
1800.010	Sales, Last 12 Months	1776	1802	1830	1860	1892	1926	1962
1800.020	Profits, Last 12 Months	172	189	206	224	242	262	282
1800.030	Dividends, Last 12 Months	17	17	17	28	28	28	39
1800.040	EBIT, Last 12 Months	325	356	388	421	455	490	526
1810.010	Return on Assets, Cur	13%	13%	14%	14%	15%	16%	17%

Figure A-10. Values of the formulas for ratios and running totals

Appendix B

COLUMN RESET MACRO FOR 1-2-3 VERSION 1A

If you have 1-2-3 Version 1A, use the following macro as a substitute for the macro COLUMNS presented in Figure 2-5.

```
          Reset the width through Column R.
          ------------------------------------
columns   {GOTO}a1~/WCS9~                A
          {RIGHT}/WCS26~                 B
          {RIGHT}/WCR~                   C
          {RIGHT}/WCR~                   D
          {RIGHT}/WCR~                   E
          {RIGHT}/WCR~                   F
          {RIGHT}/WCR~                   G
          {RIGHT}/WCR~                   H
          {RIGHT}/WCR~                   I
          {RIGHT}/WCR~                   J
          {RIGHT}/WCR~                   K
          {RIGHT}/WCR~                   L
          {RIGHT}/WCR~                   M
          {RIGHT}/WCR~                   N
          {RIGHT}/WCR~                   O
          {RIGHT}/WCR~                   P
          {RIGHT}/WCR~                   Q
          {RIGHT}/WCR~                   R
          {RIGHT}/WCR~                   S
          {RIGHT}/WCR~                   T
          {RIGHT}/WCR~                   U
          {RIGHT}/WCR~                   V
          {RIGHT}/WCR~                   W
          {RIGHT}/WCR~                   X
          {RIGHT}/WCR~                   Y
          {RIGHT}/WCR~                   Z
          {HOME}
          /XR
```

Appendix C

UPDATING @SUM FORMULAS WITH VERSION 1A

Using a macro to create an @SUM formula isn't difficult in Version 1A, but it does take some work. Here's the approach. Begin by modifying the bottom of Figure 2-14 to look like what is shown in Figure C-1. You will see that two changes have been made.

First, the string formulas have been replaced by '5 (apostrophe 5). This label represents the row number of the first row of data in the Data Bank. The range name ROWNUM has been assigned to the cell with this label.

The second change is the addition of the table of column numbers and letters. Each number in this table is a label. Each of these number labels is the range name for the letter to its right. In other words, if you entered the command **GOTO 11**, the cell pointer would go to cell AX207, the cell containing the letter K.

To create this table, go to an unused section of your spreadsheet (*not* to the section shown in Figure C-1). Use the **/D**ata **F**ill command to create a column of numbers from 11 through 57. Then use the following macro to turn these numbers into labels:

```
\x {DOWN}{EDIT}{HOME}"~
   /XG \X~
```

Place your cell pointer in the cell above the 11. When you issue the ALT-X command, the macro will turn each successive number into a label. Watch the macro, though. It won't stop when it runs out of numbers. You'll have to stop it. To do this, simply press CTRL-BREAK. The display will show an ERROR message. Then press ESC.

```
         AU        AV        AW        AX        AY        AZ        BA        BB        BC        BD        BE
196      |                                                                                                   |
197      |                   --------------------------------------------------------------------------------|
198      |                   FORMULAS                                                                        |
199      |                   =========                                                                       |
200      |                     NAME         COL#                                                             |
201      |                   -----------------            ROWNUM                                             |
202      |                   THIS_BEGC        36          5         <<Label of the row number of the         |
203      |                   THIS_ENDC        47                      first row of data in Data Bank.        |
204      |                   LAST_BEGC        24                                                             |
205      |                   LAST_ENDC        35                                                             |
206      |                   --------------------------------------------------------------------------------|
207      |                         11 K                27 AA               43 AQ                             |
208      |                         12 L                28 AB               44 AR                             |
209      |                         13 M                29 AC               45 AS                             |
210      |                         14 N                30 AD               46 AT                             |
211      |                         15 O                31 AE               47 AU                             |
212      |                         16 P                32 AF               48 AV                             |
213      |                         17 Q                33 AG               49 AW                             |
214      |                         18 R                34 AH               50 AX                             |
215      |                         19 S                35 AI               51 AY                             |
216      |                         20 T                36 AJ               52 AZ                             |
217      |                         21 U                37 AK               53 BA                             |
218      |                         22 V                38 AL               54 BB                             |
219      |                         23 W                39 AM               55 BC                             |
220      |                         24 X                40 AN               56 BD                             |
221      |                         25 Y                41 AO               57 BE                             |
222      |                         26 Z                42 AP                                                 |
223      |                                                                                                   |
224      |                                                                                                   |
```

Figure C-1. Version 1A modification of Figure 2-14

To the right of each number label, enter the letters shown in the table. Then move these columns to the area of your spreadsheet shown in the figure. Finally, issue the /**R**ange **N**ame **L**abel **R**ight command three successive times, each time highlighting a different column of number labels shown in the table.

Figure C-2 shows the additional macros that are necessary to update the

```
          Updates UPSUM macro with column address labels.
          ------------------------------------------------------------
loadlab   /Cthis_begc~tb1~                       Copy column numbers to this macro.
          /Cthis_endc~te1~                         "
          /Clast_begc~lb1~                         "
          /Clast_endc~le1~                         "
          {GOTO}tb1~{EDIT}{CALC}{HOME}'~         Turn column numbers into labels.
          {GOTO}te1~{EDIT}{CALC}{HOME}'~           "
          {GOTO}lb1~{EDIT}{CALC}{HOME}'~           "
          {GOTO}le1~{EDIT}{CALC}{HOME}'~           "
          /Crownum~rn1~                          Copy the label representing the top
          /Crownum~rn2~                            row of the Data Bank to the
          /Crownum~rn3~                            UPSUM macro.
          /Crownum~rn4~                            "
          /C                                     Treating column number labels as
tb1       36                                       range names, copy the column
          ~tb2~                                    letter labels in these ranges to
          /C                                       the UPSUM macro.
te1       47                                       "
          ~te2~                                    "
          /C                                       "
lb1       24                                       "
          ~lb2~                                    "
          /C                                       "
le1       35                                       "
          ~le2~                                    "
          /XR                                    Return.


          Updates summary formulas with @SUM.
          ------------------------------------------------------------
upsum     /XCloadlab~                  Load labels into the following macro.
          {GOTO}cur_tot~               Go to the top of the current summary column.
          @SUM(                        Place @SUM formula here.
tb2       AJ                             "
rn1       5                              "
          ..                             "
te2       AU                             "
rn2       5                              "
          )~                             "
          {GOTO}last_tot~              Go to top of the comparison summary column.
          @SUM(                        Place @SUM formula here.
lb2       X                              "
rn3       5                              "
          ..                             "
le2       AI                             "
rn4       5                              "
          )~                             "
          /XR                          Return.
```

Figure C-2. Macros for updating the @SUM formulas

```
         AA      AB       AC        AD        AE        AF        AG        AH        AI        AJ        AK
166      |                                                                                                 |
167      |                Updates spreadsheet with revised summary formulas.                               |
168      |                ------------------------------------------------------------------------------   |
169      |       formup   /Cdates~dates~              Calculate the dates.                                 |
170      |                /Cformulas~formulas~        Calculate the formulas.                              |
171      |                /XCupsum~                   Update first @SUM formulas.                          |
172      |                /XCunpark~                  Restore the DATA range.                              |
173      |                {GOTO}summary~              Go to the top of the summary column.                 |
174      |                /Csummary~.{END}{DOWN}~     Copy formulas to Summary Section.                    |
175      |                /Cmisc_dat~first_mo~        Add dates to report.                                 |
176      |                /Creport~report~            Recalculate the report                               |
177      |                /Creport~report~            Recalculate the report                               |
178      |                /XR                         Return.                                              |
179      |                                                                                                 |
180      |                                                                                                 |
```

Figure C-3. Modification version of the FORMUP macro

@SUM formulas. These two self-modifying macros use the table of column numbers and letters in Figure C-1.

Notice in Figure C-2 that the ranges for data all have data in them. (The range names are three characters long.) When you write the macros, it won't matter whether you enter the numbers and letters shown in these ranges. When the macro first runs, it will enter new data into the ranges as necessary.

Figure C-3 shows the modified version of the FORMUP macro that you will need. (The original version of FORMUP is in Figure 2-13.)

Appendix D

DERIVATION OF THE FINANCIAL PLANNING EQUATION

I = Interest payments

g^* = Sustainable growth rate

b = Earnings retention ratio

T = Tax rate

O = Operating earnings (EBIT)

A = Assets at the beginning of the period

B = Total debt at the beginning of the period

W = Net worth at the beginning of the period

i = The average interest rate

R = Return on equity

$$g^* = bR$$

$$= b \cdot (1-T) \cdot \left(\frac{O-I}{W}\right), \text{ looking only at } \left(\frac{O-I}{W}\right):$$

$$\left(\frac{O-I}{W}\right) = \frac{A}{W}\left[\frac{O-I}{A}\right], \text{ and since } \frac{A}{W} = 1+\frac{B}{W},$$

$$= \left[1+\frac{B}{W}\right]\cdot\left[\frac{O}{A}-\frac{I}{A}\right]$$

$$= \frac{O}{A}+\frac{B}{W}\left[\frac{O}{A}-\frac{I}{A}\right]-\frac{I}{A}$$

$$= \frac{O}{A}+\frac{B}{W}\left[\frac{O}{A}-\frac{I}{A}-\frac{I}{A}\cdot\frac{W}{B}\right]$$

$$= \frac{O}{A}+\frac{B}{W}\left[\frac{O}{A}-\left(\frac{IB}{BA}+\frac{IW}{BA}\right)\right]$$

$$= \frac{O}{A}+\frac{B}{W}\left[\frac{O}{A}-\frac{I}{B}\left(\frac{B}{A}+\frac{W}{A}\right)\right], \text{ and since : } \frac{B+W}{A} = 1, \text{ and } \frac{I}{B} = i,$$

$$\frac{O-I}{W} = \frac{O}{A}+\frac{B}{W}\left[\frac{O}{A}-i\right], \text{ and therefore,}$$

$$g* = b \cdot (1-T) \cdot \left[\frac{O}{A}+\frac{B}{W}\left(\frac{O}{A}-i\right)\right] = \text{Financial Planning Equation}$$

INDEX

D